“Cover Photo Courtesy of Virginia Historical Society (2010.1.38)”

“Members of the 1st VA at the hanging of John Brown
in Charlestown VA, December of 1859.”

The Bloody First

A History of the 1st Regiment of Virginia Volunteers in the American Civil War

ANTHONY POWELL

Interior Image Credit: Anthony Powell maps

LifeRich Publishing is a registered trademark of The Reader's Digest Association, Inc.

LifeRich Publishing books may be ordered through booksellers or by contacting:

LifeRich Publishing
1663 Liberty Drive
Bloomington, IN 47403
www.liferichpublishing.com
1 (888) 238-8637

ISBN: 978-1-4897-1656-9 (sc)
ISBN: 978-1-4897-1657-6 (hc)
ISBN: 978-1-4897-1655-2 (e)

Library of Congress Control Number: 2018903945

Print information available on the last page.

LifeRich Publishing rev. date: 04/25/2018

Dedicated to My Family,

To my brother Mike, who not only encouraged me to write this book but also instilled in me a love of history when we were youngsters, so many years ago. If not for his support and encouragement I would never have completed this work.

To my son Brian, who spent countless hours editing and correcting my many grammatical errors. His insight and dedication to this project made its completion possible.

To my wife Sue, and my daughter Melanie, who showed great patience with me over the years, while I turned our kitchen into an office.

I would also like to thank my good friend, Bob Mullauer, who gave me unlimited access to his vast library. He generously allowed me use of the "Official Records" for months at a time, which proved to be invaluable to tell this story.

A very special thank you to Mr. Bill Rose who spent many years researching the 1st VA and shared every page of that research with me. This book would not have been possible without his generosity and selflessness. His contribution to this book cannot be overstated.

The following institutions supplied me with documents and information. It is reassuring to know that our nation's history is in the hands of such competent institutions.

> University of North Carolina at Chapel Hill, Southern Historical Collection.
> The American Civil War Museum, Formerly The Museum of the Confederacy.
> New York Public Library, Manuscript and Archives Division.
> Gettysburg National Military Park, National Park Service.
> Virginia Historical Society, Richmond VA.
> Maymont in Richmond VA.

University of Virginia Charlottesville, Albert and Shirley Small Special Collections.

And finally, I want to thank those who I have served with in the 1st VA, Company "D," (reenactment unit) over the past 25+ years. Their names are too numerous to mention but their dedication to keeping history alive and their portrayal of the 1st VA has been a huge inspiration and source of encouragement to me throughout this endeavor. A special mention to Mr. Bob Lyons who not only kept the reenactment unit alive but also dedicated a large portion of his adult life to the memory of the Confederate soldiers.

TABLE OF CONTENTS

INDEX OF MAPS

INTRODUCTION

This is the story of a group of young men who left their families, their friends and their sweethearts to answer the call from their home state of Virginia. The regiment was made up of Companies from Richmond and the surrounding counties. Some of those companies had distinguished pasts dating back to the French and Indian War. They fought in the American Revolution and the Mexican War, proudly fighting under the flag of the United States. Other Companies were formed anew in those heady days leading up to Virginia's secession from the Union. When the fateful decision was made to secede on April 17, 1861, the men of the 1st VA were organized, ready and even eager, to defend their state. They were immediately sworn into service and their four year journey into the depths of war began.

They marched out of Richmond full of pomp and bravado, completely unaware of the hardships and pain that awaited them on the field of battle. They believed their vigorous training had prepared them for anything that the Union Army could send their way. On the banks of Bull Run, three days before the Battle of Manassas, they were the first Confederate unit to meet the Union army when it ventured out from the confines of Washington, D.C. Their initial success filled their heads with visions of glory, a short war and a return to Richmond and their families. It did not take long for the severity of their struggle to set in.

The men of the 1st VA were Richmond's favorite sons and the newspapers followed their progress as they moved from battlefield to battlefield. The soldiers themselves left us their letters, articles and memoirs to tell their story of survival, death and even levity in a war that ravaged their homeland before their very eyes. They watched as their ranks were thinned to the point of disbandment, only to be saved from obscurity by Robert E. Lee, himself.

This book is their story as they crisscrossed Virginia, meeting a determined foe at every stop. As part of the Army of Northern Virginia, they bravely marched into battle at Williamsburg, the Peninsula, and Manassas. They traveled into Maryland with ranks so thinned that the entire regiment was less than a full-sized company. These courageous young men secured their place in history on July 3, 1863, when as part of Kemper's brigade in Pickett's division they made that immortal charge up Cemetery Hill in the small Pennsylvania town of Gettysburg. Their own accounts take us step by step up that blood stained hill on a hot July day where they suffered the highest percentage of casualties in Kemper's brigade.

For two more years they withstood the agonies of war, traveling to North Carolina and returning to trenches that defended Richmond and Petersburg. They were present at the devastating losses at Five Forks and Sailor's Creek. They had the distinction of being the first to meet the Union army back in 1861 and finally their remnants were there at Appomattox when Gen. Lee surrendered in 1865.

But this was not the end of their story. In post-war Virginia men of the regiment formed the Old 1st VA Association. Through this association they continued to work for the benefit of the living veterans and memory of those that died on both sides of the conflict. They joined forces with the veterans of the Philadelphia Brigade of the Union army, the same men with whom they had fought so violently on Cemetery Hill in Gettysburg. These two organizations showed the same dedication to binding the wounds of a divided country as they did while inflicting those wounds. Two men in particular, Edward Payson Reeve and Charles Loehr, were instrumental in keeping alive the memory of the 1st VA while at the same time recognizing their roles as loyal citizens of the postwar United States. Both of these men were original members of the 1st VA and both somehow managed to survive the entire war, suffering wounds and hardships throughout.

Along with their comrades in Virginia's 1st Regiment, they carved their names in the history of the American Civil War and this is their story.

PREWAR HISTORY

They were men of Virginia. Some belonged to families who had lived in the city of Richmond for generations; others came from surrounding counties. Some were born in the northern states and relocated in the south. And still others were born overseas; they came from countries such as Ireland, Germany, Italy and Poland. They represented virtually every occupation, including carpenters, machinists, doctors, lawyers, clerks, and farmers. Some were discharged for being too young and others for being too old. For all of their differences, they had one thing in common: when their state called, they were all men of Virginia. They were the men of the 1st VA.

Although this history will focus on the years of the American Civil War, the First Regiment of Virginia Volunteers traces its lineage back to colonial Virginia, through the militias of Henrico and Chesterfield counties as well as Richmond City. Colonial Virginia was dependent on individual companies of Militia for their defense. In times of peril the Governor and the Virginia Legislature called for a muster of the troops and the various militias responded. Such a need occurred in 1754 in response to French incursions along the contested Ohio River. The French, in an effort to expand their territory in North America, moved along the Ohio from Canada and began to build fortresses. British subjects who lived and traded in the area were arrested and sent back to Canada as prisoners. Governor Dinwiddie of Virginia requested the legislature to sanction a military force to be sent to the Ohio River in an effort to counter the threat posed by the French incursion. On February 16, 1754, the Virginia Council confirmed the resolution of the House of Burgesses in support of the Governor. With this resolution the Governor formed the "Virginia Regiment" which was composed of the various militia units including those from Henrico and

Chesterfield counties. It can be argued that this was the birth of the 1st VA Infantry.[1]

The regiment left Alexandria under the command of a prominent Virginian, Col. Joshua Fry and Major George Washington. During the expedition Col. Fry died from injuries received when he fell from his horse and George Washington, a newly commissioned Colonel as of June 4th, 1754, took over command. Washington was defeated at Great Meadows and the regiment returned to Alexandria in the latter part of July. The British government, in London, determined the incursions of the French could not be tolerated and sent two regiments of British regulars under the overall command of Major General Edward Braddock. The size of the Virginia regiment was increased to 1,000 men before it joined the newly arrived British troops in a second expedition to the Ohio River region. On the 9th of July, 1755, Braddock's force was defeated by the French and returned to Virginia where the regiment spent the next two years fighting hostile Indians on Virginia's borders. The local events in the colonies became globalized when England declared war on France on May 17th, 1756.[2]

In 1758 the regiment was increased to 2,000 men and separated into two separate regiments with the designations 1st and 2nd Virginia regiments. George Washington retained command of the 1st Virginia. The regiment took part in a third expedition against the French that was successful and culminated in the capture of Fort DuQuesne, which the colonists rebuilt and renamed Fort Pitt. The Virginians returned home and the 2nd regiment was disbanded. The 1st regiment was sent to southwest Virginia where they continued to serve against hostile Cherokee Indians. The regiment was mustered out in 1762 and the men reverted back to service with their individual militia companies.[3]

In March of 1775 Virginia held a convention to discuss the current

---

[1] M. C. Jackson, Captain 1st Infantry, Virginia National Guard, "The Romantic Record of the First Virginia Infantry", 1931; Captain John C. Weckert and Captain Henry G. Dickerson, "The Old First Virginia Infantry, The Military Apprenticeship of George Washington", Supplement to the Rattlesnake (Magazine), Richmond VA, 1933, Pgs. 8-13, Hereinafter – "Weckert".

[2] Encyclopediavirginia.org, Cassandra Britt Farrell; Weckert, pgs. 13-22.

[3] Weckert, Pgs. 22-23.

hostile situation between the colonies and Great Britain. Many of the delegates were skeptical of joining their neighbors to the north in a rebellion against the king. On the 23rd Patrick Henry gave his famous "Give Me Liberty or Give Me Death" speech which persuaded the convention to approve Henry's resolutions. One of these was to establish a state militia for the protection of Virginia. The convention approved the formation of two regiments and the 1st VA was restored with Patrick Henry as its commander. The Royal Governor abandoned Williamsburg and moved to Portsmouth. The colonists quickly occupied Williamsburg and Patrick Henry chose the college of William and Mary in that city as the rendezvous point for his regiment. The first to arrive was the company from Henrico County on October 14th, 1775. The regiment was incorporated into the Continental Line but Patrick Henry resigned his commission after being passed over for promotion. The men of the regiment were outraged and threatened to leave the army. In an impassioned speech, Patrick Henry persuaded the troops to remain in the army and fight for the new nation's independence. The regiment went on to join Washington's Continental Army and participated in the battles of Trenton, Princeton, and Monmouth. The regiment then went south and fought in the battles of Eutaw Springs, Ninety-Six, and Guilford Court House. They returned to Virginia and took part in the Battle of Yorktown which culminated in the surrender of Gen. Cornwallis's command.[4]

After the revolution the regiment once again reverted back to individual companies within the militia system. The Richmond City militia was separated from the Henrico County militia in 1791. In 1792 the militia units were given numeric designations, Richmond City was known as the 19th, Henrico County the 33rd and Chesterfield County the 23rd. The regiments continued in this capacity serving their individual jurisdictions until the War of 1812 when they were once again called into Federal service. After peace was restored with Great Britain the regiment returned to militia duties until they were called upon to serve in the War with Mexico in 1846. The First Virginia Regiment was reformed with companies from Henrico County and other jurisdictions in the state. The regiment sailed to Mexico where they spent most of the war guarding supply trains for General Taylor. After their return from Mexico

[4] Encyclopediavirginia.org/Henry_Patrick_1736-1799; Weckert Pgs. 29-34.

the regiment was once again mustered out, in 1848, and the companies returned to their home units. [5]

The 1st Regiment of Virginia Volunteers that would fight in the American Civil War began its career on May 1, 1851 with the issuance of General Order #1 which follows:

"Adjutant General's Office
Richmond, Va. May 1, 1851

General Orders
No. 1

The Commander in Chief directs that the volunteer corps of the 19 and 179 Regiments and attached thereto, with those (if any) of the 23 Regiment, Chesterfield and 33 Regiment of Henrico, shall from this date constitute a new regiment to be denominated the First Regiment Virginia Volunteers, headquarters at the city of Richmond.

The senior captain will immediately assume the command until field officers shall be chosen, and will assemble the officers of the Regiment as speedily as may be for the purpose of prompt and effective organization. The election of field officers may be made without further orders from this department at any time most acceptable to the officers of the Regiment, but the Regimental muster shall be during the present month.

Officers will send their commissions to the Adjutant General that they may be made comfortable to the new organization.

By Command:
Wm. H. Richardson
Adj. Genl.

A copy:
Walter H. Harrison
Adj. 1st Regt. Va. Volunteers"

This order combined the various militia companies (the 19th, 23rd, 33rd, and179th regiments of militia) of Henrico and Chesterfield counties with the militia companies of Richmond into a single regiment of volunteers.

[5] Weckert, Pgs. 33-34.

And thus started the career of a valiant regiment of Virginians, who came to be known for their bravery on the battlefield and their frivolity in the camp. Their nicknames of "The Bloody First" and "The Rowdy First" proved to be most fitting.

The officers of the regiment were elected on May 2, 1851. Walter Gwynn was elected the Colonel and commander of the 1st VA. Gwynn graduated from West Point in 1822 and served in the United States Army until 1838. He also served in several militias, both in North Carolina and Virginia. Christopher Tompkins was elected Lt. Colonel. Tompkins was also a graduate of West Point, class of 1836, and served in the Seminole and Mexican Wars. Thomas Pearson August was elected Major. August was a prominent lawyer in Richmond and also served in the Virginia legislature. During the Mexican War he served with the Richmond Grays as a Lieutenant. On May 5, 1851, Lt. Col. Tompkins issued orders listing the following nine companies that formed the regiment: the Richmond Light Infantry Dragoons, the Richmond Fayette Artillery, the Richmond Light Infantry Blues, the Richmond Grays, the Montgomery Guard, the Richmond Eagle Infantry, the German Rifles, the Richmond Young Guard and the Caledonian Guard. [6]

During the peacetime years of the 1850's, the regiment formed for parades and public celebrations usually marking some patriotic anniversary such as the 4th of July, Washington's Birthday or the Battle of New Orleans. These anniversaries were commemorated with the firing of salutes by the Richmond Fayette Artillery, after which the entire regiment, dressed in their finest uniforms, paraded through the streets of the city culminating with a formation at Capital square. At the conclusion of the ceremonies each company held a banquet which normally involved a round of patriotic toasts. Individual companies hosted balls throughout the year, sometimes to celebrate the anniversary of the company's formation. Several companies hosted annual moonlight excursions on the James River complete with refreshments, music and dancing on board the steamers CURTIS PECK and GLEN COVE. Occasionally, the regiment would escort dignitaries

[6] Lee Wallace, "1st Virginia Infantry" H.E. Howard Inc., Lynchburg, VA, 1985, pg. 1; Robert K. Krick, "Lee's Colonels: A Biographical Register of the Field Officers of the Army Of Northern VA", Morningside Press, Dayton OH, 1991 pg. 40; Richmond Whig, Friday, May9, 1851, pg.1.

who visited the city of Richmond. Such was the case when President Millard Fillmore came to Richmond on June 27, 1851. Besides the pomp of parades and ceremonies the regiment was expected to perform as a military unit in defense of the state. Therefor regular drills, shooting competitions and instruction in the military arts were scheduled throughout the year. The 1st VA was an integral part of Richmond society and their activities were widely reported in all of the Richmond newspapers.

Throughout the 1850's the regiment went through many changes, with some companies being disbanded and new companies joining the ranks of the 1st VA. Colonel Gwynn resigned in 1853 and was replaced by Major August as commander of the regiment. The 1st VA continued to move toward a "regimental concept" as opposed to the old system of individual companies. In 1856, the companies began to use lettered designations. Order #5, dated January 1, 1856, which was posted in the local newspapers, appointed Ensign Oscar G. Cosby of Company "H" as regimental color bearer and forbade the carrying of company colors at regimental musters and parades.[7]

On July 5, 1858, the 1st VA took part in the ceremonies for the re-interment of President James Monroe at Hollywood Cemetery in Richmond. The fifth President of the United States died at his daughter's house in New York, 27 years before, on July 4, 1831. Through the efforts of Governor Henry Wise, President Monroe a native Virginian, was coming home to Richmond to be buried. After being exhumed on July 2, 1858, Monroe's body was taken to City Hall in New York where he laid in state till the following day. Monroe's remains were escorted to the docks by the 7th New York Regiment, who along with their magnificent 45-piece band accompanied the deceased president to Richmond.

On the morning of July 5, the 1st VA and other militia units marched down Main Street to the public wharf in Richmond, known as Rocketts. The steamer JAMESTOWN approached with the remains of President Monroe and the steamer GLEN COVE followed behind carrying the 7th New York Regiment. The 1st VA came to "present arms", saluting their northern counterparts, as the 7th New York disembarked. The troops took

---

[7] Lee Wallace, introduction to "War History of the Old First Virginia Infantry Regiment" by Charles Loehr, Reprint by Morningside Bookshop, 1978; Unknown Richmond Newspaper.

part in a procession which escorted the remains of the President back up Main Street to the sound of church bells, the firing of salutes by the guns belonging to the Fayette Artillery and the music of the band belonging to the 7th NY. At Hollywood Cemetery the troops stood in formation around the grave as the casket was lowered into the ground. Following the ceremonies the 7th NY was treated to a sumptuous banquet in Richmond. An otherwise auspicious occasion was marred by the death of one soldier from the 7th NY who apparently drowned during the festivities. The drowned New Yorker, was Lawrence Hamilton, the grandson of Alexander Hamilton.[8]

At the time of President Monroe's interment at Hollywood Cemetery, the 1st VA consisted of the following seven companies:

Co. A – Richmond Grays: Capt. Wyatt Elliott
Co. C – Montgomery Guard: Capt. Patrick Moore
Co. D – Rocky Ridge Rifles: Capt. F. Clopton
Co. E - Richmond Light Infantry Blues: Capt. William Fry
Co. F – Richmond Fayette Artillery: Capt. Charles Robinson
Co. I – National Guard: Capt. J. H. Johnston
Co. K – Virginia Rifles: Capt. Alfred Lybrock

The first rate military appearance of the 7th New York left a positive impression on the people of Richmond, in general, and the 1st Virginia in particular. The individual companies of the 7th New York were all outfitted in the same cadet gray uniforms, unlike the companies of the 1st Virginia which were clothed in their own distinctive uniforms of different style and color. The uniformity of the 7th New York so impressed the members of the 1st VA that they slowly adopted a standard uniform of gray frock coats for each of the individual companies within the regiment. Some companies continued to use their company uniform for company events, but donned the new Frock coats for regimental events. The appearance of the 7th New York in Richmond also helped in recruiting for the 1st VA. Within a year two new companies were raised and added to the regiment. [9]

---

[8] Richmond.com, Richmond Times-Dispatch, Time Capsule by Larry Hall, posted July 4, 2007.

[9] Wallace, "1st Virginia Infantry", pg. 6

The following year, the abolitionist John Brown and his followers attacked Harper's Ferry in an attempt to seize the arsenal and arm a slave rebellion. Governor Wise ordered several companies of the 1st Virginia to that place in October of 1859 to help quell the uprising. When they arrived in Washington, where they were to board the trains for Harper's Ferry, the regiment was told the crisis had passed and they would not be needed. On the 19th of November, Governor Wise received a dispatch from Col. Davis, the officer in command at Charlestown Virginia, which stated "A large force, armed with pikes and revolvers is marching from Wheeling." John Brown was being imprisoned in Charlestown and the rumored force from Wheeling presumably had plans to free him. Within 3 hours of the alarm being given, seven companies of the 1st VA were boarding trains headed for Charlestown. The rumors proved to be false and no rescue of John Brown was ever attempted. But the 1st VA remained in Charlestown as a precaution and witnessed the hanging of John Brown on Dec. 2, 1859. Among the ranks, although not a member of the regiment, was the actor and future Presidential assassin, John Wilkes Booth. Booth happened to be performing in Richmond, at the Marshall Theater, when the alarm was sounded. Ironically he was performing in a production of "My American Cousin", the same comedy that was playing at Ford's Theater when John Wilkes Booth assassinated Abraham Lincoln in 1865. The 1st VA boarded their train directly across the street from the theater. Booth appeared at the door to the baggage car and asked the two guards inside, George Libby and Louis Bossieux, both of whom were members of the Richmond Grays, if he could go with them to Charlestown. The actor was promptly told that only men in uniform were allowed on the train. At which point he quickly offered to buy a uniform. After some discussion the guards allowed Booth to board the train, giving him enough articles of clothing to pass muster. Booth remained with the men of the 1st VA while they were stationed in Charlestown and even regaled them with recitations from Shakespeare around the camp fire in the evenings. In this way he was able to stand in their ranks and watch as John Brown was hung.[10]

---

[10] Richmond Dispatch, November 21, 1859, pg. 1; George W. Libby, "Confederate Veteran Magazine", Vol. 38, 1930, 138-139. The author was a member of the Richmond Grays and was with Booth at Charlestown. His eyewitness account was written many years after the war.

Philip Whitlock, a twenty-one year old Polish immigrant and a private in Company "A", the Richmond Grays, stood next to Booth and left us this account: "John Wilkes Booth, being about the same height as I, was right next to me in rank. When the drop fell, I noticed he got very pale, and I called his attention to it. He said that he felt very faint and that he would give anything for a good drink of whiskey. Of course, he did not get it then." Because of the John Brown crisis Southerners feared there would be more insurrections. This fear caused recruitment into the regiment to soar. [11]

A welcome addition to the regiment came in April of 1860 when the Armory Band, under the leadership of James B. Smith, was detached from the Public Guard and transferred to the 1st Virginia. Smith, who was born in England in 1811, joined the Armory band in the mid 1850's. The Armory Band boasted thirteen pieces and was considered one of the premier bands in Richmond. They also performed in various cities along the East Coast. Following a parade in Philadelphia, where the Armory Band accompanied the Richmond Light Infantry Blues, the Baltimore Clipper newspaper wrote that the band, "could be excelled in the execution of music by but few bands in the country." Shortly thereafter, the 1st Virginia formed a regimental drum corps, with fourteen drummers. Sergeant Rudolph Maximilian Pohle of Company K was appointed Drum Major. Pohle was a Prussian immigrant, born near Leipzig in April of 1821. His father was General Carl Golieb Von Pohle, the military governor of Mayence. After living in New York, he moved to Richmond where he worked for Tredegar Locomotive Works and joined the Virginia Rifles, which became Company "K" of the 1st VA. The addition of the two musical organizations greatly enhanced the appearance and reputation of the regiment.[12]

In September of 1860 Colonel August resigned as commander of the 1st Virginia after being appointed Brigadier General of the Second Brigade, Fourth Division, Virginia Militia. Captain Patrick T. Moore of the Montgomery Guard, Company "C", was elected colonel to replace him. Moore was born in Galway, Ireland on September 22, 1821. His family immigrated to Canada in 1835 and later moved to Boston when his father was appointed British consul. Moore then moved to Richmond where he

---

[11] Philip Whitlock, "The Life of Philip Whitlock, Written by Himself"

[12] Wallace, "1st Virginia Infantry" pg. 8

became a successful merchant. In 1849 Moore was instrumental in the formation of the Montgomery Guards militia company. The company was predominantly, if not entirely, formed from Irish Americans who lived in the Richmond area. The founders of the company used St. Peter's Catholic Church in Richmond to organize the unit. Moore was elected the company's first commander, a position he held until being promoted to colonel of the 1st VA.[13]

In addition to the promotion of Col. Moore, there were other changes of regimental officers in the 1st VA. William H. Fry took over as Lt. Colonel on Sept. 18, 1860. Fry was born in Fredericksburg on October 8, 1821. Before the war he was a merchant in Richmond where he joined the Light Infantry Blues, rising to the rank of Captain. At the same time, William Munford was appointed Major of the regiment. Munford was born in Richmond on Aug. 16, 1829. He joined the Richmond Light Infantry Blues in 1850 and also served as Captain in the Eagle Infantry in 1855. He also served as Adjutant of the regiment from 1856-1860.[14]

As tensions between the north and south grew in the waning months of 1860, so did the ranks of the 1st VA. The threat of secession and possibly war caused the Regiment's drill to take on a more serious tone. The crowds of onlookers grew to record numbers when the regiment marched in parades or conducted maneuvers at the fairgrounds. The reality of the Union breaking apart was apparent in Richmond as is evidenced by a seemingly minor incident in early January. Each year on the 8th of January, the regiment would parade to commemorate the American victory over the British at the Battle of New Orleans in the War of 1812. January 8, 1861 was no exception; the regiment formed and marched through Richmond. However as The Richmond Dispatch reported, "After returning to the Square the Regiment was reviewed by Col. Moore and we noticed that the band instead of playing National airs as on similar anniversaries heretofore played the Marselleise." Clearly, allegiances in Virginia had shifted. The next large patriotic event, which took place on February 22, 1861, was the

---

[13] "Historical Times, Encyclopedia of the Civil War" Patricia Faust, Editor, 1986, Harper and Row publishers, Pg. 508; "John Dooley's Civil War, An Irish American's Journey in the First Virginia Infantry Regiment", Edited by Robert Emmett Curran, 2012, University of Tennessee Press/Knoxville. Introduction Pg. XIX.

[14] Wallace, "1st Virginia Infantry", pgs. 94, 108.

celebration of Washington's Birthday and the crowds grew even larger. Governor Letcher was among the many dignitaries who attended the parade. The Richmond dispatch reported, "When the regiment formed on the square, where they were reviewed by the largest collection of fair women and brave men that we ever recollect to have seen congregated there on a similar occasion." By the time of Washington's Birthday celebration, seven southern states had seceded. [15]

New companies of militia were being formed throughout the state of Virginia. What was later to become Company "D" of the 1st VA was organized in March of 1861 as the "Old Dominion Guard." Much of what was later written about the 1st VA came from the men of Company "D." Charles Loehr, Edward P. Reeve, Howard Malcolm Walthall, Edwin H. Chamberlayne Jr. and John Dooley Jr. all wrote of their war time experiences and all were members of Company D. The organizers of "The Old Dominion Guard" used a vacant storefront on Main Street as their recruiting center. With the fervor of the times, they soon had enough recruits to form their company and offer their services to the State of Virginia. Joseph W. Griswold, a 26-year old Richmond lawyer was elected Captain of the "Old Dominion Guard." Also elected were 1st Lieutenant William H. Palmer and 2nd Lieutenant Henry Harney. The "Old Dominion Guard" soon numbered over 80 men and went into barracks on Main Street between 7th and 8th streets. Not long afterward they were attached to the 1st Virginia Infantry as Company "D", becoming the newest company in the old regiment. Originally, they were not as well equipped as the more established companies in the regiment, but they took their training and drill very seriously and soon began to look like soldiers. [16]

As Virginia neared secession and the country headed toward a heretofore unthinkable war, the 1st Virginia was comprised of the following officers and companies:

---

15 Richmond Dispatch, January 9, 1861, pg. 1; Richmond Dispatch, February 22, 1861

16 Howard Malcomb Walthall, "A Memoir", pg. 4; Charles Loehr, "War History of the Old First Virginia Infantry Regiment." William Ellis Jones, Book and Job printer, 1884, Richmond VA., Kessinger Publishing Rare Reprints, Pg. 5.

Colonel – Patrick T. Moore
Lt. Colonel – William H. Fry
Major – William Munford
Adjutant –Samuel P. Mitchell
Surgeon – Dr. J.S.D. Cullen
Asst. Surgeon – T.F. Maury
Quartermaster – LT. W.G. Allan
Commissary – Capt. DV Bridgeford
Paymaster – J. Adair Pleasants

Non-commissioned Staff
Sergeant Major – William O Harvie
Quartermaster Sergeant – C. E. Gronwald
Commissary Sergeant – E.P. Hudgins
Ensign – E.P. Reeve
Company A – Richmond Grays, Capt. Wyatt M Elliott
Company B – Richmond City Guard, Capt. James K Lee
Company C – Montgomery Guard, Capt. John Dooley
Company D – Old Dominion Guard, Capt. Joseph W. Griswold
Company E – Richmond Light Infantry Blues, Capt. O. Jennings Wise
Company F – Capt. R. Milton Cary
Company G – Capt. William H. Gordon
Company H – Howitzer Company, Capt. George W. Randolph
Company I – Capt. Robert Morris
Company K – Virginia Rifles, Capt. Florence Miller
Band – Captain James B. Smith
Drum Corps – Drum Major, Sergeant Rudolph Maximilian Pohle[17]

[17] Loehr, "War History of the Old First Virginia", Pg. 6

BAPTISM OF FIRE

Immediately following Virginia's secession from the Union, Governor Letcher called for the mobilization of the state's volunteers on April 17, 1861. The 1st Virginia went through several significant organizational changes in these first few days following the state's secession. The first change was the removal of the Howitzer Company from the regiment. The Howitzer Company became the nucleus used to form the Richmond Howitzers, a new artillery battalion. Captain Randolph was promoted to Major of this new battalion.[18]

The Howitzers were just the first of four companies that were to be taken from the 1st Virginia. Since the older companies of the 1st VA were already established, they were equipped, trained and ready to take the field immediately. In these early days there was a sense of urgency that the fighting could commence at any time. Therefore, established units were in great demand to protect vulnerable points within the state. Company "A", the "Richmond Grays", was sent to Norfolk on April 21, 1861 never to be returned to the regiment. Instead they were eventually incorporated into the 12th Virginia. On April 24, Company "E", the "Richmond Light Infantry Blues", and Company "F" were sent to Fredericksburg in response to the news of an enemy landing at Aquia Creek. The reports turned out to be unfounded, but the companies remained in Fredericksburg. According to a letter from the commander at Fredericksburg, Daniel Ruggles, to General Richard Garnett, Adjutant General, Virginia Forces, the return of the two companies to the 1st VA would cause "irreparable injury" to his command. He also wrote, "I have also to state (on information) that the officers and men in said companies are anxious to remain here, to be incorporated with

[18] Wallace, "1st Virginia History", pg10

a regiment about to be organized. Their return to Richmond, it is said, would give the greatest dissatisfaction and very probably break up these fine companies." In fact Captain Cary, of Company "F", had petitioned John B. Baldwin, the inspector-general of his unwillingness to be mustered into the 1st VA from the beginning. The Captain wished for his company to be mustered into the service of Virginia as an independent company. Cary was told this would result in a total disorganization of the regiment and his company was mustered in as a part of the 1st VA. The reasons for Captain Cary's unhappiness is unknown, perhaps a personal dislike of Col. Moore, the regiment's stern commander. If this was the feeling among the men of the two companies, or just a few disgruntled officers, it was by no means universal. After spending some time at their new location, some of the men passed around a petition to have the companies returned to the 1st VA. The petition was not successful and Companies "E" and "F" were never returned to the regiment. [19]

In both the Union and Confederate armies, a regiment at full strength consisted of ten companies, of approximately one hundred men each, for a total of about one thousand men. On the day Virginia seceded the regiment met those criteria. With the loss of the four companies the 1st VA would now start the war undersized. This was a serious problem that would plague the regiment throughout the entire war. On April 22, The Daily Dispatch in Richmond reported, "The First Regiment, Col. P.T. Moore, paraded for inspection and drill on Broad St. yesterday morning. We estimated the number, including the Fayette Artillery at fully 1,000." On May 27, only a month later the same newspaper reported the regiment's numbers at 850, which was probably exaggerated. Including the band, this left seven companies of the 1st Virginia to start the rigors of a war time regiment.[20]

The Hermitage Fairgrounds (Camp Lee) just west of Richmond was chosen as the Camp of Instruction for the new regiments being formed

---

[19] Charles Loehr pg. 7: "The War of the Rebellion: A compilation of the Official Records of the Union and Confederate Armies", Washington Printing Office, 1884, Reprinted by The National Historical Society, Harrisburg PA, 1971, Reprinted 1985 by Historical Time, Inc. Series 1, Vol. 51 Part 2, pg.28. Hereinafter referred to as "Official Records"; Philip Whitlock, pg. 2

[20] The Richmond Dispatch, Aril 22, 1861; The Richmond Dispatch, May 27, 1861

in Virginia. The corps of cadets from the Virginia Military Institute was brought to Camp Lee under the command of Colonel William Gilham, Commandant of the Corps, to train the new volunteers. With Richmond as their hometown, the 1st VA was among the first of the infantry regiments to arrive at Camp Lee and pitch their tents. After being officially sworn in on April 21, 1861 they arrived at the camp on April 27. [21]

While at Camp Lee the regiment increased in size with the addition of Captain Francis J. Boggs's Richmond Grays #2 which was designated as Company "H", replacing the Howitzer Company. Boggs, who was born in Pennsylvania in 1821, was pastor of a Methodist church in Richmond prior to the war. He was appointed regimental chaplain in April of 1861, a post he promptly resigned after being elected Captain of Company "H" later that same month. It was said the company was efficiently supplied and armed.[22]

An incident involving Sergeant Edward P. Reeve occurred while at Camp Lee which shows the mindset of the army before any lethal action took place. At the time of Virginia's secession, Reeve was a twenty-nine year old pharmacist who lived in Richmond. He was one of the first men to join Company "D" when that company was formed and he was quickly appointed sergeant. Sergeant E.P. Reeve was married on May 13, while the regiment was training at Camp Lee. He was allowed to go home every night, if not on special duty, to be with his new bride. One morning he was a bit late returning to camp and had forgotten his white gloves. For this infraction of the rules he was given an extra hour of guard duty. Within a few short months, forgetting his white gloves would seem trivial, indeed. [23]

Not everyone was thrilled to be under the tutelage of the young cadets from VMI as Howard Walthall wrote after the war, "drilling under those squirty little cadets who lorded it over us like they were seasoned soldiers". After about one month of constant drilling, orders came for the regiment to

[21] John C. Shields, "The Old Camp Lee" Southern Historical Society Papers, Originally Published 1876, Richmond VA, Reprint by Kraus Reprint Co., Millwood, NY 1977, Vol. 26 pgs. 241-246.

[22] The Richmond Dispatch, May 4, 1861, pg. 2

[23] "Civil War Reminiscences of Captain Edward Payson Reeve", Edward Payson Reeve, unpublished. "Edward Payson Reeve Papers", Southern Historical Collection, University of North Carolina at Chapel Hill (#1828), Hereinafter "EP Reeve Reminiscences".

move to Manassas Junction on May 24. Most of the men were given leave to say goodbye to their family and friends. The next morning the camp was bustling with activity. Tents were being struck and the regiment was packing their gear for war. The camp was full of teary eyed civilians who came to see their loved ones off, perhaps for the last time. At approximately ten o'clock in the morning the regiment formed in line and Captain Boggs led them in prayer. After invoking God's blessing, Smith's band began to play and the soldiers boarded the trains for Manassas and unimaginable adventures. All along the route the trains were met at the various stations by the ladies of Virginia who gave the soldiers baked goods, flowers and other tokens of their genuine esteem. The trains passed through Ashland, Fredericks Hall, Tolersville and Louisa. It was on the morning of the 26th of May when the trains pulled into Manassas Junction, a small hamlet which consisted of a tavern, two stores and several houses. [24]

The encampment at Manassas was given the name Camp Pickens and was under the overall command of General Milledge Bonham, of South Carolina, who was later relieved by the "Hero of Charleston", General Pierre Gustave Beauregard of Louisiana. The regiment's time was filled with drill, inspections, guard duty and dress parades. They made a "splendid appearance" at the dress parades which were attended by many spectators including General Beauregard and his staff.[25]

During their time at Camp Pickens there were constant rumors of enemy activity which caused alarm. On one such occasion the report seemed serious enough that the regiment was formed up and marched out to meet the invading Yankees. Many of those in the hospital, fearing they would miss the action, grabbed their muskets and joined their comrades on the march. The exhilaration and adrenalin of finally meeting the enemy carried them along the march. Once it was found to be a false alarm, most of them "gave way completely" and had to be carried back to camp.[26]

On the 1st of June, Companies B, D, G and K were sent to Fairfax Court House under the command of Major Munford. Prior to their arrival at that place, the Warrenton Rifles engaged some enemy cavalry there,

---

[24] Howard Malcomb Walthall, unpublished memoirs, pg. 5; Charles Loehr, "War History of the 1st Virginia" pg. 8; Lee Wallace, "1st Virginia History" pg. 14.

[25] Charles Loehr, "War History of the Old First Virginia", pg. 9

[26] E.P. Reeve, "Reminiscences".

and in the process, their Captain, John Quincy Marr, was killed. The four companies of the 1st Virginia were sent there on outpost duty to watch for any further Union movements. While there, the men slept in an abandoned barn. Sergeant E. P. Reeve wrote to his new bride about the duty they were performing, "I think there can be no more trying duty in the soldier's life than that we are now performing. It requires the most ceaseless vigilance night after night of constant watching." He continued, "There are so many posts to guard and so few men and officers that it is almost constant. I have been on three nights this week and am on again tonight." It was during this operation that the regiment had their first encounter with death; not one of their own but the brother of a member of the 1st VA, and not at the hands of the Federals, but a case of mistaken identity and "friendly fire." The brother, who was in another regiment, was shot and killed by a Confederate picket when he did not give the proper countersign after being challenged. E. P. Reeve wrote, "I never saw anyone more distressed than his brother." Unfortunately, death would soon become a constant companion to the men of the 1st VA. The Federals made no further forays in this area and on June 21 the companies returned to Camp Pickens after being relieved by troops from South Carolina. [27]

The monotony of camp life continued to be broken up by many false alarms of enemy movements. So much so that E.P. Reeve wrote his wife, "I shall not in the future give you an account of an expected engagement as there are so many false rumors and it would tend to make you uneasy."[28]

As the army began to assemble on the plains of Manassas, individual regiments were grouped together into brigades. As part of that organization, Gen. Beauregard placed the 1st VA in the fourth brigade along with the 11th and 17th Virginia. The brigade was placed under the command of Brigadier General James Longstreet on July 2, 1861. James Longstreet was born in South Carolina on January 8, 1821. His father was a farmer and soon after James's birth moved the family to Augusta, Georgia. After his father's death, James and his mother moved to Somerville, Alabama and it was through an appointment from that state that he entered the United States

---

[27] E.P. Reeve, letter to his wife, June 14, 1861 from Fairfax Court House. "Edward Payson Reeve Papers", Southern Historical Collection, University of North Carolina at Chapel Hill (#1828).

[28] E.P. Reeve, letter to his wife, June 9, 1861, from Fairfax Court House.

Military Academy at West Point in 1838. His classmates included men who would play an integral part in the upcoming war, such as U.S. Grant, Henry Halleck, Irvin McDowell, George Thomas and William Sherman. His ranking upon graduation, 54 in a class of 62, did not accurately project the military career that awaited him. He was commissioned a 2nd Lieutenant and served in Missouri, Louisiana and Florida before the Mexican War. He served honorably throughout the war with Mexico and was wounded at Chapultepec. He was brevetted a Major and held that rank until he resigned his commission on June 1, 1861 and offered his services to the Confederate States Army. He was commissioned a Brig. General on June 17, 1861 and became the first brigade commander to lead the 1st VA in battle. Longstreet went on to become one of the iconic figures of the Army of Northern Virginia and indeed of the entire Civil War.[29]

As the 1st VA waited on the plains of Manassas for hostilities to begin the regiment grew with the addition of the Washington Volunteers from the District of Columbia, who were designated as Company "E" on June 22, 1861. This company replaced the original Company "E" known as the "Light Infantry Blues" which was sent to Fredericksburg immediately following Virginia's secession.

The Union Army in and around Washington DC was under the command of Gen. Irvin McDowell. He was under intense pressure from northern politicians, including President Abraham Lincoln, and the American public to invade Virginia, defeat the Confederate army and end the rebellion. McDowell, a West Point graduate, felt his green troops needed more time to train before they could offer battle to the rebel army congregating in Northern Virginia. But the political pressure increased and he finally relented and moved his army further south into Virginia toward Centreville.

On the Confederate side, General Beauregard also needed more time to concentrate his forces. He was waiting on troops from the Shenandoah Valley under Gen. Joseph Johnston to arrive. Beauregard abandoned his position at Centreville and took up a defensive position along Bull Run Creek in an attempt to put more distance between him and McDowell while he waited on Johnston.

---

[29] Patricia Faust, editor, Historical Times, Encyclopedia of the Civil War, pgs. 444-445

This would be the first of many horrific battles between these two great armies, costing many thousands of lives on both sides. The first Confederate troops that McDowell's Union Army would encounter at Bull Run would be the men of the 1st VA.

At 8:15 AM on July 18, General McDowell set in motion the events that would begin the wartime career of the 1st VA with the following orders to Brig. Gen. Daniel Tyler.

"General: I have information which leads me to believe you will find no force in Centreville and will meet with no resistance in getting there.
Observe well the roads to Bull Run and to Warrenton. Do not bring on an engagement, but keep up the impression that we are moving on Manassas."[30]

With these instructions, General Tyler's division left their camps and headed toward Centreville. The lead brigade (1st Massachusetts, 12th New York, 2nd and 3rd Michigan Regiments) was under the command of General Israel Richardson. Out in front of the brigade was a force of light infantry made up of 40 men from each of the regiments in Richardson's Brigade, under the command of Captain Brethschneider. A section of 20 pounder rifled guns of the 2nd U.S. Artillery followed behind the light infantry. Tyler's troops cautiously entered Centreville and found that it was indeed recently abandoned by the Confederate troops. After passing through Centreville, the brigade rested, while Generals Tyler and Richardson personally pushed on toward Bull Run with Brethschneider's light infantry, to reconnoiter at Mitchell's and Blackburn's Fords.[31]

The Manassas-Centreville road crossed Bull Run at Mitchell's ford. The Federal officers found that crossing to be well defended by a large brigade under South Carolinian General M. L. Bonham. Bonham's troops were also supported by cannon from the Alexandria Artillery. A farm road veered off to the left of the Manassas Centreville Road and crossed

[30] "The War of the Rebellion: A compilation of the Official Records of the Union and Confederate Armies", Washington Printing Office, 1884, Reprinted by The National Historical Society, Harrisburg PA, 1971, Reprinted 1985 by Historical Time, Inc. Series 1, Vol. 2, pg.312 Hereinafter referred to as "Official Records",

[31] Official Records, Series 1, Vol. 2, pages 310-313. "Reports of General Tyler and General Richardson.

the run at Blackburn's Ford. Feeling that Bonham's position was too well defended, the Federal officers rode off to investigate the approaches to Blackburn's Ford.[32]

On the day before Gen. McDowell wrote his directive to Gen. Tyler, reports circulated through the Confederate camps of enemy movement from Washington toward Manassas. This time it was no false alarm. Company "C" was in the middle of their 10 o'clock drill when Captain Armistead, the Adjutant General of the Brigade, rode up to Captain Dooley and ordered, "Captain Dooley, march your company in and prepare to march at a moment's notice." After months of the monotony of camp life, the men were eager to finally see some action. The camp was a flurry of activity as the men took what they thought they would need and boxed up the remainder of their belongings. Frank Potts, a thirty-six year old Irish immigrant and a private in Company "C", along with his messmates (James Mitchel, John Keiley, and Joseph Whittaker) packed some rations and filled their canteens with brandy and water, except for Whittaker who filled his with whisky. The roll of the drums summoned the men to fall in. When the regiment was formed up and ready to march off, Company "I" was ordered to remain behind and guard the camp. The men of Company "I" were "mortified" at the thought of missing the first and possibly the only big battle of the war. At approximately 11PM that night, a rider galloped into camp and relayed orders for Captain Taylor to strike the tents and prepare his company to rejoin the regiment at daybreak. Within two hours the men of Company "I" not only struck their own tents, but also the tents of all the companies who had marched off earlier in the day. At 8 O'clock in the morning on the 18th of July, Company "I" happily marched out of camp and met up with their comrades who had taken up positions at Bull Run. [33]

---

[32] Bradley M. Gottfried, "The Maps of First Bull Run", Savas Beatie, 521 Fifth Av., Suite 3400, New York, NY,10175, 2009, Pg. 14, Map #7.

[33] Frank Potts Diary, Sunday July 27, 1861," Camp near Centreville"; The Daily Dispatch, July 22, 1861, this article was written by a correspondent who was imbedded with Company I throughout the battle.

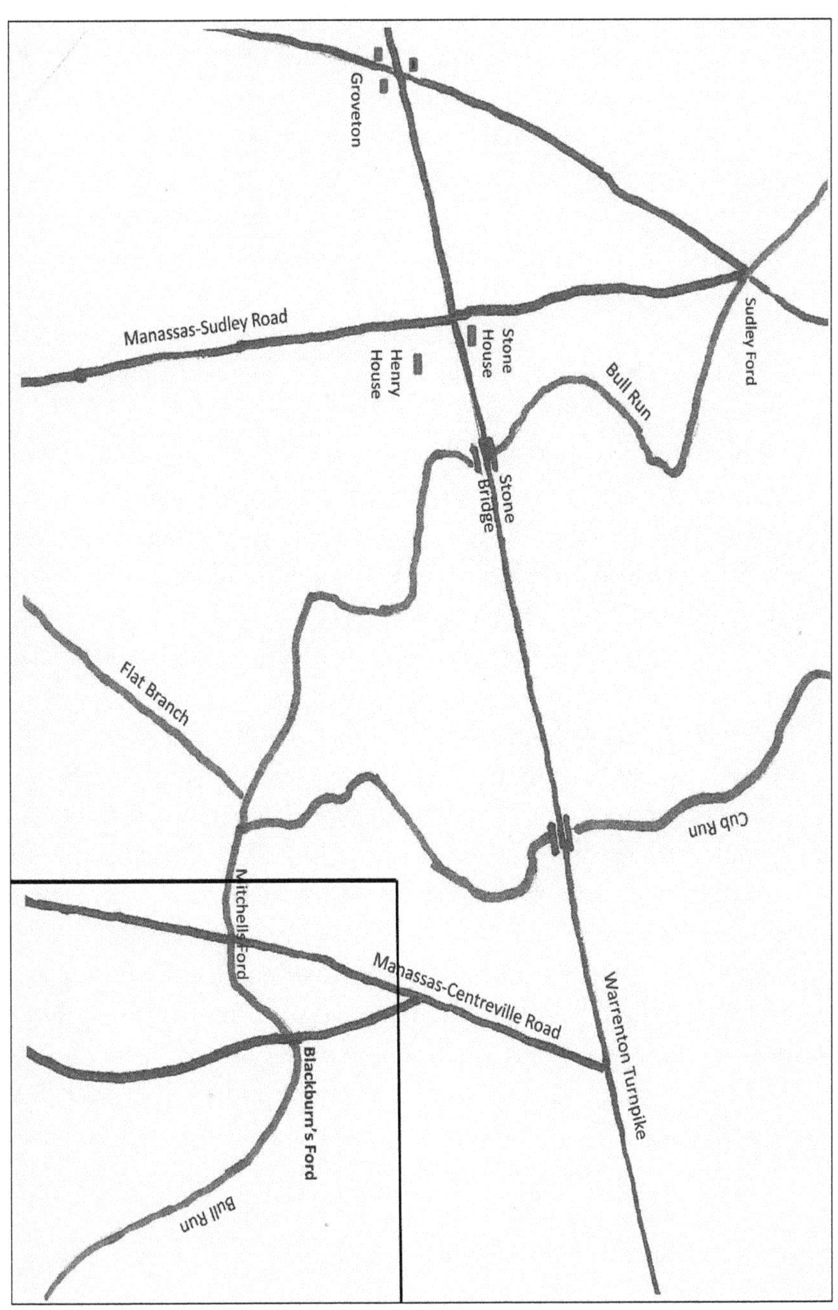

Overview of the Bull Run Battlefield

The rest of the regiment arrived at Bull Run on the evening of the 17th. They crossed over at Blackburn's Ford and halted on the north bank. On the morning of the 18th of July, they re-crossed the run and took up their positions among the trees and underbrush on the south bank and waited to contest any approach by the enemy. Company "D" was on the right, deployed as skirmishers, and to their left was the newly formed company "E" from Washington D.C. To their left was company "K" whose left flank rested on the 17th VA. Next to the 17th was the 11th VA holding Longstreet's left flank. Companies B, C, G and H, of the 1st VA, were held in reserve in an open field to the rear of Blackburn's ford. Company "I" fell in behind Company "D" upon their arrival. [34]

The infantry was supported by 2 six pounder cannon of the famed Washington Artillery from New Orleans. The guns were under the command of Lt. Garnett. The artillery had orders from Gen. Longstreet to retire from the field the "moment it was ascertained that our pieces were commanded by those of the enemy". [35]

General Tyler ordered his Federal artillery to open fire upon the position of the 1st VA and the rest of Gen. Longstreet's brigade at approximately 12PM. He had hoped the cannon fire would result in the Confederate troops disclosing their numbers and position by returning fire. Not wishing to expose their position, the Virginians endured the cannon fire in silence. After a half hour the fire was answered by the two Confederate cannon who quickly found themselves outgunned. Longstreet ordered the guns to the rear "until a fairer opportunity was offered them." At approximately 1 PM, Tyler ordered three companies of the 1st Massachusetts and Captain Brethschneider's light infantry battalion to advance on Blackburn's Ford. The men of the 1st Massachusetts wore grey uniforms which immediately caused them some confusion. They came upon skirmishers from the 1st VA, who of course were also wearing grey uniforms, and were unsure if they were friend or foe. Lieutenant William Smith, of the 1st Massachusetts, ran forward and shouted "Who are you?"

The Confederates replied "Who are you?"

---

[34] Charles Loehr, "War History of the Old First Virginia", pg. 9

[35] Official Records, Series 1, Volume 2, pg. 466, "Report of Maj, John B. Walton, Washington Artillery, of Operations July 18"; "Report of Gen. James Longstreet", pg. 461.

Smith proudly answered "Massachusetts men"

The Virginians fired a volley and Smith was killed instantly.

The skirmishers fell back across the creek where the main line of the 1st VA anxiously awaited the Union troops in the tree line. [36]

Although General McDowell's orders were to "not bring on an engagement", the Union commanders continued to escalate the action. General Tyler was still uncertain how many Confederates were in his front. He ordered two of his howitzers under the command of Capt. Ayres to advance to within 500 yards of Bull Run. Colonel Richardson also sent in the men of the 12th New York. [37]

On the south side of the run the men of the 1st VA were heavily engaged with the 1st Massachusetts troops who were firing from the north shore. E. P. Reeve was a sergeant in Company "D", but on this day he held the post of honor as color bearer for the regiment and was attached to Company "G" who was in the center of the regiment's line. He reported that eleven of the Virginians were felled by the first round of fire they faced in the war. As the volley ripped into the color guard a corporal in line next to Reeve, was among the first to fall. Forty-three year old Lt. Humphrey Miles of Company "G" leaned over to give the wounded corporal a drink of water when Miles, himself, was struck and killed by an enemy bullet.[38]

Colonel Patrick Moore in command of the 1st VA was severely wounded in the left arm and breast while sitting on his horse directing the troops. He was replaced by Major Frederick Gustavus Skinner who had just recently replaced Major Munford. Major Skinner was born on March 17, 1814 in Annapolis, MD. His father, John Stuart Skinner, played an important role in the War of 1812. During the British campaign in the Chesapeake Bay, John Skinner was the United States government's designated prisoner of war agent. In 1814, the British captured a physician, Dr. Beanes, and John Skinner was tasked with obtaining his release. Accompanying Skinner on this mission was a young Maryland lawyer named Francis Scott Key.

---

36 "From Manassas to Appomattox", James Longstreet, Mallard Press, 666 Fifth Ave. New York, NY 10103, 1991, pg. 38: Warren Handel Cudworth, "History of the 1st Regiment Massachusetts", 1883, Boston Walker Fuller and Company. Pg. 42-43.

37 JoAnna McDonald, "We Shall Meet Again", White Mane Publishing Company Inc., P.O. Box 152, Shippensburg, PA, 17257, 1999, pg. 28.

38 E.P. Reeve, "Civil War Reminiscences.

Skinner and Key joined the British fleet and negotiated Dr. Beanes release. The Americans were not allowed to leave the British ships until the current operation, the bombardment of Baltimore, was completed. Skinner and Key paced the deck of their ship throughout the night of September 13-14, watching the British bombardment of Fort McHenry in Baltimore. It was during this time that Francis Scott Key penned the immortal words to his famous poem. Had Key not accompanied John Skinner on that fateful mission, "The Star Spangled Banner" may never have been written. [39]

John Skinner was also a close friend of the Revolutionary War hero, the Marquis de Lafayette. In 1824 Lafayette made a celebrated visit to the United States. When Lafayette returned to France, John Skinner's ten year old son, Frederick, accompanied him and received a premium education there with Lafayette's grandchildren. Upon his return to the United States Frederick entered the United States Military Academy in 1831 but did not graduate. After the death of Lafayette in 1834, President Andrew Jackson appointed Frederick Skinner as ambassador to carry messages of condolences to Lafayette's family and the French government. When Virginia seceded, Skinner enlisted in the 1st VA and was appointed Major. Now in their first engagement he found himself in command of the regiment.[40]

From the tree line on the south shore of Bull Run, the intense musket fire from the 1st VA held the Massachusetts troops in check. When Longstreet saw the Union lines being reinforced by the 12th NY he ordered the reserve companies of the 1st VA to be brought forward and the additional fire power stopped the New Yorkers from crossing the ford.

For several hours, in this, their first battle, the men of the 1st VA endured artillery fire and repeated attacks by Union Infantry. For the first time they had live shells and minie balls crashing through the trees around them and showering them with debris. For the first time they saw their friends and messmates brutally killed and maimed. Yet, they held their position. At one point when it looked as though the Confederate line might break, General Longstreet unsheathed his sword and rode behind the lines

[39] Steve Vogel, "Through the Perilous Fight", Random House Publishing Group, New York, 2013, Pgs. 253, 332.

[40] Marsha Rader, Civil War News, November 1993, pg. 33; Skinner obituary in Unknown Newspaper.

rallying the troops. The Virginians promptly returned to their place in line rather than face the wrath of their brigade commander.[41]

General Tyler brought up the remainder of his brigade which consisted of the 2nd and 3rd Michigan Infantry. Longstreet also called for reinforcements, which included cannon from the Washington Artillery of New Orleans. The artillery consisted of three rifled 6 pounders and four smoothbore 6 pounders including the two guns that retired earlier. The battery was under the command of Captain Eshelman and Lt. Squires. The 7th VA and 7th LA from Col. Jubal Early's brigade also answered Longstreet's call for reinforcements. The 7th VA took up a position directly behind the 1st VA. As they came onto line, the enemy musket fire was exceedingly heavy and the woods were full of smoke and deadly projectiles. This threw the men of the 7th into some confusion and they blindly fired their muskets with the 1st VA in their immediate front. It is unclear if any of the casualties sustained by the 1st VA were from this act of "friendly fire." [42]

At one point, either through miscommunication or fear, the 12th NY began to retreat. This caused some confusion among the Union troops. Longstreet, seeing the Union troops in a state of disorganization, ordered his troops to charge across the creek and attack the Union lines. The 1st VA crossed Bull Run, led by color bearer Sergeant E. P. Reeve. Since the troops had never fought in a battle prior to this day, nor had they ever been drilled in crossing a ford under fire, the attempt was confusing and slow going. But several companies of the 1st VA and some of the 17th VA did manage to break through and engage the enemy on the north shore. Those that got across Bull Run were advancing up the hill on the far side of the stream when orders came for them to fall back to their original positions. [43]

After the war, Color Sergeant Reeve wrote of meeting Gen. Longstreet after he crossed back over Bull Run to the Confederate side. Longstreet

---

[41] James Longstreet, "From Manassas to Appomattox" pg. 39.

[42] Official Records, Series 1, Volume 2, "Reports from the Washington Artillery, July18" pgs. 465-467; "Report of Col. Jubal A. Early, Twenty Fourth VA infantry, of action at Blackburn's Ford", Pgs. 463-464.

[43] John Hennessy, "First Battle of Manassas, An End to Innocence, July 18-21, 1861", Lynchburg, VA, 1989, pg.22

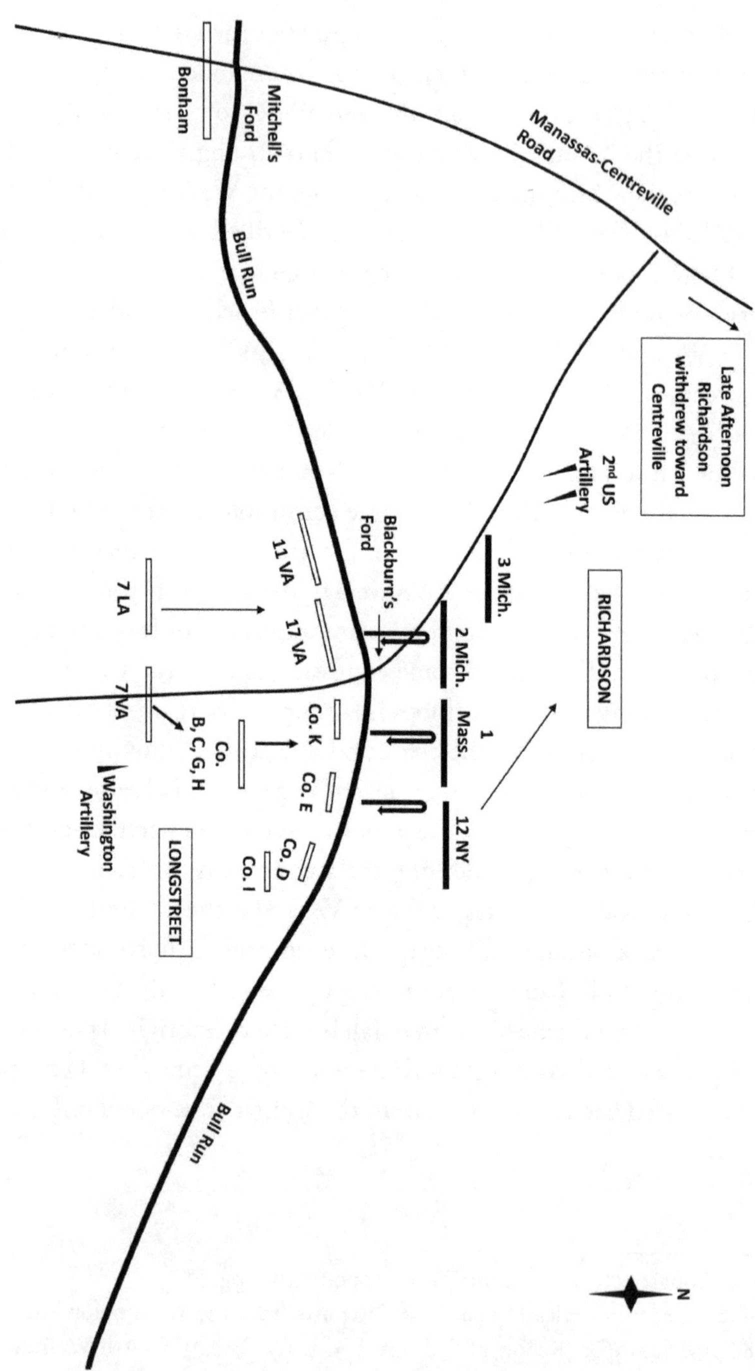

Battle of Bull Run at Blackburn's Ford
July 18, 1861

asked why he had returned to this side of the stream. Reeve told him he was on the other side but was ordered to fall back and that he would gladly carry the colors back over if the General so wished. Longstreet declined the offer and ordered Reeve to rejoin the regiment. Longstreet never forgot Reeve after this encounter. Throughout the war he referred to him as "The Big Sergeant" and said, "He was charging the enemy with the flag of the old First." [44]

Late in the afternoon General Tyler ordered Richardson's brigade to fall back to Centreville leaving the Confederates in possession of the field. The remainder of the afternoon was taken up with artillery fire from both sides. That evening, the 1st VA was relieved by the 7th VA, and the 17th VA was relieved by the 7th Louisiana. Both regiments fell back to the rear for a well-deserved rest. The 1st VA had met the enemy for the first time and handled their baptism of fire remarkably well. Longstreet's brigade suffered fifteen killed and 58 wounded. Thirteen of those killed were members of the 1st VA, along with at least 27 wounded. That such a high percentage of the Brigade's casualties were incurred by the 1st VA was proof enough that they faced the brunt of the Union attack. Their valor that day did not go unnoticed. The next day when Gen. Beauregard and his staff were riding past the men, one of his staff inquired as to the name of the regiment. Lt. Michael Seagers of Company "C" answered, "Tis 1st Regiment, VA Volunteers." Hearing this, Gen. Beauregard turned in his saddle and responded, "And a noble regiment it is." [45]

Years after the war's end, on July 20, 1883, Gen. Longstreet wrote the following;

"The old First Regiment was with me at Bull Run on the 18th of July and made the first fight of Bull Run which drove the Federals and forced them around Sudley Springs. This move on their part was the cause of delay that gave us time to draw our troops down from the Valley and concentrate for the fight of the 21st. The heavy part of the fight was made by the Old First Regiment so that it can well claim to have done more towards the success of the First Manassas than any one regiment. This too was their first battle and I can say

[44] E. P. Reeve, "Civil War Reminiscences".

[45] Charles Loehr, "War History of the Old First Virginia", pgs. 10-11; Frank Potts diary, July 27, 1861, Camp near Centreville.

that its officers and men did their duties as well if not better than any troops whose service came under my observation."[46]

In a very complimentary article printed on July 22, 1861, The Daily Dispatch wrote, "Honor to whom honor is due. The color guard acted most heroically. While the fight was the hottest Sergeant Reeve with Corp. Norvell and four privates passed the creek with flying colors, having to wade up to their waist through the water and planted the glorious bars and stars on the hill under an incessant fire from the enemy."[47]

All of this attention that the men received was quite overwhelming. So much so that E. P. Reeve wrote to his wife, "The boys and the officers and I behaved well and certainly have been praised sufficiently to make me vain if I did not remember to give the glory to God to whom it belongs."[48]

The accolades received by the 1st VA for their performance at Blackburn's Ford were well deserved. The battle on the 18th has been overshadowed by the crushing Confederate victory in the much larger battle of 1st Manassas, which was fought 3 days later on the 21st of July. But by the determined defense of the ford on the 18th against superior numbers and superior artillery, the 1st VA bought the Confederate high command enough time to bring Johnston's troops to Manassas from the Shenandoah Valley. Had the Union troops broke through on the 18th, the argument could be made that the Battle of 1st Manassas could have turned out quite differently or not been fought at all.

The 1st VA remained in the vicinity of Blackburn's Ford for the next two days awaiting the Federal advance that was sure to come. The men only had what supplies they carried with them when they left their camp at Manassas on the 17th. They had no tents, so they slept on the ground with whatever blankets they thought to bring. Fires were forbidden, so as not to give away their position to the enemy. Therefore their meals consisted of crackers and raw bacon. The Virginians quickly learned that life in the field was far more uncomfortable than the life to which they were accustomed.[49]

---

[46] Charles Loehr, "War History of the Old First Virginia". pg. 11

[47] "The Daily Dispatch", July 22, 1861, The fight at Manassas, Thursday (From Our Own Correspondents) Bull Run, July 19,1861

[48] E. P. Reeve, Letter to his wife, July 20, 1861

[49] E.P. Reeve, letter to his wife dated July 25, 1861, Centreville.

On the 20th of July, the regiment was marched back down to Bull Run. They were happy to see that the resourceful troops who were there before them built breastworks for the defense of the strategic ford. The men lay down behind the works, posted guards, and tried to get some sleep. The noise coming from the Union camps that night left the men to speculate on the coming battle. There were drummers beating to the march and bands playing all manner of patriotic songs. At 3AM the men were awakened and told to take their place in the trenches. [50]

During the morning, two Texan officers rode off to scout the Union lines for Gen. Longstreet. They were Colonels Benjamin Franklin Terry and Thomas Saltus Lubbock. They made a reconnaissance of the Union position and noted heavy infantry columns moving toward the Confederate left. On a second mission they noted the position of the batteries facing Longstreet's brigade at Blackburn's Ford. These two Texans earned the respect of the men of the 1st VA for their bravery under fire and were also praised in Gen. Longstreet's official report. Terry went on to organize the 8th Texas Cavalry (Terry's Rangers) and was commissioned its colonel in September of 1861. Lubbock went with Terry and was commissioned Lt. Colonel in the 8th Texas Cavalry. Sadly, both men died within 6 months of their exploits at the Battle of Manassas. Terry was killed in battle at Woodsonville, KY on Dec. 17, 1861. Lubbock was commissioned Colonel to replace Terry; but he died of typhoid fever on Jan. 9, 1862, the day after being commissioned. [51]

Apparently the music and other commotion in the Union camps to the front of Longstreet's brigade on the previous night was a ruse. As reported by the Texans, much of the infantry had moved off toward the left flank of the Confederate lines. In an attempt to calm his nervous troops, Captain John Dooley of Company "C", the "Montgomery Guards", walked along the lines and told the men, "Keep cool men and fire low, should they attempt to cross and jump over the ditch, give them the bayonet. Let each of us commend ourselves to God and pray to him for courage and with

---

50 Frank Potts Diary, Sunday July 27, 1861, Camp near Centreville

51 "Official Records, "Report of Gen. James Longstreet, C.S. Army, Commanding Fourth Brigade, First Corps" Series I, Volume 2, Pgs. 543-544: Bruce S. Allardice, "Confederate Colonels: A Biographical Register, University of Missouri Press, Columbia, 2008.

our hopes and confidence in him we cannot be beaten." Soon after that, the Union cannonade began.

Major Skinner, who had been in command since the wounding of Col. Moore on the 18th, met with General Longstreet around 10AM. Major Skinner returned and marched the regiment out of the trenches, across the run and up the hill on the other side toward the Union batteries. The regiment halted near the top and awaited further instructions, all the while watching Union shells fall dangerously close. While they stood in this vulnerable position the men could hear the sounds of the main battle that was raging off to their left.[52]

Captain Dooley of Company "C" was ordered to report directly to Gen. Longstreet. Company "C", the largest of the 1st VA's companies, was selected to make a charge on the enemy battery of guns that were causing so much havoc on the brigade. The Irishmen of Company "C" marched forward leaving the rest of the regiment behind. They tried to use the terrain and woods to cover their advance as much as possible. When they did come out into the open the Union gunners quickly targeted them. The stress of the moment was alleviated when the men were attempting to cross over a ravine and Private Frank Potts grabbed hold of a dead tree in an effort to pull himself over. The branch broke and Potts landed on his backside in the ditch. His comrades had a good laugh and fortunately for Potts, the only wound he sustained was to his pride.[53]

The men were ordered to drop everything they carried except their muskets and accoutrements. They moved into the tree line closest to the Union battery which continued to belch forth fire and death. The company was to act as skirmishers for the assault on the cannon. They thought this rather strange, since they were the only company in the regiment not drilled in skirmish tactics. The Union gunners began to pour canister and grape shot, along with musket fire from the supporting infantry, into the tree line. Gen. Longstreet, seeing that the Confederate company's position was untenable, ordered them to return to the trenches. The men scurried back over the hill as quickly as possible, dodging Union shells as they went.[54]

---

[52] Fran Potts Diary, Sunday July 27, 1861, Camp near Centreville.

[53] John D. Keily, Letter to his mother dated July 23, 1861, from Bull Run

[54] John D. Keily, letter to his mother dated July 23, 1861, from Bull Run.

They returned to the trenches bordering Bull Run and in some cases had to force their way into the already crowded works. While the shells continued to fall around them they could hear the battle that continued to rage on their left. Gen. Longstreet sat on his horse with a cigar clenched in his mouth, when a courier galloped up and handed him a message. After reading the paper, Longstreet stood high in the saddle and loudly proclaimed, "The day is ours, the enemy has fled." Cheers rose up and down the lines of Bull Run Creek. Then the orders came for the brigade to leave their breastworks and join the pursuit of the defeated Union Army. The regiment went back up and over the hill on the north bank of the creek. They came to the abandoned position of the Federal artillery which had harassed them throughout the day. They continued on and came out into the open fields where they could see the remnants of the defeated Union army complete with the civilian onlookers who traveled from Washington to witness the battle. As two guns of the Washington Artillery passed them on the road, cheers erupted from the ranks of the 1st VA, in recognition of the cannoneers support during the battle on the 18th. The cheers continued as Generals Longstreet, Bonham and Cocke went by at a full gallop.[55]

After marching about two miles they saw the litter of a routed army. Knapsacks, weapons, accoutrements and provisions of all sorts were strewn about the road where the Yankees had dropped them to lessen their load and speed their retreat. Many in the 1st VA had not eaten for 24 hours so they feasted on the discarded food they found and made good use of the blankets and other supplies the Yankees had left behind. The pursuit was halted outside of Centreville and the 1st VA was ordered back to their original position at Blackburn's Ford. For years after, many of the men in the brigade including Gen. Longstreet felt the pursuit of the defeated Union army should have continued all the way to Washington. [56]

That night it began to rain and it continued all the next day, making it quite unpleasant for the men since they had no tents to shelter them.

---

55 Frank Potts, diary Sunday July 27, 1861, Camp near Centreville.

56 John D. Keily, letter to his mother dated July 23, 1861, from Bull Run; Every firsthand account makes mention of what the men thought was a missed opportunity, those that were written within days of the battle and those that were written years afterward.

Some of the men went back up and over the hill that they had fought over for 4 days and toured the Manassas battlefield. The grisly sight of dead and mangled bodies sickened these men who had been soldiers for less than 6 months. The rows of dead bodies awaiting burial brought home the dreadful grotesque realities of war.[57]

Thus ended the first of many deadly encounters with the Union Army that the 1st VA would have to endure over the coming four years. And for the first time they had to add up the human cost of that struggle. The Richmond newspapers informed their interested readers in regards to funeral services for the fallen members of the 1st VA whose mortal remains were returned to the city. Family members in Richmond also studied the casualty lists, printed in the local newspapers, fearing the possibility of seeing the name of a loved one.

Throughout the war casualty lists both official and unofficial were somewhat inaccurate, therefore casualty lists should be considered as partial lists. The following is a partial list of casualties sustained by the 1st VA at Blackburn's Ford, July 18, 1861 and Manassas on July 21, 1861:

Regimental Staff: Wounded- Col. Patrick T. Moore, Maj. Frederick G. Skinner, Quartermaster William G. Allen.

Company B: Killed – Capt. James K Lee, Private John E. Allen. Wounded – Lieut. William W. Harrison, Sergeant William J. Lumpkin, Privates Frederick Lutz, Nathaniel Kessler, John H. Charles, James Henry Cobb.

Company C: Killed – Sergeant Patrick Rankin, Privates James W. Driscoll, Michael Redmond. Wounded – Lieut. William English, Privates Joseph L. Whittaker, Michael Hughes, John Hamilton, Andrew W Forsyth (died from wounds), Lawrence McCabe, John Kavanaugh*.

Company D: Wounded – Privates Isaac T. Porter, David S. Edwards*, Edward R. Miller*.

Company E: Killed – James E. Marron. Wounded – Privates Philip K. Reiley, Thomas Collins, Charles M. Henning*, George B. Jarboe*.

Company G: Killed – Lieut. Humphrey H. Miles, Privates J. Scott Mallory, Souther S. Wilkerson. Wounded – Privates, Henry Ashby, George

57 Charles Loehr, "War History of the Old First Virginia", pg. 12

F. Knauff, James A. Royster, William. S. Ware, Robert Crump, George W. Allen, Benjamin H. Hord.

Company H: Killed – Private Milton A. Barnes. Wounded – Sergeant James L. Bray, John H. Morgan, John H. Hartman, Russell S. Betts, Walter B. Eggleston, Thomas E. Jackson.

Company I: No Casualties.

Company K: Killed – Private Wolfgang Diacont, Friedrich Gutbier. Wounded – Privates William E. Cree, Philip Derhardt, Henry Dubel, Andrew Hatke, Julian Alluisi*, Adam Diacont*.

(* Denotes casualty sustained on the 21st of July, 1861)

Estimated casualties for the regiment were 11-13 killed and approximately 35 wounded.[58]

It seems even the surgeons of the 1st VA were worthy of praise in the Manassas campaign. After the battle, reports surfaced in the northern newspapers accusing the Confederates of mistreating Union prisoners who were wounded. In contradiction to those reports, the following was written by Richard Dunne, a member of the 69th NY: *"Having voluntarily become a prisoner of the Southern Confederacy, for the purpose of alleviating, as far as it is in my power, the sufferings of the wounded of the U.S. soldiers, prisoners at Centreville, and mainly induced to do so in consequence of some of the Northern doctors leaving their post. I feel myself called upon to contradict such statements as have appeared in Northern papers, representing the treatment of our wounded in an unfavorable light. Nothing could exceed the kindness and attention both of citizens and soldiers that have fallen under my personal observation since the eventful 21st ult. It gives me pleasure to award to the surgeons of the 1st Virginia Regiment, Drs. Cullen and Maury, and Dr. Alexander of this village, that praise to which they are justly entitled. They have been unremitting in their attentions."* Dr. Cullen, along with some of the other surgeons in the brigade, also received a special mention in General Longstreet's report. The General said they, "were in the heat of the action

[58] Daily Dispatch, August 1, 1861: Lee Wallace, "1st Virginia Infantry", pgs81-123: "Record of the Richmond City and Henrico Co. Virginia Troops", Compiled by E. H. Chamberlayne, Jr., Richmond 1879.

much oftener than their duties required and were exceedingly active and energetic."[59]

On July 25, 1861 Generals Beauregard and Johnston issued the following proclamation to the army:

Soldiers of the Confederate States:

One week ago a countless host of men, organized into an arm, with all the appointments which modern art and practical skill could devise, invaded the soil of Virginia. Their people sounded their approach with triumphant displays of anticipated victory. Their generals came in almost royal state; their great ministers, senators, and women came to witness the immolation of our army and the subjugation of our people, and to celebrate the result with wild revelry.

It is with the profoundest emotions of the gratitude to an overruling God whose hand is manifest in protecting our homes and our liberties, that we, your generals commanding, are enabled, in the name of our whole country, to thank you for that patriotic courage, that heroic gallantry, that devoted daring, exhibited by you in the actions of the 18th and 21st, by which the hosts of the enemy were scattered and a signal and glorious victory obtained.

The two affairs of the 18th and 21st were but the sustained and continued effort of your patriotism against the constantly recurring columns of an enemy fully treble your numbers, and their efforts were crowned on the evening of the 21st with a victory so complete, that the invaders are driven disgracefully from the field and made to fly in disorderly rout back to their intrenchments, a distance of over thirty miles.

They left upon the field nearly every piece of their artillery, a large portion of their arms, equipments, baggage, stores, &c., and almost every one of their wounded and dead, amounting, together with the prisoners, to many thousands. And thus the Northern hosts were driven from Virginia.

Soldiers, we congratulate you on an event which insures the liberty of our country. We congratulate every man of you whose glorious privilege it was to participate in this triumph of courage and truth-to fight in the battle of Manassas. You have created an epoch in the history of liberty, and unborn nations will call you blessed. Continue this noble devotion, looking always to the protection of a just God and before the time grows much older we will be hailed as the deliverers of a nation of ten millions of people.

---

[59] Daily Dispatch, August 10, 1861; Official Records, Series 1, Vol. 2, pg. 463

Comrades, our brothers who have fallen have earned undying renown upon earth, and their blood, shed in our holy cause, is a precious and acceptable sacrifice to the Father of Truth and of Right. Their graves are beside the tomb of Washington; their spirits have joined with his in eternal communion. We will hold fast to the soil in which the dust of Washington is thus mingled with the dust of our brothers. We will transmit this land free to our children, or we will fall into the fresh graves of our brothers in arms. We drop one tear on their laurels and move forward to avenge them.

Soldiers, we congratulate you on a glorious, triumphant, and complete victory, and we thank you for doing your whole duty in the service of your country.

J.E. Johnston,
General, C.S. Army.
G.T. Beauregard,
General, C.S. Army.[60]

This proclamation was read to the troops at dress parades and church services. The men commented on it widely and seemed to take great pride in their General's appreciation.

The regiment marched to Bull Run on the 17th of July as raw green troops and they marched out on the 24th of July as battle tested soldiers. They returned to Centreville and set up camp. Along the march and in Centreville itself, many of the houses and farms had been deserted by their owners trying to escape the ravages of war. Most of the vacant buildings were being used as hospitals to treat the many wounded of both armies. There were signs of vandalism from the brief occupation by the Union Army that angered some of the men. E.P. Reeve, a religious man, angrily wrote of the desecration of a "neat little Episcopal church" in Centreville. The railings around the church were broken and the walls were covered with abusive graffiti left by the Union soldiers. The wanton destruction brought the pastor, Mr. Brown, to tears. Reeve and the rest of the regiment had no way of knowing that this destruction would pale

[60] Official Records, Series 1, Volume 2, pg. 574

in comparison to what their native state of Virginia would suffer over the next 3 ½ years. [61]

On the 25th of July, 1861, General Beauregard, the Confederate commander, issued Special Orders no. 169 to the First Corps, Army of the Potomac. In this order he reorganized the brigades under his command. General Longstreet remained in command of the 4th Brigade which now included: the First Virginia Regiment of Volunteers under the command of Col. P.T. Moore, the Seventh Virginia Regiment of Volunteers under the command of Col. J.L. Kemper, the Eleventh Virginia Regiment of Volunteers under the command of Col. S. Garland Jr., and the Seventeenth Virginia Regiment of Volunteers under the command of Col. M.D. Corse. This order formed the core of what eventually became known as Kemper's Brigade. Confederate brigades normally consisted of four or five regiments and were the primary fighting unit in the army. Brigades usually traveled together, camped together and fought together. The experiences of one regiment within the brigade were basically the same as every other regiment in that brigade. Strong bonds were formed between the officers and men of the various regiments within their brigades. [62]

After facing death in their first battle, the return to the monotony of camp life made some of the men a little restless. Many ventured into the adjacent town and villages, with or without passes, where they partook of alcoholic beverages and engaged in disruptive behavior. On August 6, a picket was sent out to round up all who were away without leave. Francis McNamara of Company "C", the "Montgomery Guard", had to hide in a corn field to escape the provost. Upon his return to camp he protested to his Company Officers, "What in the name of God do they mean by driving us at the point of the bayonet through the streets, making us a laughing stock for the men of other regiments." In an effort to curtail this type of behavior no more than 5 men from each company were allowed to leave camp at any one time.[63]

By all accounts the most memorable event of their time at Centreville was the visit of Prince Jerome Napoleon of France in early August. The Prince, nicknamed "Plon Plon," was the nephew of the great French

---

[61] E.P. Reeve, letter to his wife, Hester, on July 29, 1861 from Centreville.

[62] Official Records, Series 1 Volume 2, pg. 1000.

[63] Frank Potts, diary, Tuesday August 6, 1861

Emperor Napoleon Bonaparte and the cousin to the current Emperor, Napoleon III. Although the Prince was in North America on an unofficial visit, it was well known that he was a close confidant to Napoleon III. After visiting in Washington, where he had a very awkward meeting with President Abraham Lincoln, the Prince came through the Confederate lines on August 8.[64]

Major Skinner, due to his French education, fluency in the French language and perhaps his family's ties to Lafayette, was tasked with escorting the Prince while he was within the Confederate lines. On the morning of August 9th, the order was passed down to prepare immediately for a grand review. The 1st VA, preceded by Smith's band, marched out onto a large open field where most of the army was forming up for inspection. The Prince rode up in an open carriage along with several officers including General Johnston, the commander of the army. Due to the extreme heat of the day, it was proposed that only one regiment from each of the three brigades assembled, would parade for the Prince. General Longstreet picked the 1st VA for that honor. Smith's band played while the 1st VA passed in review of the Prince and the high command of the army. Being a military man himself and being more familiar with the large "professional" armies of Europe, the Prince was very interested in the concept of a "volunteer" army. The regiment marched past in such a fine fashion that the Prince, in a remark to Major Skinner, thought they must be Confederate Regulars, going as far as complimenting the troops on their marching and soldierly appearance. Skinner replied, "Those men you see were all, a few months ago, clerks or mechanics from Richmond." Napoleon found this hard to believe. He also commented on the disrepair of the uniforms, especially in the seats of the pants. The Major proudly replied that the regiment "has not given the enemy a chance to observe their rears." On the night before the review, E. P. Reeve was invited to meet the Prince at Longstreet's headquarters but he believed it to be a prank staged by his comrades and did not go. Reeve was rather disappointed when he later found out the invitation was genuine. Following the review, Major Skinner escorted the Prince on a tour of the battlefield at Manassas. Afterwards, Prince Jerome

[64] Adam Goodheart, "A Peevish Prince, a Hairy-Handed President, a Disastrous Dinner Party", Napoleon.org, August 2, 2011

Napoleon went back through the lines and continued on his journey of North America. He left the south with a favorable impression of the Confederate Army in general and the 1st VA in particular, but not the Confederate cause. It was later thought that he counseled his cousin, the French Emperor against recognizing the Confederacy. [65]

[65] Richmond Daily Dispatch, August 14, 1861; Charles Loehr, "War History of the Old First Virginia" pg. 12; E. P., Reeve, Letter to his wife Hester, August 9, 1861 from Centreville.

CAMP HARRISON AND WINTER QUARTERS

By all recollections August 10, 1861 was one of the hottest days any of the men could remember. That was the day the 1st VA left Centreville and marched north to Fairfax Court House. The extreme heat caused many of the men to fall out of line along the route of march, including thirty-two year old Captain William Gordon of Company "G" whose sun stroke was so severe it was feared he might die. The Captain recovered and the regiment made it to Fairfax C.H. Unfortunately their tents were still in Centreville and they were met by torrential rains upon their arrival. Their first night at this new location proved to be most uncomfortable. The wagons finally arrived with their tents on the following day and the regiment set up camp, which was designated Camp Harrison[66]

When the 1st VA arrived at Camp Harrison they numbered 681 rank and file among the eight companies. Of that number, 570 of the men were present for duty. The regimental staff, band and drummers accounted for an additional 38 members. The regiment would never be this large again. During this time, a company of approximately 60 men from Washington, D.C. was added to the regiment with the designation Company "F." The new company suffered from disciplinary problems and at one point refused to serve under one of their Lieutenants who had struck a man with his sword. Fearing the entire regiment's morale would suffer because of the internal problems of Company "F", they were quickly removed from the regiment by Gen. Longstreet in early September. [67]

The 1st VA received their long awaited pay in early August, although

[66] Frank Potts Diary, Thursday August 15, 1861

[67] Charles Loehr, pgs.12, 13, "Muster roll of August, 1861 at Camp Harrison, Fairfax Courthouse, VA.": Edgar M. Ferneyhough, letter to Father, September 12, 1861, Fairfax Court House, Library of Virginia.

some of the companies were only paid off to the 1st of July. Many of the men sent their money home to help their families. This was the case with Sergeant E. P. Reeve, who paid off his debts and sent his wife forty-one dollars, keeping only enough for incidentals. Edgar Ferneyhough, a private in Company "D", also sent forty-one dollars home to his father. He requested that twenty-six dollars be used to pay his dentist bill and his father could keep the rest. He closed the letter to his father with, "Today I am eighteen years old."

Perhaps the noblest use of their recent financial gain was by the men of Captain Boggs' Company "H". These men took up a collection and sent sixty-six dollars to Richmond to be used for the care of the sick and wounded soldiers in hospitals there. A list of names of the contributors was printed in the Richmond "Daily Dispatch" along with the following letter; "Editor of the Dispatch, Sir: enclosed you will find a list of the names of the members of Company "H", Captain Boggs, 1st Virginia Regiment of Volunteers, who have contributed a portion of their pay towards the relief of the sick and wounded soldiers at the various hospitals now in this State and also the amount contributed - $66. You are requested by the members of the company through me to see that this sum is properly appropriated. They feel willing to leave it entirely to your judgment to say where it can be best used. Being confident that your application of it will be judicious and that from your superior knowledge of the location and situation of the sick and wounded soldiers, that you would be better able to further their object than they would, should they attempt the application themselves. L. Ringold Thomas, I am very respectfully your obedient servant." Considering the meagre pay of a Confederate soldier, this act of charity towards their wounded and sick comrades in arms speaks volumes as to the character of these men. [68]

While camped at Fairfax C. H., the regiment performed picket duty around Falls Church, under the command of Colonel J.E.B. Stuart. Picket duty normally lasted for four days at a time. The citizenry of Falls Church fled the onslaught of war leaving their houses empty, which the men of the 1st VA occupied while stationed there. On the 25th – 27th of August

---

[68] E.P. Reeve, letter to his wife, Hester, August 15, 1861, Fairfax Court House; Edgar Ferneyhough, letter to his father, August 21, 1861, Commissary Dept. Library of Virginia.: Daily Dispatch, August 27, 1861

several companies participated in a skirmish that resulted in the capture of Munson's Hill. A new drum and 2 prisoners were captured in the skirmish. From the conquered heights the men could gaze down on the enemy capital of Washington. The following day they witnessed a balloon ascension from Alexandria. Captain Rosser's Washington Artillery fired a few shots in the direction of the balloon and it was quickly returned to earth. A few weeks later there was another skirmish involving the 1st VA at Mason's Hill. These missions and skirmishes kept the men in constant danger and continued throughout the regiment's stay at Fairfax C.H. On several occasions the entire brigade was formed up and marched out of camp to meet the Union army, which was reportedly on the move. These reports either turned out to be false or the Federal units retreated before they could be engaged.[69]

When not detailed on picket duty at Falls Church, the regiment took part in the mundane duties that accompanied life in camp. At Camp Harrison, drill for the 1st VA began at 9:00 AM, followed by musket cleaning at 11:00 AM. The entire brigade (1st, 7th, 11th and 17th VA regiments) would drill together at 4:00 PM. As with soldiers of all wars since the invention of black powder weapons, the soldiers of the 1st VA understood the value of maintaining their muskets. Frank Potts, who was promoted to Sergeant in Company "C", found some rust on the back of his piece during an inspection one morning and spent the next two hours cleaning it. Such was the value placed on a well maintained weapon. Once a week the men were required to drop their tents and leave them down from 9:00 AM to 3:00 PM to allow the ground underneath to dry. At the tap of the drums the rows of tents would all fall together. In the afternoon, the tap of the drums would bring them back up in their former positions.[70]

There were several command changes while the regiment was stationed at Fairfax Court House. Major Munford left the 1st VA to accept the colonelcy of the 17th VA. Lt. Col. William Fry unexpectedly resigned his

---

[69] Charles Loehr, "War History of the Old First Virginia", Pg. 14; Richmond Daily Dispatch, December 13, 1861, "Correspondence of the Richmond Dispatch, Camp near Centreville, Dec. 4, 1861"

[70] Frank Potts diary, August 16 & August 21, 1861; E. P. Reeve, letter to his wife Hester, October 6, 1861.

commission and left the regiment. Major Skinner was promoted to Lt. Colonel to fill Fry's vacated spot. [71]

The immensely popular Captain John Dooley of Company "C" was promoted to Major. Dooley, who was born in Limerick, Ireland some fifty years previous, came to America in 1832. In his early twenties he landed in Baltimore and promptly moved to Alexandria where he married his cousin Sarah. It is believed that John and Sarah met on the ship during their voyage to America. They eventually moved to Richmond where Dooley took a job as a clerk before starting his own hat manufacturing business. The Great Southern Hat and Cap Manufactory and Depot was located at 81 Main Street in Richmond and advertised "a splendid stock of Goods, for Wholesale and Retail, which in quality and quantity cannot be excelled by any other house in the South". Dooley's store did quite well making him one of the wealthiest men in Richmond. As a prominent citizen, Dooley became active in civic organizations and religious groups at St. Peter's Catholic Church. He joined his Irish brethren in helping to organize the Montgomery Guard and served as 1st Lieutenant of the company when it was established in 1849. Dooley was elected Captain when Patrick Moore vacated the position to become colonel of the 1st VA. Dooley had three sons, the eldest George, died prior to the war. Dooley's two remaining sons served in the 1st VA. James, the older of the two, enlisted in Company "C", The Montgomery Guards, at the outbreak of war and served with his father. John, the youngest of the Dooley sons, enlisted in 1862 in Company "D". The promotions of both Skinner and Dooley met with the complete satisfaction of the men.[72]

During their time at Camp Harrison, the worn out uniforms that caught the attention of Prince Napoleon were replaced by the City of Richmond. The regiment seemed to be well supplied with everything except drawers, which the men requested from their loved ones at home. At one point provisions became short due to an accident on the rail line

---

[71] Richmond Daily Dispatch, December 13, 1861.

[72] Curran, "John Dooley's Civil War, An Irish American's Journey in the First Virginia Infantry Regiment", Introduction pgs. XIX-XX: John Dooley, "John Dooley, Confederate Soldier, His War Journal", Edited by Joseph T. Durkin, S.J., Professor of American History, Georgetown University, Georgetown University Press, 1945, Introduction pg. XIV: Richmond Directory, Advertisement 1859

from Richmond. During that stretch of time the men subsisted on what they had and those with money purchased produce and meals from the surrounding farms.[73]

Since the war had not yet ravaged the southern states, food was plentiful for the Confederate army. The men of the 1st VA, being in close proximity to their hometown of Richmond, found it relatively easy to get food, whiskey and other articles sent from home. So much so that they were stockpiling some of their army rations, much to the dismay of their brigade commander, Gen. Longstreet, who thought the men were being wasteful and extravagant. He forewarned his men, they would need those provisions before the end of the war.[74]

The camp of the Washington Artillery was near that of the 1st VA. The officers of the Washington Artillery came from wealthy families in New Orleans and they did not allow distance to hamper their supply situation or quality of life. At this point in the war, communications with Louisiana had yet to be interrupted and the people of New Orleans forwarded to their favorite sons everything they could to make their stay in the army as comfortable as possible. Col. Skinner, who had several friends in the Washington Artillery, including their commander Col. James B. Walton, was a frequent dinner guest at their table. The dinners were enhanced with table cloths, an elegant dinner service and the best wines of Europe. Col. Skinner, who was a fair chef himself, competed in culinary competitions with Major Roberdeau Wheat of the Louisiana Tigers and Major Lewis Cabell, the Chief Quartermaster. During this quiet time in the war, Skinner and his friends from Louisiana were feasting on delicacies such as ox head, cooked on coals overnight, and game birds stuffed with fresh oysters.[75]

President Davis visited the army at Fairfax around the 1st of October. The army fell out for inspection by the President and the scene was described by Sergeant E. P. Reeve, "We had quite a military display here a few days ago when we were reviewed by President Davis. The troops were drawn up in line of battle for several miles. Of course, we could see but

---

[73] E. P. Reeve, letter to his wife Hester, Aug. 5 and 15, 1861, Fairfax C.H.

[74] E.P. Reeve, Reminiscences.

[75] Frederick Skinner, Turf, Field and Farm Magazine, Dec. 16, 1887, Reminiscences of an Old Sportsman

a small part of them. I was sorry to see our President looking so thin and careworn but not much surprised as he must have a great deal to do and feel heavily the responsibility."[76]

On the 16th of October, the Confederate Army, which at that time was designated the Army of the Potomac, under the command Joseph E. Johnston, moved back to Centreville and began to prepare winter quarters. The regiment performed regular picket duty at Germantown, where they also worked at fortifying the defensive position.[77]

The men began work on creating a more permanent campsite at Centreville in anticipation of the coming winter. Chimneys made of rocks or barrels were attached to the tents to provide warmth on the cold nights that were sure to come. Each tent slept six men and were set up in wide streets accommodating a company of about 100 men. Wood for the fires had to be hauled from half a mile away, as well as fresh water. With the food that was sent from home and their army rations, the men fared well and by all accounts this was the most pleasant winter of the war. Groups of men, normally tent mates, banded together to form a "mess". If they had extra money the messmates would hire a cook or servant to handle the cooking and other mundane duties of camp life. If not, those duties were shared by the members of the mess. [78]

Picket duty was undertaken by individual companies, with each company going out for three or four days at a time. Recently promoted, Lt. E.P. Reeve wrote to his wife of one such mission in early December. He writes, "We had a pretty hard march of six miles through a cold drizzling rain. I, being in command of my company, Captain Griswold being too unwell to accompany us. We reached our headquarters about noon, I took up my abode in a small hut on the road side where I was sheltered from the rain but not from the cold wind which found entrance in many places where the planks had been torn off. The second day about eleven O'clock we left our temporary camp and marched some three miles below Fairfax C. H. to form an ambuscade for the enemy who had been in the

---

[76] E. P. Reeve, letter to his wife, Hester, October 6, 1861, Fairfax, C.H.

[77] "Record of Captain B.F. Howard's Company "I" 1st VA Infantry Regiment", B.F. Howard, pg. 22, American Civil War Museum, Hereinafter referred to as "B. F. Howard"

[78] Howard Malcomb Walthall, A Memoir, pg. 8.

habit of coming up that road every day for some time past. It looked like a cold blooded stealthy proceeding as we marched quietly and stealthily forward taking advantage of every piece of woods and intervening hill to screen us from observation. We reached our destination a little after noon and took our position in a piece of woods near the road where we quietly awaited the approach of the enemy. I confess I liked the ritual very little, it was necessary for me to think of all the wrongs done and intended to reconcile to me the thought of lying in wait thus for blood. Our situation was very unpleasant in other respects we had to leave our overcoats and brought no food with us. It was necessary in order to keep perfectly still we suffered with the cold and rain and hunger. I felt all the responsibility of my position expecting every moment to engage in a fierce conflict with my entire company looking to me for guidance. But the enemy did not come and we left about night fall and had a very unpleasant march as it rained all the time and the roads were very muddy. I think I was never more exhausted from the combined effect of cold, hunger and fatigue but a hearty supper and a good night's rest restored me for the last night I was on picket and as it still rained I of course had a disagreeable time but all things come to an end and so did my time of picket." [79]

On October 30, the Governor of Virginia, John Letcher, arrived in camp and presented large blue state flags to each of the Virginia regiments. The 1st VA was away on picket duty at the time and although they hurried back to camp they were too late for the presentation. Col. Moore, who was too sick to accompany the regiment on their detail, was present for the ceremony and received the flag on behalf of the 1st VA. The following day there was a grand review in honor of the Governor, in which the regiment participated.[80]

About this time the regiment also received their first battle flag of what was to become known as the Army of Northern Virginia. This flag was approximately 4 foot by 4 foot with a red background overlaid with a blue St. Andrew's cross. Unlike later versions, which featured 13 stars with one in the center of the cross, this early version of the battle flag had 12

---

79 E.P. Reeve, letter to his wife, Hester, December, 3, 1861, Centreville.

80 E. P. Reeve, letter to his wife, Hester, November 1, 1861, Centreville.

gold stars overlaid on the arms of the St. Andrew's cross, with no center star. The flag was made of silk dress material by the ladies of Richmond.[81]

Weather gave the Confederates at Centreville more trouble than the Union Army during the winter of 1861/62. Cold rain frequently drenched the men and caused the camp grounds to become a sea of mud. On November 2, a tremendous nor'easter inundated the camp with torrential rains and strong winds that knocked down all of the tents of Company "H" along with many of the others. The men spent the rest of the night, soaking wet, huddled together around fire pits stoked with damp smoldering logs. On the 28th of February, the regiment was out on picket duty when what was described as a hurricane tracked furiously across northern Virginia. The area was pummeled with high winds and heavy rain. The men returned to camp only to find all of their tents lying flat on the ground and their homemade chimneys blown completely away. [82]

Over the winter there were several command changes, starting at the top of the brigade. On October 7, James Longstreet was promoted to Major General and given command of the division, which included the 4th Brigade and 5th Brigades. Brig. Gen. Richard Ewell was given command of the 4th brigade. This was short lived as Gen. Ewell was promoted to Major General on January 23, 1862 and given a divisional command under Gen. Thomas (Stonewall) Jackson in the Shenandoah Valley. The new brigade commander was Ambrose Powell Hill a Virginian, born in Culpeper on November 9, 1825. He graduated 15th in his class from West Point in 1847. Hill served in the Mexican War and the Seminole War, along with a variety of postings in the U.S. Army. He resigned his commission on March 1, 1861 and entered into service with the Confederate Army where he was commissioned a Colonel and assigned to command of the 13th VA. He held that position until being promoted to Brig. General and given command of the 1st Brigade, 2nd Division. Although their brigade designation changed from 4th Brigade to 1st Brigade, the 1st, 7th, 11th and 17th VA regiments

---

[81] 1909 Richmond Newspaper, This flag survived the war and is in the possession of the American Civil War Museum (The Museum of the Confederacy), Richmond VA. Additional information was obtained from the Museum's worksheet.

[82] Richmond Daily Dispatch, December 13, 1861, "The First Virginia Regiment, Their Experience in Camp"; Charles Loehr, "War History of the Old First Virginia", pg. 14.

remained together. In time, Confederate brigades would be known more for their commander's name than the numeric designation.[83]

General Longstreet issued the following proclamation to his former brigade:

General Order No. 17

In relinquishing the command of the Fourth Brigade, First Corps, Army of the Potomac, the commanding General expresses his sincere thanks to the officers and soldiers of the command, for the kindly patience, the soldierly fortitude, and cheerful obedience which they have invariably exhibited during the many hardships and privations of a long and trying campaign.

The command of a brigade, second to none, is well worthy the boast of any General, and even regret may well be felt at promotion which removes it a step at least from him.

By Command of Maj. Gen. Longstreet.

G. Moxley Sorrell
Capt. and A.A.G.[84]

The regiment remained under the command of Col. Patrick Moore, although, there seemed to be widespread dissatisfaction with him throughout the rank and file. This was at least in part due to his heavy handed discipline and his tendency to refuse most furlough requests. After Bull Run, Col. Moore was absent from the regiment, nursing his wounds. There were also several occasions over the winter when illness removed him from active command. During those periods of time, Lt. Col. Skinner was in command. Skinner seemed to be popular with the men as there was no doubting his bravery, although some thought he was too reckless with their lives. The day to day operations of the regiment were under the purview of the much beloved Major John Dooley.[85]

There were also several command changes within the individual

83 Historical Times, Encyclopedia of the Civil War. Pg. 360.

84 "History of the Seventeenth Virginia Infantry, C.S.A.", George Wise, pg. 41, Kelly, Piet, & Company, Baltimore, MD, 1870.

85 Frank Potts, Diary August 6, 1861: Edgar Ferneyhough letter to his mother, Jan. 29, 1862, Camp near Centreville, Library of Virginia.

companies during the regiment's stay at Centreville. The Richmond Daily Dispatch printed the following list of company commanders on December 13, 1861:

Company B – Captain, Randolph Harrison; 1st Lt. William Harrison; 2nd Lt. James Cobb Jr; 2nd Lt. T. Herbert Davis.

Company C – Captain, William English; 1st Lt. David King; 2nd Lt. James Mitchel.

Company D – Captain, Joseph Griswold; 2nd Lt. George Norton; 2nd Lt. E. Payson Reeve.

Company E – Captain, Charles Sherman; 1st Lt. William Barker; 2nd Lt. George W. Jarvis; 2nd Lt. William Maxwell

Company G – Captain, William Gordon; 1st Lt. Frank Langley; 2nd Lt. Eldridge Morris; 2nd Lt. John McDonald.

Company H – Captain, John Greaner; 1st Lt. James Vaughan; 2nd Lt. William Tysinger Jr; 2nd Lt. Oscar Hough.

Company I – Captain, J. W. Tabb; 1st Lt. Benjamin Howard, 2nd Lt. John Tyree; 2nd Lt. William McKaig.

Company K – Captain, Florence Miller; 1st Lt. F.W.E. Lohman; 2nd Lt. Fred Hagemeyer Jr; 2nd Lt. Herman Paul.

One notable promotion on this list was E. P. Reeve who, as Color Sergeant, had courageously carried the colors across Blackburn's Ford, was promoted to Lieutenant of Company "D."

Some of the changes in command were due to the expansion of the Confederate armies, which opened opportunities for existing officers to gain promotion in new or enlarged units. Unfortunately this took experienced officers from their original units and the 1st VA was no exception. Others were due to casualties at Bull Run and Manassas, officers resigning from the service or being detailed to some government post in Richmond. The latter became a serious detriment to the 1st VA as not only officers but enlisted men were sent to the Capital to work. The Confederate government and its military contractors were in need of essential personnel for the war effort. When the Confederate government moved to Richmond, they began to build a bureaucracy and needed skilled workmen to fill the various posts. Since the 1st VA was from Richmond, family members in the capital established relationships with many of the government officials. In an effort to remove their loved ones from harm's way, they lobbied those officials to have their family members who were serving in the 1st VA detailed to safe jobs in Richmond. Since many of the men were more than qualified for the positions, they took advantage of the opportunity to get away from the drudgery of army life, not to mention the death and destruction of battle. Much to the chagrin of the regimental officers, who could not fill these vacancies with recruits as fast as the men were being detailed to Richmond.[86]

On a few occasions the men themselves tried to help family members or friends get back to civilian life. Such was the case with Private Edgar Ferneyhough, from Company "D", who tried to get his younger brother, Strother, discharged due to illness. Edgar wrote to his father, "I think you would do well to apply to the Secretary of War immediately for his discharge." In the same letter he later writes, "You may be able to get him off on account of his age." Edgar got his wish and his younger brother was discharged on October 9, 1861 when the army realized he was only fifteen years old. [87]

Lt. E. P. Reeve also tried to help someone get out of the army when he felt sympathy for a pair of brothers in Company "I" whose father passed away, leaving their mother and sister destitute and dependent on the brother's meager army pay. He wrote to his wife, "I went so far as to give Tommy a letter to Judge Robinson asking his influence in trying to get a discharge for Joseph who has a situation open in Richmond at any time which would enable him to provide for his mother and sister."[88]

This rate of attrition caused a drastic decrease in the number of soldiers ready for active duty within the already undersized regiment. In early August of 1861, the 1st VA numbered almost 700. By April of 1862, that number decreased to approximately 400. This made the 1st VA the smallest regiment of the four in the brigade, a trend that would continue throughout the war. At that time, the 7th VA numbered 700, the 11th VA numbered 750 and the 17th VA numbered 600. Rogers Battery of Artillery, also attached to the 4th Brigade, had a strength of 62 artillerists. This gave

---

86 Charles Loehr, "War History of the Old First Virginia", pg. 15.

87 Edgar Ferneyhough, letter to his father, August 24, 1861, Fairfax Court House, Library of Virginia: E.H. Chamberlayne Jr., Record of the Richmond City and Henrico County Virginia Troops, Richmond 1870.

88 E. P. Reeve, letter to his wife Hester, August 15, 1861, Fairfax C. H.

Brig. Gen. A.P. Hill a total of approximately 2512 men in his brigade when the army marched out of their winter quarters in March of 1862.[89]

A much larger manpower issue loomed in the future of the Confederate Army. Expecting a short war, most of the regiments, including the 1st VA, enlisted for one year terms and those enlistments would come due during the spring campaigning season. The Confederate Congress debated this issue over the winter months and came up with a set of regulations to reorganize the army. This act of Congress was approved in December and issued as General Orders No. 1 on January 1, 1862. The regulations provided for a fifty dollar bounty to any private, musician or non-commissioned officer who reenlisted in the army for another two years or the duration of the war. The soldier would also get a thirty day furlough, plus travel time not to exceed sixty days, to be taken at a time "compatible with the public Interest." Those that reenlisted would also be able to reorganize their companies and regiments by holding elections for officers of their respective units.[90]

In an effort to appeal to the patriotic duty of the Confederate soldiers, Gen. Johnston issued the following statement on February 4, 1862. Surely it was of great interest to every member of the 1st VA.

General Orders. No. 21.

The commanding general calls the attention of the twelve-months troops under his command to General Orders, No. 1(January 1, 1862) from the War Department, on the subject of their re-enlistment under the act of Congress approved December 11, 1861.

Soldiers! Your country again calls you to the defense of the noblest of human causes. To the indomitable courage already exhibited on the battle-field you have added the rarer virtues of high endurance, cheerful obedience, and self-sacrifice. Accustomed to the comforts and luxuries of home, you have met and borne the privations of camp life, the exactions of military discipline, and the rigors of a winter campaign. The rich results of your courage, patriotism, and unfaltering virtue are before you. Intrusted with the defense of this important frontier, you have driven back the immense army which the enemy had sent to invade our country and to establish his dominion over our people by the wide

[89] Official Records, Series I, Volume 2, part 3, pg. 481

[90] Official Records, Series 1, Volume 5, pgs. 1016-1017, "General Orders, No. 1."

spread havoc of a war inaugurated without a shadow of constitutional right and prosecuted in a spirit of ruthless vengeance. By your valor and firmness you have kept him in check until the nations of the earth have been forced to see us in our true character, not dismembered and rebellious communities, but an empire of Confederate States, with a constitution safe in the affections of the people, institutions and laws in full and unobstructed operation, a population enjoying all the comforts of life, and a citizen soldiery who laugh to scorn the threat of subjugation.

Your country now summons you to a nobler duty and a greater deed. The enemy has gathered up all his energies for a final conflict. His enormous masses threaten us in the West, his naval expeditions are assailing us upon our whole southern coast, and upon the Potomac, within a few hours' march, he has a gigantic army, inflamed by lust and maddened by fanaticism. But the plains of Manassas are not forgotten, and he shrinks from meeting the disciplined heroes who hurled across the Potomac his grand army, routed and disgraced. He does not propose to attack this army so long as it holds its present position with undiminished numbers and unimpaired discipline; but, protected by his fortifications. He awaits the expiration of your term of service. He recollects that his own ignoble soldiery, when their term of service expired, "marched away from the scene of the conflict to the sound of the enemy's cannon," and he hopes that at that critical moment southern men will consent to share with them this infamy.

Expecting a large portion of our army to be soon disbanded, he hopes that his immense numbers will easily overpower your gallant comrades who will be left here and thus remove the chief obstacle to his cherished scheme of Southern subjugation. The commanding general calls upon the twelve-month men to stand by their brave comrades who have volunteered for the war, to re-volunteer at once, and thus show to the world that the patriots engaged in this struggle for independence will not swerve from the bloodiest path they may be called to tread. The enemies of your country, as well as her friends, are watching your action with deep, intense, tremulous interest. Such is your position that you can act no obscure part. Your decision, be it for honor or dishonor, will be written down in history. You cannot, will not, draw back at this solemn crisis of our struggle, when all that is heroic in the land is engaged, and all that is precious hangs trembling in the balance.

By command of General Johnston [91]

[91] Official Records, Series 1, Volume 5, pgs. 1060-1061, "General Orders, No. 21"

Whether it was the General's words or the conscience and patriotic fervor of the men, the majority of the men of the 1st VA re-enlisted in the army. But not all, approximately 70 men took their discharges. Enough of the men in Companies "E" and "K" took their discharges that those two companies were disbanded. The remaining men from those two companies were integrated into the remaining companies of the regiment. For the 1st VA, none of these changes would take place until April 21, 1862 when their original enlistments expired. Although some of those who re-enlisted early took advantage of the thirty day furlough.

After the humiliating defeat suffered at Manassas by the Union Army, General McDowell was cashiered and the command was given to Major Gen. George B. McClellan. McClellan spent the winter rebuilding and training the Union Army in preparation for a spring offensive. Like his predecessor, he was being pushed by the politicians in Washington to engage the Confederate Army and end the war. Gen. McClellan had such a plan and, after getting the President's approval, he began to put it in motion. His plan was to move his army from Washington, by boat, to the peninsula between the York and James Rivers in Virginia. From there he intended to march on Richmond before Gen. Johnston could move the Confederate army from Centreville to block the approach to the capital.

Meanwhile, back in Richmond, the Confederate high command, including President Davis, Gen. Lee and Gen. Johnston, were formulating plans of their own to meet the Northern invasion that they anticipated would begin as soon as the weather permitted. To better cover the approaches to Richmond and put the army in a better defensive position, it was decided to pull the Rebel army back behind the Rapidan and Rappahannock Rivers.

The 1st VA, along with the rest of A.P. Hill's brigade moved out of their winter quarters at Centreville on March 8, 1862. This was one of the very few times during the war when the Confederate army had more supplies on hand than they could use or move. The men were told to take all that they could carry. As the army moved out, the leftover supplies were destroyed. The 1st VA had ridden the trains into Centreville back in May of 1861, but their withdraw from Centreville was by foot, under what can only be described as extremely harsh conditions.

On the 9th of March, they reached Gainesville and camped for the night. The next day they marched approximately 18 miles and camped at Warrenton. On March 11, another 18 miles brought the regiment to Annesville. The 12th saw them through Little Washington, Sperryville and after 20 miles, they camped near Woodville. Although the men had been in the army for almost a year, had successfully fought their first battle and had survived the winter in camp, this was the first time they were required to make such a forced long distance march. They learned quickly what they needed to carry and discarded all of their non-essential items along the roadside. Some of the men began to fall out of the ranks and straggle behind the column. On the 13th of March they crossed the Hazel River and halted for 3 days of rest. This allowed the stragglers to catch up and rejoin their units. The march was resumed on the 16th and after 12 miles the regiment camped at Culpepper Court House. The next day they finally crossed the Rapidan and camped just north of Orange Court House. After a couple of days they were moved one mile south of Orange C.H. and set up camp on a farm belonging to one Dr. Taylor. They remained here for 13 days.

About this time, McClellan's plans of a move up the peninsula were becoming clear to the Confederate high command. On the night of April 3, the 1st VA in a forced march, left Dr. Taylor's farm and headed in the direction of Fredericksburg along the Plank Road. About 1:00 AM on the 4th, they halted for a few hours sleep before starting out again at 6:00 AM. That night they camped a few miles below Vidiersville. On the 5th they reached Macedonia Church and on the 6th they marched into Louisa Court House, making 25 miles over 2 days. They had been marching in a winter storm of snow, sleet and rain. They were cold, soaking wet and covered in mud. Feeling sympathy for the bedraggled men, Gen. A.P. Hill treated the entire brigade to a drink of whiskey at his own expense. This act of kindness was never forgotten by the grateful soldiers of his brigade.

After resting a day at Louisa C.H., they marched out on the 8th of April on the final leg of the journey that would take them back to their hometown of Richmond. That night they camped south of Tolersville on Mountain Road. On the 9th they made 20 miles and camped at Brick Store. The next day, another 18 miles after which they reached Ground Squirrel Church. Finally, on the 12th of April, they camped outside of Richmond at Young's Mill Pond. Some of the men took advantage of being in such close proximity to their homes and went to see their families, most having not been home since they left Camp Lee almost a year prior. Some obtained furloughs, such as Lt. E. P. Reeve, who went to see his daughter, born just 3 days before. Many of those that could not get a furlough decided it was worth the risk of dodging the Provost Marshal and left without leave to see their loved ones before the army moved out again. [92]

[92] B.F. Howard, pg. 23: E.P. Reeve, "Reminiscences": Charles Loehr, "War History of the Old First Virginia", Pgs. 16-17.

WILLIAMSBURG

On the 16th of April, after being on such a strenuous march for a little over a month, the 1st VA, led by Smith's band, marched through the streets of Richmond. Along with the rest of the brigade they made their way to the docks. Awaiting them there was the side wheel steamer GLEN COVE, which was to take them up the James River to Yorktown. Once again, the people of Richmond turned out to see their sons off to war. The docks were full of friends, family and well-wishers. The men boarded the ship, Smith's band struck up a tune, and the GLEN COVE eased out into the James River carrying the 1st VA into harm's way.[93]

The Union army, under the command of Gen. McClellan, had been congregating on the tip of the peninsula at Fortress Monroe for almost a month. In order to counter the Federal threat, Gen. John Magruder was fortifying a line of defenses at Yorktown. For months his men were digging trenches and building redoubts across the peninsula from the York to the James River. Through a series of ruses, Magruder completely fooled the ever cautious McClellan and his intelligence officer, the famed private detective Allan Pinkerton, into believing his force was much larger than it actually was. McClellan believed the Yorktown defenses too strong for an assault and he settled in for a siege. This bought time for Gen. Johnston's Confederate army to assemble and position themselves within Magruder's defenses on the peninsula.

On the 17th of April, the GLEN COVE landed the 1st VA at King's Mill Wharf on the James River near Yorktown. The steamer GLEN COVE must have seemed surreal to the men of the 1st VA. On their pre-war cruises aboard this ship the decks were full of gentleman in their dress militia

[93] B.F. Howard, pg. 24

uniforms accompanied by the belles of Richmond in all their finery. Now the decks of the steamer were crowded with scruffy soldiers intent on stopping a deadly foe from invading their country. After disembarking the regiment marched to the rear of Magruder's defenses and camped near Wynn's Mill. The next day they were placed in the muddy trenches. The persistent spring rains made life in the trenches most uncomfortable. Their time was spent fortifying their position and dodging artillery shells fired from the nearby Union earthworks. Behind the trenches were log cabins built by Magruder's men over the previous winter. The men of the 1st VA used the cabins as refuge from the tenacious cold and rainy weather. On one occasion, when some of the men were sheltering in the cabins the Federal artillery began to lob shells into the Confederate lines. Fearing the gunners would use the cabins as targets, an officer ordered the men out. Just as they were exiting the cabin, a shell burst in one of the doorways. And with that shell burst, 18 year old Private Edgar Ferneyhough, the soldier who months before had sent money home to pay his dentist, became the first member of Company "D" to die in the war. Four days earlier Edgar had written to his mother, "We are all well and in fine spirits. We are very near the enemy. They have been shooting their cannon at our men all day." In a letter to Edgar's parents, Lt. E.P. Reeve wrote, "I never knew a young man more universally respected and beloved his loss has cast a gloom not only over his company but the entire regiment." A few days later, the regiment was taken out of the trenches and moved to the rear. [94]

On April 20, 1862, Col. Moore posted in the Richmond papers a list of 183 names of members of the 1st VA who were absent without leave. Those that did not immediately report to the regiment would be arrested as deserters. Eventually eleven names on that list would indeed be listed as deserters. A few of the officers on the list, resigned from the army and about ten of the men transferred to the artillery, cavalry and the navy. Perhaps the long difficult forced march from Centreville had something to do with these men wanting out of the infantry. While 62 of the 183 men did return to the regiment, what must have been most alarming to the officers of the

---

[94] Southern Historical Society Papers, Vol. 21, pg. 104, "The First Virginia Infantry in the Peninsula Campaign", by Charles Loehr, 1893, Southern Historical Society, Richmond VA 1893, Reprint Kraus Reprint Co. Millwood, New York, 1977: E. P. Reeve, Letter to Mr. Ferneyhough, "Camp Near Yorktown, April 24th 1862".

regiment were the 75 names who managed to obtain discharges or were detailed to Richmond to work for the government. It is unclear how many of the 75 discharged soldiers may have joined other branches of the service or other regiments after being released from the 1st VA. [95]

The one year enlistment period for the 1st VA expired on the 21st of April. Those that reenlisted were now allowed to elect their officers under the new system of reorganization passed by the Confederate Congress back in December. On the 26th of April, elections were held and Lewis B. Williams was elected Colonel of the 1st VA. The 29 year old Williams was a native Virginian, born in Orange County. He attended the Virginia Military Institute and graduated with distinction in 1855. Upon graduation he was appointed Asst. Professor of Mathematics and Asst. Instructor of Tactics at the Institute. At the same time, he attended law school and was admitted to the bar in 1858. At the beginning of hostilities, he raised and trained a company of infantry which he marched to Harper's Ferry on April 17, 1861 and offered their services to the state of Virginia. Soon thereafter he was commissioned a Lt. Colonel by Governor Letcher and was attached to the 7th VA, where he served in that capacity until being elected Colonel of the 1st VA.[96]

Frederick Skinner was re-elected Lt. Colonel. William H. Palmer was elected Major, replacing the 51 year old Major John Dooley who resigned from the army due to his advanced age. Palmer was born on October 9, 1835 into an old established Richmond family who had resided in the city for generations. He enlisted as a private in Company "F" of the 1st VA when the regiment was formed in April of 1861. In a month's time, he was promoted to 1st Lt. of Company "D" and in August of 1861, he was made Adjutant of the Regiment. In October of that year, he was made Assistant Adjutant General of the First Brigade under Gen. Ewell and maintained that position for Gen. A.P. Hill when he assumed command of the brigade. Palmer continued as the Assistant Adjutant General of the brigade until he was elected Major of the 1st VA.[97]

The six companies that remained in the regiment also held elections for company officers and the following were elected Captain of their respective companies:

---

95 E. H. Chamberlayne, "Record of the Richmond City and Henrico County, Virginia Troops", Richmond; Henry Schottt, "The State" Building, 1879

96 Baltimore American Newspaper, February 16, 1896

97 Richmond Times Dispatch, Thursday July 15, 1926. Obit.

Company B: Captain T. Herbert Davis
Company C: Captain James Mitchel
Company D: Captain George F. Norton
Company G: Captain Frank H. Langley
Company H: Captain William E Tysinger
Company I: Captain J.W. Tabb

The former Captain of Company "C", William English, who was wounded in the right leg at Bull Run, found it too painful to continue in the infantry. He left the regiment and went back to Richmond where he formed a cavalry company and continued to serve the Confederacy in the environs of Richmond.

In his place the predominately Irish company "C" elected Lt. James Mitchel to be their Captain and commander. Captain Mitchel's father was considered a radical Irish nationalist and was well known among the Irish in America. In Ireland, John Mitchel Sr. edited a magazine in which he advocated armed resistance against the British occupation of his homeland. For his troubles the British exiled Mitchel, first to Bermuda and then to Tasmania. He eventually escaped and made his way with his family to New York. While there, he began to edit another paper, "The Citizen," geared toward the many Irish immigrants in the United States. As the sectional crisis engulfed the country, Mitchel wrote articles in support of the south and the institution of slavery. In his view the Irish immigrant workers in the ghettos of the north were treated worse by the capitalists then were the slaves in the south. He moved to Knoxville, TN and renamed his paper the "Southern Citizen" where he found a more willing cliental for his views. Mitchel compared the struggle of the south against the north akin to Ireland's struggle against Britain. Over the years he befriended John Dooley Sr., so it was no surprise when his son joined Dooley's all Irish "Montgomery Guard" at the outbreak of hostilities. Mitchel's oldest son, John Mitchel Jr., was in a Confederate artillery unit stationed at the famed Fort Sumter in Charleston South Carolina. The elder Mitchel could not serve in the army due to his age and health problems, so he remained in Richmond editing for both the Richmond Enquirer and Richmond Examiner. James Mitchel, who enlisted in April of 1861, was elected

Lieutenant in August of the same year and continued in that position until being elected Captain of Company "C".[98]

Another aspect of the reorganization that must have been a great source of sadness to the men of the 1st VA was the disbanding of Smith's Band. The band served an important role within the regiment, playing martial tunes as the men marched through the towns and cities of Virginia. Their music also made lonely nights in camp a little more tolerable for the homesick soldiers. Most of the band's members were deemed overage for military service, which was the reason given for their dismemberment.[99]

About this time, the 1st VA's strength was down to approximately 400 men, and it remained the smallest regiment in the brigade. The 11th VA was the largest regiment with approximately 750 men, followed by the 7th VA with 700 men. The 17th VA had 600 men, which gave A.P. Hill's brigade a combined total of 2,450 infantry to start the Peninsula Campaign. Roger's Battery of artillery was also attached to the brigade.[100]

From the time Gen. Johnston arrived on the Lower Peninsula, he was of the opinion that the Yorktown line could not be held once the Union army brought up its siege guns. These guns were far superior to anything the Confederate Army had at Yorktown. He was also concerned that Gen. McClellan could outflank his lines by transporting Union troops down the York and James Rivers and landing them behind Gen. Magruder's line of trenches. Johnston felt the position so weak that he claimed, "No one but McClellan could have hesitated to attack." Johnston waited for the Union engineers to get their siege guns in place, at which time he simply abandoned his position at Yorktown. On the 3rd of May, the Confederate army began evacuating the trenches and started moving up the peninsula toward Richmond. [101]

---

[98] "John Dooley's Civil War, An Irish American's Journey in the First Virginia Infantry Regiment", Edited by Robert Emmett Curran, Pgs. Introduction Pgs. XVIII –XIX.

[99] Charles Loehr, pg. 18

[100] Official Records, Series 1, Volume 11, part 3, pg. 481, "Organization of the Army of Northern VA, Commanded by Gen. Joseph E. Johnston, on the Peninsula, about April 30, 1862"

[101] Douglas Southall Freeman, "Lee's Lieutenants, A Study in Command", One Volume Abridgment by Stephen W. Sears, Simon and Schuster, 1998

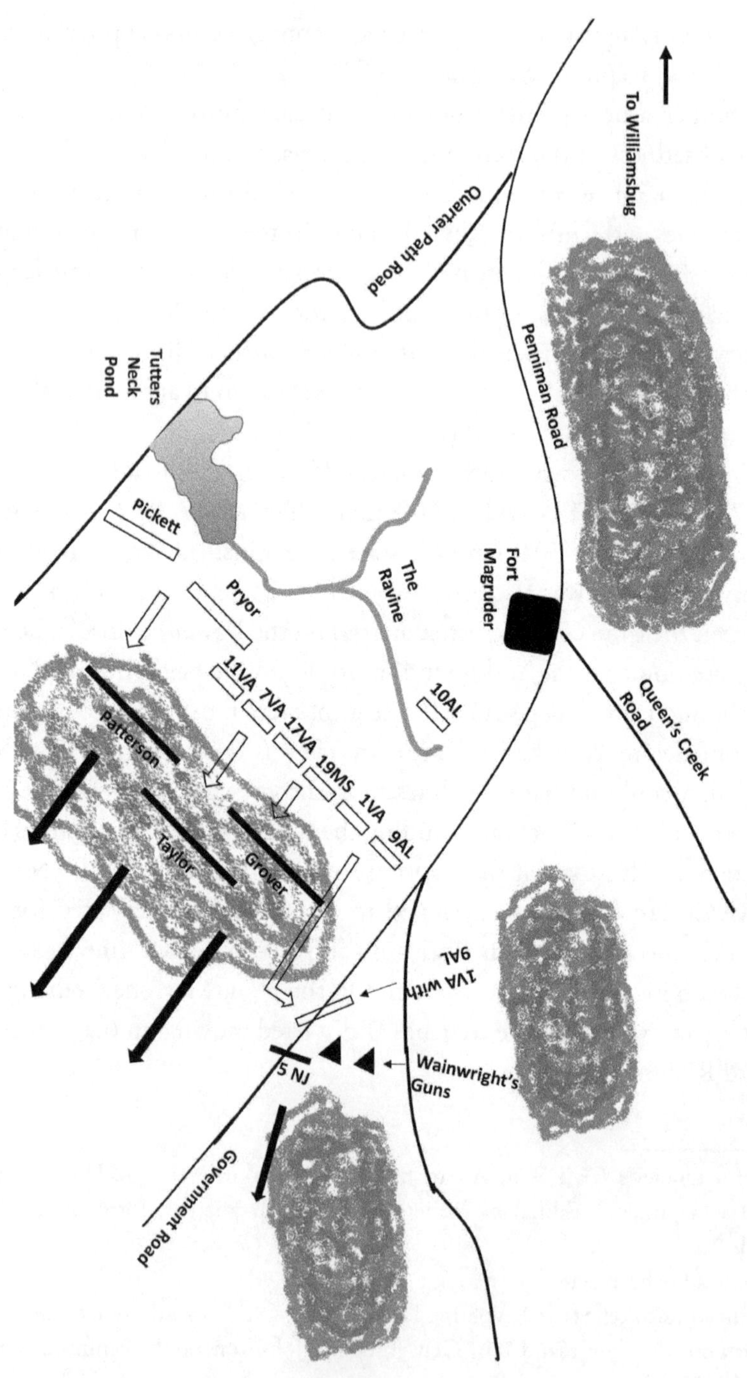

Battle of Williamsburg
May 5, 1862

Longstreet's division, including the 1st VA, was designated as the rear guard for the Confederate army's retreat. The regiment marched about 5 miles and halted by an old church. While they rested, they could hear explosions coming from Yorktown. The sounds they heard were the Confederates destroying the excess munitions and supplies to keep them from falling into enemy hands. Taking up the march later that night and during the next day, the regiment reached Williamsburg. They halted near the asylum on the western edge of town and bivouacked for the night.[102]

As soon as the Federals realized that the way through Yorktown was clear, they began their pursuit of the Confederate army. The 5th of May dawned wet and dreary in Williamsburg. Skirmishing broke out on the eastern side of town as the Union army caught up to the rear guard of the retreating Confederates. About ten o'clock, A.P. Hill received orders from Gen. Longstreet to move his brigade back through town to meet this new threat. Specifically, Longstreet ordered Hill to support the artillery at Fort Magruder on the East side of town. The 1st VA, which fielded approximately 195 men (the remainder of the regiment was on furlough, detailed to other duties or sick in hospital), marched back through Williamsburg, stopping to leave their backpacks at a private residence. They then moved to the right of and slightly behind Fort Magruder, which was manned by the Richmond Fayette artillery and two guns of the Richmond Howitzers under the command of Gen. R. H. Anderson. Upon arrival, Anderson informed Gen. Hill that he was not in need of infantry support. Hill then moved his brigade to the support of Gen. Cadmus M Wilcox, who had also requested re-enforcement. Wilcox's brigade, which consisted of the 9th Alabama, 10th Alabama and the 19th Mississippi, was heavily engaged with a Union brigade under the command of Brig. Gen. Cuvier Grover in a thicket of woods to the front and right of Fort Magruder. Grover's command consisted of the 1st Massachusetts, the 2nd New Hampshire, the 11th Massachusetts and the 26th Pennsylvania. Grover's Brigade was reinforced by a brigade of New Jersey regiments under the command of Brig. Gen. Francis Patterson and the 72nd New York from the brigade commanded by Col. Nelson Taylor. The increased firepower from these

---

102 Charles Loehr, Southern Historical Society Papers, Vol. 21, pg. 104 "The First Virginia Infantry in the Peninsula Campaign.

Federal reinforcements began to push Wilcox's outnumbered Confederates back toward Williamsburg.[103]

A. P. Hill's brigade moved at the double quick under heavy artillery fire, "which was borne with all the steadiness of veterans." After passing Fort Magruder, they immediately formed a battle line. The 7th VA was first in the column and went onto line just as some of Wilcox's troops began to break for the rear. The 11th VA followed the 7th and extended their line on the right. They were followed by the 17th VA which moved to the left of the 7th. To the left of the 17th was the 19th MS, of Wilcox's brigade, who was already in place. The 1st VA moved to the left of the 19th MS and connected with the 9th AL, also of Wilcox's brigade. From right to left the brigade, intermingled with Wilcox's brigade, formed a battle line as follows: 11th VA, 7th VA, 17th VA, 19th MS, 1st VA, and on the extreme left the 9th AL. The conglomeration of regiments pushed forward into the woods slowly driving the enemy before them. The Union soldiers were pushed back to an area of felled timber that formed a natural abatis, offering them excellent cover. General Wilcox described the terrain in his report, "This consisted of large full grown pines that had been felled, forming such an entangled mass of logs and brush as to render it difficult to penetrate." This strong natural defensive position, and the arrival of additional regiments from Patterson's and Taylor's Union brigades, allowed the Yankee troops to rally and make a determined stand. The 1st VA and the rest of the brigade formed a new line about 30 yards from the Union line. The intense fighting continued at this position for approximately 2 hours. When the ammunition started to run low, the order was given to fix bayonets and charge the enemy position. Col. Williams was seen out in front encouraging his men as they and the rest of the brigade charged the Yankee lines. The bayonet charge was too much for the tired Union soldiers and they were forced from the position. Both sides continued to escalate the violence with the addition of fresh troops. The Rebels extended their line further to the right, where the increased pressure helped to force

---

[103] Official Records, Series 1, Volume 11, Part 1, "Report of "Report of Brig. Gen. Ambrose P. Hill, C. S. Army, commanding First Brigade, Second Division.", pgs. 575-579; "Report of Brig. Gen. Cuvier Grover", pgs. 472-474; "Report of Brig. Gen. Francis E. Patterson", pgs. 487-488.

the Federals slowly back. On the extreme left of the Confederate line the 1st VA continued to push on through the dense woods.[104]

Although excellent for defense, the felled trees made it impossible to maintain cohesion for troops trying to maneuver through the obstacles. Formations on both sides of the struggle were confused and the 1st VA became separated from the rest of the brigade. One or two companies of the 9th Alabama attached themselves to the 1st VA and together they continued to fight their way forward through the trees. The regiment came out of the woods and into a clearing that was occupied by a battery of six Union cannon, with five more in an adjacent field to the right.[105]

The guns belonged to Battery "H" of the 1st United States Artillery, under the command of Captain Weber. In the adjoining field was the 6th New York Artillery under the command of Captain Bramhall. The entire combined battery was under the overall command of Major Charles Wainwright, Chief of Artillery in Brig. Gen. Joseph Hooker's Division. The cannoneers of Battery "H" had been driven from their guns earlier in the day but were rallied by Maj. Wainwright and Captain Weber. The 6th NY came up later and was placed in a muddy field to the right of Battery "H". The guns were supported by the 5th NJ infantry. Wainwright's guns had been dueling with the Confederate artillery for approximately seven hours when the 1st VA burst out of the woods on the left of the battery and drove off their infantry support. The cannoneers of Battery "H" had no choice but to abandon their guns, leaving them and two flags in the hands of the 1st VA. The men of the 6th NY Artillery held out as long as possible, but were soon forced from their guns as well.

An aide to Gen. Longstreet arrived and ordered Col. Williams to form a detail of men to take the cannon from the field. Being shorthanded, Williams informed the officer he could not spare anyone to remove the guns. Men from the 19th VA, who recently arrived on the scene, were detailed for the task. The rain continued to fall for most of the day, sometimes in torrents. Some of the guns were hopelessly mired in the mud and the 19th VA could only carry off four of them. Three were Parrott guns

---

104 Official Records, Series 1, Vol. 11, Part 1, "Report of Brig. Gen. Ambrose P. Hill, C.S. Army, commanding First Brigade, Second Division" pg. 575; "Report of Brig. Gen. Cadmus M. Wilcox", pgs. 589-594.

105 Charles Loehr, SHSP, Vol. 21, pg. 107

and the fourth was a twelve pounder howitzer. They also removed one caisson, 40 horses and 2 flags, one of which had "To Hell or Richmond" inscribed on it. [106]

In the following days the use of the 19th VA to remove the cannon caused a bit of controversy as to who actually captured the guns. A letter was written to the "Richmond Enquirer" signed by "A. B. C." from the 28th VA, who claimed the 1st VA was not on the field when the guns were captured by the 19th VA. There were several rebuttal letters written to the Richmond newspapers debating the issue. Below are some excerpts of those eyewitness accounts:

(Excerpt) The issue is one of veracity. Colonel Williams is wounded and a prisoner. When being borne from the field he said that the battery would be claimed by the Nineteenth Virginia, because, when the First Virginia passed through it, he had no men enough to take it off, and requested Colonel Strange to make a detail from his regiment to do so. The colors of the battery were placed on a caisson by a member of the First Virginia regiment. On the third day after the battle I had a conversation with Colonel Strange, in the presence of several witnesses, on the subject of the battery, and understood him to concede the fact that the First Virginia had taken it.

William Palmer,
Major Commanding.

I was with the First Virginia regiment in an engagement near Williamsburg, on the 5th of May, and during that engagement we succeeded in capturing a battery from the enemy. The First Virginia had passed through said battery and formed line when the Nineteenth Virginia had crossed the road and formed on our right. Colonel Williams then requested Colonel Strange to send the battery to the rear, giving as a reason for applying to him, that the First had so few men he could not spare any for the purpose. Soon after Colonel Strange passed, with a few men and a flag from the Nineteenth on our right, to our left, where

---

[106] Official Records, Series 1, Vol. 11, part 1, pg. 470, "Report of Maj. Charles. S. Wainwright, Chief of Artillery"; "Report of Brig. Gen. S.P. Heintzelman", pg. 458; "Report of "Report of Brig. Gen. Ambrose P. Hill", pgs. 575-579: Charles Loehr, "War History of the Old First Virginia", pg. 18.

the guns were, and immediately afterwards all went into action and left the battery to our rear. Who took the guns off I cannot say, but the First Virginia was the first to clear it of live Federal soldiers.

James W. Tabb,
Captain Company I, First Virginia Regiment.

With regard to the above, I have only to state that when the battery on the main road was charged through and taken by the First Virginia regiment, Colonel Strange and his regiment had not come upon the ground. It was not until having obtained permission from Colonel Williams, I had made a detail from my company, of a Lieutenant and some men, for the purpose of manning one of the guns and turning it on the then retreating enemy, that they arrived, coming up on our right, when, as I then understood from Col. Williams, he made arrangements with Colonel Strange for its removal. Anyone who was on the field at that time will see the absurdity of the statement of "A. B. C.," Twenty-Eighth Virginia, in article in the "Enquirer" of the 23rd instant.

James Mitchel,
Captain Company C, First Virginia Volunteers.

I was present at the capture of the battery spoken of in the foregoing article, and after the First Virginia regiment had passed through it and formed twenty steps beyond, Colonel Strange came from the right and said to Colonel Williams, by whose side I was standing, "Williams, you ought to send a detail to take that battery off the field," to which Colonel Williams replied, "Colonel, it is impossible for me to do it, as I have only one hundred and fifty men, but I wish you would do it." Colonel Strange then ordered the battery to be spiked, but eventually some of them were carried from the field by a detail from the Nineteenth regiment.

William T. Fry,
First Lieut. and Adjutant First Reg't. Va. Vols.

After the eyewitness accounts were documented, it was ascertained by the Brigade commander that the 1st VA, along with members of the 9th AL, should be given credit for capturing the Union batteries. [107]

After capturing the battery the 1st VA carried on with the fight, crossing an open field and into another section of woods. The fighting had become very confused, with Union and Confederate forces passing each other in the dense forest of pine trees. At one point, it seemed the bullets were whizzing from every direction. Just as the regiment had become detached from the brigade, individual companies became separated and were forced to fight their way back to the regiment. Eventually, the 1st VA fell back and regrouped near the spot where the remaining captured cannon sat idly in the mud. Some of their muskets had fouled so badly they could not be reloaded and most of the men were running low on ammunition. As they moved, they collected weapons and ammunition from the dead and wounded that were strewn across the battlefield. About six O'clock, Col. Williams was severely wounded through the body and carried from the field. Major Palmer, who was also slightly wounded, took over command of the regiment. The woods were full of soldiers, both Union and Confederate, who were separated from their units. Without the manpower to guard prisoners, those lost and wandering Union soldiers who came upon the 1st VA were simply given directions to the Confederate rear. The Virginians were too wet and too tired to care if the Yankees went into captivity or not.

Yankees were not the only soldiers lost and stumbling through the woods. As the sun was setting, Major Palmer ordered Private Charles Loehr of Company "D" to make contact with a North Carolina regiment that was positioned in a patch of woods to the right of the 1st VA. By the time Loehr found the unit and started back to his own regiment, the sun had disappeared and darkness fell over the battlefield. He saw a line of men that he presumed to be his own unit and called out to them. He quickly realized he was within the Yankee lines when his call was answered with a burst of musket fire. After escaping that threat, he found himself approaching another group of soldiers. Thinking they too were Union troops and being too tired to run, he shouted out, "Don't shoot,

---

[107] Richmond Whig, May 12, 1862; Richmond Dispatch, May 25, 1862; as quoted in "War History of the Old First Virginia", by Charles Loehr, pgs. 18-21.

I surrender." A voice shouted back, "What regiment is yours?" When he answered, "1st Virginia" he was much relieved to find that he had wandered into the lines of the 2nd Mississippi. After being told that the 1st VA had marched off in the direction of Williamsburg, Loehr continued toward the town in search of his comrades. His path to Williamsburg led him to the front of Fort Magruder where the Confederate cannon were busily firing at the Union lines. As the guns were fired, he lay in the mud and waited for the shot to pass over. He finally caught up with his comrades in a vacant house on the western side of town. After a very long tiring day, the men settled down for a good night's sleep.[108]

The next day, having bought the necessary time for Gen. Johnston to move his wagons out of the reach of Union forces, Longstreet's Division left Williamsburg. Colonel Williams, who was too severely wounded to travel, was left in Williamsburg to become a prisoner of the approaching Union troops. Newly elected 1st Lt. E. P. Reeve of Company "D", who had suffered a severe wound to his right shoulder during the afternoon of the previous day, also stayed behind on the recommendation of a surgeon that he not be moved.

After becoming prisoners of war, both men obtained paroles which allowed them to live at the private residence of Mrs. Judge Tucker in Williamsburg, while they recovered from their wounds. After a few weeks of recuperation Lt. Reeve felt as though he was well enough to travel and, in the hopes of being exchanged, he surrendered his parole and turned himself in to the authorities. He was sent to Hampton Roads and remained there about a week. Eventually, he boarded a steamer and was shipped to the prisoner of war camp at Fort Delaware.[109]

In this, their second major engagement, the regiment continued to show great valor and bravery in the face of the enemy. In his official report, Gen. Longstreet wrote, "The brigades of Generals C.M. Wilcox and A.P. Hill were long and hotly engaged. Ably led by those commanders, they drove the enemy from every position. The latter brigade, from its severe loss must have been in the thickest of the fight. Its organization was perfect

---

[108] Charles Loehr, Southern Historical Society Papers, Vol. 21, pgs. 108-109 "The First Virginia Infantry in the Peninsula Campaign

[109] E.P. Reeve, Reminiscences,

throughout the battle, and it was marched off the field in as good order as it entered it."[110]

Brig. Gen. A.P. Hill in his report stated, "We drove the enemy from every position he took, captured all his knapsacks and never suffered him to regain an inch of lost ground. My own brigade was fortunate in taking seven stands of colors, about 160 prisoners and shared with the Ninth Alabama the honor of taking eight pieces of artillery." He continues, "Colonel Williams, being separated from the brigade, acted pretty much throughout the day upon his own judgment, and I have to thank him for the admirable manner in which he handled his regiment." Also, receiving praise in Gen. Hill's report was Captain James Mitchel of Company "C", who received the swords of two enemy officers; Thomas H. Mercer, an 18 year old cadet who was assigned to the regiment for his "coolness and daring"; and Corporal Lee M. Blanton of Company "D" who sustained a wound to his head but stayed on the field and captured General Patterson's carpet sack with his commission papers.[111]

The 1st VA, as well as the entire brigade paid a terrible price for their gallantry on the field of battle at Williamsburg. Out of the 195 soldiers in the regiment that were reported to have started the battle, 9 were killed, 32 were wounded (of which 13 were also captured) and 3 men were captured outright, for a total of approximately 44 casualties. Among the dead was the regiment's Ensign, Canellem Fowlkes, who was shot down while bravely carrying the colors of the 1st VA. The other regiments in the brigade, which were larger, incurred higher numbers. The 7th VA suffered 77 total casualties with 12 killed and the 17th VA had 74 casualties with 14 killed. The 11th VA suffered worst of all. With a reported strength of 750 before the battle, they sustained 134 total casualties with 25 of those men being killed.

---

[110] Official Records, Series 1, Volume 11, Part 1, pg. 567, "Report of Major General James Longstreet, C. S. Army, commanding second Corps", May 16, 1862.

[111] Official Records, Series 1, Volume 11, Part 1, pg. 578, "Report of Brig. Gen. Ambrose P. Hill, C.S. Army, commanding First Brigade, Second Division. (Note- There seems to be some discrepancy as to how many cannon were captured by the 1st VA, Union General Wainwright's report lists 11 guns between the 2 batteries. But most Confederate accounts list 8 or 9. Either way, everyone agrees that only 4 of the guns were carried off. Along with a caisson and 2 stands of colors.

A.P. Hill's brigade, as a whole, suffered 67 killed, 245 wounded, and14 missing for a total of 326 casualties. [112]

A Partial list of the casualties suffered by the 1st VA at the battle of Williamsburg is as follows:

Field and Staff – Wounded: Colonel Lewis B. Williams (left in enemy hands) and Major William H. Palmer.

Company B – Killed: Corporal Charles D. Beale, Privates Jordan Pleasants and Peter Moss. Wounded: Privates Mungo P. Buchanan, Joseph T. Shiflett and Adam Smith.

Company C – Killed: Private Patrick Keeting. Wounded: 2nd Lt. James Hallinan, Private Michael Consadine. Wounded and Captured: Corporal Timothy Costello, Corporal Peter McCauley, Private James Dooley.

Company D – Killed: Private George Logan. Wounded: Sergeants Leigh M. Blanton and James M. Finn; Privates Ezekial Priddy and David S. Edwards. Wounded and Captured: Lt. Edward Reeve, Private Thomas H. Haley. Captured: Private William H. Stewart.

Company G - Killed: Ensign Canellem C. Fowlkes. Wounded: Private Hezekiah Gary, William F. Hord. Wounded and Captured: Corporal Alfred Snead.

Company H – Killed: Private Robert D. Swords. Wounded: Captain William.E. Tysinger, Private John J. Chadick. Wounded and Captured: Sergeant Thomas S. Riddick, Privates Calvin P. Hansford, Edwin Gilman, George A. Rae, and Allen O. Clayton. Captured: Robert E. Dignum.

Company I – Killed: Private John G. Grammer. Wounded: Captain James W. Tabb, Lieutenant William A. Caho, Sergeant Richard M. Jones, Corporal Calvin L. Parker, Privates John T. Ayers, Aurelius Rudd and Thomas Senior. Wounded and Captured: Julius F. Devaux. Captured: Simon Holsman.[113]

---

112 Official Records, Series 1, Vol. 11, Serial 12, pg. 569, "No. 61, Return of Casualties, in the Confederate Forces", (Note- These numbers were compiled from the battle reports and may be incomplete but they give a good indication of the casualties suffered by the brigade.)

113 "War History of the Old First Virginia", Charles Loehr, pgs. 21-22: Lee Wallace, "1st Virginia Infantry", pgs81-123: "Record of the Richmond City and Henrico Co. Virginia Troops", Compiled by E. H. Chamberlayne, Jr., Richmond 1879.

DEFENDING RICHMOND

As the Confederate army abandoned Williamsburg, the incessant spring rains that seemed to plague Virginia in 1862 continued. The roads became bottomless with wagons, cannon, horses and even men getting stuck in the thick mud. After the first day of marching, the regiment reached Burnt Ordinary, a location which Howard Malcomb Walthall remembered as a name befitting the place, "everything surely was ordinary." On the 7th of May, while stopped near the Chickahominy River, they received some meagre rations. There was only enough for each man to get a mouthful, but this was the first food they received since leaving Williamsburg two days before. Thankfully, on the next day, they met a large supply train coming from Richmond. The men loaded up their haversacks and cooked their first full meal in days. On the 9th of May, they reached Long Bridge where the regiment halted and rested for six days. The march towards Richmond continued on the 15th, the regiment moved to within 15 miles of the capital where they camped on the River Road for another six days. They then moved about five miles to Clark's farm, near Darbytown, where they camped for another six days. On the 27th of May, the regiment moved to the Mechanicsville Turnpike, one mile below the Fairfield Race Course. They remained at this location until May 31, 1862.[114]

During this march up the peninsula the men of the 1st VA maintained their good humor. They had been through quite an ordeal over the last 2 months. They endured the grueling march from Centreville, which led to their stay in the water logged trenches at Yorktown, followed by the vicious engagement at Williamsburg. Now they were once again on a forced march in foul weather, across roads that made every step a struggle. But when

114 B.F. Howard, pg. 28

the brigade halted for the night and the campfires were lit, the sound of laughter and songs emanated from the 1st VA camp.[115]

Throughout this first year of war, the honor of commanding this valiant brigade (1st, 7th, 11th and 17th VA) was a fast track to promotion. Following in the footsteps of James Longstreet and Richard Ewell, A. P. Hill became the third brigade commander in less than a year to be promoted from Brigadier General to Major General. On May 27, he was given command of his own division comprising the brigades of Gen. J.R. Anderson, Gen. O.B. Branch, Gen. M. Gregg and Gen. C.W Field.[116]

Col. James Kemper, who commanded the 7th VA, took over command of the brigade, although his promotion to Brig. Gen. was not official until June 3, 1862. Col. Tazewell Patton replaced Kemper as commander of the 7th VA. [117]

James Lawson Kemper was born in Madison City, VA on June 11, 1823. He attended the Virginia Military Institute and graduated from Washington College in 1842. He became a lawyer, but that career was interrupted when the United States went to war with Mexico. Kemper went to Washington and lobbied the Virginia congressmen for a commission in the Virginia volunteers. He was appointed Quartermaster of the 1st VA regiment, pending his commission as Captain from the U.S. Senate, which was obtained on February 1, 1847. While in Washington, he developed contacts with many of the men who became future leaders of the Confederacy. For instance, upon joining the 1st VA at Fortress Monroe, his roommate was Major Jubal Early, then adjutant of the regiment, and a future Lt. General in the Confederate Army. After he returned from Mexico, Kemper practiced law until he was elected to the Virginia House of Delegates, eventually becoming Speaker of the House. He was very interested in, and supportive of, the militia companies of Virginia. Kemper has been given a lot of the credit for the advanced state of Virginia's militia companies at the outbreak of the Civil War. When Virginia seceded from the Union, Kemper accepted the Colonelcy of the 7th VA and served in that capacity until being promoted to Brig. General and command of the same

[115] Howard Malcomb Walthall, pg. 13

[116] Official Records, Series 1, Volume 11, part 3, pgs. 554-555, "Special Orders No.119."

[117] Official Records, Series 1, Volume, 11, part 3, pg. 574 "special Orders No. 123."

brigade in which he had served since the beginning of the war. Perhaps more so than any other commander, his name would be eternally linked with this brigade of Virginians. The brigade was designated 1st Brigade in the 2nd Division, under the command of Gen. Longstreet. Gen. Kemper did not have long to get acclimated to his new role as brigade commander, before he faced the Union army in a pitched battle. In fact, his promotion to Brig. General was not even official until after his first engagement as brigade commander. [118]

Throughout history, soldiers have written of a camaraderie that can only be understood by those who have faced the horrors of battle together. Over the past year, the men of the 1st VA had developed that same camaraderie. And not only among themselves, but also with members of the other three regiments within the brigade. Charles Loehr wrote, "Never, to my knowledge was there the slightest discord or strife between the various regiments composing this brigade. An insult to a member of this brigade was an insult to be resented by every individual man of the brigade. Right or wrong, they would assist and stand by each other; on relying on the other with implicit faith – these were Kemper's men." [119]

Being camped so close to their hometown of Richmond was too much of a temptation for the men of the 1st VA and many took the opportunity to visit with family and friends. On May 30th, torrential rains flooded the camp. Col. Skinner, who was in command of the 1st VA since Col. Williams had been captured, turned a blind eye and most of the men escaped the downpour by sneaking into Richmond. The following morning, the drums unexpectedly sounded for the brigade to fall in under arms, but because of the absentees, there were very few members of the 1st VA present to answer the call. These men fell in with the 7th VA and the brigade marched out of camp toward Seven Pines. Along the route of march, most of the wayward men of the 1st VA caught up with the brigade.

---

[118] "Major General James Lawson Kemper, CSA, The Confederacy's Forgotten Son", Harold Woodward Jr, Rockbridge Publishing, Natural Bridge Station, Virginia, 1993, pg. 12; "Historical Times, Illustrated Encyclopedia of the Civil War", Patricia L. Faust, Editor, Harper and Rowe, New York, NY, 1986, pgs. 411-412.

[119] Charles Loehr, "War History of the Old First Virginia", pg. 23.

Some of the men even brought friends and relatives along with them to bolster the regiment's numbers.[120]

As Gen. McClellan's Union army slowly approached Richmond, it became evident to the Confederate high command that a long siege would be in McClellan's favor. The Confederates needed to attack the Union army in such a way as to limit McClellan's numerical superiority. That opportunity presented itself at the end of May, when McClellan's army was split by the Chickahominy River. The Confederate plan was to strike the Union troops south of the creek before reinforcements could reach them from the north side. It was this plan that put Kemper's brigade into motion on the 31st of May.

The brigade reached the vicinity of Seven Pines at approximately one o'clock in the afternoon. Gen. D.H. Hill's division began the attack an hour later and his entire division was engaged by 3PM. Kemper's brigade was held in reserve until approximately 4PM when they moved down the Williamsburg Road at the double quick. The brigade formed a battle line and moved across an open field where they received heavy artillery and musket fire. A large pile of wood near the "Barker house" offered the men a temporary refuge from the enemy fire.[121]

The enemy troops in front of the 1st VA were made up of men from Pennsylvania, Maine and New York, and were part of the division commanded by Brig. Gen. Silas Casey. Casey's troops arrived at this position on the 29th of May. Since that time, they had been busy fortifying their camp by digging trenches and rifle pits and constructing an abatis, formed from sharpened tree limbs facing the enemy. The work was not yet completed and men were actually working with picks and spades on the fortifications when Gen. D.H. Hill's troops attacked on the 31st. As reports of the Confederate advance reached Casey, he recalled the men working on the breastworks and put his division under arms, including the placement of his artillery.[122]

After regrouping behind the wood pile, the 1st VA continued its forward movement. They were out in front of the brigade and were quickly

---

120 Charles Loehr, "War History of the Old First Virginia", pg. 23.

121 Charles Loehr "War History of the Old First Virginia", pg. 24

122 Official Records, Series 1, Volume 11, Part 1, pgs. 913-917, "Reports of Brig. Gen. Silas Casey, U.S. Army, commanding Second Division."

subjected to an appalling fire that killed or wounded one-third of the men. Those still standing trudged on through the withering fire and eventually forced their way into Gen. Casey's unfinished earthworks. Once in the trenches, the 1st VA traded fire, volley for volley, with the enemy troops who had taken cover in an adjacent tree line. When the remainder of the brigade advanced to the earthworks, their combined fire eventually drove off the Union soldiers. The brigade overran the Union camp and moved into the adjoining tree line. The capture of the enemy camp netted a large amount of provisions and supplies that were left by the retreating Yankees. Gen. Casey's Headquarters tents provided shelter for weary Confederate soldiers that evening. The brigade held this position until they were relieved and ordered to fall back about 9PM. They spent the night behind the lines near the Williamsburg Road. The time spent in actual battle on this day was relatively short compared to the regiment's previous engagements but the brutality of the affair was just as bad if not worse in terms of casualties. The 1st VA lost 14 killed and 44 wounded. These were 58 casualties that the regiment could ill afford.

A partial list of casualties from the engagement at Seven Pines is as follows:

Field and staff – Wounded: Drill Master Lt. Thomas H. Mercer.

Company B – Killed: Lieutenant. Francis M. Mann; Corporal Lewis. H. Strom. Wounded: Captain Thomas H. Davis; Lt. Jesse A. Payne; Sergeants John L. Littlepage, William Harper Deane; Corporals Nathaniel T. Ernest, William I. Carter, Gustavus G. Goddin, William A. Stoaber; Privates George R. Heath, Fred Loehr, Robert. J. Pollard, Richard H. Street.

Company C – Killed: Private Tim Purcell. Wounded: Sergeant Charles Kean.

Company D – Killed: Privates Joseph A. Frith, Lucien R. Smith. Wounded: Captain George F. Norton; Lieutenants. William H. Keiningham and Adolphus Blair; Privates F.W. Gianini, Henry W. Furcron, Tazewell S. Morton, Nathaniel F. Wheat.

Company G – Killed: Privates Marcellus R. Mahone, Charles C. Taliaferro, Robert F. Tyree. Wounded: Lieutenants Eldridge Morris, Leonidas R. Shell; Sergeant George W. Ball; Corporal Thomas H. Gunn; Privates James R. Atkinson, Henry F. Brimmer, Richard D. Jordan.

Company H – Killed: Sergeant Charles R. New; Private William M. Jackson. Wounded: Captain William E. Tysinger; Lieutenant Paul C. Cabell; Corporals Richard Chadick and James A. Via; Private John J. Chadick, Edwin James.

Company I – Killed: Corporals Robert L. Tabb, Robert J. Moss; Privates Hezekiah Brooks, Armistead A. Burgess. Wounded: Lieutenant Benjamin F. Howard; Sergeants William T. White and Edwin C. Goodson; Privates Paul McGrail, Alphonso A. Figner, James Ainsko, Edwin Taliaferro, William F. Terry.

Company K – Wounded: Corporal August F. Weidenhahn; Private Julian Alluisi. [123]

Even amid this great carnage, the men of the 1st VA could find some humor. Charles Loehr related a story involving Private "Monk" Wingfield of Company "D." Prior to the battle at Seven Pines, the men were told they would be held financially responsible for their arms and ammunition. During the battle, the butt of Wingfield's musket was smashed by a piece of shell. He was told to throw it away and pick up one of the many muskets lying about with the dead and wounded. Fearing that he would be charged for losing his musket, he refused to throw it down, saying, "I am not going to pay fifteen dollars for my gun; I am going to carry it back to the ordnance wagon." Which he did the very next day and received a replacement musket.[124]

In his first engagement as brigade commander, James Kemper and the brigade that followed him into battle added new laurels to their esteemed reputations. In his report Gen. Longstreet wrote, "The attack of the two brigades under General R. H. Anderson – one commanded by Colonel Kemper (now brigadier general), the other by Colonel M. Jenkins – was made with such spirit and regularity as to have driven back the most determined foe. This decided the day in our favor." Further in Longstreet's report, he wrote, "My own troops have been so often tried

---

[123] Official Records, Series 1, Volume 11, Part 1, pg. 579, "Report of Col. Montgomery D. Corse, Seventeenth VA. Inf., of Battle of Fair Oaks or Seven Pines, May 31-June1; Charles Loehr, "War History of the Old First Virginia", pg. 24-25: Lee Wallace, "1st Virginia Infantry", Pgs. 81-123: "Record of the Richmond City and Henrico Co. Virginia Troops", Compiled by E. H. Chamberlayne, Jr., Richmond 1879.

[124] "War History of the Old First Virginia", Charles Loehr, pg. 24.

and distinguished on other fields that they need no praise from my lips. A truer, better body of men never marched upon a battle-field."[125]

In his report, Commanding General Joseph E. Johnston complimented Kemper by stating, "Kemper exercised command above his grade." President Davis was also impressed with Col. Kemper's abilities. Two days after the battle he directed the Secretary of War to promote Kemper to the rank of Brig. General. In a message to Gen. Robert E. Lee, he recommended that since Kemper had been in temporary command of the brigade, recently commanded by A.P. Hill, he should remain in that position. He left the decision to Gen. Lee who issued Special Orders No. 123, placing Brig. Gen. Kemper in command of the brigade which included the 1st VA.[126]

The Assistant Adjutant-General, Moxley Sorrel, wrote General Orders No. 18 in General Longstreet's name. In the order he wrote, "The commanding general congratulates the troops of Maj. Gen. D.H. Hill and his own upon their handsome conduct in the various attacks upon the enemy's entrenched positions and camps in the battle of the Seven Pines on the 31st ultimo, and the defense of the position on the 1st instant. After a severe struggle the enemy was driven from his stronghold and all his artillery and his entire camp captured."[127]

Of course, the biggest change in command that came from the Battle at Seven Pines was with the wounding of Gen. Joseph E. Johnston. The following day, President Davis issued Special Order No. 22 which placed Gen. Robert E. Lee in command of the Army of Northern Virginia. Both of these command changes, Lee and Kemper, had a profound effect on the men of the 1st VA. [128]

The constant battle of attrition coupled with the severe casualties sustained by the regiment at Seven Pines finally took its toll and made it doubtful if the 1st VA could survive as a viable regiment to serve under its new commanders. There was a distinct possibility that the regiment would

---

[125] Official Records, Series 1, Volume 11, Part 1, pgs. 939-941, "Reports of Maj. Gen. James Longstreet, C.S. Army, commanding Right Wing."

[126] Official Records, Series 1, Volume 11, Pg. 933, "Report of General Joseph E. Johnson"; Series 1, Volume 11, Part 3, "Davis to Lee", Pgs. 569-570.

[127] Official Records, Series 1, Volume 11, pg. 571. "General Orders No. 18."

[128] Official Records, Series 1, Volume 11, Part 1, pgs. 933-935; Part 3, pgs. 569-570, 57as4, 569.

be disbanded and its members incorporated into other Virginia regiments within the brigade. After a couple of days, it was decided to send the 1st VA, or what was left of it, to Richmond to try and recruit some new men. The regiment marched into Richmond, under the command of Captain J.W. Tabb of Company "I", on the 8th of June and took up quarters in a storefront on Cary St., near Thirteenth St. For the next two weeks the men patrolled the streets of Richmond, rounding up deserters and recruiting new members into the 1st VA. On the 23rd of June, the regiment, along with its new recruits, was ordered to rejoin the brigade at Fairfield. They marched out of Richmond, under the command of Captain G. F. Norton of Company "D." On their way to Fairfield, two of the "substitutes", who were paid to replace former members of the regiment, promptly deserted. The entire regiment reported to the brigade with approximately forty-five members, roughly half the size of a full company, but these forty-five men kept alive the proud name of the 1st Regiment of Virginia Volunteers.[129]

Although this shortage of manpower was most severe in the 1st VA, perhaps due to the discharges for men to work in Richmond, it was by no means exclusive to them. On the day the regiment was ordered to rejoin the army, June 23, 1862, Gen. Longstreet sent a communication to Governor John Letcher in Richmond. In the communication, Longstreet listed every Virginia unit in his command along with their present strength and those absent from their respective units. According to the General, he commanded twenty-three regiments and one battalion of infantry, as well as seventeen batteries of artillery. Those units should have contained a total of approximately thirty-two thousand men, but the actual combined strength of these units was closer to twenty thousand. Of those, seven thousand were absent at any given time, giving Longstreet much closer to thirteen thousand men from the Virginia units. The General writes, "In bringing this subject to your attention my object is to induce you to take some active measures if any such lie in your power, to recruit their ranks." Longstreet went on to explain the advantages of sending recruits to existing units where they could benefit from serving with experienced soldiers as opposed to starting new regiments with all green troops. Of the twenty-three regiments on the report, the 1st VA was the smallest, with a listing of "about 100 present and 200 absent." As can be seen from these

[129] B.F. Howard, pg. 29.

numbers, a large portion of a regiment's rostered members were absent and not available for duty. The absent included wounded and sick in hospital, prisoners, furloughs, etc. There were also support positions within the regiment such as commissary, quartermaster and guard details which drained rostered members from being present for actual combat. The next smallest regiment from Virginia in Longstreet's command was the 46th VA, which had 330 present and 242 absent. It must also be remembered that the 1st VA began the war with only seven companies as opposed to the normal quota of ten which helps to explain the disparity in numbers.[130]

About this time, due to the policy of the Confederate government of brigading regiments by state, the ranks of Kemper's brigade got a boost in numbers with the addition of the 24th VA. Originally, the 24th was made up of companies from Giles, Mercer, Franklin, Henry, Patrick, Floyd, Montgomery, Pulaski and Carroll counties. The regiment was formed in Lynchburg and placed under the command of Colonel Jubal Early who was later promoted to Brig. Gen. after the battle of First Manassas. Prior to their transfer, the 24th VA was in Gen. Early's brigade and had already proven itself in battle. The 24th VA was a welcome addition to Kemper's brigade whose numbers, like those of the 1st VA, had decreased significantly since arriving on the peninsula. [131]

Gen. Lee was determined to drive the Union army from Richmond before Gen. McClellan could call on reinforcements from the north. All available Confederate troops were consolidated into the Army of Northern Virginia for the upcoming offensive, which became known as the Seven Days Battles.

As part of Gen. Lee's effort to push the Yankees back, the entire 1st brigade, approximately 1,400 strong, marched out of camp on the 26th of June. The brigade consisted of the 1st VA under the command of Capt. G.F. Norton of Company "D", the 17th VA under the command of Col. M.D. Corse, the 11th VA under the command of Capt. K. Otey, the 7th VA

---

[130] Official Records, Series 1, Vol. 11, part 3, pg. 614, "Letter to Gov. John Letcher from Maj. Gen. James Longstreet."

[131] Official Records, Series 1, Vol. 11, part 3, pg. 665 "Correspondence from R.E. Lee to Jubal Early, 8/5/1862.": David E. Johnston, "Four Years a Soldier" Pg. 52, Princeton WV, 1887, Digitized by Emory University, Robert Woodruff Library.

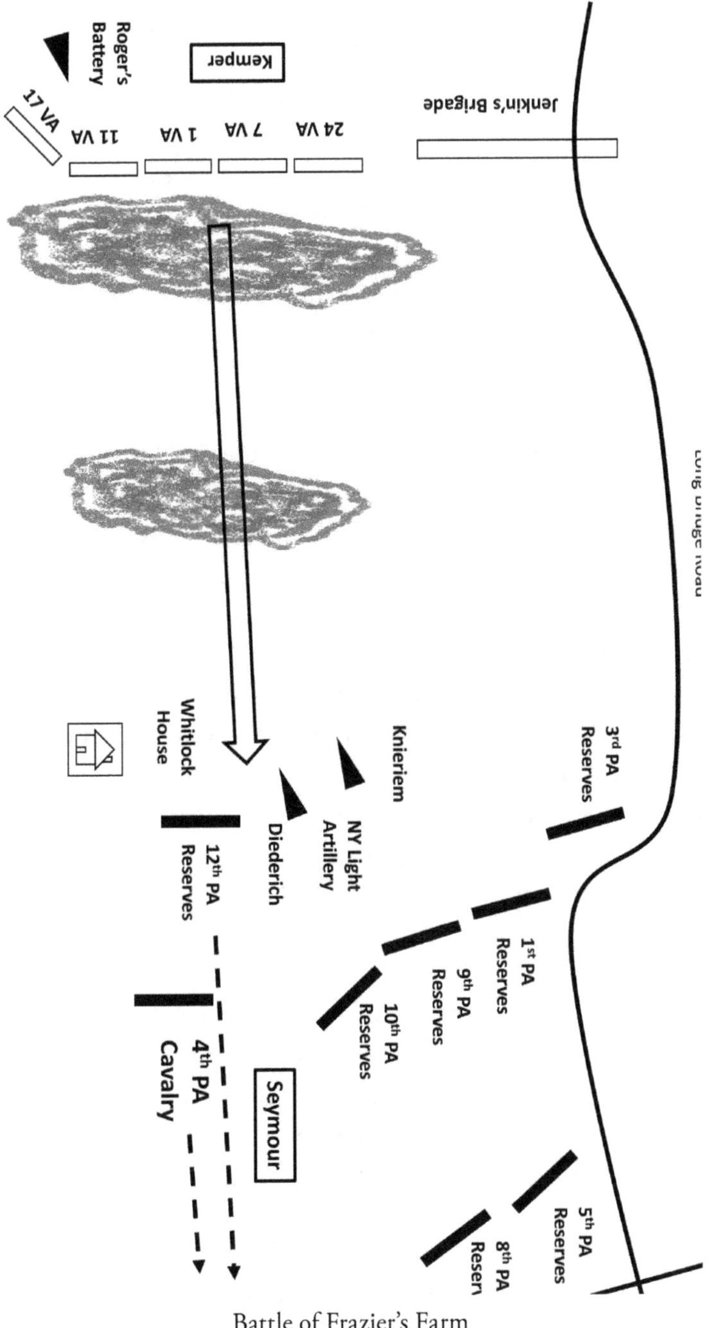

Battle of Frazier's Farm
The fight at the Whitlock House
June 30, 1862

under the command of Col. W.T. Patton, and the newly acquired 24th VA under the command of Lt. Col. Hairston.

On that day, the brigade was held in reserve during the battle of Mechanicsville. They were also held in reserve on the 27th during the battle of Gaine's Mill. After each of these battles, the Union army continued to fall back along their line of supply, with the Confederate army following close behind. The Confederates caught up with several Corps of McClellan's army in the vicinity of the crossroads at Glendale on June 30, 1862 and commenced what became known as the Battle of Frazier's Farm or Glendale.

Kemper's brigade, which constituted the extreme right of the Confederate line, formed a line of battle to the right of the Long Bridge Road. The 1st VA was in the center, with the 11th VA to their right and the 17th VA to the right of the 11th. On the left of the 1st VA was the 7th and to their left was the 24th. The brigade was supported by four guns of Roger's Battery, which were placed near the right of the line to cover their exposed flank. Kemper also faced the 17th VA to the right, at a forty-five degree angle to the rest of the brigade, to help secure his flank.[132]

They reached that position about 1PM but were held in reserve until 5PM. At that time, the order came from Longstreet for the brigade to advance, which they commenced to do in good order. The advance moved through a wooded area, which had an abundance of thick undergrowth, which made it difficult to maintain their formation. As the men tripped and stumbled through the dense vegetation, an enemy battery began to launch shells into the midst of the advancing Virginians. As the brigade came upon the enemy pickets, they promptly pushed them back and quickened their step toward the enemy lines. They hurried through the woods, through an open field and into another section of woods. The men were yelling and cheering as they went which only served to draw more attention from the Federal gunners. The 1st VA remained in the center of the brigade and was out in front. When the men exited the woods, they found themselves facing the Yankee breastworks, which were hastily constructed near a log house owned by the Whitlock family. The works were manned

---

[132] Official Records, Series 1, Volume 11, Part 2, pgs.762-766, "Report of Brig. Gen. James L. Kemper, C.S. Army, commanding First Brigade, of the battle of Frazier's Farm (Nelson's Farm, or Glendale)"

by the 12th PA Reserves, part of Brig. Gen. Truman Seymour's brigade, and supported by eight 20 pounder Parrott rifles in two batteries. The batteries belonged to the New York Light Artillery, under the command of Captains Diederich and Knieriem. Unbeknownst to the Rebels, there were also two squadrons of dismounted cavalry from the 4th PA Cavalry hidden in a ravine directly behind the 12th PA Reserves. As Kemper's men exited the woods and drew closer to the Federal lines, the gunners opened a deadly fire with canister. The field became a killing ground and yet the Virginians braved the fire and continued to move forward at a quickened pace. The brigade forced their way across the field, firing as they went, eventually driving off both the Union infantry and artillerymen. As the 12th PA tried to get away from the Confederate onslaught, they ran through the hidden position occupied by the Pennsylvania cavalry. The troopers were trying to mount their horses just as the disorganized and frightened infantrymen came crashing through. Some of the horses became spooked and made a mad dash to the rear, further disrupting the Union forces. After taking possession of the Federal works, Gen. Kemper realized that his brigade was all alone in that position with a far superior force forming in his front and moving toward both of his flanks. Being the extreme right of the Confederate line, he could not look in that direction for support. The 2nd Brigade, which was to his left, had either become separated or fallen behind during the attack and were nowhere to be seen. Kemper reformed his brigade in a line of battle. When the 10th PA Reserves began putting pressure on his left flank and Federal reinforcements continued to arrive in his front, Kemper ordered the men to fall back. As the brigade was falling back, they found the supporting brigades were finally moving forward.[133]

The 55th and 60th VA from Field's Brigade in A.P. Hill's Division advanced through the trees as Kemper was falling back. They reached the

[133] Official Records, Series 1, Volume 11, Part 2, pgs.762-766, "Report of Brig. Gen. James L. Kemper, C.S. Army, commanding First Brigade, of the battle of Frazier's Farm (Nelson's Farm, or Glendale)"; "Report of Maj. Albert Arndt, First Battalion New York Light Artillery, commanding Third Brigade, Artillery Reserve" pg. 264-265; "Reports of Col. James T. Kirk, Tenth Pennsylvania Reserve" pg. 425; "Report of Col James H. Childs, Fourth Pennsylvania Cavalry" pg. 406; "Report of Brig. Gen. Truman Seymour, U.S. Army, commanding Third Division" pgs. 309-406; "Brig. Gen. George A. McCall, U.S. Army commanding Third Division" pgs. 384-392.

abandoned battery just before the Federal troops could retake it. These fresh troops forced the Yankees back once again and followed them until, like Kemper, they found themselves alone and without support. They fell back to the position of the captured battery and managed to hold it long enough for some of the guns to be taken from the field.[134]

In his official report, Gen. Kemper remarked, "A more impetuous and desperate charge was never made than that of my small command against the sheltered and greatly superior forces of the enemy." He also gave credit to the 1st and 7th VA for making "the first daring charge, which drove the enemy from his position." It was Gen. Kemper's opinion that had the attack been better coordinated and the supporting brigades attacked in concert with his own, the enemy forces in his front would have been destroyed. Since none of the commanders on the Peninsula had ever commanded this many troops, a lack of cohesion was to be expected. Uncoordinated and unsupported attacks among the Confederate forces proved to be a problem throughout the Peninsula campaign and beyond. [135]

Miraculously, no member of the 1st VA was killed at Frazier's Farm, even though some of the men thought it the hottest battle of the war. They did suffer seven wounded and four captured. However, since they only had forty five men under arms when they marched off to Frazier's Farm, this small number still amounted to approximately 25% casualties. This percent of loss was just under the average for the brigade, which started the battle with just over fourteen hundred men and suffered four hundred and fourteen casualties, of which forty-four were killed. One of those captured in the 1st VA was Monk Wingfield, the soldier who had refused to discard his broken musket at Seven Pines. After over-running the cannon at Frazier's Farm, Monk sat on one of them to light his pipe and was still sitting there when the enemy counterattacked and he was taken prisoner.[136]

---

134 Official Records, Series 1, Volume, 11, Part 2, pgs. 846-848, "Report of Col. Francis Mallory, Fifty-fifth Virginia Infantry, of the battles of Mechanicsville, Gaines Mill, and Frazier's Farm (Nelson Farm or Gendale)."

135 Official Records, Series 1, Volume 11, Part 2, pg. 765. "Report of Brig. Gen. James Kemper."

136 "War History of the Old First Virginia", Charles Loehr, pg.25

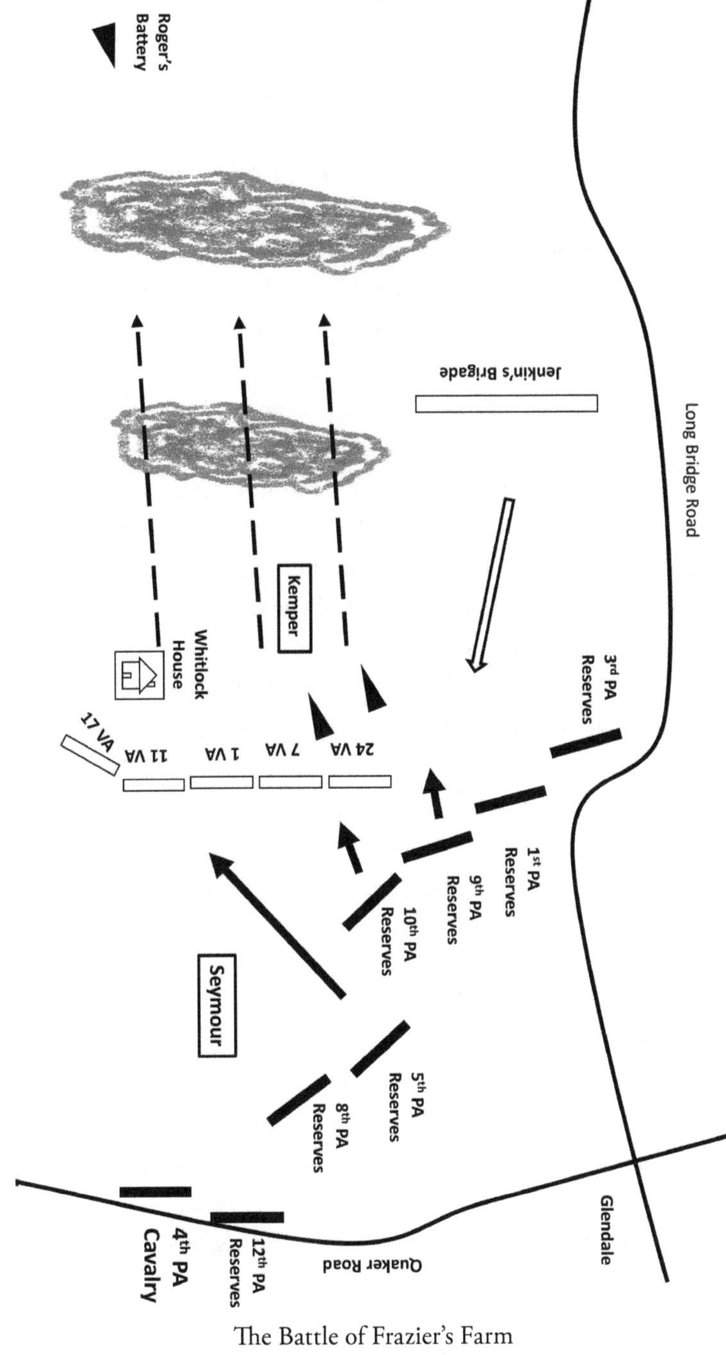

The Battle of Frazier's Farm
Kemper's Retreat

The following is a partial list of the casualties incurred by the 1st VA at the engagement at Frazier's Farm/Glendale:

Company B – Wounded: Lieutenant Logan S. Robins; Sergeants John L. Littlepage and John Q. Figg.

Company C – Captured: Private Lawrence McCabe.

Company D – Captured: Private Marcellus (Monk) Wingfield.

Company G – Wounded: Privates Gustavus A. Chapman, William J. Ferguson, George A. Wilkinson. Captured: William S. Layard.

Company K – Wounded and Captured: Corporal August F. Weidenhahn.

Chaplain Joseph E. Martin was also taken prisoner.[137]

On the 1st of July, the two armies clashed at the Battle of Malvern Hill. The 1st VA was held in reserve and did not get into the fight. Upon arriving on the battlefield afterward, they witnessed the carnage that had taken place. The sight of the mangled bodies lying about the battlefield in long grotesque rows would sicken some of the men for years to come. This was the last contest of the Seven Days Battles and McClellan's Peninsula campaign. The Army of Northern Virginia, under their new commander Robert E. Lee, had forced George McClellan and the Army of the Potomac away from Richmond and back to Harrison's Landing on the James River. Under the cover of his gunboats, McClellan was safe from attack, but the threat to the capital had been removed.

On July 5th, President Jefferson Davis issued the following proclamation to the Confederate army on the Peninsula:

To the Army of Eastern Virginia:

Soldiers: I congratulate you on the series of brilliant victories which, under the favor of Divine Providence, you have lately won, and as the President of the Confederate States, do heartily tender to you the thanks of the country whose just cause you have so skillfully and heroically served. Ten days ago an invading army, vastly superior to you in numbers and in the material of war, closely beleaguered your capital, and vauntingly proclaimed its speedy conquest. You marched to attack the enemy in his intrenchments with well-directed

---

137 "War History of the Old First Virginia", Charles Loehr, Pgs. 25-26: Lee Wallace, "1st Virginia Infantry", Pgs. 81-123: "Record of the Richmond City and Henrico Co. Virginia Troops", Compiled by E. H. Chamberlayne, Jr., Richmond 1879.

movements and death defying valor. You charged upon him in his strong positions, drove him from field to field over a distance of more than 35 miles, and despite his re-enforcements, compelled him to seek safety under cover of his gunboats, where he now lies cowering before the army so lately derided and threatened with entire subjugation. The fortitude with which you have borne toil and privation, the gallantry with which you have entered into each successive battle, must have been witnessed to be fully appreciated, but a grateful people will not fail to recognize your deeds and to bear you in loved remembrance. Well may it be said of you that you have "done enough for glory," but duty to a suffering country and to the cause of constitutional liberty claims from you yet further effort. Let it be your pride to relax in nothing which can promote your future efficiency, your one great object being to drive the invader from your soil and carry your standards beyond the outer boundaries of the Confederacy, to wring from an unscrupulous foe the recognition of your birthright, community independence.

Jefferson Davis. [138]

After a few days, the regiment headed back toward Richmond and camped a few miles from the capital at the "Poe Farm" on the Williamsburg Road, near Darbytown. When not engaged in the normal duties of camp life, the men took advantage of their location and a more liberal policy for obtaining passes to visit friends and family in Richmond. Those without passes played a game of cat and mouse with the provost on the roads in and around Richmond. On one occasion, Howard Walthall was caught by the provost and turned over to his commanding officer for punishment. On another occasion, he was rounded up by the City Guard in Richmond and taken to Gen. Winder's office, the Provost Marshall for all of Richmond. Along with other detainees he was lined up against a wall on Capital Street. Walthall, being familiar with the area, waited for the guard to be distracted and slipped through the side door of the building and out the front door on the other side. On a third occasion, he fled the provost by climbing out of a window into an alley and making good his escape. After everything these men had been through and not knowing what their future would

[138] Official Records, Series 1, Volume 11, Part 3, pg. 690

hold, no risk was too great to spend some quality time with family and friends before heading back into the field. [139]

Major William Palmer returned to the regiment after recovering from the wound he received at the Battle of Williamsburg. Upon returning, Maj. Palmer was summoned for a personal interview with Gen. Robert E. Lee. Palmer met the new commanding General at his headquarters, which was on the Nine Mile Road at former Governor Gregory's farm, "High Meadow." At this meeting, Lee instructed Palmer to reorganize, in effect to save, the 1st VA Volunteer Infantry regiment. Palmer succeeded in his task, as he managed to round up 140 men to serve, thereby saving from extinction the proud name of the regiment once again. Besides new recruits, some of the men discharged during the reorganization in April returned to the regiment. Some of the wounded who were recuperating in Richmond returned to duty, as well as Confederate prisoners who were recently exchanged. Two of the men exchanged were Lt. E.P. Reeve and Col. Lewis Williams, both of whom were wounded and captured at Williamsburg. Williams, who was still recovering from his dangerous wounds, could not immediately return to active duty.[140]

Lt. Reeve spent his captivity at Fort Delaware which he described succinctly, "My first experience in prison life was not so bad." Since he had some money with him he could buy the provisions he needed to live somewhat comfortably. They had no communication with the outside world except for northern newspapers that were smuggled into the prison. On the 4th of July, 1862, the Yankees even allowed the prisoners to purchase whiskey for the patriotic celebrations that both northerner and southerner could share. Their imprisonment was further eased by the boxes of food, clothing and all manner of articles they received from southern sympathizers in Baltimore, Maryland. The men were cheered to learn, through smuggled newspapers, of McClellan's failure to take Richmond and his subsequent retreat to Harrison's Landing. But Reeve was saddened to read in one of the northern papers that the 1st VA had been so cut to pieces that it was to be disbanded. At the time, he had no way of knowing that the regiment had subsequently been revived.

---

139 Howard Walthall, pgs. 14-16

140 Richmond Times-Dispatch, Thursday July 15, 1926, "William Palmer, Obituary."

As rumors of a prisoner exchange became a reality, Lt. Reeve left Fort Delaware and was allowed to take a steamer to Fortress Monroe at his own expense to be exchanged. His treatment up to this point had been extremely fair. At Fortress Monroe, he came under the purview of troops from the state of Maine. The prisoners were crowded onto a steamer with little food and no water. The hot August sun was beating down on the men and the lack of water was making them sick. Even those with money could not buy a drink. Finally, Reeve, too weak to stand, protested loudly to several officers who were standing nearby. He expressed his profound wish, "that the world might witness our treatment as the best commentary which could be made on Yankee philanthropy." The officers' sense of honor must have been aroused, as food and water were then handed out to the prisoners. Later that night the steamer sailed into Aiken's Landing and the prisoners disembarked as free men in their home state of Virginia. Reeve headed home where he was allowed a few days furlough to spend with his wife and infant daughter before returning to the 1st VA.[141]

The regiment remained at Darbytown for about a month, returning to the routine of camp life. They continued to fortify their position and conduct picket duty in the direction of Malvern Hill, to keep an eye on McClellan's army. The Union leaders in Washington were also keeping a close eye on Gen. McClellan. Both President Lincoln and Maj. Gen. Halleck, who was the overall commander of all Union armies, visited McClellan at Harrison's Landing. Eventually, it was decided to abandon McClellan's failed Peninsula campaign. Some of the troops from his "Army of the Potomac" were to be transferred to reinforce Gen. John Pope's newly formed "Army of Virginia", which was beginning operations in the northern section of the state. McClellan was outraged when he received his orders on August 3, 1862 to withdraw his army from the Peninsula. McClellan objected profusely to the War Department in Washington, saying that this order, "has caused me the greatest pain I ever experienced." His objections went unheeded and he reluctantly began to move his army back down the

141 E.P. Reeve, "Reminiscences."

peninsula to Fortress Monroe. The Confederate Army, and their new commander, had turned back the Union invasion, albeit at a terrible cost. The 1st VA, as part of the Army of Northern Virginia, had done their part in the successful defense of Richmond, but now the war, and the regiment, would be moving in another direction. [142]

[142] Official Records, Series 1, Volume 11, part 1, pgs. 80-81. "Correspondence between Halleck and McClellan."

BACK TO BULL RUN

President Abraham Lincoln combined several corps of Union troops to create the Army of Virginia under the command of Gen. John Pope. Pope's army moved from the vicinity of Washington south into Virginia, threatening the vital rail hub at Gordonsville. If Pope could capture Gordonsville, it would hamper the lines of communication between Richmond and the Shenandoah Valley. But Gen. Lee's immediate concern was to prevent the armies of McClellan and Pope from combining. Lee held the central position between the two armies and decided to attack Pope before his army could be reinforced by McClellan's troops. He sent Gen. Thomas "Stonewall" Jackson's Corps to hold Gordonsville while confirming McClellan's intentions. Once it was established that McClellan was no longer a threat to Richmond, Lee began moving the remainder of his army toward Gen. Pope and his Army of Virginia.[143]

On the 10th of August, the 1st VA, with the rest of Kemper's brigade, left their camp at Darbytown and marched to Richmond where they took the cars of the Central Railroad and steamed towards Gordonsville. They arrived there that evening and camped for the night. On a sultry August 11th, the brigade left Gordonsville and took up a line of march towards Orange C.H. The excessive heat and dusty roads caused quite a few of the men to straggle. At about noon, for some unexplained reason, the column was halted, about faced and marched back in the direction of Gordonsville, which they reached about sunset. The regiment moved near Mechanicsville

143 "The West Point Atlas of War, The Civil War", Chief Editor: Brig. General Vincent J. Esposito, Published by Tess Press, an imprint of Black Dog and Leventhal Publishers, Inc., New York, NY 10011.

and camped for a few days. While there, the remainder of Longstreet's Division arrived from Richmond. [144]

On August 12, a new recruit of note, nineteen year old John Dooley Jr., arrived from Richmond. John's father was Major John Dooley, who had such a large influence on the 1st VA, both prior to and during the first year of the war. As previously stated, Major Dooley just recently resigned from the army during the reorganization the previous April. John's brother, James, was also a member of the 1st VA, in company "C", and had been wounded and captured at Williamsburg. James, like E.P. Reeve and Col. Williams, was exchanged in early August. It is unclear why John did not join his father's former company, which was mostly Irish, but instead he was placed in Company "D". He immediately began to keep a journal of his war time experiences. His journal "John Dooley, Confederate Soldier" was published in 1945 and is often quoted.

The 1st VA took up the march on the 16th of August, heading north on the Orange and Fredericksburg Turnpike. They crossed the Rapidan River at Raccoon Ford on the 20th of August. Federal troops were in the area and the regiment was halted on the 21st about one half mile south of Kelly's Ford. An engagement comprising mostly cavalry and artillery was taking place near Kelly's Ford and the brigade was held in reserve, but their services were not needed. They did come under artillery fire, but no casualties were reported. Charles Loehr, of Company "D", among others, wrote of an incident that occurred while the regiment was at this location. A courier wearing a new uniform arrived from Gen. Jackson's Headquarters with information for Gen. Longstreet. Longstreet, who knew all of Jackson's messengers, did not take long to recognize that the man was a fraud and a Yankee spy. Moxley Sorrel, Longstreet's Chief of Staff, expands on this story of espionage. Sorrel claimed that the Union spy murdered a Confederate courier and was caught red-handed with the courier's papers on his person. A trial was convened, overseen by three Brigadier Generals. The man admitted he was a spy from Loudon County, Virginia but he denied murdering the courier. The man was found guilty and sentenced to hang immediately. He was mounted on his horse and a noose placed around his neck. His final seconds were described by Sorrel, "A smart blow with the flat of a saber started the horse on the jump and left

---

144 B.F. Howard, pg. 30.

the spy breathless, and there he hung until the army, continuing its march, passed almost under the tree and perhaps took the lesson to heart."[145]

The march continued past Stevensburg to Brandy Station, where the regiment camped at a farm belonging to Mr. John Minor. On the 23rd, there was an artillery duel across the Rappahannock and although they were in the vicinity, the 1st VA was not engaged. The following day they moved up the Rappahannock and crossed the Hazel River near Jeffersonton, where they spent the night. The regiment camped on the 25th near Waterloo Bridge and crossed the Rappahannock at Hinson's Ford on the 26th, spending the night at Salem. They finally reached Thoroughfare Gap on the 27th and camped for the night near White Plains. When the men had settled down for some much needed sleep, some of the horses from an adjoining camp broke loose from their tethers and stampeded through the camp of the 1st VA. At first, this caused great alarm since enemy cavalry was known to be in the vicinity. Fortunately, cooler heads prevailed and no one started shooting in the crowded environment. Things soon settled down, but not before a couple of the men were hurt. One of the injured was Sergeant Thomas Durham of Company "G", who had a piece of his ear ripped off during the stampede. Perhaps hoping the injury would get him relieved from the constant marching, he grasped the wounded ear and exclaimed, "I have got a one 'ear furlough!" It is not known if Durham's theatrics got him excused from duty.[146]

This march to Thoroughfare Gap had been particularly arduous. Since the men were separated from their supply trains, their rations were paltry at best. Their diet consisted primarily of green corn and apples. The hot August sun dried out the roads, which caused a choking cloud of dust that covered their hair and skin, making them unrecognizable. The roads were jammed with troops, which resulting in accordion style stop and go marching. At one point, Private John Dooley was sent back to find the 1st VA's supply wagons. He waited on the side of a hill and got a firsthand view of the army on the march. A stream at the base of the hill had slowed the progress of the long line of wagons to a slow crawl. This being his first

145 Charles Loehr, "War History of the Old First Virginia", pgs. 26-27: "Recollections of a Confederate Staff Officer", G. Moxley Sorrel, Neale Publishing Co., 1905, Reprinted by Bantam, November 1992, New York, New York, 10103.

146 Charles Loehr, "War History of the Old First Virginia", pg. 27.

campaign, he was impressed with the logistics involved in moving an army of this size. As he watched, he saw infantry, artillery, and all manner of wagons traversing the rugged country roads. He later wrote, "Nearly every second wagon comes to a halt in the middle of the stream, which is deep, and the wagons are heavy and the horses, unlike the well fed beasts of the Yankees, are weak and they must drink; and there is much ado about getting out of the stream and clambering up the ground on the other side of which is anything but a level plain." It made him think of the newspaper critics back in Richmond, "I wish some of the wiseacres at home who sit in their cozy offices and write censorial articles about the inefficiency of Generals in failing to follow up their victories and in annihilating this and t'other army could have stood where I did on that memorable day and watched the slow process of this immense train of wagons which was almost steadily passing here all day and at night fall scarce one half had crossed the little stream. They (the armchair strategists) might then understand what it is to move a large army over rough, muddy, and rocky roads, having but one road for troops, baggage, ordnance, ammunition, Quartermaster stores and Commissaries." Dooley eventually gave up all hope of hurrying along the wagons and he returned to his comrades.[147]

Despite the harsh conditions, Longstreet continued to push his men forward. Gen. Lee had hoped to catch the Union Army in a trap between Gen. Jackson's Corps already in the vicinity of Manassas, and Longstreet's troops which were approaching from the south and west. Jackson had already engaged Pope's army and captured the Union supply depot at Manassas Junction. When confronted with an overwhelming force, Jackson burned what his men could not carry and withdrew to a strong defensive position to wait for Lee and Longstreet. Pope was moving more troops into the area of operations hoping to defeat Jackson before he could be united with the rest of the army. This sense of urgency kept the Confederate Army and the men of the 1st VA moving on a forced march along those dusty roads.[148]

The command structure for this march and the ensuing battle had

---

147 Durkin, "John Dooley, Confederate Soldier, His War Journal", pg.11.

148 Official Records, Series 1, Volume 12, Part 2, pgs. 554-555, "Reports of Robert E. Lee, C.S. Army, Commanding Army of Northern Virginia, of operations August 13 – September 2."

changed somewhat from that which the regiment operated during the Peninsula Campaign. The Army of Northern VA, under the overall command of Gen. Robert E. Lee, was split into two corps with Gen. Longstreet in command of one, which in this case encompassed the right wing of the army. Gen. Thomas "Stonewall" Jackson was in command of the other corps or left wing. Gen. Kemper took over temporary command of Longstreet's old division from Gen. George Pickett, who was recuperating from a wound he received during the Peninsula Campaign. Kemper took Maj. Palmer, of the 1st VA, as his Chief of Staff. Col. Corse, of the 17th VA, took over command of the Brigade in Kemper's absence. Lt. Col. Frederick Skinner was in command of the 1st VA as Col. Williams was still recuperating from the wound he received at Williamsburg.[149]

The 1st VA approached Thoroughfare Gap on August 28th. They heard the sounds of fighting in their front as the lead elements of Longstreet's Corps forced their way through the mountain pass. The next day, as they marched through the gap they witnessed the unburied bodies of Union Soldiers who had tried to stop the Confederate advance. They descended down the mountain onto the Plains of Manassas, the scene of their baptism of fire a little over a year before.

About noon on the 29th, the regiment, along with the rest of the brigade, formed a battle line and was placed on the right of the Confederate line, adjacent to the Manassas Gap Railroad. The order was given and the brigade moved forward, crossing over to the east side of the railroad. They continued to advance another four hundred yards, occupying a woods at that location. This entire movement was done in full view of and under intense artillery fire from a Union battery located about twelve hundred yards distant. Some of the shells landed in close proximity of the brigade's advancing line, showering the men with dust and dirt. The enemy fire, coupled with the blazing August sun, made for a most unpleasant afternoon, especially for the new recruits who were "seeing the elephant" for the first time. The regiment made it to a fence, where they were ordered to lie down. They remained at this location, under sporadic fire, until they were relieved by Gen. T. F. Drayton's brigade. The entire brigade then

---

149 Official Records, Series 1, Vol. 12, part 2, pgs. 546-551, "Organization of the Army of Northern Virginia during the battles of the August 28 – September 1, 1862": Charles Loehr, "War History of the Old First Virginia", pg. 27-28.

moved back to the rear of Hood's Brigade of Texans, where they remained for the night, near the railroad.[150]

The morning of August 30th, 1862, dawned with the two armies facing each other on the old battlefield at Manassas. It was obvious to the men of the 1st VA that there was going to be a major engagement on this day. Lt. E.P. Reeve, who had just recently returned to the regiment after his recuperation, took a few minutes to write to his wife and describe the sights and sounds going on in the Confederate camp. He wrote, "There is so much excitement around me watching the approach of the enemy that I had stopped writing for a time. It seems now very doubtful which way the enemy are traveling as we can only see the columns of dust which they raise. I will write you again the first opportunity I have. In the fight yesterday, we were under a heavy artillery fire much of the time, but had no one seriously hurt. While I write, the batteries around us are playing away at each other, but I am getting accustomed to the sound again." Within hours, he would once again be in the midst of a great struggle.[151]

During the day the Union army was concentrating on Jackson's position on the left of the Confederate line. When Pope shifted troops from his own left to bolster his attack on Jackson, Generals Longstreet and Lee saw an opportunity to get behind Pope's army and destroy a major portion of it. A rise in the terrain known as Henry Hill dominated Pope's avenue of retreat along the Warrenton Turnpike from the Manassas battlefield. If Longstreet's troops could get around the Union left flank, which now appeared to be inadequately defended, and capture that hill, they would cut off Pope's ability to retreat. He would be trapped between Jackson's and Longstreet's corps.

Longstreet put his plan in motion using all the troops at his disposal. Gen. John Bell Hood's Brigade of Texans would lead the attack as the "column of direction." Evans's brigade of South Carolinians would follow Hood as support. Kemper, in command of Pickett's Division, would

---

150 Official Records, Series 1, Volume 12, Part 2, pgs. 625-627, "Reports of Col. Montgomery D. Corse, Seventeenth Virginia Infantry, commanding brigade Kemper's Division, of the battles of Groveton and Manassas": SHSP, Vol. 38, pgs. 262-265, "Report of Capt. F. A. Langley on the part taken by the 1st VA at the Battle of Groveton "(Manassas): John Dooley, "Confederate Soldier" pgs. 18-19

151 E.P. Reeves, Letter to his wife Hester, August 30, 1862, "Camp near Gainesville."

move on Hood's right. The three brigades within Kemper's division were positioned with Col. Eppa Hunton's Brigade of Virginians and Brig. Gen. Micah Jenkins Brigade of South Carolinians in the front. Kemper's Brigade, with the 1st VA, followed behind Hunton and Jenkins in support. As previously stated, the brigade was under the command of Col. Corse and the 1st VA was under the command of Lt. Col. Skinner. [152]

A little after 4:00 PM in the afternoon the Confederate troops began to advance. Hood's Texans with the Hampton Legion and the 18th GA attacked the 10th New York scattering them back onto the 5th New York Zouaves. The Texans pushed on and riddled the Zouaves with a devastating fire. The New Yorkers tried to make a stand but they were quickly overwhelmed, suffering 300 casualties in the first ten minutes. The Zouaves broke and Hood's brigade continued to advance at a quick pace. Men from the 11th and 12th Pennsylvania Reserves, with a battery of cannon, were hastily thrown in the path of Hood's attack, but to no avail. The Texans overran this position and captured the guns. The brigades, including Kemper's, tasked with supporting Hood had longer routes of march and the Texans had moved so fast they outpaced the other Confederate brigades.

Meanwhile, Gen. Irwin McDowell, who was in command of the Union Army at 1st Manassas, was now in command of the left wing and realized the peril his men were in. Not wishing to be routed twice on the same battlefield, he needed to slow Longstreet's advance long enough to fortify Henry Hill. Earlier he had placed a brigade of infantry consisting of the 73rd, 25th, 75th and 55th Ohio regiments, under the command of Col. Nathaniel McLean, on Chinn Ridge. In support of the Ohioans, McDowell placed a battery of four Parrott guns of Battery "I" of the First New York Artillery, under the command of Capt. M. Wiedrich. At this point in the battle, the hopes of the Union Army depended on this brigade of Ohioans and their supporting guns to hold Chinn Ridge long enough for McDowell to organize a defense of Henry Hill. [153]

The Ohioans watched as the decimated Zouaves ran in their direction,

---

[152] James Longstreet, "From Manassas to Appomattox", pg. 188: Official Records, Series 1, Volume 12, Part 2, pgs. 625-627, "Reports of Col. Montgomery D. Corse."
[153] John J. Hennessy, "Return to Bull Run, The Campaign and Battle of Second Manassas", pgs.367-378 Simon and Schuster, Rockefeller Center, NY, NY 10020

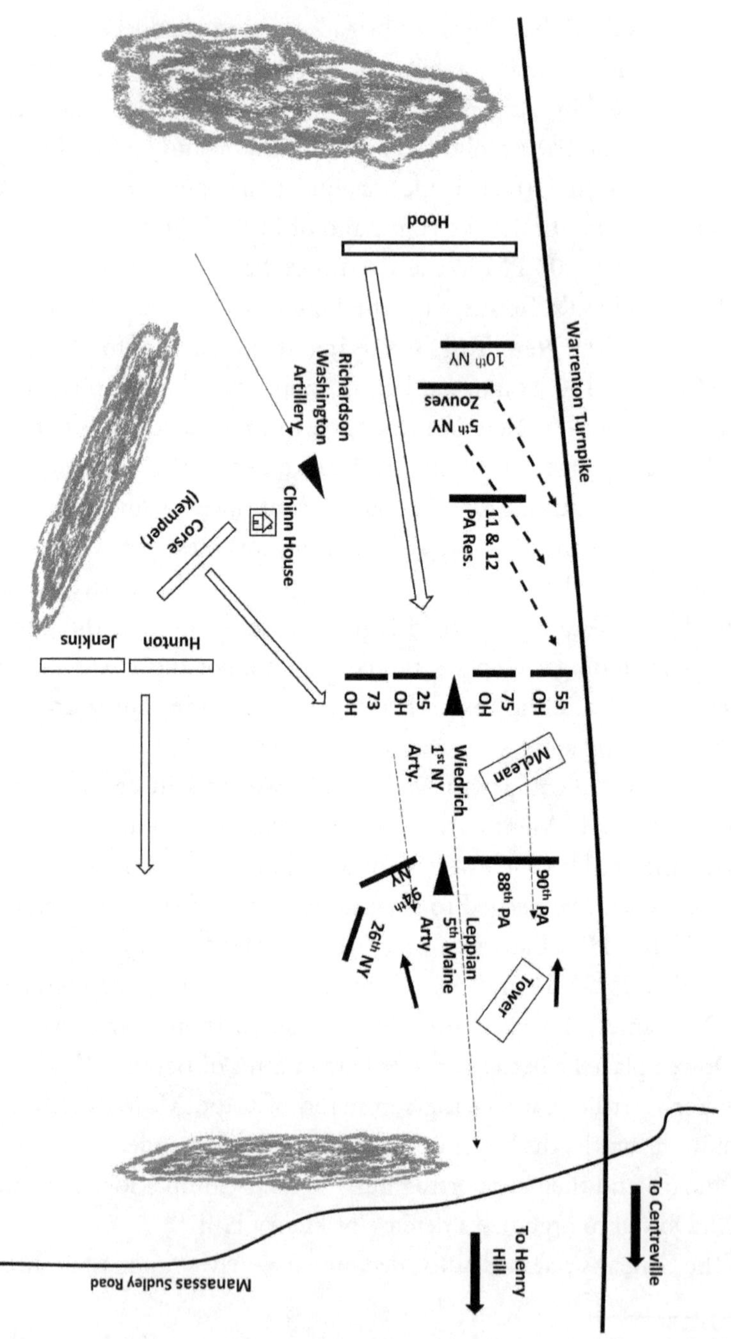

Battle of Second Manassas
The Fight for Chinn Ridge, August 30, 1862

followed closely by Hood's Confederates who were also advancing toward their position at a rapid pace. After the retreating Union troops cleared their front, Wiedrich's guns opened fire on the Texans. As the Confederates moved closer, Wiedrich switched to canister and the Union infantry opened a destructive fire. Finally, after covering more than a mile, Hood's exhausted troops came to a halt and slowly retreated back down the hill, away from Chinn Ridge and into the woods to regroup.

As Hood's troops were withdrawing, Kemper's division, including the 1st VA, finally caught up and entered the battlefield through some trees on the left flank of the Ohio troops holding Chinn Ridge. As the Confederates entered the clearing, they were fortunate to benefit from confusion within the Union lines. At first, McLean gave the order to turn two of the cannon toward this new threat, but quickly countermanded it "upon the assurance of someone who professed to know" that the approaching troops were Union reinforcements. McLean turned his attention back to his front where the Confederates had regrouped and the remnants were advancing again.[154]

The Federal commanders were not the only officers dealing with confusion that day. Through some misinterpretation of orders, the front two brigades, Hunton and Jenkins, of Kemper's three brigade division, marched off to the right, away from the battle, instead of turning left toward Chinn Ridge. Col. Corse, seeing the opportunity of striking the Yankees in the left flank and rear, turned his brigade, including the 1st VA, toward the critical ridge. The brigade maneuvered around the Chinn house and reformed their battle line, after which they continued toward the Union flank. At the same time, individual regiments from Hood's and Evans's disorganized brigades continued to assault the ridge from the front. This new frontal attack drew the attention of the Yankees away from Corse's brigade until they were within 50 yards of the Union flank. The surprised Ohioans finally realized that Corse's brigade was indeed Confederate troops and unleashed a terrific volley into the Virginians.

[154] Official Records, Series 1, Vol. 12, pgs. 286-287, "Reports of Col. Nathaniel C. McLean, seventy-fifth Ohio Infantry, commanding Second Brigade of the battles of Groveton and Bull Run."; pgs. 303-305 "Report of Capt. Michael Wiedrich, Battery I, First New Your Light Artillery, of operations August 22-30."

McLean moved the 55th Ohio to his left and they became hotly engaged with Corse's brigade and the 1st VA. [155]

Even with their flank turned, the Ohioans put up a fierce defense of their position, trading volley after volley with the Confederate forces. Once again the guns of the Washington Artillery, from New Orleans, came to the support of the 1st VA. Specifically, it was Capt. J.B. Richardson who moved his battery to the left of the Chinn house and opened fire on the Federal position. By day's end his battery had fired 178 rounds in support of Corse's brigade.[156]

About this time Wiedrich's Union gunners on Chinn ridge claimed they were out of ammunition, hitched up their cannon and beat a hasty retreat, leaving the infantry to fend for themselves against the ever increasing Confederate pressure. The attack on their left flank was more than they could handle and McLean's troops began to waver, just as fresh troops came to their support. Brig. Gen. Zealous Tower arrived with his brigade and attempted to bolster the sagging lines in an effort to hold Chinn Ridge. His brigade, which consisted of the 26th and 94th New York and the 88th and 90th Pennsylvania, moved onto the ridge at the double quick. As Tower's troops tried to form a line, some of the Ohio troops broke for the rear with Wiedrich's battery. The caissons and the retreating infantry drove through Tower's Brigade, disrupting their attempts to form a proper battle line. The confusion grew even greater as the officers tried to wheel their regiments to the left to face Corse's brigade who were getting ever closer. The New York and Pennsylvania regiments, with some of McLean's remnants, finally stabilized the line and commenced a fierce exchange with the Virginians. A new battery, Capt. George Leppien's 5th Maine Light Artillery, arrived on the scene and quickly unlimbered to aid in the Union defense.[157]

---

[155] Official Records, Series 1, Volume 12, part 2, pgs. 625-627"Reports of Col. Montgomery D. Corse"; John J. Hennesy, "Return to Bull Run" pgs.389-390. Pgs. 292-293; "Report of Col. John Lee, Fifty-fifth Ohio Infantry, of the battle of Bull Run"

[156] Official Records, Series 1, Volume 12, Part 2, Pgs. 575-576, "Report of Captain J.B. Richardson, Washington Artillery, of battle of Manassas";

[157] Official Records, Series 1, Volume 12, Part 2, pgs. 389-390, "Report of Richard H. Richardson, Twenty –sixth New York Infantry"; Pg. 391, "Report of Maj. George W. Gile, Eighty-Eighth Pennsylvania Infantry."

Seeing this new battery unlimber, Col. Corse called out for the brigade to charge and capture the guns. In a war chocked full of individual acts of heroism, what happened next deserves special praise. Col. Frederick Skinner with the sword he brought home from France as a young man and, that some say, was one of the heaviest swords in the Confederate Army, spurred his horse forward. He yelled back to his men, "Forward, the Old First, follow me." Racing thirty yards ahead of the advancing infantry of the 1st VA, he got in among the gunners of Leppien's Maine Battery. As one of the cannoneers was preparing to pull the lanyard, which would have caused devastating casualties to Skinner's men in the 1st VA, he slashed down on the man's collar bone killing the gunner instantly. A second man reached for the lanyard only to suffer the same fate from Skinner's heavy sword. A third gunner, with pistol in hand, grabbed the bridle of Skinner's horse and fired point blank at the Colonel's face. Skinner moved just quickly enough that the bullet only grazed his ear. His French sabre came down again, killing the third gunner. By this time the infantry of the 1st VA was swarming over the battery, forcing the Union soldiers to surrender or flee for safety. When the melee ended, it was determined that Col. Skinner had in fact been shot three times during his heroic attack on the battery. And yet when his men reached him, his first words were to complement his horse, "Didn't old Fox behave splendidly?" he is to have said. [158]

According to Private John Dooley, Col. Skinner was bleeding profusely when he came upon him. He told Dooley, "Jack, bear me witness that I was the first man on that battery." Dooley assured the Colonel that he would and he helped his comrades bind up Skinner's wounds. Besides the wound to his ear, he had also been shot in the side and his arm was "torn from wrist to elbow." Skinner was later carried off the field. His wounds were so serious that they kept him from returning to active duty for the remainder of the war. Near the end of his life he is quoted by his daughter

---

[158] Official Records, Series 1, Volume 2, pgs. 625-626, "Report of Col. Montgomery Corse": Joshua Brown, Confederate Veteran Magazine, Nashville Tenn., June 1894, pg. 184: John Hennessy, "Return to Bull Run", pg. 398.

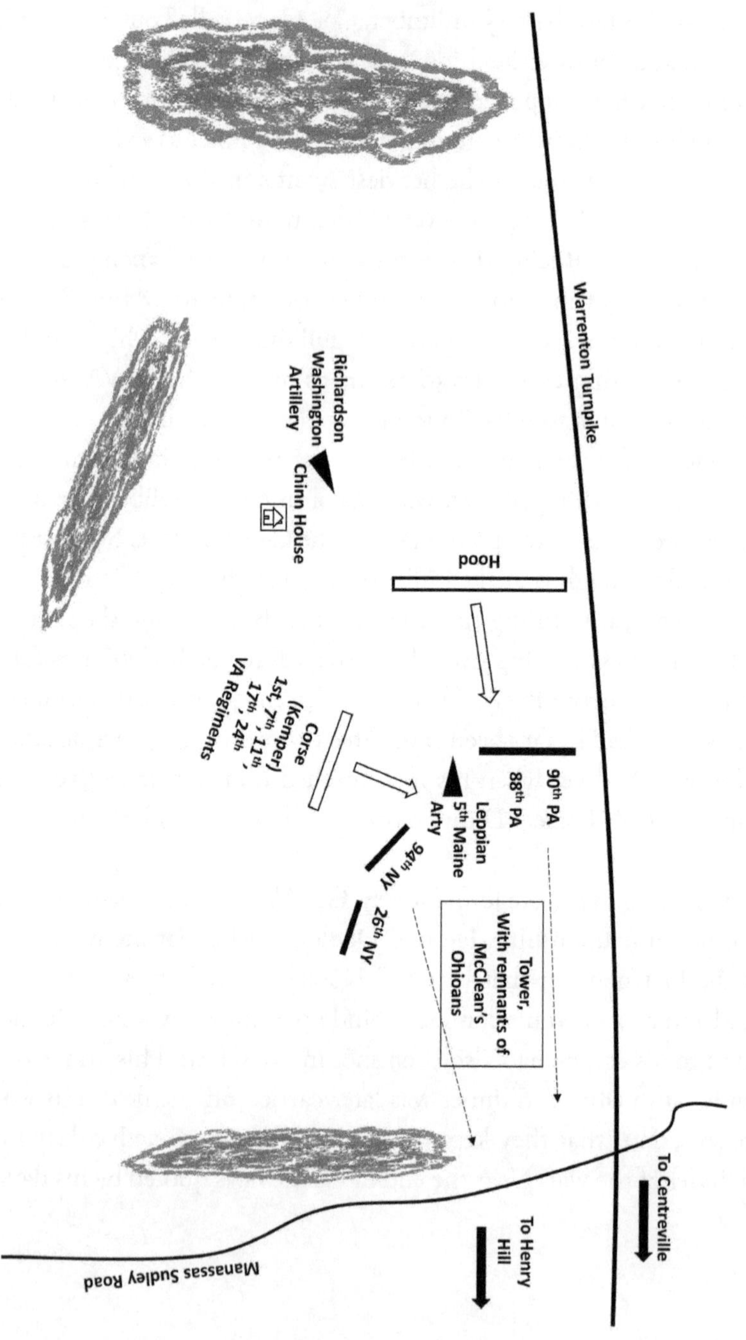

The Battle of 2nd Manassas
The Attack on Leppian's Battery

as saying," I hated to kill those brave men. How splendidly they stood by their guns".[159]

No less than five different regiments from three different brigades claim to have captured Leppien's battery on Chinn Ridge. This is a testament as to how confused and intermingled the Confederate forces had become in their attack on the ridge. Although there were many who claimed to have captured the battery, there is absolutely no debate as to who was the first person to get in among the guns. That honor belongs to Lt. Col. Frederick Skinner of the 1st VA.

Although they were in disarray, the Confederates swarmed over the ridge and continued to pursue the Yankees down the other side. Some of the rebels remained in a semblance of companies, while others moved across the field in jumbled groups. A few of the men from the Washington Artillery, with the help of some infantry, turned the captured guns and began to fire at the fleeing Union soldiers. A group of about fifty members of the 1st VA banded together and followed a group of Union soldiers into a nearby patch of trees. When they came out on the other side, they had a panoramic view of the Plains of Manassas. Although under sporadic fire, from this vantage point they watched the spectacle of the battle that was raging in the open fields below. The 1st VA held this position until darkness brought an end to the fighting. The day was a significant victory for the Confederate forces, but they failed in their quest to take Henry Hill and surround Pope's army. The Union Army's survival was due in no small part to the gallant defense of Chinn Ridge by McLean's and Tower's troops holding up Longstreet's advance just long enough for the rest of the army to adequately defend Henry Hill. During the night, Pope made good on his escape from Manassas and moved his defeated army towards Centreville and eventually the outskirts of Washington. [160]

Once again the 1st VA proved their gallantry and steadfastness on the battlefield and once again they paid a terrible price. The following is a

---

[159] Durkin, "John Dooley, Confederate Soldier, His War Journal", pgs.21-22: T.C. DeLeon, "Belles, Beaux and Brains of the 60's", pg. 248, G.W. Dillingham Company, New York, NY, 1909.

[160] Official Records, Series 1, Volume 12, Part 2, Pgs. 575-576, "Report of Captain J.B. Richardson, Washington Artillery, of battle of Manassas": Durkin, "John Dooley, Confederate Soldier", pgs. 22-24.

partial list of the casualties suffered by the regiment at what became known as the battle of 2nd Manassas.

Staff – Wounded: Lt. Col. Frederick Skinner. Ensign Jacob R. Polak.

Company "B" – Killed: Corp. Gustavus G. Goddin. Privates Charles C. Carter, John W. Ratcliffe, Joseph T. Shiflett. Wounded: Sergeants Benjamin M. Crow, Lewis W. Odgen. Privates William H. Crigger, John Q. Figg, William A. Stoaber, Richard H. Street. Captured: Sergeant John L. Littlepage.

Company "C" – Killed: Lieutenant John H. Donahue. Wounded: Captain James Mitchel. Sergeant Henry Sullivan.

Company "D" – Killed: Sergeant William A. Morris. Wounded: 1st Lt. Edward P. Reeve. Privates George L. Meanley, Tazewell S. Morton, Isaac T. Porter, Albert G. Steger, Lemuel R. Wingfield. Captured: Howard M. Walthall.

Company G – Wounded: Private Robert G. Stuart.

Company H – Killed: Captain William E. Tysinger: Private William M. Wight. Wounded: Sergeant John W. Wynne. Privates John A. Meanley, Edward G. Nuckols.

Company I – Killed: Captain James W. Tabb, Private Jacob H. Smith. Wounded: Lieutenant Henry C. Ballow. Corporal Calvin L. Parker. Privates John T. Ayres, Joseph Ainsko, Germain R. Glenn.

Total Casualties for the regiment were approximately 10 killed and died from wounds, 25 wounded and 2 captured.[161]

The tributes to Col. Skinner for his gallantry that day lasted throughout his lifetime and beyond. His heroism was immediately acknowledged in the official reports of 2nd Manassas. Captain Langley, who filed the report for the 1st VA wrote, "Here, Colonel, allow me to call attention to the gallant bearing of Lt. Col. Skinner, who at the head of his Regiment, rode into the battery, cutting down two of the enemy at their guns." Col. Corse in filing his report for Kemper's Brigade, wrote, "Lieutenant Colonel F. G.

---

161 Lee Wallace, "1st Virginia Infantry", Pgs. 81-123: "Record of the Richmond City and Henrico Co. Virginia Troops", Compiled by E. H. Chamberlayne, Jr., Richmond 1879. Charles Loehr, "War History of the Old First Virginia", pg. 28-29: Southern Historical Society Papers, Vol. 38, Edited by R.A. Brock, Published by the Society, Richmond VA, 1910, Reprinted by Kraus Reprint Co., Millwood NY, 1977, "Reports of The First, Seventh, and Seventeenth Virginia Regiments in 1862", pgs. 262-267.

Skinner, First Virginia, dashing forward in advance of the whole line, was the first to reach the battery, and I saw him dealing deadly blows with his saber to the Yankee gunners." Skinner's attack on the 5th Maine Battery was the subject of countless newspaper and magazine articles for years to come.

In 1866, in his very popular history of the war, E.A. Pollard wrote of the 1st VA at 2nd Manassas, "Still farther to the right is Longstreet's old brigade, composed of Virginians – veterans of every battlefield – all of whom are fighting like furies, The First Virginia, which opened the fight at Bull Run on the 18th of July, 1861, with over six hundred men, now reduced to less than eighty members, is winning new laurels; but out of the little handful, more than a third have already bit the dust." [162]

That night and the following morning the men cared for the wounded and buried the dead. By the afternoon the army was on the move again in pursuit of the retreating Yankees. As the 1st VA left Manassas they crossed the battlefield and once again they viewed the horrors of war, as the fields were littered with the mangled bodies of the previous day's combatants. The regiment pushed on and crossed Bull Run at Sudley's Ford on September 1. This was the first leg of a trek that would, for the first time, take the regiment out of their native Virginia.

---

[162] E. A. Pollard, "Southern History of the War", pg. 462, C.B. Richardson Publisher, 540 Broadway, New York, 1866, Digitized by the Internet Archive 2011.

MARYLAND

As the 1st VA marched away from Manassas, they did so without Private Howard Walthall of Company "D." Walthall became separated from his comrades during the advance on Chinn Ridge and fell into the hands of the Union army. Along with other captives, he was marched off to Alexandria where they were held in a building known as "The Slave-Pen." The makeshift prison was guarded by men of the 68th Illinois who "were as lenient as possible" with their unfortunate captives. The guards even allowed the people of Alexandria to visit the prison with gifts of food and clothing for their fellow Virginians. Many friendships were formed between the incarcerated soldiers and the populace of Alexandria. After two weeks, the prisoners were marched out of the Slave-Pen and headed to the wharf for transport to Washington. Many of their new found friends from Alexandria turned out to see the Confederate soldiers off. Upon their arrival in the capital, it became abundantly clear the friendly atmosphere they enjoyed while in Alexandria was over. As they marched through the streets, they were not allowed to communicate with any of the civilian population. The prisoners were taken to the Old Capital prison which Walthall described as "clean and orderly." After a couple of weeks, Walthall and some of the other prisoners were once again herded toward the wharf and loaded onto another steamer. Not knowing their destination, their spirits rose when the boat passed Fortress Monroe and turned up the James River, confirming their hopes of being quickly exchanged. The boat was crowded and many of the men slept on the deck. Unlike E.P. Reeve, who made a similar journey a few months before, Walthall and his fellow prisoners were well fed and even had hot coffee to drink. Coffee had become almost non-existent in the south, so the men stole whatever they could to take home to their families. After being released at Aiken's

Landing, Walthall headed straight to his father's office in Richmond. His parents, not knowing if he was dead or alive, were elated to see their son in good health. Under the terms of being paroled, Howard Walthall was not allowed to rejoin his company until he was formally exchanged. He remained in Richmond with his family, for what must have seemed like a four month vacation until he was permitted to return to the 1st VA.[163]

Meanwhile, after leaving Manassas by way of Sudley's Ford on September 1, 1862, the 1st VA moved on to Germantown VA, near Fairfax Court House. Gen. Jackson's troops had fought there earlier in the day and the risk of further conflict had everyone on edge. The brigade was sent into the woods during the night, where they marched and countermarched through the darkness. They were finally halted and put into a line of battle to await the enemy that was thought to be nearby. Even for these well trained veterans with experienced officers, marching to and fro through the darkness proved to be a confusing proposition. As the dawn's light began to pierce the treetops, the regiment realized their battle line was facing their own wagon train and the enemy was nowhere in sight. The forced march continued until the regiment arrived at White's Ford on the Potomac on September 3rd. Anticipating the hard march ahead, all of the sick and barefoot men in the army were sent to Winchester. The rest of the men cooked three days rations in preparation for the upcoming campaign. Those that remained with the regiment continued the march, passing through Leesburg on the 5th of September. While at Leesburg, the brigade was attached to Brig. Gen. David R Jones's Division. After being temporary division commander, this organizational change allowed Kemper to return to the command of his brigade. The 1st VA waded across the Potomac into Maryland that night, and after marching 17 miles the following day, the regiment spent their first night on Union soil near Buckstown, MD. On the 7th of September, they reached Frederick Junction where they finally rested for three days.[164]

---

163 Howard Malcomb Walthall, pgs. 17-21.

164 Charles Loehr, "War History of the Old First Virginia", pgs. 29-30: Harold Woodward, "The Confederacy's Forgotten Son", pg. 67: Official Records, Series 1, Vol. 19, Part 1, "Report of Maj. Gen. David R. Jones, C.S. Army, Commanding Division, of Operations September 2-19" pgs. 885-87.

David Johnston of the 7th VA wrote an excellent account of life on the march in Kemper's brigade:

"A cloth haversack, canteen and blanket was the sum of our baggage. We had no change of clothing – a grey cap, jacket, pants and colored shirt made up all we had in the way of clothing, and when we thought we would like to have a clean shirt, we took off the soiled one, went to the water and without soap, gave it a little rubbing hung it out in the sun and then hunted a shade, waiting for it to sufficiently dry to put on again. We rolled our blankets, tied the ends together and threw them over one shoulder. When on the march in pleasant weather, we carried as little as possible, and at night, if the weather was warm and dry, we would spread down a blanket, and with the cartridge box for a pillow and without removing our clothing, would lay down to sleep. If the weather was cool, two or three would join together, putting down one blanket and covering with the others. If rain came upon us we would drive down two small forks and lay a pole on them, and then stretch a blanket or a rubber cloth, if we chanced to have it, over the pole, tying the ends to stakes set in the ground and then crawl under. To protect our muskets from the rain we usually stuck the bayonet in the ground so as to leave the muzzle down, that no water could get into the bore. Frequently our guns became very rusty in wet damp weather and while we were required to keep them bright and clean, this requirement was very little looked after when actively engaged in the field – indeed after the first year of the war our officers were not very exacting in this matter."[165]

The foot sore and weary men took advantage of this respite from the constant marching at Frederick Junction. They bathed in the Monocacy River, scrubbing off the layers of thick dust that covered their bodies. Actual meals were cooked and consumed as opposed to the rations and raw corn they ate on the march. While camped at Frederick Junction, some of the men of the 1st VA were detailed to help the Confederate engineers with the destruction of a railroad bridge that was nearby. The

[165] "Four Years a Soldier, A Member of Company D, 7th Virginia Infantry and Sergeant Major of the Regiment", David E. Johnson, Originally published by Princeton WV, 1887, Digitized by Emory University, Robert W. Woodruff Library. Pg. 192.

iron bridge belonged to the Baltimore and Ohio Railroad and consisted of three spans, each measuring 115 feet long. B. F. Howard described it as "the magnificent iron bridge across the Monocacy River." The bridge was blown up on September 8th, along with the water station, pump house and an engine.[166]

When the 1st VA left the outskirts of Richmond less than a month before, it is doubtful they had any idea they would be invading the north. After the battle of 2nd Manassas, Pope's army fell back on the defenses of Washington and was again put under the command of Gen. George McClellan. With the Union army protecting the Capital, Gen. Lee saw the opportunity to take the fight to the north, thereby relieving Virginia from the ravages of war.

In a letter to President Davis on September 3, 1862, Gen. Lee put forth his reasoning for an invasion of Maryland. It was his belief that the Army of the Potomac was "much weakened and demoralized." Although the armies of Pope and McLellan were now united around Washington, in Lee's estimation it would take time for them to be reorganized into an operational force. It was his desire, "to give material aid to Maryland and afford her an opportunity of throwing off the oppression to which she is now subject." The General's main concern was the current condition of the army. The men were in desperate need of clothing and shoes. But it was his belief that if the army could be supplied with provisions and ammunition, the campaign into Maryland had a good chance of success.[167]

Gen. Lee was hoping to receive a warm welcome from the people of Maryland and to increase his ranks with recruits from the border state. He issued General Order No. 102 which stated, "This army is about to engage in most important operations, where any excesses committed will exasperate the people, lead to disastrous results, and enlist the populace on the side of the Federal forces in hostility to our own. Quartermaster and commissaries will make all arrangements for purchase of supplies needed by our army, to be issued to the respective commands upon proper requisitions, thereby removing all excuse for depredations." The order

---

[166] B. F. Howard, pg. 33; Daniel Toomey, "The Civil War in Maryland", Toomey Press, Baltimore, MD. 1993, pgs. 48-49; Charles Loehr, "War History of the Old First Virginia", pg. 30

[167] Official Records, Series 1, Vol. 19, part 2, pgs. 590-591.

continued with guidelines for a strict provost marshal to be instituted in each brigade to keep men from leaving the ranks. "A provost guard, under the direction of Brig. Gen. L.A. Armistead, will follow in rear of the army, arrest stragglers, and punish summarily all depredators, and keep the men with their commands, Commanders of brigades will cause rear guards to be placed under charge of efficient officers in rear of their brigades, to prevent the men from leaving the ranks, right, left, front or rear, this officer being held by brigade commanders to a strict accountability for proper performance of this duty." The order also called for harsh treatment for stragglers. "Stragglers are usually those who desert their comrades in peril. Such characters are better absent from the army on such momentous occasions as those about to be entered upon. They will, as bringing discredit upon our cause, as useless members of the service and as especially deserving odium, come under the special attention of the provost-marshal and be considered as unworthy members of an army which has immortalized itself in the recent glorious and successful engagements against the enemy, and will be brought before a military commission to receive the punishment due to their misconduct. The gallant soldiers who have so nobly sustained our cause by heroism in battle will assist the commanding general in securing success by aiding their officers in checking the desire for straggling among their comrades." [168]

Many of the men in the 1st VA disagreed with this order, considering the vast devastation that the war and the Union army brought to Virginia. Sparing the farms of Maryland, many of which were owned by Union sympathizers, was too hard a thing for many of the hungry soldiers. But the regimental officers took Gen. Lee's orders seriously, as is evidenced by an incident that occurred on September 7th. Col. Corse, who was still acting Brigade Commander until Gen. Kemper returned, was in the midst of his morning prayers when he witnessed a group of stragglers who were pillaging a nearby cornfield. The Colonel, who was infuriated began to scream, "You thieves, you robbers, you miserable skulking wretches! Sergeant, take a guard of men and arrest these rascally thieves; I'll teach them to rob the people in this style!" It is not known what regiment or

[168] Official Records, Series 1, Vol. 19, part 2, pgs. 592-593.

brigade the stragglers were from, but the scene must have left an indelible impression on the men of the 1st VA and the entire brigade.[169]

In his continuing effort to bring the people of Maryland over to the side of the Confederacy, Gen. Lee issued the following proclamation on September 8;

"To the people of Maryland:

It is right that you should know the purpose that brought the army under my command within the limits of your State, so far as that purpose concerns yourselves. The people of the Confederate States have long watched with the deepest sympathy the wrongs and outrages that have been inflicted upon the citizens of a commonwealth allied to the States of the South by the strongest social, political and commercial ties. They have seen with profound indignation their sister state deprived of every right and reduced to the condition of a conquered province. Under the pretense of supporting the Constitution, but in violation of its most valuable provisions, your citizens have been arrested and imprisoned upon no charge and contrary to all forms of law. The faithful and manly protest against this outrage made by the venerable and illustrious Marylander, to whom in better days no citizen appealed for right in vain, was treated with scorn and contempt; the government of your chief city has been usurped by armed strangers, your legislature has been dissolved by the unlawful arrest of its members; freedom of the press and of speech has been suppressed; words have been declared offenses by an arbitrary decree of the Federal Executive, and citizens ordered to be tried by a military commission for what they may dare to speak. Believing that the people of Maryland possessed a spirit too lofty to submit to such a government, the people of the South have long wished to aid you in throwing off this foreign yoke, to enable you again to enjoy the inalienable rights of freemen, and restore independence and sovereignty to your state. In obedience to this wish, our army has come among you and is prepared to assist you with the power of its arms in regaining the rights of which you have been despoiled.

This, citizens of Maryland, is our mission, so far as you are concerned. No constraint upon your free will intended; no intimidation will be allowed within the limits of this army, at least. Marylanders shall once more enjoy their ancient freedom of thought and speech. We know no enemies among you and will protect all, of every opinion. It is for you to decide your destiny freely

[169] Durkin, "John Dooley, Confederate Soldier", Pgs. 25-26.

and without constraint. This army will respect your choice, whatever it may be; and while the southern people will rejoice to welcome you to your natural position among them, they will only welcome you when you come of your own free will."[170]

It remained to be seen how the people of Maryland would react to this invasion by their southern brethren.

The depredations of the campaign were somewhat lessened for John Dooley while camped outside of Frederick. Ned Haines, a black servant belonging to the Dooley family showed up with letters, money and a much needed new pair of shoes. Ned was no stranger to soldier life within the 1st VA, having served with John's father, Major John Dooley during the 1st Manassas campaign. When Major Dooley resigned from the army, Ned served with John's brother James until he was wounded and captured at Williamsburg. Now, Ned was in camp to help make John Dooley's life in the army a little easier. It was somewhat common for officers in the 1st VA to band together in a "mess" and hire servants to help with the cooking, washing, etc. But it was a rarity for an individual enlisted man to have his own servant. Dooley's discomfort was also pleasantly relieved when he went into Frederick to visit the local Novitiate, which housed the Catholic priests, and look for acquaintances from his days at Georgetown. He was instantly recognized by the Jesuits and invited in to their home, where they fed him and gave him a new set of clothes. Dooley was also treated to an actual bath, which was quite the luxury after the long march from Virginia.[171]

On September 9th, Gen. Lee's plans for the army were set forth in Special order #191. The details of the army's movement were as follows:

"The army will resume its march to-morrow, taking the Hagerstown road. General Jackson's command will form the advance, and after passing Middletown, with such portion as he may select, take the route toward Sharpsburg, cross the Potomac at the most convenient point and by Friday morning take possession of the Baltimore and Ohio Railroad, capture such of them as may be at Martinsburg, and intercept such as may attempt to escape from Harper's Ferry."

"General Longstreet's command will pursue the main road as far as Boonsboro, where it will halt, with reserve, supply and baggage trains of the army."

---

170 Official Records, Series 1, Vol. 19, part 2, pgs. 601-602.

171 Durkin, "John Dooley, Confederate Soldier", pgs. 26-27.

"General McClaws, with his own division and that of General R.H. Anderson, will follow General Longstreet. On reaching Middletown will take the route to Harper's Ferry, and by Friday morning possess himself of the Maryland Heights and endeavor to capture the enemy at Harper' Ferry and vicinity."

"General Walker, with his division, after accomplishing the object in which he is now engaged, will cross the Potomac at Cheeks' Ford, ascend its right bank to Lovettsville, take possession of Loudoun Heights, if practicable, by Friday morning, Keys' Ford on his left, and the road between the end of the mountain and the Potomac on his right. He will, as far as practicable, co-operate with Generals McLaws and Jackson, and intercept retreat of the enemy."

"General D.H. Hill's division will form the rear guard of the army, pursuing the road taken by the main body. The reserve artillery, ordnance, and supply trains, Etc., will precede General Hill."

"General Stuart will detach a squadron of cavalry to accompany the commands of Generals Longstreet, Jackson, and McLaws, and with the main body of the cavalry, will cover the route of the army, bringing up all stragglers that may have been left behind."

"The commands of Generals Jackson, McLaws, and Walker, after accomplishing the objects for which they have been detached, will join the main body of the army at Boonsboro or Hagerstown."[172]

This order separated the confederate army, putting the 1st VA back on the road and, within days, back into harm's way.

The next day, September 10th, in accordance with special order #191, Longstreet's corps moved out of Frederick junction and passed through Frederick on their way to Boonsboro. Dooley returned to the Novitiate to thank his benefactors and to bid them farewell. Several other former students from Georgetown, along with a few paroled Union officers, were visiting the Jesuits when Dooley arrived. One of the visitors was Jack Davis, a former classmate of Dooley's. Davis was a Unionist from Washington, but in this house of peace Confederates and Unionists were cordial and even friendly with one another.[173]

---

172 Official Records, Series 1, Vol. 19, part 2, pgs.603-604.

173 Curran, "John Dooley's Civil War, An Irish American's Journey in the First Virginia Infantry Regiment", Pg. 36.

Despite Gen. Lee's attempt to win the hearts and minds of the Marylanders, the people of Frederick were less than enthusiastic to host the Confederate army in their town. Unwilling to accept Confederate money, many of the shop owners simply closed their stores. The soldiers of Kemper's brigade received a "lukewarm" reception, at best, as they passed through Frederick. Some of the residents treated the men to half-hearted cheers and clapping while others went as far as to openly display Union flags, much to the dismay of the visiting confederates.[174]

After passing through Frederick, the regiment crossed over South Mountain and bivouacked outside of Boonsboro on the 11th of September. Longstreet received orders to push on through Boonsboro and proceed to Hagerstown, presumably to protect the northern flank of the disjointed army. In Hagerstown, as in Frederick, the citizenry was amazed at the ragged condition of the Confederate army. The dirty worn uniforms brought many a remark from the bystanders as the troops marched by. While passing through Hagerstown, a woman asked, "Why the soldiers wore such dirty, bad clothes?" To which 26 year old Sergeant Patrick Woods of Company "C" remarked, "Well Madam, we don't put on our good clothes to kill hogs".

The regiment arrived outside of Hagerstown during the evening of the12th and set up camp in a wooded area near the edge of town on the road to Williamsport. Early the next morning, Ned Haines went into Hagerstown in search of provisions for himself and John Dooley. Haines ingratiated himself to a local family, including the mistress of the house, who tried to persuade him to leave Dooley and run away to the north and freedom. According to Dooley, Haines declined the offer and returned to camp with bunches of grapes and other treats. In telling the story to Dooley, Haines said, "It wouldn't do for me to leave you here in dat way,

---

[174] "Before Antietam: The Battle for South Mountain", John Michael Priest, pgs. 61-66, White Mane Publishing Company Inc., P.O. Box 152, Shippensburg, PA 17257, 1992.

for if you gets wounded or anything happens to you, who going to take care about you and tell the folks at home when you are well?"[175]

As the 1st VA rested on the outskirts of Hagerstown neither they, nor the Confederate high command, had any idea that the Union army was in possession of Gen. Lee's special order #191. In one of the great intelligence coups of the war, albeit accidental, a copy of Lee's orders was left in a field outside of Frederick MD, wrapped around some cigars. The order was coincidently found by Union soldiers at a campsite and sent up the chain of command to General McLellan. With this intelligence the Union commander was well aware of the fact that the Confederate army was spread out from Harper's Ferry to Hagerstown.

Up until this point, McClellan and his superiors in Washington were unsure if the entire Confederate army was in Maryland or if this was a diversion to draw the Army of the Potomac away from the Federal capital. McClellan wrote to the President and General Halleck, informing them of his acquisition of Lee's plan. It was now clear that the entire Army of Northern Virginia was taking part in this campaign and that Gen. Lee was in command. As was the norm for McClellan and his intelligence officer, they completely overestimated the strength of Lee's army, which they believed was over 120,000 men. In fact, the Confederate force numbered around 50,000 men. With the threat to Washington removed, McLellan put the Army of the Potomac, well over 85,000 strong, into motion toward Frederick. His goal was to force his way through the passes over South Mountain and attack the disjointed Confederate army piecemeal.[176]

As the Union army paraded through Frederick, they received a very different reception from that of the Confederates. According to a member

---

175 Durkin, "John Dooley, Confederate Soldier, His War Journal", pgs. 31-32: "Four Years a Soldier, A Member of Company D, 7th Virginia Infantry and Sergeant Major of the Regiment", David E. Johnson, Originally published by Princeton WV, 1887, Digitized by Emory University, Robert W. Woodruff Library. Pg. 192: Wallace, "1st Virginia Infantry", pg. 123.

176 Official Records, Series 1, Vol. 19, part 2, pgs. 281-281: "The U.S. Army War College Guide to the Battle of Antietam" Edited by Jay Luvaas and Harold W. Nelson, Harper Collins Publishers Inc., 10 East 53rd St., New York, NY1022, 1987. Pg. 302 (The numbers for the opposing armies vary and are estimates, The War College Guide puts them at: Army of the Potomac-87,100 and the Army of Northern Virginia-51,800).

of McClellan's staff, the residents of the town were out in force. Houses were adorned with the national flag, women were waiving their handkerchiefs and throwing bouquets of flowers at the passing troops. The day had all the elements of a national holiday, as opposed to the prelude of a terrible battle. The spectacle, compared to the halfhearted reception received by the Confederates, was proof enough of the strong unionist sentiment in this part of the border state.[177]

The only obstruction between the Union army in Frederick and the Confederate army was South Mountain. The passes through South Mountain were initially guarded by J.E.B. Stuart's Confederate cavalry and two brigades of infantry under the command of Gen. D.H. Hill. Hill also had three brigades of infantry in nearby Boonsboro. It was the Confederate commander's hope that the passes could be held until Harper's Ferry fell to Gen. Jackson and the army could be reunited before facing McClellan's Army of the Potomac. When it was discovered that a large portion of the federal army was moving toward South Mountain from Frederick, Longstreet's command was ordered to march back to Boonsboro from Hagerstown. Toombs brigade and some of the cavalry were left in Hagerstown to maintain a guard at that place. The rest of Longstreet's corps, including the 1st VA, started for Boonsboro on the morning of the 14th of September. The day became exceedingly hot and the roads turned to dust. Straggling became a serious problem, with some estimates reaching fifty percent of the soldiers falling out of ranks on the side of the road. The 1st VA was the lead regiment in Kemper's brigade, under the command of Captain George Norton of Company "D". The rest of the brigade was composed of the 17th VA commanded by Col. M. D. Corse, the 11th VA commanded by Major Adam Clement, the 7th VA commanded by Major Arthur Herbert, and the 24th VA under the command of Col. W.R. Terry.[178]

---

[177] "The Civil War Archive, The History of the Civil War in Documents", Edited by Henry Steele Commager, Black Dog and Leventhal Publishers Inc., 151 West 19th St., New York, NY 10011, 2000, Article by David Strother a member of McClellan's staff, pg. 171.

[178] "The Maryland Campaign, of September 1862, Vol. 1, South Mountain", Ezra A. Carmen, Edited and annotated by Thomas G. Clemens, Savas Beatie LLC, 521 Fifth Ave, Suite 1700, New York, NY 10175, 2010, pgs. 345-46, 358.

South Mountain was crossed by three main passes. From north to south, they were Turner's Gap, Fox's Gap and Crampton Gap. Kemper's brigade was marching with Garnett's and Walker's brigades. Brig. Gen. Richard Garnett was temporarily in command of Gen. George Pickett's brigade and Col. Joseph Walker was in command of Gen. Jenkin's brigade. The three brigades were heading for Turner's Gap when they were rerouted to meet a perceived threat farther to the south. After marching an extra mile or more, the column was halted, about faced and returned to the National road. This detour added to the misery of the exhausted men, who were now ordered to march at double time to meet the ever worsening situation at Turner's Gap. The men reached the National Road, dropped all their non-essential items at the base and started the march up South Mountain. The road became steeper with each arduous step, further inducing many of the footsore and exhausted soldiers to fall out of line.[179]

The battle on the summit had been raging for most of the day. The valley between Middletown and the mountain was full of Union soldiers marching in long blue columns toward the mountain gaps and the rebel army. The Confederate commanders were in a race against time to get enough troops up the mountain to hold back the ever increasing numbers of enemy soldiers. As Kemper's brigade moved at the double quick up the mountain, the wounded from the battle were making their way down. The 1st VA passed an ambulance and were saddened to learn it contained the remains of fellow Virginian, Gen. Samuel Garland Jr. Garland was the grand-nephew of former President James Madison and he was a graduate of the Virginia Military Institute as well as the University of Virginia Law School. He had organized a company of militia in 1859 which was later mustered into the 11th VA as company "C" upon the outbreak of war. Garland was quickly elected Colonel of the 11th VA and served in that capacity for the first year of the war. He was well liked and respected by the men of not only the 11th VA, but the entire brigade including the 1st VA. He was wounded at Williamsburg and promoted to Brig. General shortly thereafter. His brigade was one of the original units defending Fox's gap that morning and he was killed while commanding his men. A member of

[179] Longstreet, "From Manassas to Appomattox', pg. 224.

the 17th VA later wrote that he was, "loved and honored for his gentlemanly courtesy and noble bearing by all the brigade".[180]

The men pushed on, climbing the steep grade of the mountain. As they neared the summit, the sound of musketry and cannon grew louder. After passing the Mountain House on the National Road, they veered off to the left onto Dahlgren Road. The incline grew steeper and the lane was narrow and rutted. The regiment was marching in a column of fours when they came under the fire of artillery belonging to the Pennsylvania Light Artillery, Battery "D", under the command of Captain George W. Durrell. Accurate artillery fire was difficult on the mountain top due to the sharp incline and broken terrain, but Durrell had a good position and he had been sighting his guns on the road all afternoon. The solid shot was crashing into the trees and rock outcroppings along the road, causing the men much distress. A spent six pound shot struck Private John H. Daniel of Company "H", knocking him off his feet. Miraculously, Daniel was not seriously hurt, although he sustained a deep bruise on his hip. Daniel was originally part of Company "A", one of the companies that had left the 1st VA in the early days of the war. He was discharged from that unit in July of 1861 and reenlisted with the 1st VA a month later.[181]

As the brigade was making its way up Dahlgren Road, Gen. Kemper, Moxley Sorrel of Longstreet's staff, Captain Thomas Beckham, the A.D.C to Kemper and Major William Palmer of the 1st VA rode ahead to reconnoiter the ground. They traversed the summit and started down the eastern slope when they ran into a long line of Union troops advancing up the reverse slope of the mountain. The Yankees quickly fired on the group of officers, killing Captain Beckham's horse and putting a hole in Gen. Kemper's coat, which was draped across his saddle. The Confederate

---

180 "Historical Times Illustrated, Encyclopedia of the Civil War", Patricia L Faust, editor, pg. 299: "History of the Seventeenth Virginia Infantry, C.S.A.", by George Wise, Originally published by Baltimore, Kelly Piet & company, digitized by Cornell University Library, pg. 111.

181 "The Maryland Campaign, of September 1862, Vol. 1, South Mountain", Ezra A. Carmen, pg. 358: Official Records, Series 1, Vol. 19, part 1, "Organization of the Army of the Potomac, Maj. Gen. George B. McClellan, U.S. Army Commanding, September 14-17, 1862", pg. 178: Charles Loehr, "War History of the Old First Virginia", pg. 30: Wallace, "First Virginia Infantry", pg. 89.

officers abruptly turned and galloped back to the top of the hill as fast as possible to align the brigade.[182]

The Yankees that Kemper and the other mounted officers inadvertently encountered were the thirty-five hundred men of Brig. Gen. John Hatch's division. They had been making their way up the east side of South Mountain while the 1st VA was climbing the western slope. Gen. D.H. Hill, who had the unenviable task of trying to stop the Federal onslaught at South Mountain, witnessed the approach of Hatch's division. Hatch's men moved toward the summit in three lines of battle, each line composed of a brigade. The first brigade in line was under the command of Brig. Gen. Marsena Patrick. Behind him was the brigade of Col. Walter Phelps Jr, who was in temporary command of Hatch's brigade. And the third brigade was under the command of Brig. Gen. Abner Doubleday, of Fort Sumter fame. D.H. Hill described the advance of the Federal division as "grand and imposing." Hill continued, "Hatch's general and field officers were on horseback, his colors were all flying, and the alignment of his men seemed to be perfectly preserved." From Hill's position, the sight was "grand and sublime." When Hatch's lines first appeared, Kemper's men had not yet arrived on the scene, so D. H. Hill called for artillery to try and slow the union troops. Col. Cutts from the reserve artillery came up, placed his guns and began to fire at the advancing blue lines. Due to the broken ground and inexperience of the Confederate gunners, D. H. Hill described their fire as, "harmless as blank cartridge salutes in honor of a militia general." It was not until after this ineffectual cannon barrage that Kemper's brigade, followed by Garnett's, arrived on the field and took up their positions in an attempt to hold back the impressive Yankee division.[183]

After running the gauntlet of Union cannon fire on Dahlgren Road, Kemper's brigade finally made it to the top of the mountain. The ground leveled off somewhat forming a plateau on the summit which was crisscrossed with fields of corn and other crops. The fields were separated

---

182 Letter from William Palmer to Ezra Carmen, dated August 26, 1899. "Ezra Carmen Papers", Manuscripts and Archives Division of the New York Public Library, 476 Fifth Ave, New York, NY 10016.

183 "Battles and Leaders of the Civil War", Vol. 2, "North to Antietam", published by A.S. Barnes and Co. Inc., 1956, "The Battle of South Mt. or Boonsboro" by Daniel H. Hill, Lieutenant-General C.S.A. pgs. 573-74.

by wooden fences and stone walls. Some of the open areas were dotted with large rocks protruding from the ground. Other sections were not cleared and were heavily wooded. The Confederate column was met by Gen. Kemper and the other mounted officers who had just made their fortunate getaway. The brigade was quickly formed in a line of battle across Dahlgren Road with the 1st VA centered on the road. The 11th VA was to their immediate right, with the 17th VA to the right of the 11th. To the immediate left of the 1st VA were the 7th VA and the 24th VA. The strength of the brigade when it reached the battlefield is difficult to determine. Most estimates put it at approximately 400, though this number may not accurately reflect the heavy straggling during the long march from Hagerstown. It is safe to say the entire brigade numbered less than one-half of a full regiment. The 1st VA probably numbered less than thirty muskets, a far cry from the one thousand in a full regiment. According to Capt. B.F. Howard, Company "I" had only 6 members present.[184]

General Garnett's brigade followed Kemper onto the field and formed a line of battle along a fence to the right of Kemper's line. From left to right his line consisted of the 56th, 28th, 19th, 18th, and 8th VA regiments. There was a gap between the two brigades which Garnett filled by moving the 56th VA to connect with the 17th VA of Kemper's brigade. Garnett's brigade was not much larger than Kemper's, probably numbering just over 400. It was up to these 800 Virginians to slow the tide of the 3,500 men in Gen. Hatch's Federal division which had also reached the summit and was advancing on Kemper's and Garnett's position.[185]

It was late in the afternoon when Hatch deployed two regiments from his leading Union brigade to act as skirmishers and advance toward the line of Virginians. The remaining two regiments of Patrick's brigade followed the skirmishers as support. A gap opened between the two regiments on the left, the 35th and 23rd NY, and the two regiments on the right, the 80th and 21st NY. The 2nd U.S. Sharpshooters, from Phelps' brigade, were moved forward and pushed out to the extreme right of the Union line. Patrick's brigade soon became engaged with Garnett's and Kemper's men. Phelps'

---

[184] Priest, "Before Antietam, the Battle for Antietam", pg. 252: Howard, "Record of Captain B.F. Howard's Company "I", First Virginia Infantry", pg. 33.

[185] "The Maps of Antietam", Bradley M. Gottfried, Published by Savas Beatie LLC, P.O. Box 4527, El Dorado Hills, CA 95762, pg. 65.

brigade, which was second in line, was pushed forward to fill the gap that had formed in the center of Patrick's line. The Confederates held their line under a ferocious fire from the two Federal brigades. General Hatch was riding along the Union lines, encouraging his men to push forward and drive the Confederates from their position, when he was seriously wounded and forced to turn over command of the division to Gen. Doubleday, after which he was removed from the field.[186]

The overwhelming force of the Yankee formations began to push the undersized Confederate brigades back. The Confederates tried to use every fence, tree and rock as cover in their attempt to stem the blue tide. Doubleday pulled Phelps' brigade, "who had suffered severely," back and replaced them with his own fresh brigade of one thousand men. The Confederates tried to counterattack and disrupt the Union advance to no avail. As the Virginians continued to fall back, organized lines of battle disintegrated into groups of men banding together to continue the struggle. As the sun was setting in the western sky, the Confederates rallied enough to form a line and prolong the battle into darkness. Private John Dooley was fighting the temptation to turn and run when Captain Mitchell of the 11th VA gave him a slap on the back saying, "Hurrah for you! You are one of the 1st VA. I know you'll stand by us to the last!" The words of encouragement were enough to bolster his nerve and keep Dooley at his post. It was near dark when Walker's brigade arrived to help steady the Confederate lines. The Federals brought up more fresh troops in the form of a brigade from General Ricketts's division replacing Doubleday's men. The shooting continued till well after dark, with each side aiming in the direction of their antagonists muzzle flashes. Eventually the firing died away and Kemper's brigade was ordered to fall back to the base of the mountain.[187]

The Confederate high command realized that they could not counter the initial Union success on the mountain with the forces they had on hand. Therefore at approximately 11:00 PM, the men of Kemper's brigade, including the 1st VA, were ordered to march away from the mountain and

---

186 Official Records, Series 1, Vol. 19, part 1 "Reports of Brig. Gen. Abner Doubleday" pgs. 221-23.

187 Durkin, "John Dooley Confederate Soldier", pgs. 37-38; Official Records, Series 1, Vol. 19, part 1, "Reports of Brig. Gen. Abner Doubleday" pgs. 221-23.

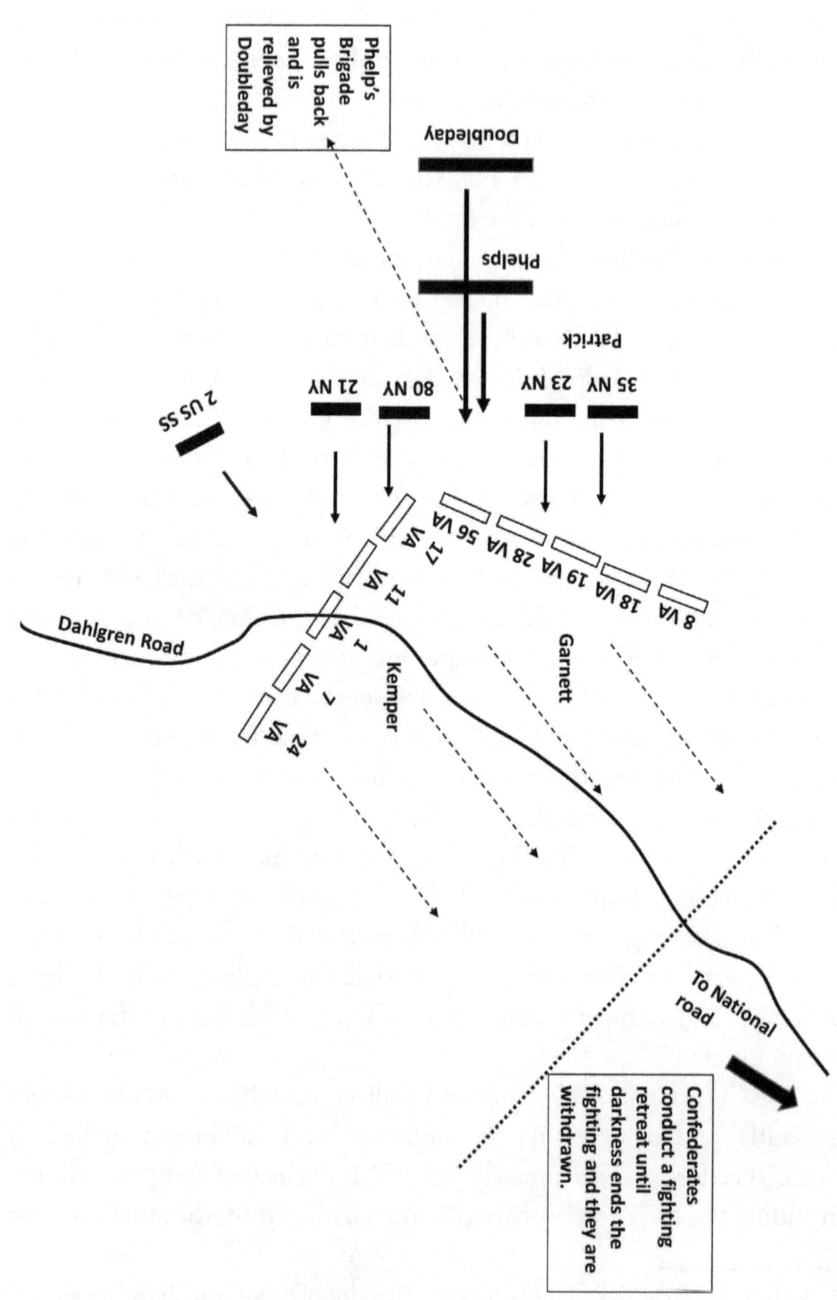

The Battle of South Mountain
The Fight at Turner's Gap, September 14, 1862

back toward Boonsboro. Their eventual destination was the small town of Sharpsburg, near the Potomac River, where Lee hoped to reunite with Gen. "Stonewall" Jackson. The strain of the twenty mile march from Hagerstown, culminating in the Battle of South Mountain, had exhausted the men to a point that even the threat of enemy cavalry patrols could not keep them from seeking rest. After passing through Boonsboro, Private John Dooley and Capt. Norton, both of Company "D", fell out of line and snuck into a nearby field to get some much needed sleep. The pair awoke the next morning and found that they were alone on the road. They nervously walked at a quick pace until they caught up with the rear guard of the army. They pushed on, until they eventually found the brigade at rest on the side of the road, where they were reunited with their comrades in the 1st VA.[188]

Both Generals Longstreet and Hill contended after the battle that if Longstreet's troops could have been in position on the mountain earlier on the 14th, before the attack began, that the Federals could very well have been repulsed. As it happened, by the time the Confederates reached the battlefield the enemy had already gained favorable positions for their artillery and infantry, forcing the Confederates to enter the fray in a piecemeal fashion after an exhausting march.[189]

The lopsided fight on South Mountain was not in vain. Harper's Ferry capitulated to Gen. Jackson on the 15th of September, freeing his force to rejoin Gen. Lee's Army at Sharpsburg. The short but extremely fierce fight on top of the mountain cost Kemper's brigade eleven killed, fifty-seven wounded and seven missing for a total of 75 total casualties, or approximately nineteen percent of the four hundred men engaged. Garnett's brigade, who fought next to Kemper, suffered one hundred and ninety-six casualties or forty-eight percent of their force engaged. The casualty figures would suggest that Garnett's brigade faced the brunt of the Union attack. The 1st VA suffered seven casualties, five wounded and two captured, of the twenty-five plus who were engaged. Those casualties were as follows: Wounded: Company D - Lieutenant William H. Keiningham.

---

[188] "John Dooley's Civil War, An Irish American's Journey in the First Virginia Infantry Regiment", Edited by Robert Emmett Curran, pg. 43

[189] Official Records, Series 1, Vol. 19, part 1, "Report of Lieut. Gen. James Longstreet", pg. 839; "Report of Maj. Gen. Daniel H. Hill", pg. 1018.

Company H - Privates John H. Daniel, William H. Smith and William F. Pumphrey. Company I – Private Andrew T. Minor. William Pumphrey was severely wounded and had to be left on the mountain, where he was captured. Also captured was John Willey of Company "B" and Alfred Jeff Vaughan of Company "G".[190]

The gallantry of the two small brigades is apparent, having lasted as long as they did against four brigades of Union Infantry, with all but one being larger than the combined brigades of Kemper and Garnett. The Federal brigades that were relieved by fresh troops reported being low or out of ammunition, indicating the volume of fire hurled at the Virginians. Gen. Doubleday reported that he had learned from a wounded prisoner that he was engaged with four to five thousand Confederates. That he believed such an exaggerated false report implies that the eight hundred men of the two Confederate brigades put up a fight worthy of many times their numbers. After the war, Gen. Longstreet wrote about the stand of Kemper, Garnett and Walker, after describing their grueling march and ascent of the mountain. He claimed they were "thinned to skeletons of three or four hundred men to a brigade." He went on to praise the tiny brigades by saying, "That they succeeded in covering enough of the position to conceal our retreat after night is sufficient encomium of their valorous spirit." [191]

The 1st VA continued their march to Sharpsburg, where they arrived about noon on the 15th. After resting for a couple of hours on the outskirts of the town, they were moved to a position on the south side of Sharpsburg, atop a hill between the town and Antietam Creek. Across the fields from their position was a stone bridge, known locally as Rohrbach's bridge. As was the case with most days when not fighting or marching, their time was spent resting and looking for something to eat.[192]

The Union army followed close behind the retreating Confederates

---

[190] "Before Antietam", Priest, pg. 324: Loehr, "War History of the Old First Virginia Infantry Regiment", pg. 30. Lee Wallace, "1st Virginia Infantry", Pgs. 81-123: "Record of the Richmond City and Henrico Co. Virginia Troops", Compiled by E. H. Chamberlayne, Jr., Richmond 1879.

[191] Official Records, Series 1, Vol. 19, part 1 "Reports of Brig. Gen. Abner Doubleday" pgs. 221-223: Longstreet, "From Manassas to Appomattox", pg. 226

[192] Curran, "John Dooley's Civil War, An Irish American's Journey in the First Virginia Infantry Regiment", pgs. 43-44.

from South Mountain to Sharpsburg. The lead elements arrived in the vicinity of Sharpsburg during the afternoon of the 15th. As dawn broke on the 16th of September, Longstreet's corps, along with D.H. Hill's division, formed a thin gray line of defense between the town and Antietam Creek. Gen. Jackson was hurrying his divisions along the roads from Harper's Ferry to Sharpsburg trying to reach that place before the overly cautious McClellan could attack with overwhelming numbers. The Confederates anxiously watched as the remaining columns of blue clad Union soldiers arrived on the scene and took up positions across Antietam Creek in preparation for an assault on the outnumbered Confederates. An artillery duel erupted between the armies during the day. On the section of line held by the 1st VA, the shells flew over the hills and landed within Sharpsburg, doing more damage to the structures in town than to the Confederate soldiers. Jackson's troops began to arrive during the afternoon and Gen. Lee placed them on the left of the rebel lines. Gen. A.P. Hill's division was left behind in Harper's Ferry to handle the details of the surrender and take control of the captured property. Both armies settled down for a night of uneasy sleep, frequently interrupted by musket fire, as nervous sentries shot at the slightest sound coming from the enemy's direction.

The twenty-four hundred men of Confederate Gen. David R. Jones's division were responsible for defending the entire line from the Boonsboro pike on the east side of Sharpsburg, wrapping around to Harpers Ferry Road on the south side of town. The length of the line and the depletion of the ranks left gaps between most of the brigades. Garnett's brigade was on the far left of the division anchored on the Boonesboro Road. To Garnett's right was Jenkins's brigade, which remained under the command of Col. Joseph Walker. To Walker's right was the brigade of Gen. Thomas F. Drayton, positioned to the left of and adjacent to Kemper's brigade, constituting the extreme right of the Confederate line. The 20th GA and the 2nd GA of Toombs' brigade, also part of Jones's division, were placed well in front of the line defending the approaches to Rohrbach's Bridge, which crossed the Antietam Creek in this sector. [193]

The 1st VA and the rest of Kemper's brigade were positioned in a

---

193 Official Records, Series 1, Volume 19, Part 1, "Report of Major Gen. David R. Jones, C.S. Army, commanding division, of operations September 2-10" pgs. 885-887: Bradley M. Gottfried, "The Maps of Antietam", pgs. 210-211.

ravine that gave them some protection from the Union artillery. The position overlooked a series of rolling hills which eventually sloped down to the Antietam creek where the two regiments of Toombs' brigade were stationed. The ground in front of the 1st VA was crisscrossed with farm fields separated by fences and stone walls.

Early on the morning of September 17th, the sounds of battle were heard on the far left of the Confederate line, out of sight of the men of the 1st VA. The fight was exploding around landmarks whose names would become famous: Dunker Church, The Cornfield, and Bloody Lane. During the morning the reverberations of battle became louder and louder as the fight cascaded down the Confederate lines from left to right, moving in the direction of the less than twenty-five men in the tiny regiment. Eventually the men could see the fight that was taking place to their left. They watched as the Confederates were pushed back, followed by long battle lines of blue clad soldiers. The Union lines were ravaged by artillery fire, punching huge gaping holes in their ranks. Eventually, the Yankees came to a halt and the reorganized Confederates held them in check. But it was the ominous activity in their immediate front which now demanded the attention of the 1st VA and the rest of Jones's division.[194]

During the morning, the 24th VA followed by the 7th VA, the two largest regiments in Kemper's brigade, were sent farther to the right to support Confederate artillery on the road to Harpers Ferry and to protect the right flank of the division. This reduced the effective strength of the brigade to less than 200 men. Across the creek, Kemper's men watched as the Union 9th Corps, under the command of Major Gen. Ambrose Burnside, continued to make repeated assaults on the stone bridge, which was stubbornly defended by two regiments of Georgians under the command of Brig. Gen. Toombs. The Georgians were supported by artillery placed on the hill by Gen. Jones. The open ground on the far side of the creek left the advancing Union troops vulnerable to the cannon and musket fire as they approached the bridge. Undaunted, the Federal troops continued to endure the rebel fire and gallantly attack the bridge. After suffering numerous casualties and running low on ammunition, the Georgians were forced to yield their position after the bridge was attacked by the 51st New York and the 51st PA, at approximately one o'clock. The Union 9th Corps poured across the bridge

[194] David E. Johnston, "Four Years a Soldier", pgs. 199-200.

and began to form lines of battle on the Confederate side of Antietam Creek, facing Jones's division and the 1st VA.[195]

Toombs's weary men fell back to the far right of Kemper's brigade where they were joined by several fresh regiments from their own brigade who recently arrived on the field. Their position left yet another large gap between their left and Kemper's right. Confederate artillery continued to bombard the enemy as they tried to organize their lines for the final assault. It took Burnside's men approximately two hours to get their divisions over the creek and begin their advance. By this time, much to the relief of the infantry posted on the top of the hill, advance units of Gen. A.P. Hill's division were seen drawing close to the battlefield. [196]

At approximately four o'clock, the men of the Union 9th corps started up the hill toward Sharpsburg. Kemper's brigade was called to arms, leaving the protection of the ravine, and moving forward to a wooden fence to await the enemy. Drayton's brigade, on the left of Kemper, also moved forward to prepare for the enemy attack and found they were fortunate enough to form behind a stone wall, which offered better protection. The Confederate batteries cut holes in the Union ranks, which were quickly filled, and the lines continued cautiously forward. Union cannon were also busy preparing the field for their infantry with a barrage of shot and shell. One shell burst directly above the 17th VA, who were in line next to the 1st VA. The shrapnel ripped into the body of a member of Company "E" of the 17th, killing him instantly and splattering his comrades with blood. Eventually, either from lack of ammunition or the overwhelming Yankee counter-fire, the Confederate guns limbered up and galloped off in the direction of Sharpsburg. This left only the thin line of infantry to stop the wave of Union soldiers advancing up the slope. Due to the undulating ground, the blue lines would disappear in the valleys only to reappear as they ascended the next slope. Private Alexander Hunter of the 17th

---

[195] Official Records, Series 1, Volume 19, Part 1, "Report of Brig Gen. Robert Toombs", pgs. 888-893; "Report of Maj. Gen. Ambrose E. Burnside, U.S. Army, commanding right wing, Army of the Potomac, of operations September 7-19; "Report of Col. Montgomery D. Corse, Seventeenth Virginia Infantry, Battle of Sharpsburg", pg. 905.

[196] Official Records, Series 1, Volume 19, Part 1, "Report of Brig Gen. Robert Toombs", pgs. 888-893.

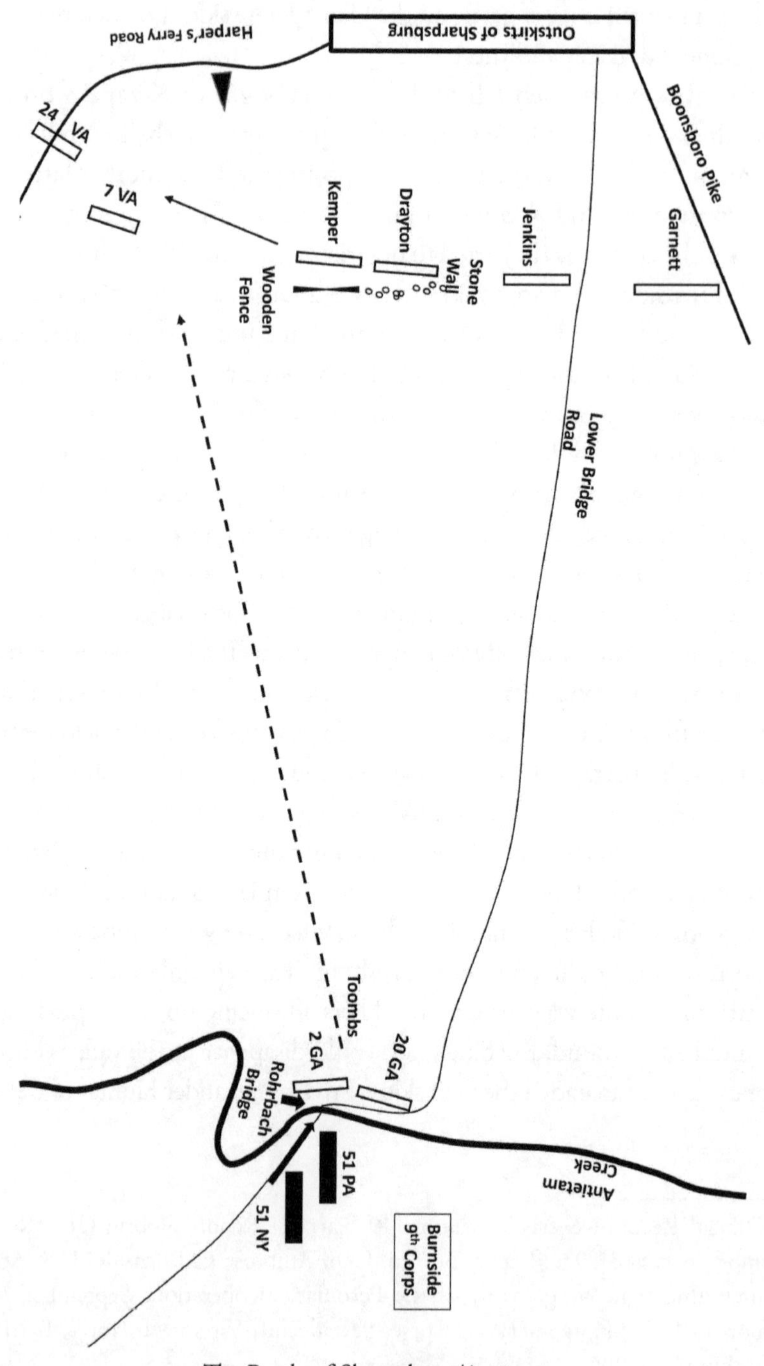

The Battle of Sharpsburg/Antietam
September 17, 1862

VA gives a description of the sight that beheld the brigade that afternoon as they waited for the Yankees to crest the final hill:

"Each man sighted his rifle about two feet above the crest, and then, with his finger on the trigger, waited until an advancing form came between the bead and the clear sky behind.

The first thing we saw appear was the gilt eagle that surmounted the pole, then the top of the flag, next the flutter of the Stars and Stripes itself slowly mounting – up it rose; then their hats came in sight; still rising, the faces emerged; next a range of curious eyes appeared, then such a hurrah as only the Yankee troops could give broke the stillness, and they surged towards us."[197]

Hunter was watching the 9th, 103rd and 89th New York regiments, who were brigaded under the command of Col. Harrison S. Fairchild. Along with Hunter, the men of the 1st VA waited anxiously for the Yankees to crest the hill. They leveled their muskets along the fence and stared down the barrels until the blue clad soldiers presented themselves as targets. When the approaching lines were within sixty yards, the Confederates fired a deadly volley of lead, dropping many soldiers and staggering the blue lines. The Yankees answered with a murderous volley of their own shattering the wooden fence and the rebel soldiers behind it. The men loaded and fired as fast as they could but the overpowering weight of the Union lines made the outcome of the contest a foregone conclusion. Within minutes, the Federals charged the fence line. There was a brief bout of hand to hand fighting during which time Lieut. W. W. Athey, of Company "C" 17th VA, captured the regimental colors of the 103rd NY Infantry. However, the power of the Union advance proved to be too much for the Confederates. For the first time in the war, the 1st VA, along, with the rest of Kemper's brigade, broke and ran. Drayton's brigade met with a similar fate and the entire Confederate line seemed to be collapsing back toward Sharpsburg. The hasty retreat took the men through a cornfield, the tall stalks of corn slowing their progress to escape the enemy. Fortunately for the fleeing rebels, the New

---

[197] Southern Historical Society Papers, Vol. 11, Edited by Rev. J. William Jones D.D., Published by the Society, Richmond VA, 1883, Reprinted by Kraus Reprint Co., Millwood NY, 1977, "A High Private's Sketch of Sharpsburg" by Alexander Hunter, Pgs. 10-21

Yorkers stopped at the scene of their victory, throwing their caps in the air and cheering their success. The men of the brigade ran to the very outskirts of town, where they stopped and began to reform their units. The ground behind the fence, now under Union control, was littered with the Confederate dead and wounded. One of the wounded, and now a prisoner, was Col. Montgomery Corse, the commander of the 17th VA and the man who commanded the brigade at Second Manassas.[198]

While Kemper's brigade was locked in mortal combat with Fairchild's New Yorkers, Gen. A.P. Hill's division was joining the fight on the Yankee's left flank. After their forced march from Harper's Ferry, Hill's infantry and artillery went directly into the fray. At the same time, Gen. Toombs, whose troops were resupplied and reinforced began a counter attack on the Union lines. Soldiers from the 1st VA, along with the 11th and 17th VA, were attempting to reorganize their shattered brigade in the rear. Captain Troup, a staff officer in Toombs's brigade, saw the disorganized Virginians and helped to rally them back to the fight. Troup placed the reformed remnants of Kemper's brigade on the left of Toombs' battle line. The guns of A.P. Hill's newly arrived division, along with the vaunted Washington Artillery, began to pound away at the stunned Yankees. As A.P. Hill drove in the Union left flank, Toombs ordered his command to advance from the front and they began to push the Federal troops back down the hill toward the bridge. The men of Kemper's brigade, their pride restored, were being led by Major Herbert of the 17th VA. Many of the Union soldiers in this sector were inexperienced "green" troops and they could not stand up to the counterattack conducted by battle hardened Confederate veterans. In addition, some of A.P. Hill's men were wearing new blue uniforms from the recently captured supplies at Harper's Ferry, causing even more confusion among the inexperienced Yankees. The Rebel assault recaptured the lost ground and a battery of Confederate guns that were lost during the Union advance. Also liberated was Col. Corse, who was still on the field when his captors left him and retreated down the hill. As night fell, the Confederates had regained all that was lost during the day except for the Rohrbach Bridge

---

198 Official Records, Series 1, Volume 19, Part 1, "Report of Col. Montgomery D. Corse, Seventeenth Virginia Infantry, Battle of Sharpsburg", Pg. 905: Curran, "John Dooley's Civil War, An Irish American's Journey in the First Virginia Infantry Regiment", Pg. 48-49.

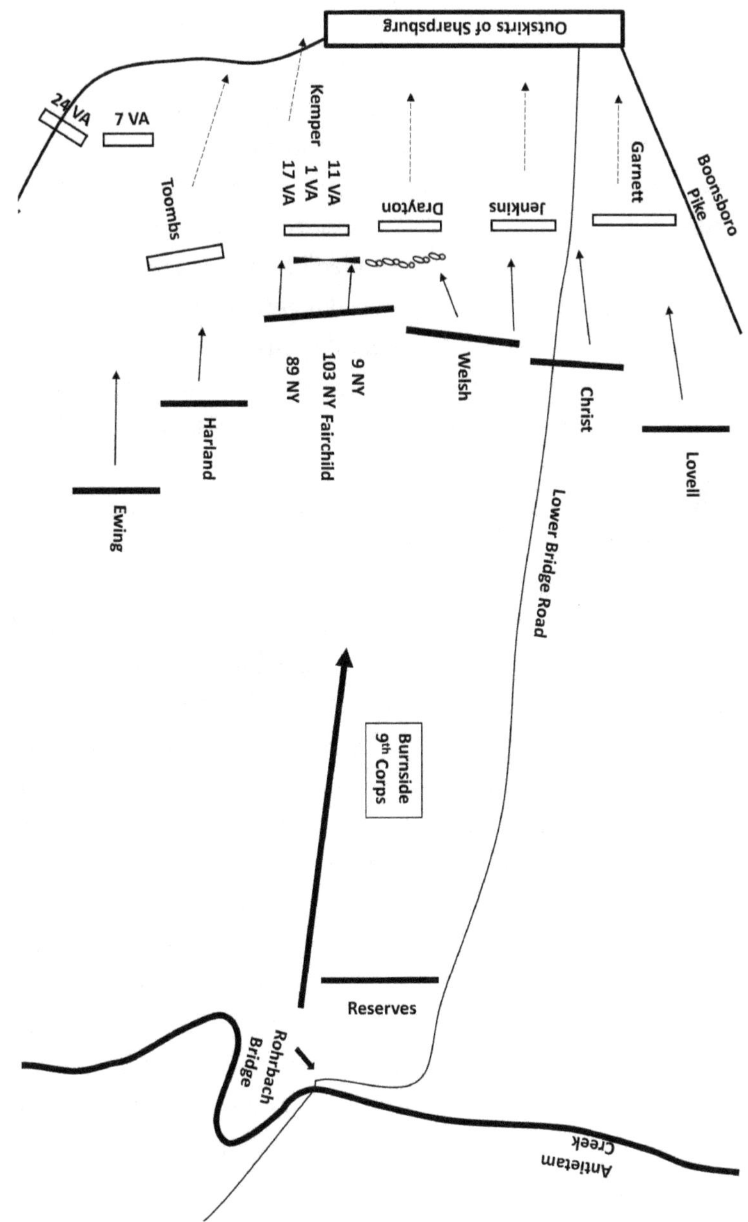

The Battle of Sharpsburg
The Advance of the Union 9th Corps

itself, which forever after this day would be known as Burnside Bridge.[199]

The night was spent caring for the wounded and, when possible, burying the dead. The men were fatigued and slept with their muskets by their side since they expected a resumption of hostilities in the morning. As the sun rose on the 18th of September, it illuminated a ghastly field of death and destruction between the two armies. Most of the Confederate wounded were within the rebel lines and had been taken to the makeshift hospitals overnight. Between the lines of skirmishers, however, many of the Union wounded lay unattended. Some of the more compassionate rebels tried to go between the lines and help the wounded enemy soldiers. These missions of mercy into "no man's land" were a dangerous proposition, since the skirmishers of both armies were actively shooting at each other. A member of the 7th VA was shot and killed by a Yankee sharpshooter while trying to aid the enemy wounded. This incident abruptly halted the charitable missions and the wounded continued to lie in agony unattended.[200]

As the morning wore on, the two armies eyed each other nervously while they waited for their commanders to decide if the battle would resume. The quiet of the day was occasionally broken by the sound of the skirmishers but no serious fighting took place. The weary men of the 1st VA even found time to take a much needed nap during the lull. Part of the day was also used cleaning the battlefield of muskets, cartridges and other discarded tools of war. As the sun began to sink in the western sky, orders were received to plan for the evacuation of Sharpsburg. As the 1st VA was preparing to leave, a detail was sent to fill the regiment's canteens with water for the march back to Virginia. The detail came upon a warehouse where whiskey was being stored, guarded by a group of Confederate soldiers from Georgia. The men of the 1st VA marched up to the warehouse, convinced the Georgians they were there to relieve them, and promptly filled the regiment's canteens with whiskey. Charles Loehr credits thirty-eight year old Corporal Lawrence Carroll of Company "C" with engineering the prank, while John Dooley gives the credit to twenty-five year old Private James McCrossen, also of Company "C." Perhaps they

---

[199] Official Records, Series 1, Volume 19, Part 1, "Report of Brig Gen. Robert Toombs", Pgs. 888-893.

[200] David E. Johnston, "Four Years a Soldier", pg. 204: "John Dooley Confederate Soldier", Durkin, pg. 50.

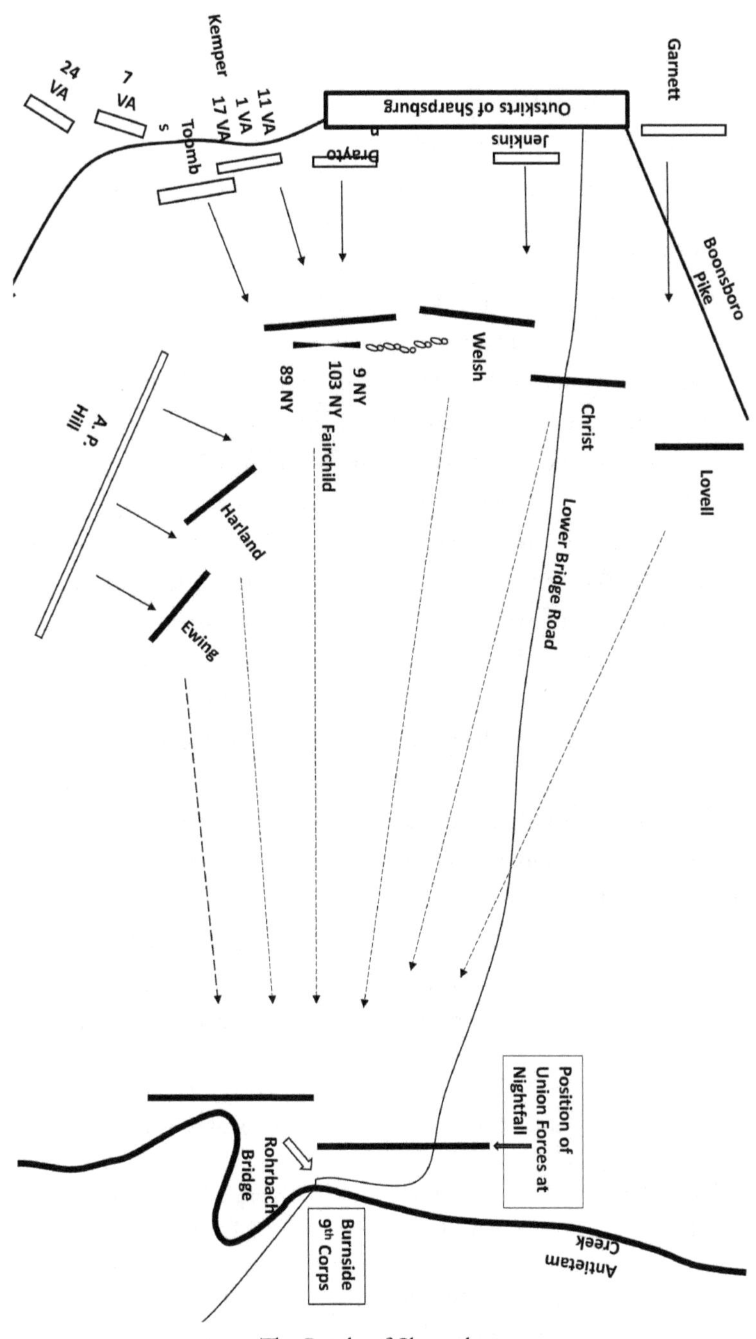

The Battle of Sharpsburg
The Confederate Counterattack

were both part of the conspiracy. Regardless of who was responsible, their ingenuity "caused the step of most of the men to be rather uncertain in fording the stream." With this comical incident, the Maryland Campaign of 1862 came to an end for the 1st VA. [201]

Unfortunately, there does not seem to be an accurate accounting for the number of men engaged from the 1st VA in the Maryland campaign, which consisted of both the Battles of South Mountain and Sharpsburg. William Palmer, after the war, claimed the 1st VA had "only about twenty-four at Sharpsburg." Allowing for straggling and the casualties at South Mountain, it is safe to assume the regiment entered Maryland with thirty to forty soldiers, less than one half a full sized company. Of the approximately twenty-four men present at the battle of Sharpsburg, Charles Loehr lists only one wounded and that was Private William J. Mallory of Company "B." John Clarence Head of Company "I" was reported as captured during the fighting at Sharpsburg. These casualties, added to the seven casualties sustained at the Battle on South Mountain, corresponds closely with the report of Surgeon Lafayette Guild, the Medical Director for the Army of Northern Virginia, which claims eight wounded for the 1st VA in the Maryland campaign. It would seem miraculous that the regiment only suffered two casualties at Sharpsburg, considering the 17th VA, who was fighting adjacent to the 1st VA, took fifty-five men into the battle and suffered forty-one casualties including ten men taken prisoner. The Union brigade of Col. Harrison S. Fairchild, comprising the 9th, 89th and 103rd NY regiments, who opposed the 1st and 17th VA, claimed a total of four hundred and fifty five total casualties. It is unclear how many of those casualties were a direct result of the combat with the Virginians.[202]

The five regiments in Kemper's brigade, by most estimates, totaled

---

[201] Charles Loehr, "War History of the Old First Virginia Infantry Regiment", Pgs. 30-31: Durkin, "John Dooley Confederate Soldier", pg. 51: Lee Wallace, "1st Virginia Infantry" Pgs. 86 &104.

[202] Charles Loehr, "War History of the Old First Virginia Infantry Regiment", Pg. 30: Official Records, Series 1, Vol. 19, Part 1, "Report of Surg. Lafayette Guild, C. S. Army, Medical Director Army of Northern Virginia". Pg. 810: "Report of Col. Montgomery Corse, Seventeenth Virginia Infantry", Pg. 905: "Return of Casualties in the Union Forces at the battle of Antietam", Pg. 197. Lee Wallace, "1st Virginia Infantry", Pgs. 81-123: "Record of the Richmond City and Henrico Co. Virginia Troops", Compiled by E. H. Chamberlayne, Jr., Richmond 1879.

fewer than four hundred men, at the onset of the Maryland campaign. This is less than half the size of one full regiment. In total, the brigade suffered approximately fifteen killed, one hundred and two wounded, and twenty-seven missing for a total of one hundred forty-four casualties during the campaign.[203]

The hardships endured by the men in this campaign are best summed up by their corps commander, Gen. James Longstreet, who wrote in his report, "*The name of every officer, non-commissioned officer, and private who has shared in the toils and privations of the campaign should be mentioned. In one month these troops had marched over 200 miles, upon little more than half rations, and fought nine battles and skirmishes, killed, wounded, and captured nearly as many men as we had in our ranks, besides taking arms and other munition of war in large quantities. I would that I could do justice to all of these gallant officers and men in this report.*"[204]

After evacuating Sharpsburg the regiment crossed the Potomac near Shepherdstown. McClellan made a half-hearted attempt to stop the fleeing Confederates and the brigade was halted when Union forces skirmished with the rear guard of the army. The attack was beaten off and the brigade continued on their march. On the 21st of September they forded the Opequan Creek and camped nearby on the outskirts of Martinsburg. On the afternoon of the 21st, the Chaplain of the 1st VA held a service for the men of the brigade. His sermon was appropriately from the text of the Second Epistle of Paul to Timothy, "I have fought the good fight, I have finished my course, I have kept the faith."[205]

---

203 "Battles and Leaders of the Civil War", Vol. 2, "North to Antietam", "The Opposing forces in the Maryland Campaign, Pg.601.

204 Official Records, Series 1, Vol. 19, Part 1, "Report of Lieut. Gen. James Longstreet", Pgs. 839-843.

205 George Wise, "History of the Seventeenth Virginia Infantry, C.S.A.", Pg. 121.

FREDERICKSBURG

After leaving Maryland, Gen. Lee consolidated his army in the vicinity of Winchester. The 1st VA arrived within three miles of that place and camped at Washington Spring on the 27th of September. The ragged men were in a deplorable state. They were in desperate need of clothing and especially shoes. Straggling during the Maryland Campaign was a serious detriment to the army, despite Gen. Lee's attempts to limit the practice. The long marches, combined with the lack of proper shoes, proved too much for even the most dedicated veteran soldiers. Thousands of stragglers were spread out over the countryside in the wake of the army's line of march. In a communication with his two corps commanders, Longstreet and Jackson, Gen. Lee voiced his concern over "this growing evil." Many of the stragglers threw away their weapons to lighten their load, compounding the loss to the army.

The commanding general instituted a more stringent set of rules for the brigades to counter the problem of straggling. He ordered that a strict adherence to morning roll calls be conducted at reveille. The men were forced to appear under arms in order that company commanders could verify that each soldier was in possession of his weapon. Brigade guards would follow each brigade, increasing their efforts to round up all stragglers and return them to their proper commands. Lee was very cognizant of the damage done to surrounding neighborhoods when a hungry army passed through and how this could negatively affect public opinion toward the cause of the Confederacy. Brigade guards were ordered to place sentinels to protect private property in the vicinity of the army's camp sites. The men of the 1st VA were not immune to the habit of straggling. On the march out of Maryland, several of the men dropped out of line and were resting in a hay stack when Gen. Lee, himself, happened upon them. Lee asked,

"My good men, what regiment do you belong to?" The men being both frightened and ashamed showed the general their bruised and bloody feet and explained they could not keep up with the rapid march. They answered the general's question, telling him they were members of the 1st VA. To which Lee replied, "What, members of the glorious 1st! The first regiment that Virginia placed in the field and which has never yet proved recreant to its duty! No, no; rise, my good fellows and rejoin your regiment." The men returned to the regiment both ashamed of their actions and more dedicated to Gen. Lee than ever.[206]

On October 2, 1862, General Lee issued the following well deserved congratulatory message to the men in his command:

General Orders, No. 116

"In reviewing the achievements of the army during the present campaign, the commanding general cannot withhold the expression of his admiration of the indomitable courage it has displayed in battle and its cheerful endurance of privation and hardship on the march. Since your great victories around Richmond, you have defeated the enemy at Cedar Mountain, expelled him from the Rappahannock, and, after a conflict of three days, utterly repulsed him on the plains of Manassas, and forced him to take shelter within the fortifications around his capital. Without halting for repose, you crossed the Potomac, stormed the heights of Harper's Ferry, made prisoners of more than 11,000 men, and captured upward of seventy-five pieces of artillery, all their small-arms, and other munitions of war. While one corps of the army was thus engaged, the other insured its success by arresting at Boons borough the combined armies of the enemy, advancing under their favorite general to the relief of their beleaguered comrades. On the field of Sharpsburg, with less than one-third his numbers, you resisted from daylight until dark the whole army of the enemy, and repulsed every attack along his entire front of more than 4 miles in extent. The whole of the following day you stood prepared to resume the conflict on the same ground, and retired next morning without molestation across the Potomac. Two attempts subsequently made by the enemy to follow you across the river have resulted in his complete discomfiture and being

---

206 Official Records, Series 1, Vol. 19, Part 2, correspondence dated September 22, 1862 addressed to Generals Longstreet and Jackson, pg. 618: Durkin, "John Dooley Confederate Soldier", pg.55.

driven back with loss. Achievements such as these demanded much valor and patriotism. History records few examples of greater fortitude and endurance than this army has exhibited, and I am commissioned by the President to thank you in the name of the Confederate States for the undying fame you have won for their arms. Much as you have done, much more remains to be accomplished. The enemy again threatens with invasion, and to your tried valor and patriotism the country looks with confidence for deliverance and safety. Your past exploits give assurance that this confidence is not misplaced.

R.E. Lee
General Commanding."[207]

During the month of October, the regiment took part in several reviews and inspections as the army tried to recuperate and reorganize after months of actively campaigning. On the 6th of October, Gen. Kemper reviewed his brigade, followed three days later by a review of the entire division by Gen. James Longstreet. Later in the month, an even larger review of a portion of Longstreet's Corps was conducted, allegedly for the benefit of a group who the men remembered as, "some visiting English Lords." The "English Lords" were actually two English reporters, Francis Lawley, a correspondent for the London Times and Frank Vizitelly, a correspondent and artist for The London Illustrated News. Both of the journalists were reporting on the Confederacy for their respective papers back in Britain. The third Englishman of the group was Colonel Garnet Wolseley of the British Army. Wolseley was a reputed soldier in his own right having fought in the Crimea, India, Egypt, the Sudan and other British conflicts. He was later promoted to the rank of Field Marshall as Viscount Wosely in the peerage of England. At the time of his visit to the Confederacy, Wolseley was stationed in Canada and crossed through the lines to get a personal soldier's view of the Army of Northern Virginia. Judging from his later writings, his impression of the Confederate army was first rate. When writing of the review he witnessed that day, which included the 1st VA, the Field Marshal wrote, "I have seen many armies file past in all the pomp of bright clothing and well-polished accoutrements; but I never saw one composed of finer men, or that looked more like work,

[207] Official Records, Series 1, Vol. 19, Part 2, "General Orders No. 116", pg. 644-45

than that portion of Gen. Lee's army which I was fortunate enough to see inspected." He also placed Gen. Lee in the top tier of commanders among the likes of Marlborough and Wellington, two of England's most accomplished Generals. He described Lee as a "True Hero" and "the most perfect man I ever met".[208]

While the regiment rested at Winchester, some of the men who were wounded on the Peninsula and at 2nd Manassas began to return to their respective companies. One of them was Col. Lewis B. Williams, who shortly after being elected Colonel of the regiment in April was seriously wounded and captured at the battle of Williamsburg. After being paroled and then exchanged, Williams finally returned to the command of the 1st VA. The regiment also lost a very competent officer in Major William Palmer who was transferred to become Chief of Staff for Gen. A. P. Hill. Kemper's brigade also lost the services of Col. Corse, commander of the 17th VA, who was promoted to brigadier general and given command of Gen. Pickett's former brigade. [209]

If the 1st VA was associated with the name of any Confederate General besides James Lawson Kemper, it would be Gen. George Edward Pickett. Like many of the men in the 1st VA, Pickett was a native of Richmond, born there on January 28, 1825. He attended the military academy at West Point, where he graduated last in his class in 1846. During the war with Mexico, he was brevetted 1st lieutenant and then captain for his gallant service in several battles, including the capture of Mexico City. After the Mexican War, he remained in the U.S. Army until 1861 when he resigned his commission and offered his services to the Confederate government. Pickett was promoted to brigadier general in January of 1862 and commanded a brigade under Longstreet. On October 10, 1862, he was promoted again to major general and was put in command of a division in which Kemper's brigade was a part. Longstreet and "Stonewall"

---

208 "History of the Seventeenth Virginia Infantry", George Wise, pg. 121: "Recollections of a Confederate Staff Officer", G. Moxley Sorrel, Pgs. 94-95: "The American Civil War, An English Point of View" by Field Marshal Viscount Wolseley, Published by Stackpole Books, 5067 Ritter Road, Mechanicsburg, PA 17055, 2002, Pgs. 40, 51, 53.

209 Charles Loehr, "War History of the Old First Virginia Infantry Regiment", Pg. 31.

Jackson were both promoted to lieutenant-general and placed in command of the 1st and 2nd Corps, respectively, in Gen. Lee's army. When all of the promotions and transfers were complete, the 1st VA Volunteer Infantry Regiment under the command of Col. Lewis B. Williams was in Kemper's Brigade, Pickett's Division, Longstreet's 1st Corps, Army of Northern VA.[210]

For the second time since taking over command of the Army of Northern Virginia, Robert E. Lee used his influence to try and help fill the ranks of the 1st VA. In a correspondence with Major Gen. Gustavus Smith, who was in command of the defenses around Richmond, Lee wrote, "If I send the First Virginia Regiment to Richmond, where it was originally raised (but now has very few for duty in the field), could you fill it up with conscripts?" Whether or not Lee made any such appeal, perhaps through private channels, prior to this is not known. But, previous to Lee's letter on the 24th, the regiment did in fact receive the much needed recruits. Lieutenant E.P. Reeve, who was recuperating in Richmond from the wound he received at 2nd Manassas, wrote to his wife on the 26th of October, "I learn that my regiment is in better condition than it has been for some time there being some two hundred men present for duty, there seems to be no chance of its being disbanded soon." Since Reeve had knowledge of the increase in manpower on the 26th, it is obvious the recruits arrived before Gen. Lee wrote to Smith in Richmond on the 24th. The fact that Lee wrote the letter at all is proof enough of his concern in keeping the 1st VA as an active military unit. The additional troops were a welcome relief to the regiment. Charles Loehr stated that few of the recruits were from Richmond because in that city, where the 1st VA was formed, they had a reputation as "a bad luck regiment" because of the many battle losses incurred.[211]

With the reorganization of the army and the addition of the conscripts

---

210 "Historical Times, Encyclopedia of the Civil War" Patricia Faust, Editor, pg. 583-584: Official Records, Series 1, Vol. 19, part 2, "Special Orders No. 234, Pgs. 698-699.

211 Official Records, Series 1, Volume 19, Part 2, "Correspondence to Major Gen. Gustavus W. Smith from R.E. Lee" dated October 24, 1862: E.P. Reeve letter to his wife Hester, dated October 26,1862: Charles Loehr, "War History of the Old First Virginia Infantry Regiment", pg. 31.

came a renewal of daily drills, much to the chagrin of the veterans who had not had to drill since they left Richmond in August. The regiment returned to the normalcy of camp life. The supply lines were open and the men were getting regular rations. When not drilling they spent their days doing maintenance on the camp and their equipment. Guard duty, reviews and dress parades were common occurrences. Gen. Pickett reviewed his new division on the 16th of October and the division was reviewed again by Gen. Robert E. Lee on the 22nd. At night, the men sat around their campfires talking of home and the various campaigns that they had taken part in. The stories of the veterans must have been both exciting and horrifying to the young new recruits, who had yet to fire a shot in anger. At night, Sergeant William Deane of Company "G" and his vocal troupe would entertain the men with their renditions of "Nelly was a Lady," "Come to de ol'gum tree" and many of the old Negro songs. The men regularly received packages and letters from Richmond by way of a black man who is only described as "Old Reuben". Reuben called on the families, picking up the parcels, and then made the trek to Winchester to complete his delivery. Unfortunately, Reuben "always happens to be robbed of about one half of his goods." The soldiers, who were starved for news from home, were happy to get the deliveries even if some of the articles were lost in transport.

Guard duty during this time normally required the men to spend the night protecting private homes and farms from foragers and stragglers who strayed from the Confederate camps. Since the threat of an enemy attack was minimal, the men did not take this duty very seriously. Private John Dooley was on one such detail on a very cold night in October. The men were wrapped up in their blankets around a raging campfire telling stories until they all, shirking their duty, fell fast asleep. The winds picked up and began to blow the hot embers from the campfire into a hollow apple tree nearby. When the men awoke, the apple tree, where they had hung their cartridge boxes, was ablaze. The scorched boxes were quickly retrieved just before the gunpowder inside could explode and cause injury to the negligent sentinels.[212]

After the battle of Sharpsburg, the Union army remained motionless in

---

212 "History of the Seventeenth Virginia Infantry", George Wise, pg. 121: Durkin, "John Dooley Confederate Soldier", pgs. 54-67:

Maryland, much to the annoyance of President Lincoln. Gen. McClellan finally began moving south and crossed the Potomac on Oct. 26th, 1862. Unsure of McClellan's intentions, Gen. Lee began moving his own army to cover the approaches into Virginia. Lee ordered Gen. Longstreet to move his corps in the direction of Culpeper Court House on October 28. In a second communication that day, Lee wrote to Longstreet, "I desire that you will expedite the movements of General Pickett as much as possible, as circumstances may render it very desirable that he should reach his destination with the least delay." With this order, the 1st VA broke camp and took up the line of march.[213]

The brigade marched through Winchester on their way to Front Royal. The removal of the army left Winchester vulnerable to occupation by the federal forces and yet, applause and cheers greeted the men from the townspeople who lined the streets and leaned out of the open windows. The reception they received by their fellow Virginians was in stark contrast to the treatment accorded them in Frederick and Hagerstown by the people of Maryland. The men passed Front Royal and crossed over the mountains at Chester Gap. While marching through the Shenandoah Valley, the men could not help but notice the damage that war had brought to the once beautiful valley. The brigade arrived in the vicinity of Culpeper Court House about the 31st of October and set up camp to await the consolidation of Longstreet's Corps.[214]

While in camp at Culpepper C.H., men continued to return to the regiment. One of them was Lt. E.P. Reeve of Company "D". Reeve, who was shot in the chest at 2nd Manassas, had been convalescing in Richmond with his family. While there, he was offered a permanent position at Camp Lee, which would have taken him out of harm's way and out of the ranks of the 1st VA. After learning that the regiment had been refurbished with recruits and was in no immediate danger of being disbanded, Reeve declined the position in order to return to his comrades. He left Richmond on October 27th, in charge of eighty-four exchanged Confederate prisoners who were also returning to their respective commands. By the time Reeve reached Winchester with his charges, the 1st VA had already vacated that place and moved on to Culpepper C.H. After completing his assignment,

---

213 Official Records, Series 1, Vol. 19, Part 2, pgs. 686-87

214 Durkin, "John Dooley Confederate Soldier", pgs. 68-70

Reeve continued on in search of his regiment, reaching their camp in early November.[215]

Another new recruit worthy of note joined the regiment at Culpepper C. H. William "Willie" Mitchel was the brother of Captain James Mitchel of Company "C" and the youngest son of John Mitchel, the Irish nationalist and close friend of Major John Dooley who had adopted the Confederate cause as his own. Not yet seventeen, Willie had already seen more of the world than most men of this period would see in a lifetime. He had spent time in Tasmania while his father was in exile there because of his anti-British activities in Ireland. After they escaped from that place, Willie was then left in France to get an education while the rest of the family moved on to America. John Mitchel returned to France to fetch his son and, after a harrowing adventure sneaking through Union lines, they returned to Virginia, where Willie promptly enlisted in the 1st VA Company "D." Willie, like E.P. Reeve, went to Winchester looking for the regiment. Not finding them there, he too hurried on to Culpeper C.H., where he caught up with Kemper's Brigade. Willie's brother James was no longer the Captain of Company "C", having been wounded at 2nd Manassas and subsequently transferred to the staff of Brig. Gen. John Gordon of Early's division in Stonewall Jackson's 2nd Corps. The presence of John Dooley and the close relationship between the two Irish families gave Willie a companion in Company "D." Although it is doubtful the two ever met before Willie arrived in the company, he and John Dooley instantly bonded and became the best of friends. They teamed up with twenty-two year old Sergeant Major Robert "Tante" Jones and formed a mess, which meant the three of them would camp together and share their equipment and food.[216]

Meanwhile, back in Washington, President Lincoln, who had grown weary of Gen. McClellan's arrogance and lack of substantial results, finally removed him from command of the Army of the Potomac on November 5, 1862. In his place, Major General Ambrose Burnside, former commander of the 9th corps, whose troops had clashed with the 1st VA at Sharpsburg, was ordered to take command. Burnside was immediately ordered to

---

[215] E.P. Reeve, Letter to his wife, Richmond 0ct. 26, 1862.

[216] Robert Emmett Curran, "John Dooley's Civil War; An Irish American's Journey in the First Virginia Infantry Regiment", Pgs. 73-74 & 445.

propose a plan of action for the Union army, which he did on November 7th. The new commanding general reorganized the command structure of the Army of the Potomac by splitting this large army, over 110,000 men, into three "Grand Divisions." Burnside's plan was to make a feint toward Culpepper or Gordonsville and then make a rapid move with the entire army toward Fredericksburg, crossing the Rappahannock at that city and continuing on toward Richmond. [217]

As Burnside began to put his plan in motion, the men of the 1st VA continued the monotony of camp life. The dense woods where the regiment originally camped were now barren of trees. The weather was growing colder and rain turned the roads and the campsite into a sea of mud. As most men expected military operations to cease for the winter months, rumors abounded as to the possible destinations of the 1st VA. There was even a strong belief that the regiment would be sent back to Richmond to be filled with recruits. In a letter to his wife regarding this expected move to Richmond, Lt. E.P. Reeve wrote, "I have heard enough to make me think it highly probable though I do not think it by any means certain." Perhaps Reeve, who had relationships with some high ranking officers, including Longstreet, may have had knowledge of Gen. Lee's letter to Gen. Smith in regards to sending the regiment to Richmond for refurbishing. Whether at Richmond or somewhere else, everyone expected the army to go into winter quarters and await the coming of spring before hostilities resumed. Some of the officers were already looking to hire servants to handle the cooking while in winter quarters.[218]

As October turned into November and the temperatures in Northern Virginia began to drop, the men suffered accordingly. The newly formed mess of Sergeant Major Jones, John Dooley and Willie Mitchel found an ingenious if not comical way to keep warm at night. With three men and four blankets, the mess mates decided to pool their scanty resources. Lying together, they laid one blanket on the ground and covered themselves with the other three. The width of the blankets only proved to be sufficient if all three men lay in the same position. If any of the three rolled over, one of the men on either end quickly found himself uncovered and exposed to the elements. To counter this dilemma, the men agreed that if any one

---

[217] Official Records, Series 1, Volume 19, Part 2, Pgs. 545-554.

[218] E.P. Reeve, letter to his wife Hester, from Culpepper C. H., November 19, 1862.

of them decided to change position during the night, he would wake the other two and all three men would make the change simultaneously. The man in the middle would be responsible for giving the command "right or left turn," at which time the move would be made with all the precision of well-trained soldiers. All the while, the ever present Ned Haines wrapped himself in a blanket and slept next to the fire. Although Ned had unlimited opportunities to escape the bondage of slavery, he remained a loyal servant to John Dooley, sharing in the hardships of the Confederate soldiers.[219]

There were several organizational changes in the month of November that affected Kemper's brigade and the 1st VA. As mentioned earlier, the War Department continued the policy of grouping regiments from a particular state into the same brigade. There were three regiments from the state of Florida in the Army of Northern Virginia and two of them, the 2nd and 8th FL, along with the 3rd VA and the 14th AL were in the brigade of Brig. Gen. Roger A. Pryor. On November 10th, Pryor's brigade was disbanded to allow for the formation of a brigade composed of all three Florida regiments under the command of Colonel E. A. Perry, who was also from Florida. Longstreet was ordered to assign the 3rd VA from Pryor's now defunct brigade to a new brigade made up entirely of Virginia regiments. The 3rd VA, under the command of Colonel Joseph Mayo Jr., was assigned to Kemper's brigade, further increasing their numbers. Events were now put into motion that nearly altered the history of the 1st VA completely. Gen. Lee sent Pryor to Richmond with the intention of his getting a command in the Blackwater region south of the James River. Pryor reported to the commander in Richmond, Gen. Gustavus Smith, and a plan was devised wherein the 1st and 61st VA were to be sent to Petersburg to form the nucleus of a brigade under the command of Pryor. Apparently the plan had the approval of the Secretary of War, who requested on November 12th that Gen. Lee send the two Virginia regiments to Petersburg. This transfer would obviously have removed the 1st VA from their comrades in Kemper's brigade, with whom they had shared so much thus far in the war and would also have taken them from the Army of Northern Virginia. Gen. Lee was not willing to part with the 1st or the 61st VA regiments when he wrote to Gen. Pryor on November 25th, "I regret my inability to detach from this army the two regiments you

---

[219] Durkin, "John Dooley, Confederate Soldier", Pg. 71-71

desire to constitute a brigade, to operate on the Blackwater, under your command. As far as I am able to judge, troops are more wanted here than there." A few days later, Lee expressed the same concerns in a dispatch to the Secretary of War, James A. Seddon. This ended the matter and the 1st VA remained with their comrades in Kemper's brigade. It is probable that the men in the 1st VA knew nothing of this proposed move since there is no mention of it in any of their writings. The 61st VA also remained in the Army of Northern VA after being transferred to Mahone's Brigade.[220]

Union Gen. Burnside's plan to attack at Fredericksburg put an end to the expectations of a winter repose. On the 17th of November, it was discovered that the Right Grand Division of the Army of the Potomac, under the command of Gen. Sumner, was moving toward that town. Longstreet immediately began to move with two divisions toward Fredericksburg, and the rest of his corps was ordered to follow on the 19th. Pickett's division acted as the rear guard for the corps on the march to Fredericksburg. This made the journey more difficult for the men of the 1st VA, as the movement of horses, wagons and thousands of marching men to their front turned the muddy roads into a deep sticky sludge as the army passed over them.[221]

The brigade crossed the frigid waist deep water of the Rapidan River at Raccoon Ford and headed toward Fredericksburg. The next day, they marched through the desolate pine forests known as the Wilderness and camped at the hamlet of Chancellorsville. On the 21st of November, after three days of hard marching over very bad roads, the brigade crossed over Telegraph Road and camped on the outskirts of Fredericksburg. Pickett's division was placed on a hill in the woods behind McClaw's division, which was placed in a sunken road across from Telegraph Road. The area, known as Deep Run Valley, was named after a stream of the same name which meandered through it. As Longstreet's divisions were establishing a defensive position on the heights behind Fredericksburg, Burnside's Union

---

220 Official Records, Series 1, Volume 19, Part 2, Pgs. 708,709,712, 715; Volume 21, pgs. 1032, 1036.

221 James Longstreet, "From Manassas to Appomattox", pg. 292-93.

troops were concentrating on Stafford Heights, opposite the town on the other side of the Rappahannock River.[222]

Just prior to their arrival at Fredericksburg, the men of the 1st VA witnessed a review of a large portion of Stuart's cavalry on the outskirts of the city. For most of the men, it was the largest conglomeration of horsemen they had ever seen. The grand spectacle was the main topic of their camp fire chatter upon reaching their destination that evening.[223]

Since returning to Virginia from their foray into Maryland, the Army of Northern Virginia had swelled to approximately seventy thousand men. This increase in numbers helped to boost the morale of the individual soldiers who felt they now had the adequate strength to face the hosts of Union soldiers who were once again invading their country. Additionally, the lines of communication were open with Richmond, which helped in securing a relatively steady supply of rations. But the men were still in serious need of clothing and especially shoes. In a report to the Inspector General, dated November 14, 1862, it was reported that two thousand and seventy-one men out of the approximate seven thousand men present for duty in Pickett's division were in need of shoes. This problem was somewhat alleviated when over eight thousand pairs of shoes were sent from Richmond, to the Army of Northern Virginia on the 14th and 16th of November. [224]

As the rebels waited on the Union army to disclose their intentions, they spent their time building makeshift shelters to protect themselves from the ever worsening winter weather. The cold nights were spent around blazing camp fires, telling stories and singing songs, sometimes to the accompaniment of Sgt. Bill Deane's glee club. Packages from home were also a source of great pleasure to the men. Items in civilian life that would have been commonplace proved to be a luxury to the men in the field. The three man mess of Dooley, Mitchel and Jones received a quart of whiskey

---

[222] George Wise, "History of the 17th VA Infantry", Pgs. 122-23: James Longstreet, "From Manassas to Appomattox", pgs. 192-93, 297.

[223] Durkin, "John Dooley, Confederate Soldier", Pg. 78.

[224] "The U.S. Army War College Guide to the Battles of Chancellorsville and Fredericksburg", edited by Jay Luvaas and Harold W. Nelson, Harper and Row, Publishers Inc., 10 East 53rd Street, New York, NY 10022, 1989, Appendix pg. 349: Official Records, Series 1, Volume 19, Part 2, pgs. 713 & 721.

in a package from home. While camped outside of Fredericksburg on a very frigid night, the men concocted a piping hot whiskey punch with their newly acquired gift. Since they had more than they could drink, they shared the remainder with the officers of Company "D," Captain Norton, Lt. William Keiningham and Lt. Reeve. The officers, who had already fallen asleep, were awakened by the smell of the steaming punch placed next to each of their noses in a hot cup. The delicious spiked punch warmed the men, making their situation and the cold night a bit more tolerable.[225]

Col. Corse of the 17th VA, who was promoted to Brig. General in November, returned from furlough and took command of his brigade in early December. At the request of General Corse, his old regiment, the 17th VA, was transferred to his new brigade. On December 3rd, the 17th broke camp and marched off, leaving their comrades in Kemper's brigade with whom they had fought and struggled since their initial test of combat at Bull Run in July of 1861. This left Kemper's brigade with five regiments, all from Virginia;

1st VA under the command of Col. Lewis B. Williams,
3rd VA under the command of Col. Joseph Mayo Jr.,
7th VA under the command of Col. W. T. Patton,
11th VA under the command of Col. David Funsten,
24th VA under the command of Col. William R. Terry.

These five regiments would serve together for the remainder of the war. Kemper's brigade remained in Gen. Pickett's division, which also included the brigades of Generals Garnett, Armistead, Jenkins and Corse's newly formed brigade. Jenkins brigade was composed of regiments from South Carolina, the other four brigades were made up entirely of Virginians. There were also three batteries of artillery attached to Pickett's division, each under the command of Captains Dearing, Macon, and Stribling. This gave Pickett approximately nine thousand men in his division.[226]

---

225 Robert Emmett Curran, "John Dooley's Civil War; An Irish American's Journey in the First Virginia Infantry Regiment", Pg. 83.

226 Harold Woodward Jr., "Major General James Lawson Kemper, CSA, The Confederacy's Forgotten Son", pgs. 73-74: Official Records, Series 1, Volume, 21, pgs. 1071, 1075.

On the 8th of December, Major John Dooley and his friend John Mitchel, the Irish patriot and father of Willie Mitchel, visited the regiment. The elder Dooley, whose popularity in the regiment had not waned since his resignation, was welcomed as a guest of Col. Williams. Dooley's visit was twofold, in addition to visiting with his son and his many friends within the 1st VA, he was examining the situation from the perspective of his role in the Richmond Ambulance Company. After Major Dooley's resignation from the regiment in May of 1862, he continued to serve the Confederacy by helping to organize a volunteer organization that was originally known as the Ambulance Committee, of which he was chosen as their Captain. The purpose of the company was to remove wounded soldiers from battlefields and arrange transportation for them to the hospitals in and around Richmond. Prior to the efforts of this organization, the removal of wounded soldiers was haphazard at best, leaving many of the injured to suffer and die where they fell. The committee's first test came after the battle of Seven Pines, during the Peninsula campaign, in the summer of 1862. On June 12, 1862, The Richmond Daily Examiner gave a description of this invaluable service to the Confederate soldier:

The Ambulance Committee—This is a voluntary association, composed at present of about fifty gentlemen, who immediately after the battle of Williamsburg, organized themselves into a society for the removal of our wounded from future battlefields to this city. The society was called into existence by imperative necessity, the government having made absolutely no provision for attention to the wounded, or their removal to places of safety. During and after the battles of Saturday and Sunday, the value of the committee was first manifested. Under their direction, and with their assistance alone, two-thirds of our wounded were removed from the field. But for the energetic and untiring exertions, great numbers of our men who are now convalescent must have perished where they fell. Throughout the terribly dark night, the first squads of the committee, lantern in hand, traversed the woods and swamps for miles around Seven Pines, hunting up the fallen and bearing them to the roadside hospitals, where even the candles by which the surgeons plied their profession were furnished by the forethought of the committee. Indeed, but for the foresight and management of the gentlemen of this committee, all of our troops disabled in the fight of Saturday must have laid on the field for from ten to twenty-four hours, weltering in the blood, and in many cases actually dying from want of water and timely attention.

We have said so much of the performance of the committee, not by way of compliment for they are patriots who work not for praise, but to give some idea of great benefits that have resulted from their labours, and to take the occasion to urge {upon} the public the necessity of a large increase in their numbers.

Expecting a large battle at Fredericksburg in the near future, Dooley and Mitchel, who was also a member of the Ambulance Company, were there to survey the area for the unpleasant yet vital task that was sure to be asked of their organization in the coming days.[227]

With the two armies apprehensively staring at each other across the river, the regiment resumed daily drills. Occasionally they were sent on picket duty to watch for any attempt by the Federals to cross the river. The unification of the army was nearing completion with the arrival of a portion of Gen. Jackson's corps at the end of November. Every day that Burnside delayed in crossing the river gave the Confederate army another day to prepare. The Confederates meticulously placed their three hundred and six cannon on and around Marye heights overlooking the open fields leading to the town of Fredericksburg, the Rappahannock River and the Union Army. The Confederate position was also fortified with rifle pits, breastworks and parapets.

In the early morning hours of December 11th, Gen. Barksdale, whose Mississippians were guarding the river, heard a commotion from the opposite shore. Convinced these were the sounds of Union engineers preparing the pontoon bridges, Barksdale ordered his men to take their positions. He and his men waited in the pre-dawn darkness for any sign of the enemy's approach. Once he was convinced, he sent word to Gen. McLaws, his division commander, of the impending river crossing by the

---

[227] "John Dooley's Civil War; An Irish American's Journey in the First Virginia Infantry Regiment", Edited by Robert Emmett Curran, Pg. 90: "Richmond Ambulance Co., Herbig's Infirmary Co. and the Virginia Public Guard and Armory Band", Jeffrey Weaver and Lee A. Wallace Jr., H.E. Howard, Inc., Lynchburg, Virginia, 1985. Pgs. 1-4.

Union troops. McLaws gave the order for the Confederate signal guns to be fired at Five A.M.[228]

The signal guns aroused the Confederate camps, the drums began to roll and the men grabbed their cartridge boxes and muskets and fell into line. For the officers of Company "D" of the1st VA, the signal could not have come at a worse time. The night before, Lt. Reeve visited the brigade butcher and came away with a fine mess of brains. Reeve, Capt. Norton, and Lt. Keiningham were just sitting down to enjoy them for breakfast when the alarm sounded. Not wanting to waste their delicacy, it was decided the 1st Sergeant would take charge of the company and march them out, while the officers finished their meal. The regiment took their position and spent the day, under arms, listening to the battle that was taking place on the riverbank and on the streets of Fredericksburg.[229]

Back on the river, the Union bridge builders continued with their strenuous work. Barksdale's men waited patiently for the construction of the bridges to bring the engineers within range of their muskets. When the morning mist dissipated and the enemy were in plain view, the Mississippians opened a destructive fire, driving the work parties back across the bridges to the safety of the opposite shore. Several more attempts were made to complete the work on the unfinished pontoon bridges but each one was thwarted in the same manner. In an attempt to drive the deadly rebel sharpshooters from their positions, Burnside ordered an artillery barrage from the overwhelming number of batteries within range of the town. The Union shells rained down on Fredericksburg, causing massive devastation to the buildings of the city but very little damage to the rebels within. Most of the civilians fled the city prior to the battle but others remained in the town and were forced to face the bombardment huddled in their houses. The Mississippians hunkered down in basements and trenches and waited for the cannonade to stop, at which time they emerged from their holes and continued their lethal work. At about four P.M., boats loaded with Yankee soldiers began landing on the Confederate

---

228 "The Fredericksburg Campaign", Edward J. Stackpole, Stackpole Books, Cameron and Kelker Streets, P.O. Box 1831, Harrisburg, PA 17105, 1991, Pgs. 132-38: Official Records, Series 1, Volume 21, "Report of Major General Lafayette McLaws, C.S. Army, commanding McLaws Division", pg. 578

229 E.P. Reeve, "Civil War Reminiscences"

side of the river. They formed a bridgehead in an attempt to protect the workmen on the bridges. The Mississippians slowly began to fall back through the town, challenging the ever increasing number of Yankees every step of the way. Barksdale's defense of the river front bought Gen. Lee all the time he needed to bring up the remainder of Jackson's troops and he was ordered to abandon the town after nightfall. [230]

December 12th dawned with the approximately eighty thousand Confederates fully expecting to be attacked by the Union army that was pouring across the bridges over the Rappahannock at several different points. The long blue columns of the Right Grand Division, under the command of Gen. Sumner, was crossing the river at Fredericksburg and the Left Grand Division, under the command of Gen. Franklin, was crossing below the town in plain view of the Confederates. These two grand divisions totaled approximately ninety thousand men. The Center Grand Division, an additional forty-seven thousand men, commanded by Gen. Hooker, was held in reserve. As Burnside deployed his men on the east side of the river, Lee strengthened his position on the heights and the rank and file nervously waited for the battle to begin.[231]

Like everyone else in the Confederate army, the men of the 1st VA spent the day waiting for an attack that never came. They stood behind their makeshift ramparts of felled trees with their muskets at the ready. When it became apparent that the Federals were not going to offer battle that day, the brigade was ordered back to their bivouac. Having spent the night before on picket duty, the warmth of a blazing campfire was very comforting to the cold, weary men. As if it were any other night, they laughed, they sang and of course they talked about the upcoming battle. Some believed the Yankees would not attack and others thought the battle was a certainty. John Dooley Sr. and his companion John Mitchel Sr. were still in camp but were planning on leaving the next day for Richmond, unless the fighting started before their time of departure. Several veterans of the regiment caught up with the army that night and returned to duty. Others who were being held under guard for minor offenses were also

---

[230] James Longstreet, "From Manassas to Appomattox", pg. 302; Edward J. Stackpole, "The Fredericksburg Campaign", Pgs. 132-38.

[231] Official Records, Series 1, Volume 21, Pgs. 1057 & 1121.

returned to their companies. The regiment would need every able man if and when the huge Army of the Potomac finally attacked.[232]

With the rest of the brigade, the 1st VA filed out of their bivouac early on the morning of December 13th. They were placed in reserve up the hill from the front lines of the army. They formed a line of battle and peered out onto the fog covered fields below. As the fog subsided, an impressive sight was unveiled before them. Large portions of the Army of the Potomac were beginning to form up for an assault on the rebel position. The men watched as the long blue columns marched out of Fredericksburg and formed massive lines of battle which continued to move in their direction. The Confederate artillery exploded with shot and shell that cut gaping holes in the tightly massed Union troops. The cannonade was answered by the Federal guns that were now mounted on both sides of the river. They watched as the initial wave of blue clad soldiers crashed into the section of line manned by Jackson's Corps. The morning air was cold and most of the men of the 1st VA did not have proper winter clothing. They stood shivering as they watched the grand spectacle play out before them.[233]

Generals Lee and Longstreet began to move their reserves to positions where they could best support the ongoing battle. Kemper's brigade was ordered to move to their left onto Marye's Hill, more toward the center of the Confederate line. Gen. Kemper was shouting encouragement to his various regiments as they marched off. He rode up to the 1st VA and addressed the men, "Men of the First Virginia regiment – you who have on so many hard fought fields gained the name of the 'Bloody First' – today your country calls on you again to stand between her and her enemy, and I know you will do your duty." According to Charles Loehr, the speech was answered with "one of those yells that could be heard for miles."[234]

As the brigade moved from one position to another, they became increasingly exposed to enemy artillery and musket fire. Moving at the double quick along the Telegraph Road, several men in the 1st VA sustained injuries from shrapnel and spent musket balls. One of those wounded was

---

232 Robert Emmett Curran, "John Dooley's Civil War, An Irish American's Journey in the First Virginia Infantry Regiment", Pgs. 97-98.

233 David E. Johnston, "Four Years a Soldier", Pg. 212.

234 Charles Loehr, "War History of the Old First Virginia Infantry Regiment", Pg. 32.

Bill Deane, the leader of the glee club that had entertained the men on so many lonely nights. The brigade was ordered to shelter in a ravine while awaiting further orders. Enemy shells were landing in close proximity to the regiment's refuge and the men were instructed to sit along the right hand side of the trench, which offered more protection from the barrage. One of the men disregarded this order when he found a comfortable flat rock on the left side of the trench on which to rest. Capt. Norton of Company "D," fearing for the man's safety, ordered him to return to the right side of the trench. Immediately after vacating his spot, a large piece of shrapnel smashed into the rock and buried itself into the wall of the trench. Moments later, Lt. Reeve, who was sitting on a wooden plank in the gully, spied a cannon ball in mid-flight hurling toward their position. Reeve yelled out a warning and dove on the ground just as the round shot hit the wooden plank that was his seat, sending shards of wood down the trench line. Without being directly engaged with the enemy, the brigade continued to suffer casualties from the vast amount of ordinance sailing around Marye's hill.[235]

During the afternoon, Gen. Longstreet ordered Pickett to send Kemper's brigade to the support of Gen. Ransom's division of North Carolinians, who were positioned behind the stone wall at the base of Marye's Hill. Ransom's men had defended this position against repeated attacks by waves of Union infantry throughout the day. When they arrived, the 1st VA and the 7th VA were sent to the relief of the 24th NC which had suffered massive casualties in officers and men during their stalwart defense of the wall. Under fire, the 1st VA took their place behind the stone wall with the 7th VA to their left. In his official report, Gen. Ransom wrote, "Brigadier General Kemper came upon the field late, but in the handsomest style, under a galling fire, moved his command into position with the greatest alacrity and steadiness, and during this time lost a few killed and quite a number wounded." The field of battle to their front was littered with the dead and wounded of the Union attackers, testament to

[235] Edward Payson Reeve, "Civil War Reminiscences of Captain Edward Payson Reeve": Robert Emmett Curran, "John Dooley's Civil War, An Irish American's Journey in the First Virginia Infantry Regiment", Pgs. 100-102.

the ferocity of the fight that took place on this part of the ground during the day.[236]

As darkness fell upon the bloody field, the firing subsided to the occasional shot from the sharpshooters. Expecting a renewal of hostilities in the morning, the two regiments of Kemper's brigade began to strengthen their position by extending the wall across the road to protect their flank. Their work completed, the men listened to the eerie groans of the wounded and dying men who laid upon the field, begging for help. They also heard the sounds of the creaking Federal ambulance wagons crisscrossing the ground picking up their suffering comrades. The missions of mercy were conducted unmolested even though the recent memory of the Union sharpshooters at Sharpsburg was fresh in the minds of the Virginians. Some of the men slithered over the wall and crawled about the battlefield looking for dead Yankees who would no longer be in need of their shoes. Others, even though the need was great, refused to participate in robbing the dead. While some tried to fall asleep, others laid awake and listened attentively for any sound that would denote a surprise night attack. The sound of hoof beats slowly coming down the road from the direction of Fredericksburg aroused the entire regiment. Each man leveled his musket on the stone wall waiting to see if the riders were friend or foe. The hoof beats grew louder and louder until the riders were practically upon the newly constructed wall across the road. Capt. Norton stepped out in front and ordered the men to halt. Not realizing they had ridden into the Confederate lines, the horsemen asked for directions to Union Gen. Couch's headquarters. Norton promptly ordered the men to dismount and surrender. At first they thought to wheel their horses and escape, but the sound of muskets being cocked persuaded the men to acquiesce and surrender. The riders, a major, two lieutenants and an orderly were relieved of their swords and put under the charge of Sgt. Moriarty of Company "C" who escorted the Federal officers to the rear. Later that night, the aurora borealis appeared over Fredericksburg, a rarity that far south, casting an eerie light on the dead and wounded scattered about the battlefield.

At first light, the men of the 1st VA were convinced a battle line of Yankees was approaching directly in their front. The men let loose with a

---

236 Official Records, Series 1, Volume 21, "Report of Brig. Gen. Robert Ransom Jr.", Pgs. 625-627.

couple of volleys only to realize they were shooting at a wooden fence off in the distance. The embarrassed men had a good laugh at their own expense, and were forced to endure some good natured barbs from their startled comrades in the 7th VA. The rising sun revealed the horrors of the previous days fighting. A few of the Union dead were within thirty yards of the wall. The number of dead increased further back from the Confederate lines. Some of the dead laid in rows marking the position of their lines when fired into by the Carolinians, who had previously occupied the position during the battle. The Union ambulance workers from the night before, not wanting to get too close to the rebel lines, left some of their wounded in close proximity to the wall. The Confederates could do nothing to help the enemy wounded since the Federal sharpshooters had renewed their deadly craft. The sharpshooters were using the cover of nearby houses to fire at anything that moved within the Confederate lines. The men of the 1st VA tried to counter the fire, shooting at the houses, until they were ordered to conserve their ammunition. Sergeant Moriarty, having completed his task of delivering the prisoners from the night before, was returning to the regiment when he crossed behind the line of the 7th VA. His comrades in the 7th warned him of the presence of a sharpshooter behind a nearby brick house who had been particularly annoying all morning. As Moriarty cautiously continued on his way, the Yankee stepped out from his hiding place and fired his rifled musket, hitting Moriarty in the arm and causing a painful flesh wound. The regiment remained in this position for the rest of the day awaiting a renewed attack that never came.[237]

At eleven o'clock that night, the regiment evacuated the trenches, rejoined the brigade and marched back to their original bivouac. During the night, the Union army retreated back across their pontoon bridges, destroying them after their crossing, and took up positions on Stafford heights. The next morning the Confederates reoccupied the devastated city of Fredericksburg, ending the battle.

At the time, the battle of Fredericksburg was considered a huge success for Gen. Lee and the Army of Northern Virginia. The Union army suffered

---

[237] David E. Johnston, "Four Years a Soldier", Pgs. 214-16: Robert Emmett Curran, "John Dooley's Civil War, An Irish American's Journey in the First Virginia Infantry Regiment", Pgs. 107-114: Charles Loehr, "War History of the Old First Virginia Infantry Regiment", Pgs. 32-33.

more than twice as many casualties as the Confederates. More importantly, since the Federals could easily replace their casualties, Burnside's drive to Richmond was stymied and would have to be postponed for months. The battle at Fredericksburg boosted the morale of the southern soldiers and elevated their admiration of the commanding general. In this engagement, the 1st VA spent most of the day in reserve, keeping them out of direct contact with the enemy until late in the day. Compared to their previous battles, the regiment's losses were relatively small, having only nine men wounded. The total casualties for the five regiments in Kemper's brigade were two killed and forty-three wounded. The officers and men of the brigade never forgot the severe damage they witnessed to the houses in Fredericksburg caused by the Federal bombardment. The sympathy they felt for their fellow Virginians, whose homes and lives were destroyed, was heartfelt. Despite the depredations of their own situation the men of Kemper's brigade raised $2,291.50 for the citizens of Fredericksburg, which was sent to the Mayor of the devastated city during the winter.[238]

The following is a list of casualties sustained by the 1st VA at the Battle of Fredericksburg:

Company B – Wounded: William H. Deane.

Company C – Wounded: Sergeant John Moriarty, Privates Willis Clark, Daniel Sullivan.

Company D – Wounded: Private Tazewell Morton.

Company G – Wounded: Sergeant William H. Deane, Privates John Jackson, John Spraggins.

Company I – Wounded: Private William Lipscomb.[239]

---

238 Official Records, Series 1, Volume 21, Pg. 573: Harold R. Woodward Jr., "The Confederacy's Forgotten Son", Pg. 77.

239 Lee Wallace, "1st Virginia Infantry", Pgs. 81-123: "Record of the Richmond City and Henrico Co. Virginia Troops", Compiled by E. H. Chamberlayne, Jr., Richmond 1879.

SPRING OF 1863

After the battle of Fredericksburg, the regiment remained in camp until the 23rd of December at which time they were sent on picket duty. The Union army remained on the opposite side of the Rappahannock and their pickets patrolled that side of the river. Although it was against orders, some of the men of the 1st VA carried on conversations with the enemy sentinels. At least one member of the regiment crossed over the river and exchanged newspapers, tobacco and other articles with the Yankees. On December 24th, after twenty-four hours of picket duty, they returned to camp. On Christmas day the regiment shifted their camp to Guinea Station, arriving there about eleven o'clock in the morning. They were met by the mother of Lt. Keiningham and other ladies of Richmond, who brought packages from the families and friends of the soldiers. The packages contained clothing and all manner of food. In company "D" they had a Christmas feast of ham, turkey, roast beef, cold round beef, apple and peach puffs, sweet potato pudding, cotton candy, apples and loaves of bread. The evening was capped off with a "tin pail full of nice egg nog," making for a merry Christmas, considering the situation. When describing the dinner provided by "The Ladies of Richmond," a grateful member of the regiment said, "This kind and considerate action make us remember that though absent we are never forgotten by our dear friends."[240]

Expecting a lengthy stay at Guinea Station, the men immediately commenced to building more permanent structures to guard against the winter weather. Some were built using logs plastered over with mud made from the clay soil of the region, others erected large tents for their

---

[240] E. P. Reeve letter to his wife Hester, dated December 26, 1862, Camp near Fredericksburg: B.F. Howard, Pg. 35.

winter quarters and some used a combination of canvas and logs for their new abodes. No matter what the style, they all had large fireplaces with chimneys attached.

Most of the men remembered their time at Guinea Station as a pleasant period during the war. The position of their camp near the railroad allowed for easy access to Richmond. Family and friends made the trip by train to visit their loved ones in the regiment, bringing with them gifts of food and clothing to ease the distress of Richmond's favorite sons. On one such trip, the ladies of Richmond supplied a full set of clothing for each member of the regiment. Some of the men, mostly officers, even managed to obtain short furloughs to Richmond, although this was not widespread since the enemy was still in the vicinity of Fredericksburg and continued to pose a threat.[241]

The wounded and exchanged prisoners from the previous year's many campaigns continued to return to the regiment. The constant rotation of returning officers altered the command structure in some of the companies. In Company "I," for instance, 1st Lt. B.F. Howard had been absent since being seriously wounded at the battle of Seven Pines in May of 1862. While Howard was recuperating, the commander of the company, Captain James W. Tabb, died from the severe wounds he received at 2nd Manassas in early September. Howard, although absent, was promoted to Captain upon the death of Tabb but did not assume command of Company "I" until he returned to duty in February of 1863. The 1st VA also received recruits while at Guinea Station. In some cases the recruits were family members of the veterans of the regiment, as was the case with Joseph Keiningham, who enlisted in mid-January and joined his brother, Lt. William Keiningham in Company "D." According to Lt. E. P. Reeve, these recruits helped to increase the membership of Company "D"' to over thirty soldiers, still well short of the one hundred needed for a full sized company, but nonetheless the highest number since the battle of Williamsburg the previous May.[242]

---

241 E. P. Reeve letter to his wife Hester, dated December 26, 1862, Camp near Fredericksburg: "Civil War Reminiscences of Captain Edward Payson Reeve", Edward Payson Reeve: Robert Emmett Curran, "John Dooley's Civil War, An Irish American's Journey in the First Virginia Infantry Regiment", Pg. 123.

242 B. F. Howard, Pg. 35: E. P. Reeve, Letter to his wife, "Camp near Guinea Station, January 17, 1863".

With the snows of January snowball battles became the order of the day. There were engagements between the regiments within Kemper's brigade. The regiments then banded together to fight off attacks from rival brigades. Perhaps the most epic contest occurred on a cold sunny day in January when the Texans of Gen. Hood's division, many of whom had never seen snow before joining the army, attacked Gen. Pickett's camp. The mock engagement took on the characteristics of the more deadly encounters of the past year. The officers, mounted on horseback, directed long lines of troops who advanced, retreated and counter attacked, all with colors flying. At the proper command the air was full of the white frozen projectiles which rained down on the opposing "army." Camps were overrun, flags captured, prisoners taken, paroled and returned to battle. According to some witnesses, the battles reached the division level, comprising many thousands of combatants. Unlike the battles with the Army of the Potomac, the casualties were limited to black eyes, bloody noses and bruises.[243]

Mrs. Keiningham, who now had two sons in the 1st VA, and the ladies of Richmond, continued to visit the regiment, bringing with them much appreciated gifts of food, clothing and blankets. The gifts from home, coupled with army provisions, had the men well situated with supplies except for the chronic shortage of shoes. The visitors also brought ample supplies of whiskey which enlivened the camps at night and caused laughter and songs to emanate from the cabins and tents. Many of the visitors would extend their stays for several days, much to the delight of their homesick family members within the regiment.[244]

It was still wartime, however, and on January 20th the Union army began to move in another attempt to cross the river above Fredericksburg and catch the Confederates by surprise. The 1st VA, along with the rest of the brigade, marched out of their camps to meet the enemy threat. Due to the winter weather, the roads on both sides of the river were in a deplorable state, causing much anguish to the struggling infantrymen. A violent rain storm on the night of January 20th made the roads virtually

---

243 Charles Loehr, "War History of the Old First Virginia Infantry Regiment" Pg. 33: David E. Johnston, "Four Years a Soldier", Pgs. 224-25; Alexander Hunter, article in Confederate Veteran Magazine.

244 E.P. Reeve, Letter to his wife, Dated February 1, 1863.

impassable. The Federal's caissons and heavy wagons loaded with pontoons became hopelessly bogged down in the bottomless Virginia mud. This greatly amused the Confederates who watched the struggling enemy from the other side of the Rappahannock. The Yankees quickly realized the folly of this attempted winter move and returned to their camps on the 23rd of January. This ended Gen. Burnside's celebrated "Mud March" and his short tenure as commander of the Army of the Potomac, which was terminated "at his own request" two days later. Burnside's replacement, and Robert E. Lee's newest antagonist, was now Major General Joseph Hooker.[245]

On February 13th the regiment was sent to the north of Fredericksburg to work on the defenses along the Rappahannock River. While the 1st VA was engaged in this labor, the rest of Pickett's division moved out of Guinea Station in route toward Richmond. After working one day on the trenches, the 1st VA was ordered back to camp where they rested for the night. Early the following morning, the regiment broke camp and filed out onto the road to rejoin their brigade. After two days of hard marching over poor roads in appalling weather, the 1st VA overtook the brigade at Hanover Junction. The men were cold, wet and covered in mud. They were only allowed a few hours rest before the column moved out again in the midst of a tremendous snowstorm, which further increased their discomfort. After trudging through the snow, they camped that night within five miles of Richmond.[246]

The citizens of Richmond were well accustomed to seeing columns of Confederate troops marching through their city but when the 1st VA marched through their hometown it was a special occasion. As the regiment approached the outskirts of the city, they were greeted by friends and family as conquering heroes. Baskets of food were handed to the hungry men and passed from file to file. Bottles of spirits were also passed down the line as the soldiers celebrated their homecoming. The further into the city the column progressed, the larger and more boisterous the crowds of well-wishers became. Each passing step brought cheers from onlookers who gathered on the sidewalks, doorways and windows. The abundant supply of alcohol being passed from man to man made the step of the well trained

245 Official Records, Series 1, Volume 21, Pgs. 753-55: Pgs. 1004-05

246 Charles Loehr, "War History of the Old First Virginia Infantry Regiment" Pg. 33:

soldiers a bit unsteady as they exited the city limits. The regiment halted and camped for the night in Manchester on the south side of the James River. Major Dooley rode out to the camp, as he did the night before the regiment entered the city, and convinced the Colonel to allow his son John and Willie Mitchel to spend the night at his house in Richmond. It is not known how many others, if any, were allowed to visit their families while the regiment was in such close proximity to their hometown. [247]

The Confederate high command had a genuine concern that the Union army would attempt a second invasion of Virginia along the James River, just as McClellan had tried during the previous spring. The Yankees already controlled fortified areas along the coast of Virginia and North Carolina which could be used as bases to launch an army toward Richmond. To counter such a move, Gen. Longstreet was ordered south with two divisions, Pickett's and Hood's, while Gen. Lee guarded against any move by the Army of the Potomac with the remainder of his army. There were also vast amounts of produce and other supplies in the eastern counties of Virginia and North Carolina that were badly needed to support the Confederate war effort. Longstreet, from his headquarters at Petersburg, proposed a plan to use his two divisions to push the enemy back into their fortified positions while the supplies were gathered by the commissary department and sent to the Army of Northern Virginia. Gen. Lee approved the plan, provided the divisions could be easily recalled and sent north in the event the Army of the Potomac, now under the command of Gen. Joseph Hooker, made any aggressive move on Lee's army.[248]

After leaving Manchester, the brigade continued to move south, camping at Chester Station. With no tents, the men awoke to find a heavy snow had fallen overnight. This led to another snow ball battle against the South Carolinians of Jenkins' brigade, with Mother Nature providing the ammunition. About the 1st of March, the brigade passed through Petersburg and set up camp near Prince George Courthouse, where they remained for a couple of weeks. Regular camp life was resumed with drills, inspections and guard duty. The monotony was interrupted by the occasional visit from friends and family or the much sought after packages

---

[247] Robert Emmett Curran, "John Dooley's Civil War, An Irish American's Journey in the First Virginia Infantry Regiment", Pg. 128.

[248] "From Manassas to Appomattox", Longstreet, Pg. 324.

from home. The luckiest of the men managed to get short furloughs to visit their homes in Richmond. The weather was dismal with a great deal of cold rainy days, making for a miserable camp site.[249]

In any organization composed of human beings, there is going to be the occasional bad apple. In military organizations, there are deserters, cowards and even thieves who steal from their comrades in arms. Justice can be humiliating and brutal. While at Petersburg, a member of the 24th VA was found guilty of cowardice at the battle of Sharpsburg. The man was sentenced to be whipped out of the army. To make the humiliation complete, the entire brigade, including the 1st VA, was ordered to fall in and watch as the punishment was administered. The condemned was stripped to the waist and tied to a pole. The executioner stepped forward and meted out thirty-nine lashes across the man's bare back. The experience was so disturbing that the executioner himself was seen with tears running down his cheeks. The condemned man was then issued a dishonorable discharge and sent on his way. The horrifying scene was meant to be an example for all of the astonished men in the brigade. Earlier in the year, when a most despicable member of the 7th VA was caught stealing from his comrades, he was similarly whipped out of the army. In this case, each member of the company, holding a switch, formed a gauntlet through which the thief had to run. As the man ran past, his former mates swung the sticks, striking him on the back. The thief was also given a dishonorable discharge and sent away. For less serious crimes the culprits were forced to wear a flour barrel like a shirt, with holes cut in the side for the wrongdoer's arms. The hapless man was then marched around the camp in full view of his fellow soldiers for hours at a time. This was an embarrassing sentence for the accused but much less painful than the penalties for the more serious infractions.

The most serious charges of desertion or treason could bring about a sentence of death by hanging or firing squad. In many cases, the deserter was sent back to Richmond for a general court martial, where he was held at the military prison known as Castle Thunder until convicted and executed. In early October of 1862, four men convicted of desertion were taken from Castle Thunder to the fair grounds at Camp Lee for the implementation of their sentences. Two of the men were from the 14th VA

---

249 "War History of the Old First Virginia Infantry Regiment" by Charles Loehr, Pg. 33:

and two of the men, Dan Rogers and Owen Maguire, were reputed to be hired substitutes from the 1st VA, although their names do not appear on any roster from the 1st VA. Rogers and the two men from the 14th VA were sentenced to be shot, Maguire was sentenced to one hundred lashes. A hollow square made up of two thousand soldiers formed the stage for the gruesome spectacle. The Assistant Provost Marshal read the sentences announcing that Rogers had received a reprieve of fourteen days before his sentence would be carried out. Maguire's sentence was reduced to fifty lashes. Two wooden caskets were carried to the site for the unfortunate individuals from the 14th VA. The two men were blindfolded and knelt before the two twelve man firing squads. The command was given and the soldiers fired, killing the deserters instantly. After the men were placed in the caskets and carried off, Maguire was tied to a tree and the sentence of fifty lashes administered to his bare back. Rogers made good use of his reprieve, escaping from Castle Thunder by climbing out of a window a few days before he too was to be shot.[250]

On the 15th of March the regiment left Petersburg and headed for Fort Powhatan on the James River. In an attempt to block Union gun boats from moving up the James River toward Richmond, the Confederates were in the process of building the earthen fort to cover a bend in the river by placing heavy guns within its ramparts. The regiment was detailed to help with the construction. After three days labor, on March 19th, it began to snow and the 1st VA was ordered back to Petersburg. That night was spent at an abandoned farm which offered some protection against the ever worsening winter snow storm. The following day, the regiment, plowing through eighteen inches of snow, reached their camp outside of Petersburg at approximately one o'clock in the afternoon. Two hours later, they were ordered to strike the tents and the regiment moved into Petersburg where they spent the night in a large warehouse. The 1st VA was on the move again the next day, leaving Petersburg at ten o'clock in the morning on a train bound for Goldsboro, North Carolina. They stopped for the night at Goldsboro on the 22nd of March before continuing on to Kinston, NC

---

[250] Durkin, "John Dooley, Confederate Soldier", Pgs. 83, 73: David E. Johnston, "Four Years a Soldier", Pgs. 223-24: Richmond Dispatch, October 6, 1862 and October 15, 1862, Richmond Enquirer, October 21, 1862, from the website Civil War Richmond, www.mdgorman.com.

the next day. At Kinston, they were directed to set up camp on the south side of the Neuse River.[251]

While camped at Kinston, Lt. Reeve arrived from Richmond with approximately one hundred and fifty much needed recruits. In January, when the regiment was camped at Guinea Station, Reeve and another officer were sent to Richmond on a fifty day furlough to try and obtain recruits for the 1st VA. Even though their numbers had been strengthened since the Maryland campaign, upon reaching Fort Powhatan they were reported to have 206 present for duty or approximately one-fifth the size of a full regiment. Constant campaigning and the Secretary of War's policy of detailing skilled men to the capital continued to drain the manpower of the 1st VA. In Richmond, Reeve visited Camp Lee and attempted to get some of the new recruits to volunteer for the 1st VA before they were processed and assigned to other units. The blood stained reputation of the regiment preceded him however, and the recruits felt that volunteering with the 1st VA was tantamount to signing their own death warrant. Reeve spoke with some of the officers from the companies who were detached from the 1st VA at the beginning of the war and tried to convince them to return to the regiment. He was told they did not consider it proper for them to share in the laurels of the regiment since they had not shared in the hardships.[252]

Politics also played a role in the lack of recruits and conscripts who were sent to the 1st VA. Conscripts who reported for duty were processed at Camp Lee, where Major Thomas G. Peyton was in command of assigning the conscripts to the various units in the Confederate Army. Reeve received a letter, dated February 5, 1863, from his friend D.S. Minton, who was apparently working at Camp Lee. In the letter, Minton explained the situation in regards to the 1st VA. Major Peyton, according to Minton, had sought the Lt. Colonelcy in the 1st VA but was unsuccessful in his bid. Minton went on to say, "He seems to hate everything connected with the Old First." From this statement it would seem that Peyton's wounded pride was one more factor that was keeping recruits out of the ranks of the 1st VA. Reeve, who was becoming frustrated, finally obtained an order from

---

251 B. F. Howard, Pg. 37: Charles Loehr, "War History of the Old First Virginia Infantry Regiment" Pgs. 33-34:

252 Edward Payson Reeve "Civil War Reminiscences of Captain Edward Payson Reeve": Official Records, Series 1, Volume 18, Pg. 929.

the Secretary of War for 150 recruits who were not at Camp Lee, thereby side-stepping Peyton's interference, but on detached service at Staunton and Gordonsville. While detailed in Richmond, Reeve was once again offered several positions working for the army in the capital, and once again he refused the offers, preferring to return to his comrades in the field. After arranging transportation, Reeve, along with his 150 recruits, boarded the train and left Richmond, rejoining the regiment at Kinston, NC. [253]

Kemper's brigade was moved to North Carolina to guard against Yankee interference with the gathering of supplies from the eastern counties of that state and Virginia. The theatre of operations ran from the York River in Virginia to the Cape Fear River in North Carolina, under the overall command of Gen. Longstreet. Under Longstreet, Gen. D. H. Hill was in command of the troops operating at Kinston and Goldsboro. The two Federal strongholds in this sector were at New Bern on the Neuse River and thirty miles to the north at Washington, NC, on the Pamlico River. Kemper's brigade, along with Gen. Garnett's brigade, also from Pickett's division, was sent to Kinston in the hope that the enemy garrison in "Little" Washington could not only be contained but possibly captured. Simultaneously the larger Union garrison at New Bern would have to be held within their fortifications to keep them from interfering with Confederate operations.[254]

After receiving an intelligence report claiming the garrison at New Bern was being reinforced by Federal troops from Newport News, the 1st VA along with the 7th VA were sent in that direction. The two regiments, under the overall command of Col. Williams, made a demonstration in front of New Bern, marching and countermarching in the vicinity of the garrison. The Confederates formed a line of battle and sent scouts in close to the fortifications. The Federals remained within the safety of their ramparts and under the protection of their cannon. After several days, Col. Williams gained the required information and the regiments returned to Kinston. Gen. D. H. Hill concluded that the artillery defending the Federal positions at both Little Washington and New Bern far outweighed

---

[253] "Edward Payson Reeve Papers", Southern Historical Collection, University of North Carolina at Chapel Hill (#1828), Letter from D.S. Minton, Richmond, February 5, 1863: SHSP, Volume 26, "The Old Camp Lee", pgs. 241-245.

[254] Official Records, Series 1, Volume 18, Pgs. 926, 931, 933, 937.

his own, making any attempt to capture the garrisons too costly in lives to attempt. With this news, Longstreet ordered Kemper's brigade to rejoin him in Virginia. Gen. Hood's division of Longstreet's Corps had been conducting similar operations to those of Kemper in the Blackwater region of Virginia, protecting the removal of supplies from that area. Longstreet planned to combine Pickett's division with Hood's and attempt to capture Suffolk before being recalled by Gen. Lee to rejoin the Army of Northern Virginia.[255]

On April 5th, 1863, Kemper's brigade boarded the trains in Kinston and took the cars to Franklin, Virginia, leaving the swamps and dismal low lying areas of eastern North Carolina behind. The weather had begun to warm and some of the men rode on top of the box cars rather than squeeze into the hot overcrowded compartments. The trains carrying the 1st VA arrived at Franklin, Virginia, on the 6th of April. The regiment remained in this area for several days, until April 11th. Pickett's division, along with Hood' division, then started in the direction of Suffolk where they arrived on the 13th. As the Confederates approached, the enemy withdrew into the fortified confines of the city. While Longstreet's troops held the Yankees at bay, the commissariat department went about their business of collecting supplies for the army. The regiment spent their time fortifying their position and conducting picket duty. There were several skirmishes between the opposing outposts and the Federals would occasionally bombard the rebel lines with their artillery. Near the end of April the Army of the Potomac began crossing the Rappahannock and Gen. Lee called for Longstreet to immediately return to Fredericksburg with Hood's and Pickett's divisions.

At 3:00 pm On May 3rd, the siege of Suffolk was lifted and Longstreet's troops began a forced march back toward Richmond. Marching all night and most of the following day, the regiment moved about thirty miles, much to the distress of the weary soldiers. On the 5th of May, they covered twelve miles, followed by another seventeen miles on the 6th, reaching Littleton, where they camped for the night. The footsore men trudged another twenty two miles on the 7th and on the 8th of May they camped within six miles of Petersburg. The following day, the march continued

---

255 Official Records, Series 1, Volume 18, Pgs. 957, 960, 962: "B. F. Howard", Pg. 37.

through Petersburg and eventually to Chester Station, thirteen miles to the south of Richmond, where the regiment camped on the 11th of May.[256]

It had been about two and a half months since the regiment left Chester Station for their foray into the coastal regions of North Carolina and Virginia. Over that time they covered hundreds of miles over deplorable roads in the worst of conditions. The cold rains of March and April inundated the roads in the low lying areas with knee deep water, making the long marches nearly unbearable for the wet, exhausted soldiers. Although the brigade was never involved in any major engagements with the enemy, the protection they gave for the collection of vital supplies was invaluable to the Confederate cause.

While the brigade was hurrying towards Petersburg, Gen. Joe Hooker and the Army of the Potomac had crossed the Rappahannock and engaged in the battle of Chancellorsville with the Army of Northern Virginia. The men were delighted to hear of yet another southern victory, but saddened to hear of the injury and subsequent death of the illustrious Gen. "Stonewall" Jackson, who was revered by the men of Kemper's brigade, as well as the whole of the Army of Northern Virginia.

While the men moved into Chester Station, the entire senior staff rode into Richmond to pay their last respects at the funeral of Gen. Thomas "Stonewall" Jackson. Generals Kemper, Garnett and Corse, all from Pickett's division, along with Generals Longstreet, Ewell, Winder and Commodore French Forrest, of the Confederate Navy, served as Pall Bearers. The body of the fallen hero was removed from the Executive Mansion and moved by procession to the Capital Building. Among the brass bands, artillery pieces and marching troops rode Gen. Pickett and his staff. The streets were lined with mourners and the city was draped in black bunting. The General's remains were placed in the Capital building, where he lay in state and more than twenty thousand mourners passed through during the day. The next day the casket was placed on a train and

---

256 Charles Loehr, "War History of the Old First Virginia Infantry Regiment" Pgs. 34: Harold Woodward Jr, "Major General James Lawson Kemper, CSA, The Confederacy's Forgotten Son", pg. 81.

sent to Lexington, VA, where Jackson was buried. Pickett and his brigade commanders returned to their troops and the continuation of the war.[257]

Because of the Confederate victory at Chancellorsville and subsequent retreat of the Union army to the north bank of the Rappahannock, the immediate threat that sent the brigade rushing toward Richmond was negated. Pickett's and Hood's divisions had been operating independently of the Army of Northern Virginia since February and the Confederate high command was contemplating how best to employ them in the near future. With potential threats challenging the Confederacy on multiple fronts, veteran troops were needed at numerous locales. The possibility of an attack from the Atlantic coast was always a possibility but the major concern of the War Department was the ever tightening siege at Vicksburg, Mississippi, by the Union army, under the command of Gen. U. S. Grant. There were discussions in Richmond in regards to sending Pickett's and/or Hood's divisions to Tennessee in an attempt to draw off Grant's troops from in front of Vicksburg. General Lee protested, in his normal diplomatic fashion, the removal of two veteran divisions from his army, seeing as he was currently outmanned by the Army of the Potomac. Lee's position was sustained and the two divisions, including the 1st VA, remained with the Army of Northern Virginia.[258]

After four days of rest at Chester Station, Pickett's division was ordered to Hanover Junction on May 15th, 1863. The 1st VA moved north through Richmond, and although the citizens of the capital gathered on the streets to see them pass through, they were much more subdued than they were on the regiment's previous trip. The recent funeral of the beloved Stonewall Jackson left the city in a somber state. The regiment camped at Taylorsville, near Hanover Junction, and began daily drills and the routine duties of camp life. The diarist Private John Dooley, who had recently been elected Lieutenant of Company "C," perhaps due to the patronage of his father's influence, got his first taste of drilling a company in the intricacies of military maneuvers. The camp's proximity to Richmond allowed for the renewal of visits by friends and family.

---

257 "They Called Him Stonewall", by Burke Davis, Published by Wings Books, A Random House Company, 40 Engelhard Avenue, Avenal, New Jersey 07001, 1954, Pgs. 449-451.

258 Official Records, Series 1, Volume 25, Part 2, Pgs. 720 & 790.

The visitors were treated to a review of Pickett's entire division, which they found to be quite impressive. Less so for the men taking part in the review since the weather had turned quite warm and the parade grounds were covered in dust.[259]

A religious revival swept through the brigade while in camp at Taylorsville. There were daily sermons by ministers, such as the Rev. Dr. Pryor of Petersburg and the Rev. James B. Taylor from Richmond. The sermons, normally held in the morning and evening, were so well attended by the men of the brigade that the local church could not accommodate the large crowds. The ministers used a grove of trees located in the center of the brigade's camp as a makeshift chapel. Being surrounded by the death and destruction of war and the prospect of their own demise may have encouraged the men to take a greater interest in religion. [260]

On June 2nd, Gen. Lee received information of a Federal incursion at the small village of Tappahannock on the Rappahannock River. He immediately ordered Gen. Pickett to move his division in that direction to meet the Union threat. The next day the 1st VA, along with the rest of Pickett's division, marched out of Taylorsville in search of the enemy. On the first day they marched twenty-one miles, stopping in Caroline County to rest. The following day they moved another seventeen miles, crossing into King and Queen County where they spent the night. On the third day the division passed through the town of Newton, where the sheer size of the division astonished the local citizenry. They spent the night of the 5th of June between the villages of Newton and Tappahannock. No enemy raiders were found in the vicinity and the division retraced their steps, arriving back at Taylorsville on the night of June 7th. There was no rest for the weary and the regiment left Taylorsville again the following day, this time

---

259 Official Records, Series 1, Volume 25, Part 2, "Special Orders No. 116", Pg. 802: Durkin, "John Dooley, Confederate Soldier", Pgs. 92-94: "Edward Payson Reeve Papers", Letter to his wife Hester, Dated June 1, 1863.

260 "Edward Payson Reeve Papers", Letter to his wife Hester, Dated June 1, 1863: David E. Johnston, "Four Years a Soldier", Pg. 234.

moving to the northwest. After three more days of constant marching, the men reached Culpepper Court House. A large part of the army was already camped in the area as Gen. Lee was consolidating his forces for the next campaign. A campaign that would return the 1st VA to northern soil and, eventually, to a small and unassuming little town in rural Pennsylvania named Gettysburg.[261]

---

261 Official Records, Series 1, Volume 25, Part 2, Pg. 852: Charles Loehr, "War History of the Old First Virginia Infantry Regiment" Pgs. 34-35.

GETTYSBURG

After remaining in the vicinity of Culpepper C.H. for three days, the regiment was ordered to cook three days rations and prepare to march. The following day, June 16th, they marched eighteen miles to Gaines Cross Roads, where they camped. On the 17th they moved to Piedmont Station and the following day, the regiment, along with the rest of the brigade, moved to Paris in Fauquier County, VA. Here, they halted for two days before resuming the march past Upperville and over the Blue Ridge Mountains through Snickersville Gap, on the 19th. The column had been plagued by severe storms of rain and hail over the past several days which not only made their journey most uncomfortable but also swelled the waters of the Shenandoah River, which the 1st VA reached on the 20th of June. The men crossed the swift running water, which was up to their armpits, holding their muskets, cartridge boxes and blankets above their heads. That night the regiment dried out near Berryville. The following day, while camped at that place, the entire regiment was issued a new set of much needed clothing. They left Berryville on the 23rd and marched to Darkesville, where they bivouacked on the 24th. On the 25th, the brigade passed Martinsburg on their way to the Potomac River.[262]

As the brigade prepared to cross into Maryland for the second time in less than a year, some of Kemper's men had a philosophical problem in regards to an invasion of the North. Scholars and historians have argued for 150 years about the geo-political issues that caused the Civil War, but for many of these men, the men that were doing the actual fighting, it

[262] Official Records, Series 1, Volume 27, Part 3, "Itinerary of Kemper's brigade, June 15-July 24, 1863" pgs. 1090-91: Charles Loehr, "War History of the Old First Virginia Infantry Regiment" Pg. 35: Edward Payson Reeve, "Civil War Reminiscences of Captain Edward Payson Reeve".

boiled down to one thing: the defense of Virginia. They had joined the army because Virginia was under threat of invasion from Union armies and they felt it their duty to protect their homes, their families and their state. They had no interest in conquering the north and yet now they, the Virginians, were invading another sovereign state. But the men in the ranks also realized, as did the Confederate hierarchy, that the continuation of the war within the boundaries of Virginia was an unbearable hardship on the civilian population. Farms, crops, houses and indeed entire towns, such as Fredericksburg, had been devastated by the enormous battles within "The Old Dominion." If crossing the Potomac into Maryland would help in the defense of their homeland, then they would follow their flag and their comrades into the north. Another reason for the men to put aside any moral dilemmas about the invasion, and this cannot be underscored too much, was their absolute devotion to and admiration of their Commanding General, Robert E. Lee.

Just the sight of Lee riding by on his horse was worth a notation in diaries and journals. His presence among the troops brought about boisterous cheers with the men raising their hats in the air, every eye fixed on his person for as long as he was within sight. Men who were ready to drop from exhaustion claimed it was the leadership of Robert E. Lee that kept them moving forward in the ranks. It was said that he had the confidence of the entire army from generals down to raw recruits. If "Marse Robert" was going to Pennsylvania, then by God, so were they.

The regiment forded the waist deep water of the Potomac at Williamsport, MD, on June 25th. The sixty thousand men in the Army of Northern Virginia were in fine spirits as they crossed into Maryland. The resounding victories at Fredericksburg and Chancellorsville gave the men a sense of confidence and an optimistic outlook for success in the upcoming campaign. After receiving false reports of Confederate victories at Vicksburg, many believed that a major victory by their army on Union soil could very well end the war. [263]

The 1st VA entered Maryland under the command of Colonel Lewis B. Williams and Major Frank H. Langley. Most estimates put the overall strength of the regiment at approximately two hundred soldiers, broken up into six companies, each commanded by the following:

---

263 "Edward Payson Reeve Papers", Letter to his wife Hester, Dated June 22, 1863.

Company B: Captain Thomas Herbert Davis.
Company C: Captain James Hallinan.
Company D: Captain George F. Norton.
Company G: Captain Eldridge Morris.
Company H: Captain Abner J. Watkins.
Company I: Captain Benjamin F. Howard.

The 1st VA was the smallest of the fifteen regiments that made up Pickett's division.[264]

Along with the 1st VA, four other regiments composed the brigade, under the command of Gen. James Lawson Kemper. The 3rd VA was under the command of Colonel Joseph Mayo with approximately 350 rank and file. The 7th VA was under the command of W. Tazewell Patton with approximately 360 men. The 11th VA was under the command of Major Kirkwood Otey with approximately 400 men. The 24th VA, the largest regiment in Kemper's Brigade, was commanded by Colonel William Terry with approximately 450 rank and file. Together the five regiments totaled a little less than eighteen hundred men in Kemper's Brigade.[265]

Kemper's brigade remained in the division commanded by Major General George E. Pickett. At this time the organization of the army was such that a division was normally made up of five brigades. Much to the dismay of Gen. Pickett, two of his brigades were stationed in Virginia when the army moved into Maryland. Jenkins' Brigade of South Carolinians was left in the Blackwater region south of the James River guarding the approaches to Richmond from Suffolk. Corse's Brigade was left at Hanover Junction guarding the roads leading to Richmond from the north. Gen. Pickett repeatedly requested the return of the two brigades or that a replacement brigade be assigned to his division, prior to the invasion of the north, but to no avail. Realizing the reduction of his force would cause a hardship to the three remaining brigades, he wrote in a dispatch to headquarters, "for it is well known that a small division will be expected

---

264 SHSP, Volume 32, "The Old First Virginia at Gettysburg" by Charles Loehr, Pg. 38.

265 Official Records, Series 1, Volume 27, Part 2, "Organization of the Army of Northern Virginia, July 1-3", Pgs. 283-92: "Nothing But Glory", by Kathy Georg Harrison, Published by Thomas Publications, P.O. Box 3031, Gettysburg, PA 17325, 2001, Pg. 5.

to do the same amount of hard service as a large one, and, as the army is now divided, my division will be, I think, decidedly the weakest." Gen. Lee also petitioned the authorities in Richmond for a return of at least one of the two brigades detailed from Pickett's division. But, with the Army of Northern Virginia moving toward Pennsylvania, the President and the War Department were concerned the enemy might take advantage of the opportunity to strike at Richmond. Fearing the inexperienced forces in the vicinity of Richmond insufficient to deal with such an attack on the capital, they refused to release the two battle hardened brigades even at the request of Gen. Lee. To make matters worse, the two brigades left in Virginia were two of the largest in Pickett's division, totaling approximately 4,000 men. It remained to be seen just how severe the loss of these men would be to the division in the coming days as the army moved toward Pennsylvania. [266]

This left Pickett's division with three brigades for the invasion of the north. Besides Kemper's, he also had the brigades commanded by Brigadier General Richard B. Garnett and Brigadier General Louis A. Armistead. Garnett's Brigade was made up of the 8th, 18th, 19th, 28th, and 56th VA regiments. Armistead's Brigade, the largest of the three, was composed of the 9th, 14th, 38th, 53rd, and 57th VA regiments. The three brigades totaled approximately 5,800 rank and file, all from Virginia. Also attached to the division was a battalion of artillery composed of four batteries under the overall command of twenty-three year old Major James Dearing. The batteries, also from Virginia, were the Fauquier Artillery commanded by Captain R. M. Stribling, the Hampden Artillery commanded by Captain W. H. Caskie, the Richmond Fayette Artillery commanded by Captain M. C. Macon, and the Virginia Battery under the command of Captain Joseph G. Blount. The artillery battalion included two 20-pound Parrot rifled cannon, three 10-pound Parrott rifled cannon and twelve 12 pound Napoleon smoothbores. Pickett's division was part of the 1st Corps under the command of Lieutenant General James Longstreet.[267]

The 1st VA, along with the rest of Pickett's division, acted as the rear guard of the army as they moved north of the Potomac on the 26th of June. It rained on the previous night which made it impossible for the men to dry

---

266 Official Records, Series 1, Volume 27, Part 3, Pgs. 910 & 944.

267 Official Records, Series 1, Volume 27, Part 3, Pg. 284: Kathy Georg Harrison, "Nothing But Glory", Pgs. 6-7.

out after crossing the river. The roads were covered in thick mud as the men marched to Hagerstown, Maryland. They passed through the town and crossed over the Pennsylvania border, where they camped near Greencastle. The following day the column passed through Chambersburg and camped two miles beyond the town on the Harrisburg Road. Few of the residents of Chambersburg ventured out onto the streets as the division marched by. One brave fair maiden of the town took it upon herself to lecture the southern men as they passed by her garden. Her sermon was quickly drowned out by a band in the division who began to play "Dixie," much to the delight of the parading Virginians. The following day, June 28th, the regiment did not move and the men got some well-deserved rest. On the 29th of June the brigade moved back to the south side of Chambersburg and established a picket line of outposts to guard against an attack on the rear of the army.[268]

While the army was still in Virginia, Gen. Lee issued General Order #72 which governed the process of collecting supplies for the army while in enemy territory. Foraging by unauthorized personnel was strictly forbidden as was the wanton destruction of private property. By all accounts, these regulations were being adhered to by the majority of the army. Unlike the invasion of 1862 that ended at Sharpsburg, straggling and foraging were kept to a minimum and the long columns of men were in excellent spirits, disciplined and orderly. General Order #72 did not apply to public property that could be used to aid the Federal armies. Therefore, when not on picket duty the men of the division were employed in the destruction of the railroad in the vicinity of Chambersburg. Tracks were torn up, the rails were heated on bon fires until red hot, at which time they were bent around trees rendering them unrepairable. Depots, workshops and all of the machinery used in the operation of the railroad were also destroyed.[269]

During the march to Chambersburg, the 1st VA was issued a new battle

---

[268] Official Records, Series 1, Volume 27, Part 3, "Itinerary of Kemper's brigade, June 15-July 24, 1863" pgs. 1090-91: Walter Harrison, (A.A. and Inspector General of Pickett's Division), "Pickett's Men, A Fragment of War History", Published by D. Van Nostrand, 23 Murray St. and 27 Warren St., New York, NY, 1870, Digitized by Google from the collections of University of Virginia, Pgs.86-87.

[269] Official Records, Series 1, Volume 27, Part 3, Pg. 912: Walter Harrison, "Pickett's Men, A Fragment of War History", Pg. 87.

flag. The flag made of cotton and wool was square in shape, measuring forty-five inches on all sides. It was the typical Army of Northern Virginia design, with a red background that was overlaid with a blue St. Andrews cross. The cross was overlaid with thirteen white stars and the unit designation, "1st Va. Infy." was painted in white letters across the red background. It is probable, since there is no evidence to the contrary, that this new flag replaced the original silk battle flag that the regiment received back in November of 1861. For a year and a half the men of the 1st VA followed that silk flag through all the hardships of war. It led them in the battles on the Peninsula, from Yorktown back to Richmond, and it was out in front when the regiment attacked the guns at 2nd Manassas where Col. Skinner secured his place in history. It was there at South Mountain, Sharpsburg, and Fredericksburg. Its silk fabric was drenched, along with the wool uniforms of the men, in the spring rains during the North Carolina campaign. This proud, albeit somewhat faded symbol of the 1st VA was carefully folded and reverently placed in the trunk belonging to Col. Williams. The regiment would now proudly march under the furls of a new bright red banner in the coming campaign.[270]

The Union army was also on the move, following the Confederates into Pennsylvania, keeping their columns between the rebel army and the Federal capital. In his never ending quest to find a worthy opponent for Gen. Lee, President Lincoln took the bold step of replacing his army commander in the middle of an active campaign. This was the fourth change in command in the last eight months. On June 28th, Major General George Meade, former commander of the Union V Corps, replaced Major General Joseph Hooker as overall commander of the Army of the Potomac. Meade would not have much time to get acclimated to his new command before hostilities would begin.[271]

There are many controversies and debates surrounding the Battle of Gettysburg that are not within the purview of this book. However one cannot discuss the Battle of Gettysburg without mentioning the lack of

---

[270] "The Damned Red Flags of the Rebellion", by Richard Rollins, Rank and File Publications, 1926 South Pacific Coast Highway, Suite 228, Redondo Beach, California 90277, Pg. 67: American Civil War Museum/Museum of the Confederacy, Worksheet. (Both flags are in the possession of the Museum).

[271] Official Records, Series 1, Volume 27, Part 1, Pg. 4.

cavalry support for the Army of Northern Virginia. Regardless of the cause, Gen. Stuart's horsemen were not in front of Lee's army, scouting for the enemy. Subsequently on June 30th, Heth's division of A.P. Hill's corps was approaching the small town of Gettysburg when they unexpectedly realized the town was occupied by unknown Federal troops. Gettysburg was a farming community of approximately 2,400 people. It was also the county seat of Adam's County, Pennsylvania, and it boasted a college and a Lutheran Seminary. This accidental meeting of these two enemies altered the future of this peaceful little town forever.

On July 1st, Gen. Heth obtained permission from Gen. A.P. Hill to continue his advance toward Gettysburg in search of supplies that were rumored to be in the town. Once it was determined the town was occupied, Heth anticipated a brief skirmish with what he theorized to be only a cavalry patrol and maybe some local militia, which he believed could easily be swept aside, capturing the town and any provisions he found within. What he found were two stalwart brigades of Union cavalry under the command of Major General John Buford. They put up a stubborn defense of the town, frustrating the Confederate advance long enough for Yankee infantry from the 1st Corps, Army of the Potomac, under the command of Gen. John Reynolds, to arrive. Each of the combatants was reinforced and the epic struggle known as the Battle of Gettysburg began.[272]

It was not long before reports reached Gen. Lee that the Yankees in his front were from the Army of the Potomac and not mere Pennsylvania militia. Lee immediately began to consolidate the scattered sections of his own army to meet whatever threat his army had stumbled onto. Brigadier General John Imboden's Confederate cavalry was sent to relieve Pickett's division at Chambersburg. The 1st VA, along with the rest of the division, left Chambersburg about 2 o'clock in the morning on July 2nd and marched in the direction of the ongoing battle at Gettysburg, now in its second day. The weather was hot and the roads were dusty, but even with the quickened pace there was little straggling. After a forced march of approximately twenty-five miles, the column halted near the stone bridge, over Willoughby Run, on the Cashtown Road outside of Gettysburg. It was around 3 o'clock in the afternoon and the battle was raging just

---

[272] "The Gettysburg Companion", by Mark Adkin, Published by Stackpole Books, 5067 Ritter Road, Mechanicsburg, PA 17055, 2008, Pgs. 317, 333-338.

a couple of miles from where the division halted, the sounds of which could clearly be heard by the anxious soldiers. Gen. Pickett and one of his staff officers, Col. Walter Harrison, rode ahead to report their arrival to Generals Lee and Longstreet and they were told to rest the men and await further instructions.[273]

As the men of the 1st VA bivouacked for the night, it is not clear how much they learned about the fighting of the previous two days. The rumor mill must have been rife with horrific stories of the bloody conflict that had already taken the lives of so many of their comrades in the Confederate Army. If the officers and men intermingled with the participants of the battle they would have learned that on the first day the Confederates eventually massed enough troops to push the stubborn Yankees back through the town of Gettysburg. Near dark the Union troops stemmed the Confederate advance and took up a defensive position on Cemetery Hill, south of the town. Opposite the Union position and three quarters of a mile away, the Confederates formed their lines on Seminary ridge. Fresh troops joined both armies during the night of July 1st and the Federals dug in and awaited the attacks that were sure to come with the rising sun of July 2nd. The attacks came at Culp's Hill, Cemetery Hill, the Peach Orchard and the Wheatfield. Fighting raged around Devil's Den and Little Round Top. Thousands were killed and wounded and although the Union lines had been pierced the rebels could not capitalize on their gains. By the end of the 2nd day the Yankees remained on the ridge line, bloodied but stalwart.

On the morning of July 3rd, the Union lines were formed in the now famous "fish hook" shape to the south of Gettysburg. Culp's Hill, which constituted the right flank of the Union position, formed the barbed end of the hook. From there the line ran west to Cemetery Hill and then due south along the shank of the fish hook to Little and Big Round Top, which anchored the left flank of the Federal line. On the previous day the Confederates attacked both of the enemy flanks but the attacks were uncoordinated and Gen. Meade took advantage of his interior lines to

273 SHSP, Volume 34, "Pickett's Charge at Gettysburg" by Col. Joseph C. Mayo Third Virginia Regiment, pgs. 327-335: Charles Loehr, "War History of the Old First Virginia Infantry Regiment", Pg. 36

reinforce the flanks with troops from his center. Late in the day, an attack on Cemetery Hill near the center of the Union line by Georgia troops under the command of Gen. Ambrose R. Wright showed some signs of success. This convinced Gen. Lee that a massive infantry attack, preceded by an artillery barrage, at the same point could break the Yankee line. Gen. Longstreet disagreed but was superseded by Lee and the attack was ordered.

Reveille came early on July 3rd, little did they know, that for many this would be their last roll call with the 1st VA. Little did they know that by day's end more than two-thirds of these men, veterans of two years of war and those that were witnessing their first campaign, would be dead on the field, terribly wounded or a prisoner of the Yankees. What they did know was that they were the only fresh troops in the Army of Northern Virginia and General Lee would certainly have hot work for them on this day.

The 1st VA was the third regiment in line as Kemper's brigade led Pickett's division out of their bivouac in the early morning hours of July 3, 1863. The column filed out onto the Chambersburg Pike and headed toward Gettysburg. Traveling on the pike a short distance, the column turned right onto a farm road, known as Knoxlyn Road, which they traversed until turning left onto Hereter's Mill Road, which ran parallel to Chambersburg Pike. The early morning march through the farming community was pleasant enough, passing wheat fields and groves of trees. But, as they neared the Confederate lines on Seminary Ridge, burial parties and mutilated corpses from the previous days fight reminded the men of the dangerous work that awaited them just ahead. Their confidence remained high, in themselves and in Gen. Lee. They honestly believed a victory here, on the enemy's own soil, could very well end this dreadful war and return them to their homes and loved ones. The column halted behind the Confederate lines on the western edge of the woods on Henry Spangler's property. After a short delay, each of the three brigades formed a front, or battle line. Weapons and ammunition were inspected and they marched through Spangler woods, exiting on the other side into an open field.[274]

Pickett's division, being the only division in the army not engaged during the fight of the previous two days, was the obvious choice to take

[274] Kathy Georg Harrison, "Nothing But Glory", by Pg. 15.

part in the assault. Also selected to make the attack were four brigades of Major Gen. Henry Heth's division they were under the command of Brig. Gen. James Pettigrew because Heth was wounded during the fighting on the 1st day. There were also two brigades of Major Gen. William Pender's division, who were under the command of Major Gen. Isaac Trimble as Pender was wounded during the 2nd day's fight. All six of these brigades were from the 3rd Corps, under the command of Lieutenant Gen. A.P. Hill, and all six of these brigades were heavily engaged in the fighting on July 1st, suffering many casualties.[275]

The four brigades under the command of Gen. Pettigrew were aligned from left to right, north to south, in the following order: Col. John Brockenbrough's brigade, Gen. James Davis' brigade, Pettigrew's brigade, who was under the command of Col James Marshall and Archer's brigade, under the command of Col. Birkett Fry. These four brigades constituted the first line, which was followed up by Lane's and Lowrance's brigades, under Trimble's command, in the second line. Pickett's division was to the right and slightly in front of Pettigrew's troops. The division was formed with Garnett's brigade to the left of Kemper's brigade. Armistead's brigade, the largest of the three, did not have room to form on Garnett's left. Therefore, they were ordered to file in behind the other two brigades, creating a second line. To the right of Pickett's division were the brigades of Col. David Lang and Brig. Gen. Cadmus Wilcox, who were to act as support by following Pickett's division and protect his right flank.[276]

The five regiments in Kemper's brigade were formed from left to right in the following order: the 3rd VA under the command of Col. Joseph Mayo, the 7th VA under the command of Col. Walter Tazewell Patton, the center of the brigade was held by the 1st VA, under the command of Col. Lewis Williams. To the right of the 1st VA was the 11th VA under the command of Major Kirkwood Otey, and to their right was the 24th VA under the command of Col. William Terry, which was the extreme right of the brigade and Pickett's Division. The five regiments in Kemper's

---

275 James Longstreet, "From Manassas to Appomattox", Pgs. 388-389: "Historical Times, Encyclopedia of the Civil War" Patricia Faust, Editor, Pgs. 569, 579 & 763.
276 "The Maps of Gettysburg", by Bradley M. Gottfried, Published by Savas Beatie LLC, 521 Fifth Ave, Suite 3400, New York, NY, 10175, 2007, Pg. 251.

brigade totaled between 1800 and 1900 men, with the 1st VA accounting for approximately 220 of those. [277]

The division moved into the field on Spangler's farm, removing fences and obstacles as they went. In front of the men was a gentle hill, rising up toward the Emmitsburg Pike. The slope ran parallel to the pike and then veered back to the west, toward the Spangler woods. In an attempt to conceal their movements from prying eyes on Cemetery Ridge, the three brigades conformed their lines to the contour of the hill. Kemper's line ran parallel to Emmitsburg Pike and Garnett's line curved to the left, with his left flank resting in the Spangler woods. There was, however, a Union signal tower on the hill known as Little Round Top that had a partial view of the Confederate position. In order to disguise the number of regiments on the Spangler farm the color guards were ordered not to unfurl their flags until the regiments formed for the advance. The three brigades halted, the men stacked their arms and were allowed to rest. Some of the men of the 1st VA, seeking shelter from the ever increasing heat of the July sun, moved into the shade of a nearby apple orchard. Perhaps to lessen the anxiety of the coming battle, a few of the men began pelting each other with the little green apples. The men watched as officers and couriers galloped back and forth across the field. Orders were dispersed and eventually the plan of attack was explained to the men in the ranks, so that every man knew what was expected of him when the grand assault began. The men were told to lay flat on the ground when they heard the fire of two cannon, whose discharge would signal the Confederate artillery to commence the bombardment of the Union lines. Kemper specifically wanted the men to know that Gen. Lee had assigned Pickett's division "the post of honor that day."[278]

---

[277] "Official Report for Kemper's Brigade" by Col. Joseph Mayo, July 25th 1863, (Never published in the Official Records), George Edward Pickett Papers, William R. Perkin's Library, Duke University, as quoted in "Pickett's Charge, Eyewitness Accounts", edited by Richard Rollins, Rank and File Publications, 1994.

[278] Durkin, "John Dooley, Confederate Soldier", Pg. 102: SHSP, Volume 34, "Pickett's Charge at Gettysburg" by Colonel Joseph Mayo, 1906, Kraus Reprint Company, 1979, Pg. 328.

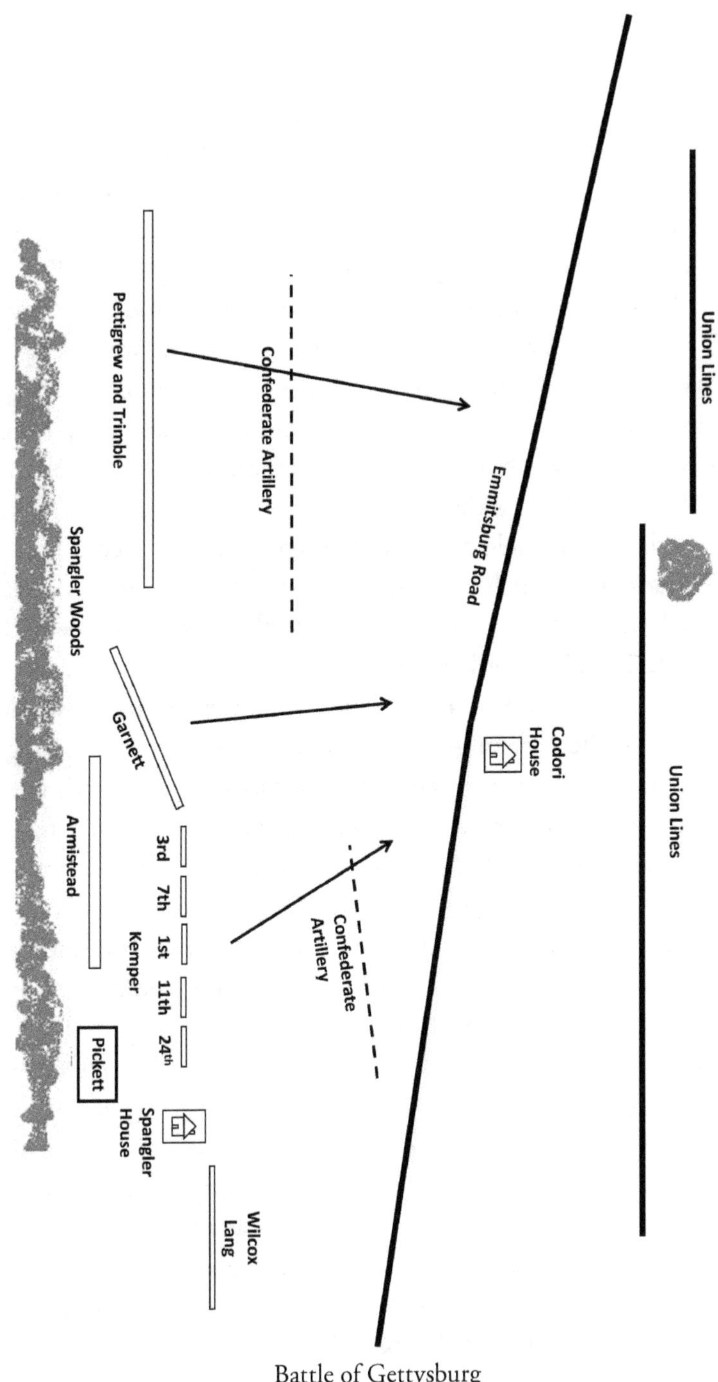

Battle of Gettysburg
Position During the Bombardment, July 3, 1863

As the men relaxed at the bottom of the hill they could see the Confederate artillery being placed at the summit, two hundred yards to their front. The cannoneers had been hard at work since three in the morning preparing their guns and caissons for whatever duty Gen. Lee called upon them to perform. Kemper's brigade was behind the section of guns attached to Pickett's division under the command of twenty-three year old Major James Dearing. The artillery of Longstreet's 1st Corps was actually under the command of Col. James B. Walton but it was the talented artillery officer Col. Edward Porter Alexander who Longstreet tasked with overseeing the bombardment on this day. Alexander had seventy-five guns from Longstreet's corps and sixty-three guns from A. P. Hill's corps with which to soften up the Federal lines for the infantry's assault. Alexander also had the services of nine howitzers from A. P. Hill's corps. He planned to hold these short range guns in reserve until the infantry attacked, at which time he would send them to protect Pickett's exposed right flank. The howitzers were sent off to a safe place behind the lines and told to wait for orders.

It was Gen. Lee's hope that such a massive array of cannon would be able to drive off the Federal guns defending Cemetery Hill, clearing the way for the infantry to storm the Union breastworks. Although the 138 Confederate guns, lined up on the ridge, presented an awe-inspiring sight, Alexander was well aware that his guns, and especially his ammunition, were inferior to that of his opponents. He also knew that after two days of heavy fighting, the army had only enough ammunition for one more large scale battle. While surveying the position of the guns, Alexander received the following note from Longstreet:

"Colonel: If the artillery fire does not have the effect to drive off the enemy, or greatly demoralize him, so as to make our effort pretty certain, I would prefer that you should not advise General Pickett to make the charge. I shall rely a great deal upon your good judgment to determine the matter, and shall expect you to let General Pickett know when the moment offers."

Alexander, being a Colonel, was not comfortable with the thought of being responsible for ordering 14,000 men into the jaws of death and he responded to Longstreet with the following:

"General: I will only be able to judge the effect of our fire on the enemy by his return fire, for his infantry is but little exposed to view and the smoke will

obscure the whole field. If, as I infer from your note, there is any alternative to this attack, it should be carefully considered before opening our fire, for it will take all the artillery ammunition we have left to test this one thoroughly, and if the result is unfavorable, we will have none left for another effort. And even if this is entirely successful, it can only be so at a very bloody cost."

Gen. Wright, who was in command of the Georgians who attacked the same position on the previous day, was with Alexander during this exchange of notes with Longstreet. While discussing the situation, Wright advised Alexander, "It is not so hard to go there as it looks; I was nearly there with my brigade yesterday. The trouble is to stay there. The whole Yankee army is there in a bunch." Wright's words and Alexander's concerns would prove to be an ominous prediction for the men of the 1st VA and the rest of the men taking part in this assault.[279]

Unlike the infantrymen at the bottom of the hill, Alexander and the rest of the artillerymen could see the imposing Federal lines along Cemetery Hill. In front of the Confederate cannon the ground sloped down to the Emmitsburg Road, which had a heavy split rail fence on both sides of the lane. This fence would have to be removed or climbed by the infantry before they could pass over the road. From there it was an uphill climb to the Federal position, which was bristling with cannon. The top of the hill was crowned with a stone wall that offered excellent protection for the Union infantry and presented one more obstacle to the attacking Confederates. The Yankees also had a strong skirmish line out in front of their main battle line. Behind the wall, the main line consisted of two lines of infantry and reserves. Once the Confederate infantry passed through their own artillery, their entire route of march to the stone wall would be under the fire of the Yankee cannon. [280]

During the previous night, Brig. Gen. Henry J. Hunt, Chief of Artillery for the Army of the Potomac, had his men replacing and refurbishing their cannon after the fighting on the 2nd of July. Damaged guns were sent to

---

279 SHSP, Volume 4, "Colonel E. P. Alexander's report of the Battle of Gettysburg", dated August 10, 1863. Kraus reprint edition, 1977, Pgs. 235-39: Battles and Leaders, Volume 3, A. S. Barnes and Co. reprint edition 1956, "The Great Charge and artillery fighting at Gettysburg" by E. Porter Alexander, Brigadier General, C. S. A. pgs. 357-368.

280 Walter Harrison, "Pickett's Men", pgs. 92-3.

the rear and new batteries ordered up from the artillery reserve. During the morning, Hunt made a personal inspection of the artillery along the entire Union line. He witnessed the placement of the Confederate cannon in front of Seminary Ridge and concluded he had seventy-five of his own guns in position to answer the Rebel threat. He also had Hazlett's battery, 5th U.S. Artillery, Battery D, on Little Round Top under the command of Lieutenant Benjamin Rittenhouse, who took over the command when Hazlett was killed on the previous day. Rittenhouse's six rifled cannon were in an excellent position to enfilade the Confederate lines.[281]

As the sun climbed higher in the sky, the day became unbearably hot. Charles Loehr, who was now a Corporal, strayed up the hill in search of water. After filling his canteen, and within sight of the Federal lines, Loehr struck up a conversation with some of the artillerists in regards to the coming attack. The cannoneers pointed out the Union defenses and the obstructions that must be overcome to reach the Yankee breastworks. Upon returning to his comrades at the bottom of the hill, Loehr remarked, "I would not give twenty-five cents for my life if the charge is made." Col. Mayo, commander of the 3rd VA, noticed that the normally happy-go-lucky members of Kemper's brigade were very quiet and pensive on this hot July morning. Walking over to Col. Tazewell Patton, the commander of the 7th VA, he said, "This news has brought about an awful seriousness with our fellows, Taz." "Yes," replied Patton, "and well they may be serious if they really know what is in store for them. I have been up yonder where Dearing is, and looked across at the Yankees." With every pair of eyes that went up the hill, the men became better informed of the task that lay before them on this hot July afternoon.

At approximately 1 PM, the Washington Artillery fired two signal guns in quick succession. The signal guns were quickly followed by the eruption of the Confederate batteries arrayed along the ridge. The largest artillery duel ever seen on the continent of North America had begun. In obedience to orders, the startled infantry dove on the ground, lying as flat as possible. The men lay under thc scorching sun, listening to the outgoing bursts of the Confederate cannon, waiting for the Federal gunners to return in kind. It was not long before the enemy shells came screaming

---

281 Official Records, Series 1, Volume 27, Part 1, "Reports of Brig. Gen. Henry J. Hunt, U.S. Army, Chief of Artillery, Army of the Potomac", pgs.228-243.

over the hill crashing into the ground among Pickett's men. Below their prone bodies, the ground shook as if a massive earthquake had struck Adams County, Pennsylvania. All manner of long range ordinance was raining down on the unprotected infantrymen. Solid shot was ripping up the ground and any unfortunate soldier who happened to be laying in its wake. Shells were exploding in the tree tops, showering the men with shrapnel and tree limbs, causing horrid wounds and killing instantly. A blanket of acrid smoke covered the field from the exploding shells and the discharges of the Confederate cannon. This combined with the sweltering heat, made the situation insufferable for the men of Kemper's brigade. [282]

Walter Harrison, a member of Pickett's staff, left this account of the bombardment: *"Such a tornado of projectiles it has seldom been the fortune or misfortune of any one to see. The atmosphere was broken by the rushing solid shot, and shrieking shell; the sky, just now so bright, was at the same moment lurid with flame and murky with smoke. The sun in his noontide ray was obscured by clouds of sulphurous mist, eclipsing his light, and shadowing the earth as with a funeral pall; while through this sable panoply, ever descending and wrapping this field of blood in the darkness of death, shot the fiery fuses, like wild meteors of a heavenly wrath; hurtled the discordantly screaming shell, bearing mangled death and mutilation in its most horrible form."*[283]

David Johnston, who himself was wounded in the barrage, was a member of the 7th VA and was in line next to the 1st VA, left this account of the bombardment; *"The very atmosphere seemed broken by the rush and crash of projectiles, solid shot, shrieking, bursting shells. The sun, but a moment before so brilliant, was now almost darkened by smoke and mist enveloping and shadowing the earth, and through which came hissing and shrieking, fiery fuses and messengers of death, sweeping, plunging, cutting, ploughing through our ranks, carrying mutilation, destruction, pain, suffering and death in every direction. Turn your eyes whiter-so-ever you would, and there was to be seen at almost every moment of time, guns, swords, haversacks, human flesh and bones, flying and dangling in the air, or bouncing above the earth, which now trembled beneath us as if shaken by an earthquake."* Johnston went on

---

282 SHSP, Volume 32, 1904, "The Old First Virginia at Gettysburg" by Charles T. Loehr, Pg. 40: SHSP, Volume 34, 1906, "Pickett's Charge at Gettysburg" by Colonel Joseph Mayo, Pgs. 328-29.

283 Walter Harrison, "Pickett's Men, A Fragment of History", Pgs.96-97.

to say; *"Over us, in front of us, behind us, and in our midst, and through our ranks, poured shot, shell and the fragments thereof, dealing out death on every hand; yet the men stood bravely to their posts – that is, those that had not been knocked out of place by shot – and all this in an open field, beneath the burning rays of a July sun."*[284]

Those who laid on the reverse slope of the hill like Wellington's men a half century before at the Battle of Waterloo would have been somewhat protected from the solid shot, but, the sheer number of projectiles and the amount of exploding ordinance among the great mass of men made a large number of casualties inevitable. The agonizing screams of the men who were being brutally maimed were intermingled with the terrific sound of explosions. Others perished without a whimper, lying next to men who were unscathed and unaware of their neighbor's misfortune. As the bombardment continued, the men were frustrated at not being able to fight back and defend themselves. Their only hope was that their adversaries on the opposing ridge were getting the worst of this long range duel. They knew when the cannonade ended it would be their turn to muster the courage to avenge their fallen comrades and. as many believed, end the war with a victory for the south. The officers did what they could to set an example for the men to follow. Major Dearing was seen riding his horse, flag in hand, from cannon to cannon rallying his men. Gen. Longstreet calmly rode along the lines, unattended, and according to Captain John Holmes Smith of the 11th VA, "He was as quiet as an old farmer riding over his plantation on a Sunday morning." The sight of the Corps commander exposing himself to such danger alarmed Gen. Kemper, who implored him to seek shelter.[285]

Like many aspects of "Pickett's Charge," the length of the bombardment is debatable. However, most accounts put it at about two hours. According to Gen. Hunt it was "about 2:30 p. m." when he ordered the Union artillery to slacken their fire and conserve ammunition for the infantry

---

[284] David E. Johnston, "Four Years a Soldier", pg. 253.

[285] Curran, "John Dooley's Civil War", pg. 158-160: "Nothing but Glory, Pickett's Division at Gettysburg", by Kathleen R. Georg and John W. Busey, Published for Longstreet House by Gateway Press, Inc., 1987, 1001 N. Calvert St., Baltimore, MD 21202, Pg. 41: SHSP, Vol. 32, "The Battle of Gettysburg, Captain John Holmes Smith's Account", pg. 190.

attack that he knew would follow the barrage. Batteries that had exhausted their ammunition were ordered off the line and fresh cannon were ordered up from the reserve.[286]

On the Confederate side, a series of miscommunications and mismanagement of the artillery reserve were some of the blunders that took place and would prove fatal for the infantrymen, especially in Kemper's brigade. Col. Alexander sent a courier to retrieve the nine howitzers that were held behind the lines in order to advance them with Pickett's division. The howitzers were no longer at their designated location and the courier returned empty handed. Gen. Pendleton, the Chief of Artillery for the Army of Northern Virginia, had moved some of the guns without notifying Alexander. On his own accord, the commander of the remaining howitzers felt his position unsafe and moved the guns to a more secure location further to the rear, also without notifying Alexander. Many of the guns on the line were either low or completely out of ammunition. Caissons were sent to the rear to refill their ammunition chests, but the supply trains had also been moved further away from the bombardment, rendering it impossible for the guns to refurbish in time to advance with the infantry. Since the plan had always been for a strong artillery presence to accompany the infantry during the attack, these unfavorable developments put Alexander and Longstreet in a precarious position. Longstreet, who was never in favor of this assault, felt it was not within his authority to cancel the operation, which Gen. Lee had ordered. Longstreet rode over to Alexander and the two officers discussed the situation. According to Alexander, Longstreet said, "I don't want to make this attack. I would stop it now but that General Lee ordered it and expects it to go on. I don't see how it can succeed." The consequences of canceling the assault were severe since the army did not have adequate ammunition for a second attempt and resupply was not an option because the army was so far from their base of

---

286 Official Records, Series 1, Volume 27, Part 1, "Report of Brig. Gen. Howard J. Hunt". pg. 239.

operations in Virginia. The only person with the authority to cancel the attack was Gen. Lee and he was not notified of the setback.[287]

When the Union fire decreased, Alexander determined it was time for the infantry to advance, before his guns were completely out of ammunition. Pickett received a reluctant command from Longstreet and orders were passed down the line. The men were finally allowed to stand and they began to form their companies, regiments and eventually the brigade. But many were unable to rise from their prone positions. There were the dead, scattered about the open field with the most hideous of injuries. Others tried to answer the call but found their wounds were too serious to join their comrades in what they believed could be the most important engagement of the war. Still others were so afflicted with heat stroke they were unable to rise to their feet. And some so paralyzed with fear after lying defenseless under the horrific bombardment that they dare not rise. In an attempt to rally the men, Gen. Pickett rode along the line, calling out to the soldiers of his division, "Up men and to your posts! Don't forget that today you are from Old Virginia," as he galloped by. With these words from Pickett, the assault that would forever bear his name began.[288]

The men grabbed their muskets and fell into line. The color bearers unfurled their new red battle flags, ready to lead their regiments to victory and onto the pages of history. The flag of the 7th VA had already seen the loss of its first color bearer, killed in the bombardment with his right hand tightly grasping the staff. As the men were forming up, Captain Robert Bright, a member of Pickett's staff, galloped up to give Gen. Kemper his orders. Kemper was told to dress on Garnett's brigade, which was to his left, and use the "red barn" as his objective. Although there was a much smaller barn on the property, the now familiar red Codori barn was not built until 1883. Therefor Bright's "red barn" was more likely the red brick Codori farmhouse which was the most visible landmark from Kemper's

---

[287] Battles and Leaders, Volume 3, "The Great Charge and Artillery Fighting at Gettysburg", by E. P. Alexander, Pg. 363: Official Records, Series 1, Vol. 27, Part 2, "Report of Lt. Gen. James Longstreet", Pg. 360: "Report of Gen. Robert E. Lee, January 1864", pg. 321.

[288] Robert Emmett Curran, "John Dooley's Civil War, An Irish American's Journey in the First Virginia Infantry Regiment", Pg. 160: David Johnston, "Four Years a Soldier", Pg. 255.

position. The farm house was to the right of the "copse of trees" that was the focal point of the entire attack.

The fear being that officers mounted on horseback would present too tempting of a target, Captain Bright relayed the order that "all officers were to go in dismounted." Kemper chose to ignore this order. Robert "Tante" Jones, former Sergeant Major, who was recently promoted to 2nd Lieutenant in the 1st VA, was a former classmate of Captain Bright. Jones called out to his old friend, "Bob, turn us loose, and we will take them." Next, Captain Bright was confronted by the commander of the 1st VA, "Captain Bright I wish to ride my mare up," implored Colonel Williams. Bright repeated the orders he had just relayed to Kemper that all officers were to go on foot. Williams persisted, claiming he was sick, and could not make the long march on foot. Bright relented, saying, "Mount your mare, and I will make an excuse for you."[289]

The three brigades of Pickett's division remained in the same formation as when they entered Spangler's field earlier that morning, with Kemper and Garnett in front and Armistead's brigade following behind. The regiments within Kemper's brigade were aligned from left to right: 3rd, 7th, 1st, 11th and 24th VA. Fifteen members of Company "D" of the 1st VA were sent out in front of the regiment as skirmishers. The color bearer was Sergeant William Lawson and the remainder of the color guard consisted of Sergeants Pat Woods and Theodore Martin, Corporal John Figg and Private Willie Mitchel. When the command was given to forward the colors, the guard stepped out four paces in front of the regiment. This was repeated throughout Pickett's division and at the command "March," fifteen regiments of Virginians, more than 5,000 men, boldly started up the hill.[290]

As they passed through the Confederate cannon, they were given salutes, cheers and well wishes. Those artillerymen who had spent the afternoon assailing the Union lines could do little more to help the infantry but give this small boost to morale. Major Eshelman of the Washington Artillery did manage to scrape together five guns with barely enough

---

289 Kathy Georg Harrison, "Nothing But Glory", Pgs. 41-42: "Pickett's Charge at Gettysburg", Confederate Veteran Magazine, Vol. 38, by Captain Robert A. Bright, Nashville, Tennessee, July 1930. Pgs. 263-266.

290 SHSP, Volume 32, "The Old 1st Virginia at Gettysburg", by Charles Loehr, Pg. 36.

ammunition to advance and support Pickett's flank. Far less artillery support than what was envisioned when the plans for this attack were devised.[291]

After cresting the hill and passing through the artillery, the Confederate line came into view of the Union troops waiting on Cemetery Hill. Through a series of left obliques, Kemper moved his brigade to the left, closing the gap between his and Garnett's brigade. Garnett's left then linked up with the right flank of Archer's brigade, which was part of Pettigrew's division. By all accounts the men performed the different maneuvers with parade ground accuracy. E.P. Alexander was watching as Pickett's division approached his position and later wrote, "Pickett's division swept out of the wood and showed the full length of its gray ranks and shining bayonets, as grand a sight as ever a man looked on." The movements even garnered the respect of their enemies who watched with great interest as they waited to repel the advance with deadly force. It was the troops of Major General Winfield Scott Hancock's 2nd corps who were stationed along the section of the line that was the target of Pickett's division. Writing of the Confederate battle line in his official report, Hancock said, "Their lines were formed with a precision and steadiness that extorted the admiration of the witnesses of that memorable scene." Gen. Henry Hunt, whose Union guns had caused so much havoc among the Rebel infantry less than one-half hour before, also wrote after the war, "The Confederate approach was magnificent, and excited our admiration." The lines of rebels also drew the unwanted attention of Rittenhouse's battery of rifled cannon on Little Round Top, which opened a deliberate fire into Pickett's right flank.[292]

As the Confederate line approached the Emmitsburg Road, they encountered Yankee skirmishers who were easily pushed back toward their own main lines. At about this point the Union artillery along Cemetery Hill exploded with a burst of shot and shell that cut gaping holes in the ranks

---

[291] Official Records, Volume 27, Part 2, "Report of Major B. F. Eshelman, Washington (Louisiana) Artillery", Pg. 435.

[292] Official Records, Volume 27, Part 2, "Report of Major Gen. Winfield S. Hancock", Pg. 373: SHSP, Volume 34, "Pickett's Charge at Gettysburg" by Col. Joseph Mayo, Pgs.331-332: Battles and Leaders, Volume 3, "The Great Charge and Artillery Fighting at Gettysburg" by. E.P. Alexander, Pg. 365 & "The Third day at Gettysburg" by Henry J. Hunt, Pg. 374.

of the advancing rebels. Some of the Yankee guns remained silent, having used up their long range ammunition in the preceding bombardment. Those guns, loaded with canister, bided their time until the Confederates closed the distance to the anxious gunners. The Confederate guns opened with whatever meagre supply of long range ammunition they had left, firing over the heads of their comrades. This in itself was a risky maneuver, owing to the unreliable fuses of the Confederate ammunition that could very well explode over friendly heads as well as that of the enemy. The Union gunners ignored the Confederate cannon and concentrated their fire on the unprotected infantry. Yet the southerners pushed on, passing through and over the fences along the Emmitsburg Road and began the ascent to Cemetery Ridge.[293]

As Pickett's division crossed the Emmitsburg Road on the extreme right flank of the attack, things had already begun to unravel on the extreme left. Brockenbrough's brigade of Pettigrew's division was being attacked on their unprotected left flank. Facing a vicious fire from the front and side by small arms and artillery, Brockenbrough's brigade eventually halted and began to fall back. Being on the far right of the exceptionally long battle line, this setback was not yet apparent to the men of Kemper's brigade. It was necessary for Pickett's division to make a series of left obliques and marching by the left flank to reach the Codori house and eventually the copse of trees in the center of the Union line. With every step the fire from the Federal lines increased. When the Virginians got within musket range, the entire Yankee line erupted with a torrent of lead and smoke. The breakdown on the left continued to multiply. As each regiment fell back, they exposed the next regiment in line to the flanking fire, causing a domino effect, from left to right, of men returning to the rear.[294]

---

[293] Battles and Leaders, Volume 3, "The Great Charge and Artillery Fighting at Gettysburg" by. E.P. Alexander, Pg. 365 & "The Third day at Gettysburg" by Henry J. Hunt, Pg. 374.

[294] Official Records, Series 1, Volume 27, "Report of Gen. Robert E. Lee, January 1864". Pg. 321.

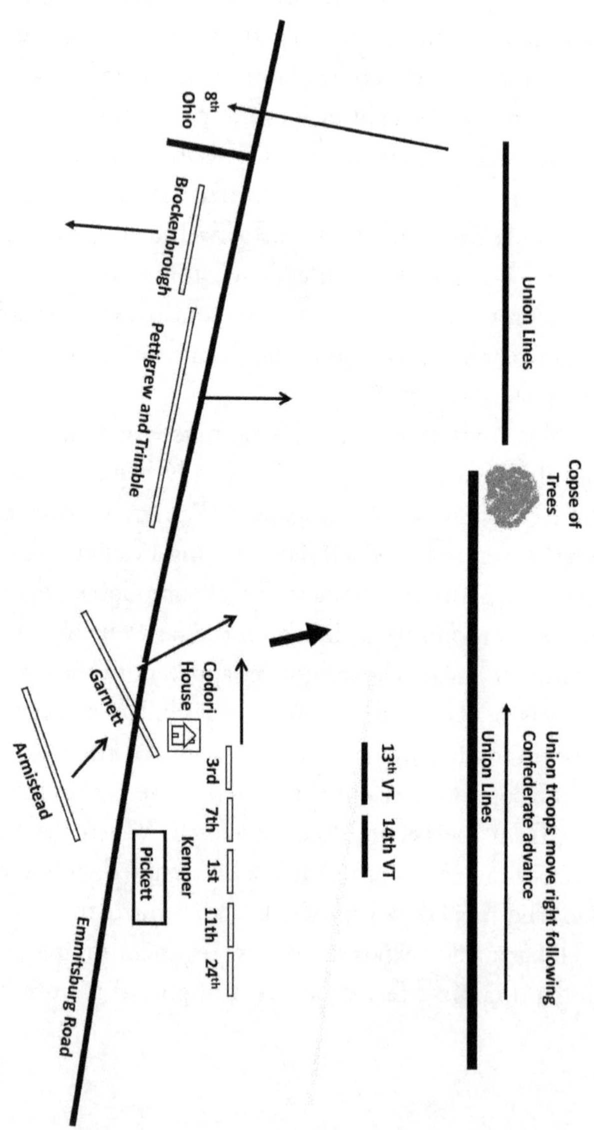

The Battle of Gettysburg
The Confederate Advance

Of more immediate concern to both the men and officers of Pickett's division was the lack of support on their own side of the field. Marcellus "Monk" Wingfield, of the 1st VA, looked back toward the Confederate line, and turning to Charles Loehr, asked, "Where are our reinforcements?" Corporal Loehr, turned his head to the rear, saw only a scene of death and destruction in the wake of the division's path and no fresh troops making the same trek, replied to his friend's question, "Monk, I don't see any." Monk replied, "We are going to be whipped, see if we don't." These prophetic words were the last that Monk Wingfield, a two year veteran, ever spoke. Moments later he was shot and killed. Gen. Pickett, who was also aware of the absence of any support, sent a courier back to find Wilcox's and Lang's brigades who were supposed to be protecting his right flank. Fearing the courier would be killed before completing his mission, Pickett sent two others to insure the message got through. All three couriers reached Wilcox, whose brigade, along with Lang's, through some unexplained miscommunication had yet to move from their starting point. The two brigades made up of Alabamians and Floridians immediately started forward.[295]

The Codori house presented an obstacle to Kemper, whose brigade was to the right of the house, but his target, the copse of trees, was to the left. This forced Kemper's brigade to pass between the house and the federal lines, marching by the left flank, in a column of fours, exposing the men to a withering enfilade fire. The brigade was directly in front of the Yankee cannon under the command of Lt. Col. Freeman McGilvery. McGilvery had fourteen 12 pounders, nineteen rifled 3 inch guns, four James rifled guns and two howitzers under his command. The thirty-nine pieces of Union artillery were trained on Kemper's brigade as they maneuvered around the Codori house and small barn. As the rebels neared the Federal lines, the artillery blasted away with double canister, causing enormous casualties among the Confederates. At this point, they were

295 SHSP, Volume 32, "The Old First Virginia at Gettysburg", by Charles Loehr, Pg. 40: "Pickett's Charge at Gettysburg", Confederate Veteran Magazine, Vol. 38, by Captain Robert A. Bright, Pgs. 263-266:

also well within musket range and the Yankees took full advantage, firing continuous volleys at the defenseless gray column in their front.[296]

Prior to the attack, Union Brig. Gen. George Stannard placed the 13th and 14th Vermont Infantry regiments among an outcropping of rocks and trees, seventy-five yards in front of the main Union battle line. The Vermonters unloaded their muskets into Kemper's right flank as the Confederates passed between their advanced position and the Codori house. The leftward movement toward the copse of trees continued, passing regiment after regiment of Union soldiers who fired from behind their breastworks. After firing at the passing Southerners, the Union soldiers moved behind their own line, to their right, mirroring the movements of the Confederate column. This gave the appearance of a crowd following an Independence Day parade with the onlookers moving behind those spectators who had front row seats. This movement tended to stack up the Federals further down the line, increasing their firepower with every step the Confederates took. After passing the Vermonters, the Virginians turned toward the stone wall and advanced in the direction of the ever increasing mass of blue clad soldiers. At this point, according to Brig. Gen. William Harrow, who commanded a division of Union troops along this section of the line, "Here the contest raged with almost unparalleled ferocity." The Virginians quickly formed a battle line after passing the red brick house and pushed on toward the copse of trees. The maelstrom of fire and smoke disintegrated the heretofore parade ground precision of the Confederate lines. The brigades of Kemper and Garnett became jumbled and yet they pressed on determined to reach their objective. Kemper rode back to Armistead encouraging him to push forward with his brigade. Armistead's men gave a cheer and picked up their pace to join their fellow Virginians.

The change of direction toward the stone wall by the Virginians presented an opportunity for Gen. Stannard's regiments, which he quickly took advantage of. The 1st company of the 13th Vermont wheeled to the right and the remainder of the 13th Vermont dressed on the 1st company. Stannard then ordered the 16th Vermont forward and they aligned themselves on the 13th Vermont. This movement put two Union regiments directly and at short range on the unprotected right flank of Kemper's

---

296 SHSP, Volume 34, "Pickett's Charge at Gettysburg", by Joseph Mayo, Pg. 332: "Nothing But Glory" by Kathy Georg Harrison, Pg. 65: Official Records, Series 1, Volume 27, Part 1, pgs. 883-884.

brigade. The Virginians were now facing musket fire from both their front and right flank. They were also forced to endure murderous blasts of canister fire from every enemy gun that could be brought to bear on the ever thinning gray lines. The remnants of the 11th and 24th VA regiments halted and turned to face the new threat presented by the Vermonters on the right flank. It is probable that some of the 8th VA from Garnett's Brigade also fell in line with the 11th and 24th VA to help fend off the attack on Kemper's right. The 16th Vermont claimed to have captured the 8th VA's flag, further evidence of the intermingling between Garnett's and Kemper's brigades at this point in the attack. [297]

Casualties within the 1st VA and Kemper's brigade were piling up at an alarming rate. Colonel Williams, immediately after giving Lieutenant E. P. Reeve an order in regards to the alignment of Company "D," was shot off of his horse. The Colonel fell onto his own sword causing a painful mortal wound to his spine. William's rider less horse charged on into the smoke and fire and was later seen returning to the Confederate lines. Major Langley was second in command, but he too was wounded. Captain Norton, of Company "D," was the senior Captain, and so he assumed command of the regiment but shortly thereafter was also among the valiant wounded. Captain Davis of Company "B" then stepped forward and led the regiment but he was also quickly shot down. Command of the regiment, what little remained, fell to 1st Lt. E. P. Reeve because no other Captain was left standing within sight of the small group of men still banded together under the banner of the 1st VA. A courier rode up from Gen. Kemper and ordered Reeve to turn the 1st VA to the right, possibly to help hold off the Vermont regiments. Men were falling as fast as Reeve could put them in line, until he finally turned to the messenger and sadly declared that he had no regiment left to conduct the movement. The courier rode off and shortly thereafter Reeve was shot and wounded in the right arm, his third painful wound since the Battle of Williamsburg, fourteen months before. [298]

---

297 Official Records, Volume 27, Part 1, "Report of Brig. Gen. George J. Stannard, U.S. Army Commanding Third Brigade", Pgs. 349-350: "Report of Brig. Gen. William Harrow, U.S. Army, Commanding Second Division", Pg. 420: SHSP, Volume 34, "Pickett's Charge at Gettysburg", by Joseph Mayo, Pg. 332.

298 E.P. Reeve, "Reminiscences": SHSP, Volume 32, "The Old First Virginia at Gettysburg", by Charles Loehr, Pg. 35.

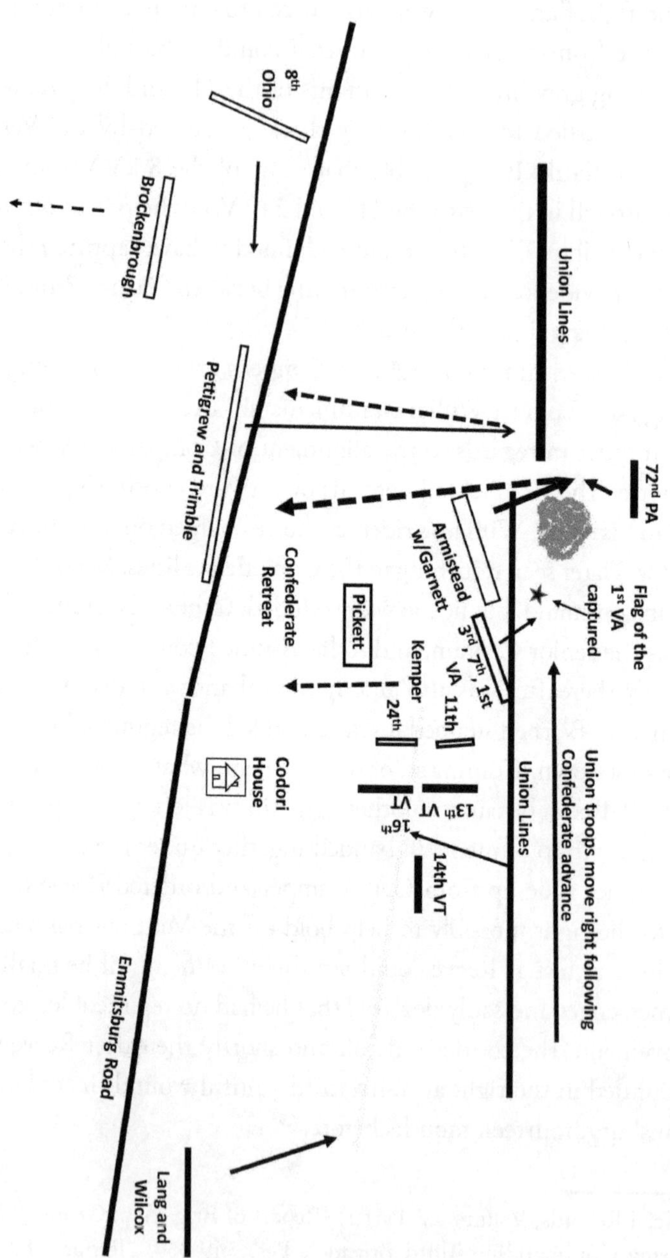

Battle of Gettysburg
The Confederate Retreat

As the officers of the 1st VA were falling one after another, the brigade was approaching an angle in the stone wall, which forever after was simply known as "the angle." General Kemper rose up in his saddle, pointed toward the wall with his sword and shouted, "There are the guns boys, go for them." What was left of his brigade fired a volley and let loose with their first and only cheer of the day before breaking into a run and charging the wall. Shortly thereafter, the gallant brigade commander was knocked out of his saddle by a projectile. Kemper later wrote that he was close enough to the wall "to observe the features and expressions of the faces of the men in front of me, and I thought I observed and could identify the soldier who shot me." He was close enough to the enemy lines that Union soldiers ran out to where the general was lying and placed him on a blanket in an attempt to carry him off the field. Confederate soldiers rescued Kemper by firing over his body, injuring or running off the would-be captors. The seriously wounded Kemper was then carried, using the same blanket, back toward the Confederate lines on Seminary Ridge. At least one of Kemper's liberators, Sergeant Leigh Blanton of Company "D," was from the 1st VA. It is unclear who assisted Blanton or what regiments they were from.[299]

The color guard of the 1st VA fared no better than the regiment's unfortunate officers. As the brave band of five men led the regiment toward the Codori farmhouse the youthful Willie Mitchel was the first of the guard to be shot. His companions pled with Mitchel to turn back and seek treatment for his wound. Willie refused and pushed on with his comrades in the color guard only to be shot again and killed near the Codori house. Mitchel, who was playfully known as "the bugoligist" because of his interest in studying insects, was only sixteen or seventeen years old. The remainder of the guard pressed on through the storm of lead, all the while proudly waving their new crimson banner aloft. The flag acted as a magnet, drawing the attention and the bullets of the Union infantrymen who aimed for the center of the regiment. One by one, Pat Woods, Theodore

---

299 Letter from James Lawson Kemper to W. H. Swallow, Dated February 4, 1886, Gettysburg National Military Park: "Report of Col. Joseph Mayo, July 25, 1863", George Edward Pickett Papers, William R. Perkins Library, Duke University, as quoted in "Pickett's Charge, Eyewitness Accounts", edited by Richard Rollins: "Third Day at Gettysburg", edited by Gary Gallagher, The University of North Carolina Press, 1994, "Pickett's Charge" by Carol Reardon, Pg. 61.

Martin and John Figg were shot down and left on the ground in the regiment's bloody wake. As the remnants of the 1st VA approached the wall near the right or south edge of the copse of trees, William Lawson, the color bearer, was all that remained of the color guard. Finally, he too was shot, the bullet shattering his right arm, which was eventually lost to the surgeons saw. The flag fell to the ground where it was scooped up by Jacob Polack, of Company "I," who was also immediately shot in the arm. The flag once again fluttered to the ground, where the noble symbol of the regiment remained as there was no one left to raise it up. Sergeant Martin McHugh of the 82nd NY, one of the regiments that followed the parade as the Confederate line moved across the Union front, ran out and captured the unattended flag. The 82nd NY also claimed to have captured the flag of the 7th VA from Kemper's brigade.[300]

Gen. Garnett was down, after being shot off of his horse, leaving Armistead as the only brigade commander left in Pickett's division. Armistead, on foot, with his hat raised on his sword, led the remnants of his brigade up to the wall, sweeping some of Garnett's and Kemper's men with him. A melee ensued, a section of the Federal line broke and the small band of southerners swept over the stones and into the Union breastworks. The rebel flags were seen in and around the copse of trees, the target of the attack that had cost the army so dearly. The Virginians having achieved their goal looked back, scanning the field and expecting to see the gray columns of support that were sure to come in order to exploit their success. To their dismay, there was no supporting column within their view and the domino collapse of the attack on the left allowed the enemy on that side of the field to now concentrate on Pickett's division. During a brief lull in the action, the Yankees continued to mass their troops on both flanks and in front of the Virginians. [301]

Brig. Gen. Alexander Webb, whose troops, the Philadelphia Brigade, had been forced back at the wall, managed to rally his men behind the lines

---

[300] SHSP, Volume 32, "The Old First Virginia at Gettysburg", by Charles Loehr, Pg. 36: Richard Rollins, "The Damned Red Flags of the Rebellion", Pg. 159: Official Records, Series 1, Volume 27, Part 1, "Report of Captain John Darrow, Eighty-Second New York", Pg. 426.

[301] Official Records, Series 1, Volume 27, Part 2, "Report of Major Charles S. Peyton, Nineteenth Virginia Infantry, commanding Garnett's brigade", Pg. 386-87.

before their retreat developed into a general rout. The Federal troops, like their enemies, had become intermingled and most regimental organization was lost. Webb's men fell back onto the reserves who were in line behind them, waiting for their opportunity to join the fray. The Philadelphians not only halted the Confederate advance, they began to reclaim lost ground. The regiments from the Union left who followed the parade were now piling up at the angle, all merging together into one large force. The combination of Federal units far outmanned the small group of Rebels who now had possession of the angle. The Union soldiers also had officers who managed to rally their men and bring some order to the mass confusion, whereas most of the Confederate line officers were wounded or dead. Gen. Armistead, the last of the Brigade commanders, went down, mortally wounded among the Union cannon. The small group of surviving Confederates could not hold the ground that so many had sacrificed their lives to gain. Without reinforcements the battle was lost and it was up to each soldier to either surrender or retreat under fire back across the open field. [302]

The dead and wounded of the 1st VA were strewn about the ground designating the route of march that the regiment took from Seminary ridge to the Union breastworks. Lt. E. P. Reeve, after being wounded, took a seat on a pile of rocks near the stone wall and watched as the chaos rage around him. He witnessed a color bearer from Armistead's brigade climb the stone wall, waving his flag and urging his comrades forward. The man advanced into the Federal lines proudly displaying his flag in defiance of the Yankee guns. The color bearer, possibly from the 38th VA, after finding himself practically alone, simply turned and walked off the field holding his colors aloft. Reeve called it, "an act of cool daring strictly in the line of his duty which I have never seen surpassed." Enemy fire made the fields over which the attack was made just as deadly for those trying to make their way back to the safety of the Confederate lines as it was during their advance. Reeve thought of his wife and daughter and decided crossing the field was worth the risk. He left his perch among the rocks and retreated toward the protection of his own lines.[303]

---

302 Official Records, Series 1, Volume 27, Part 1, "Report of Major General Winfield Scott Hancock", Pg. 374.

303 Edward Payson Reeve, "Civil War Reminiscences of Captain Edward Payson Reeve".

Lt. John Dooley was shot through both thighs and fell about thirty yards in front of the wall. Next to him was twenty-five year old 2nd Lt. William Caho from Company "B," who was shot in the knee and was suffering severe pain. Dooley laid on the ground listening as the sounds of the battle resounded all around him. Hearing the distinctive "Huzzahs" of the enemy he knew the day was lost. A nearby battery of guns opened fire on the retreating Confederates, the percussion of the blasts shaking his wounded body with every discharge. Eventually some of the Vermonters approached the wounded men and ordered them to move within the Yankee lines. Dooley moved about a hundred yards before he became dizzy from lack of blood and collapsed into a ditch where he remained for the night.[304]

Charles Loehr, who remained with the skirmish company, suffered minor wounds to his face and arm but continued to fight. He reached a position near the wall and watched as the Federals were massing to his front when he saw Col. Patton of the 7th VA fall to the ground with a severe bullet wound. Rushing to Patton's side, Loehr saw blood gushing out of the colonel's mouth from the wound that would eventually take his life in the coming days. Loehr returned to his position until the outcome of the battle was no longer in question, at which time he and the remainder of the skirmishers ran the gauntlet of fire and joined in the retreat. As Pickett's men began to fall back, Loehr witnessed the approach of Wilcox's and Lang's brigades who were far too late to change the result of the engagement. Following his orders to support Pickett's division, Wilcox pushed on toward the Federal lines. By this time Pickett's division had disintegrated into a defeated stream of men moving toward the rear. The field over which the division had crossed in such fine form was now covered with men moving in small groups or individually in the opposite direction. Wilcox could not find an organized body of men to support. As his and Lang's brigades neared the enemy lines, the Federals concentrated their fire on this new threat. The two brigades hit the Union line further to the right from where Pickett's men had attacked. The Vermont regiments that had caused so much damage to Kemper's brigade wheeled about and fired into Lang's left flank, inflicting many casualties on the Floridians. The 16th

[304] Robert Emmett Curran, "John Dooley's Civil War, An Irish American's Journey in the First Virginia Infantry Regiment", Pgs. 162-64.

Vermont captured the colors of the 2nd Florida, Lang's brigade, in addition to the flag of the 8th VA from Garnett's brigade that they had captured earlier. Realizing that Pickett's attack had failed and his small command was needlessly being annihilated, Wilcox ordered a retreat.[305]

Pickett's men, who forever after this day they would be known as "Pickett's men," straggled back to the Confederate line, gathering near the spot from where they started the assault. The disorganized mass of men mingled about looking for friends and comrades, many of whom would never grace their ranks again. So many of the men were wounded and bleeding that a nearby stream turned red as the men used the cool water to clean their wounds. Nevertheless, parched men who had emptied their canteens on the hot July day were compelled to drink the discolored water. As Gen. Pickett rode among the men, Charlie Belcher, a member of the 24th VA, began to wave his regiment's flag, one of the few not captured, and shouted, "General, let us go at them again." The sight of the seriously wounded Gen. Kemper being carried through the crowd on his way to the surgeon halted Belcher's demonstration and brought Pickett to tears.

About this time Gen. Lee and some of his staff rode up to the group of beleaguered men, one of whom was Charles Loehr. The ever loyal soldiers immediately gathered around their beloved commander. According to Loehr, the following memorable exchange took place: Lee speaking to Pickett said, "General Pickett, your men have done all that men could do; the fault is entirely my own." Lee then turned to Kemper and said, "General Kemper, I hope you are not seriously hurt, can I do anything for you?" To which Kemper replied, "General Lee, you can do nothing for me; I am mortally wounded, but see to it that full justice is done my men who made this charge." Gen. Lee answered Kemper's request with, "I will," and then he rode off, followed faithfully by his staff. After the threat of a Union counterattack subsided, the men were told to return to their wagons, rest, tend their wounds and await further orders.[306]

---

305 "War History of the Old First Virginia", by Charles Loehr, Pg. 36-37: Official Records, Series 1, Volume 27, Part 2, "Report of Brig. Gen. Cadmus M. Wilcox", Pg. 620: Official Records, Volume 27, Part 1, "Report of Brig. Gen. George J. Stannard, U.S. Army Commanding Third Brigade", Pgs. 349-350.

306 Charles Loehr, "War History of the 1st Virginia", Pg. 38: SHSP, Vol. 32, "The Old first Virginia at Gettysburg", by Charles Loehr, Pgs. 36-37.

The wounded Lt. E. P. Reeve also made it back to the Confederate line, where he went directly to the field hospital. Finding the doctors overloaded with men more seriously wounded than himself, Reeve fashioned a sling from a discarded bandage, had a drink of whiskey to numb the pain and headed toward the army hospital in Cashtown. At Cashtown, the bullet which entered near his right shoulder was extracted and Reeve rested for the night. Among the many wounded of the 1st VA who were left on the field was the newly commissioned 2nd Lt. John Dooley. He lay in the ditch where the Vermonters had placed him after the battle, behind Union lines and among the wounded of both armies. Dooley spent the night with a wounded, generous Irish Yankee who shared his canteen of water and crackers with him. He watched as the mortally wounded Gen. Armistead, whom the Yankees mistakenly believed was Gen. Longstreet, was carried past him on a blanket. During the night it began to rain and the following morning Dooley was moved from the ditch a short distance to where Col. Williams was laying. Williams' spinal injury was agonizing and no position in which he laid brought relief to the pain. With the help of a Yankee Colonel, Dooley did what he could to help alleviate Williams' discomfort. During the afternoon of July 4th, Colonel Williams was taken to one of the makeshift Union hospitals where he died a few days later. Dooley was also loaded into an ambulance and taken to a Union field hospital.[307]

After witnessing the encounter between Generals Lee and Pickett, the remnants of the division headed toward their wagons, parked near the Chambersburg Pike. Some of the men of the 1st VA found space in an abandoned mill where they spent the night. Adding to the gloom of the situation, it began to rain on the night of July 3rd and continued to douse the men and their spirits on the 4th. Just over thirty men were left to fill the ranks of the 1st VA on that rainy morning under the command of Captain B. F. Howard of Company "I." Howard had taken ill several days previous and was therefore unable to participate in the attack, leaving him as the only unharmed officer left to command the regiment. The whereabouts of most of the regiment were unknown at the time. Like Lt. Dooley, many

---

307 "Civil War Reminiscences of Captain Edward Payson Reeve", Edward Payson Reeve: Robert Emmett Curran, "John Dooley's Civil War, An Irish American's Journey in the First Virginia Infantry Regiment", Pgs. 169-170.

of the wounded who were unable to extricate themselves from the field were left to spend the night where they fell. Since most of the wounded were within or adjacent to the Federal lines and the Union sharpshooters had a reputation for shooting litter bearers and ambulance workers, the Confederates were helpless to retrieve their fallen comrades. The scene in front of the Union lines was described by a Federal soldier:

Just as the sun was setting I went to the crest of the hill and took a look at the field. No words can depict the ghastly picture. The track of the great charge was marked by bodies of men in all possible positions, wounded, bleeding, dying and dead. Near the line where the final struggle occurred, the men lay in heaps, the wounded wriggling and groaning under the weight of the dead among whom they were entangled. In my weak and exhausted condition I could not long endure the gory ghastly spectacle. I found my head reeling, the tears flowing and my stomach sick at the sight. For months the specter haunted my dreams, and even after forty-seven years it comes back as the most horrible vision I have ever conceived.[308]

The bodies of the dead still littered the field when the controversies and discrepancies surrounding Pickett's charge began. One such inconsistency involves the number of participants who were actually involved and the casualties sustained in the attack. For the 1st VA this is further complicated because the regiment was on picket duty in Chambersburg on June 30 and did not file a muster report. Due to the high casualties among the regiment's officers, post battle reports are scanty or non-existent. Postwar recollections from the regiment's members tend to deflate the numbers engaged perhaps to inflate the percentage of casualties in Pickett's division, as if the actual numbers were not horrendous enough. The large quantity of dead and wounded men left on the field or in enemy hands further complicate the matter of determining casualties. It is virtually impossible to ascertain the exact numbers of those involved but, in the 1980s, John W. Busey conducted an exhaustive study of the rosters of Confederate units engaged at Gettysburg. Those rosters were further revised for the exceptional book, Nothing But Glory, Pickett's Division at Gettysburg"

308 "Statement of Benjamin W. Thompson, October 13, 1910, GNMP, as quoted in "The Damned Red Flags of the Rebellion", by Richard Rollins, Pg. 197.

which he co-authored with Kathleen R. Georg. It is those rosters that are used as a basis here. The 1st VA carried a total of approximately 230 officers and men into Pennsylvania. Allowing for sickness, guard duty and men being detailed to other tasks it is safe to assume the regiment's strength at the time of the battle was slightly less than 230. Out of that number the following men suffered casualties:

Regimental Staff:
Killed: Col. Lewis B. Williams.
Wounded: Major Frank Langley, Capt. William T. Fry.
Captured: Surgeon Alexander Grigsby (Stayed with the wounded and captured on July 5th).

Color Guard:
Killed: Private William L. Mitchel.
Wounded: Sgt. John Q. Figg, Private Theodore R. Martin.
Wounded and Captured: Sgt. Patrick Woods, Sgt. William M. Lawson.

Company "B":
Killed: Fendall Franklin.
Wounded: Lt. Jesse A. Payne, Privates Joseph R. Daniels, H.L. Spickard, Philip J. Vermillera.
Wounded and Captured: Captain Thomas H. Davis, Cpl. William I. Carter, Privates George R. Heath, William J. Mallory, John P. Overstreet, James Stagg, Richard H. Street.
Captured: Privates Ernst A. Gotze, George M. Tilghman.

Company "C":
Killed: Captain James Hallinan, Sgt. Edward Byrnes, Sgt. Charles Kean, Privates James D. Clark, William Crenshaw, Richard E. Giles, John E Scammel, James M. Thomas, John Tompkins, Robert Youell.
Wounded and Captured: Lt. John E. Dooley, Sgt. John Moriarty, Privates Hillery W. Collins, Eli M. Davis, John N. Johnson, Benjamin J. McCary, Alex E. Powell, Richard C. Price, Samuel H. Sloan.
Captured: Cpl. Timothy Costello (possibly deserted after the battle), Privates John D. Clark, Michael Consadine.

Company "D":
Killed: Privates David S. Edwards, J. W. Freeman, Marcellus J. "Monk" Wingfield.
Wounded: Captain George F. Norton, Lt. Edward P. Reeve, Lt. Adolphus Blair, Corp. George E. Craig, Corp. Charles T. Loehr, Private James B. Angle, William J. Armstrong, Delaware McMinn, Ezekial Priddy, Chasteen M. Sublett, John F. Wheeley, Samuel L. Wingfield.
Wounded and Captured: Lt. William H. Keiningham, Sgt. James M. Finn, Privates George W. Johnson, Joseph C. Keiningham, Tazewell S. Morton, Lemuel R. Wingfield.
Captured: 1st Sgt. John H. Keplar, Private Nathaniel W. Bowe (captured while serving as a hospital nurse).

Company "G":
Killed: Corp. William T. Miller, Private Gehn Doss.
Wounded: Captain Eldridge Morris, 1st Lt. William Woody, Sgt. William H. Deane, Sgt. Thomas H. Durham, Corp. John Allen, Privates James Farrar, Charles W. Gentry, William F. Kendrick, Cornelius A. Redford, Thomas S. Rogers, Norborne L. Royster, Alfred J. Vaughan, Robert R. Walthall.
Wounded and Captured: Privates Gustavus A. Chapman, Henry C. Fergusson, Thomas W. Hay, Benjamin H. Hord, William S. Layard, William H. Martin.
Captured: 1st Sgt. George W. Ball, Privates Benjamin T. Ashby, J. Ryland Epps (captured while serving as a hospital nurse), William F. Hord (captured while serving as a hospital nurse),James R. Fuller, Augustus L. Haskins, William Patterson (captured and deserted), George Walthus (captured and deserted).

Company "H":
Killed: Sgt. Calvin P. Hansford, Corp. Richard Chadick, Privates Mathew W. Bresnahan, Stephen Farson, B. S. St. Clair, William D. Waddell.
Wounded: Captain Abner J. Watkins, 1st Lt. Ellerson W. Martin, Lt. Paul C. Cabell, Privates Allen O. Clayton, Robert N. Dunn, Ryland H. Norvell, F. M. Smith.

Wounded and Captured: Corp. Walter R. Kilby, Privates William N. Anderson, Solomon Banks, John H. Daniel, Robert E. Dignum, William H. Duerson, E. C. Fiser, H. C. Hite, William B. Mosby, Thomas Mouring, Edward G. Nuckols, James W. Payne, John J. Sinnott, Nicholas L. Vaughan.
Captured: David Flowers.

Company "I":
Killed: Lt. William A. Caho, Corp. Lemuel O. Ellett, Privates E. J. Griffin, Hugh McLaughlan, Edwin Taliaferro.
Wounded: Corp. William F. Terry, Corp. Thomas E. Traylor, Privates C. H. Chappell, George Joy, Jacob R. Polak, George W. Shoemaker, Charles A. Wills.
Wounded and Captured: Corp. Calvin L. Parker, Corp. John T. Ayres, Privates Samuel Clark, Richard O. Meredith, Silvanus S. Neal.
Captured: Sgt. John T. Crew, Sgt. Edwin C. Goodson, Sgt. William T. White, Privates James E. Robinson, William C. Taliaferro Jr.

The casualties in the 1st VA totaled 146 or approximately sixty-six percent of the regiment's strength. This was the highest percentage of casualties of any regiment in Kemper's brigade, which must have perpetuated the feeling in Richmond that enlistment in the 1st VA was a very dangerous post. More appropriately, the statistic is testament to the courage of a band of men who despite insurmountable odds endeavored to do their duty. The cost in officers in the regiment was exceptionally high. The 1st VA effectively had no field grade officers remaining as their commander Col. Williams was killed, Major Frank Langley was wounded and Lt. Colonel Skinner remained absent, recuperating from the wounds he received at 2nd Manassas and who in fact would never return to duty. Of the six company commanders who took part in the engagement, only Captain James Hallinan of Company "C" was killed. Captain Thomas Herbert Davis of Company "B" was wounded and left on the field to be captured. Captains George Norton of Company "D," Eldridge Morris of Company "G," and Abner Watkins of Company "H" were all wounded. As previously stated, Capt. Benjamin Howard of Company "I" did not take part in the battle, leaving the company's command in the hands of 1st Lt. Henry Ballow the only company commander to escape unhurt. The other ten lieutenants of the regiment were not so lucky. One was killed and eight were wounded. Of the nineteen regimental officers who left Chambersburg on July 2nd, only three, 1 Captain and 2 Lieutenants, were present for duty on the morning of July 4th.[309]

In the minds of the men of Pickett's division, the biggest controversy surrounding the attack was the lack of support the division received during the assault. In the vast majority of written accounts the Virginians believed they accomplished their goal of breaching the Union lines but were unable to hold the position because of the absence of Confederate reinforcements. The plan had called for Lang's and Wilcox's brigades to support Pickett's right flank had these two brigades been within supporting distance, they may have relieved Kemper's brigade of the devastating fire from the Vermonters who completely disrupted Kemper's advance. That is not to say that their presence would have made the attack a success. It is undeniable that the original plan called for strong artillery support of the infantry during the assault, but bad management of the artillery reserves and supply wagons made this support almost non-existent.

The domino collapse of Pettigrew's troops, to the left of Pickett, has also been a source of controversy since the close of the battle. Many of the Virginians claim they saw no other units, other than those of Pickett's division, after they penetrated the Union works. This may be true, but at least some of Pettigrew's troops made it to the enemy breastworks, if not over them. Four out of five battle flags from Archer's brigade, which was to the immediate left of Pickett, were captured directly in front of the Union lines. That being said, it is interesting to note that in his official report for Archer's brigade, Lt. Col. S. G. Shepard, wrote "I cannot particularize where so many officers and men did their whole duty. There are doubtless some, however, as is always the case, who did not do their duty, and richly deserve the severest punishment that can be inflicted." Since most officers tend to embellish their unit's performance in their official reports, it is thought-provoking that Shepard would draw attention to the failings of at least some of the soldiers in his command. This could lead one to believe

---

[309] "Nothing But Glory", Kathleen R. Georg and John W. Busey, Pgs. 237-248. "War History of the Old First Virginia", Charles Loehr, Pgs. 37-38: Lee Wallace, "1st Virginia Infantry", Pgs. 81-123: "Record of the Richmond City and Henrico Co. Virginia Troops", Compiled by E. H. Chamberlayne, Jr., Richmond 1879.

that the conduct of many of the troops on this part of the line was less than stellar.[310]

The anguish felt by the men of the 1st VA and the entire division over the lack of support must have been corroborated by their commander, Gen Pickett, in his official report following the battle. The contents of the report are unknown, but it clearly was extremely critical of one or more of Pickett's fellow officers and possibly the troops under their command who were connected with the attack. Pickett's report prompted the following response from Gen. Lee:

General George Pickett,

General: Your and your men have crowned yourselves with glory; but we have the enemy to fight, and must carefully, at this critical moment, guard against dissensions which the reflections in your report would create. I will, therefore, suggest that you destroy both copy and original, substituting one confined to casualties merely. I hope all will yet be well.

I am, with respect, your obedient servant,
R.E. Lee
General[311]

In a supposed conversation during the night of July 3rd with Confederate cavalry Gen. John Imboden, Gen. Lee also voiced his concern over the lack of support for Pickett's division. Lee proclaimed, "I never saw troops behave more magnificently than Pickett's division of Virginians did today in the grand charge upon the enemy. And if they had been supported as they were to have been, but, for some reason not yet fully explained to me, were not, we would have held the position and the day would have been ours."[312]

It is mere speculation that if any or all of the shortcomings connected with Pickett's Charge had been corrected, the attack would have succeeded. It is quite possible that the Federal position was too well defended with

---

310 Official Records, Series 1, Volume 27, Part 2, "Report of Lieut. Col. S. G. Shepard, Seventh Tennessee Infantry, of operations of Archer's brigade". Pg. 647.

311 Official Records, Series 1, Volume 27, Part 3, Pg. 1075

312 "Battles and Leaders of the Civil War", Vol. 3, "Retreat from Gettysburg", published by A.S. Barnes and Co. Inc., 1956, "The Confederate Retreat from Gettysburg" by John D. Imboden, Brig. Gen. C.S.A., Pg. 421.

seasoned soldiers and well managed artillery to be taken by a frontal assault. In a conversation with Gen. Lee, Longstreet claimed to have warned something to the effect that no fifteen thousand men could take that position. Perhaps he was correct. No matter what the cause or who was to blame for the disaster, the 1st VA and Pickett's entire division would never fully recover from the battle on July 3rd, 1863.

RETURN TO DIXIE

On the morning of the 4th of July the remnants of the 1st VA gathered in the rain near their supply wagons. Jacob Polack, his arm in a sling and a slight wound to his face, pulled a flag from one of the wagons and began to wave it over his head, intimating a renewal of the attack. The remaining men of the regiment did not see any humor in his antics and asked him to return the flag to the wagon, which he promptly did. Later in the day the remnants of the regiment, along with the rest of Pickett's depleted division, was ordered to act as provost and escort approximately 4,000 Federal prisoners of war back to Virginia. After their horrid experience of the previous day, the men and officers of the division took this duty as an insult but begrudgingly followed orders. That afternoon, the division lined both sides of the road and the Yankee prisoners filed in between them and together they marched away from the small town of Gettysburg, the scene of so much carnage. They rested that night in Fairfield and started again early on the morning of the 5th. At one point along the march, sporadic musket fire was heard coming from in front of the slow moving column, which caused Pickett's men some alarm and gave the prisoners some hope of rescue. The Yankees were soon disappointed when it was ascertained that the musket fire came from a group of Confederate soldiers who were bivouacked in a nearby woods and were cleaning their weapons. The column pushed on to Williamsport, which they reached on the 8th of July. Upon reaching Williamsport they found the Potomac River swollen from the recent rains and were unable to ford it. On the following day, while they waited for the Potomac to recede the unwanted prisoners were happily turned over to Gen. Imboden's cavalry. [313]

The perceived humiliation of guarding the prisoners was relieved when Gen. Lee sent the following letter to Gen. Pickett:

Headquarters Army of Northern Virginia

July 9, 1863

Maj. Gen. George E. Pickett

General: Your letter of the 8th has been received.

It was with reluctance that I imposed upon your gallant division the duty of conveying prisoners to Staunton. I regretted to assign them to such service, as well as to separate them from the army, though temporarily, with which they have been so long and efficiently associated. Though small in numbers, their worth is not diminished, and I had supposed that the division itself would be loath to part from its comrades at a time when the presence of every man is so essential. I therefore felt gratified to be able to assign to the charge of the prisoners a portion of General Imboden's command, which I thought could be better spared from the army at this time, and enable him to muster into service some newly organized companies that have been completed since he left Staunton, shoe his horses, and return to the army more quickly than an infantry force. It would also spare your division a long and disagreeable march.

These were the reasons that governed me, and, in my opinion, are the best for the public service. I regret that it has occasioned you and your officers any disappointment. If circumstances permitted, I should be glad to allow your division to move to Winchester, if it would afford any gratification or benefit, but I need not tell you how essential it is not to diminish this army by a single man, if possible. I still have the greatest confidence in your division, and feel assured that with you at its head, it will be able to accomplish any service upon which it may be placed. You can send an efficient officer with a portion of your division that you may assign as a guard to the prisoners, as far as Winchester,

313 SHSP, Vol. 32, "The Old first Virginia at Gettysburg", by Charles Loehr, Pg. 37: Charles Loehr, "War History of the Old First Virginia Infantry Regiment", 38-39: B.F. Howard, Pg. 40.

with directions there to collect all your convalescents and others, and to return to you as soon as possible.

In the meantime, I trust you will lend all your energies as well as those of your division to sending off our wounded prisoners and all surplus articles belonging to the army, and having them conveyed beyond Winchester. No time should be lost in accomplishing this, and I rely mainly upon you to effect it.

No one grieves more than I do at the loss suffered by your noble division in the recent conflict, or honors it more for its bravery and gallantry. It will afford me heartfelt satisfaction, when an opportunity occurs, to do all in my power to recruit its diminished ranks, and to reorganize it in the most efficient manner.

Very respectfully, your obedient servant,

R. E. Lee
General

Gen. Pickett distributed the letter to the entire division, which boosted the spirits of the men in his command. Upon turning over the prisoners to Imboden's troopers, the 1st VA's service in the Pennsylvania campaign ended. All that was left for the regiment was to cross the Potomac into Virginia and try to recover from the ill-fated operation. [314]

On July 10th, after waiting two days for the water to ebb, the 1st VA along with the 3rd and 24th VA crossed the Potomac and went into camp about a mile from the river. The 7th and 11th VA remained in Maryland supporting a battery of artillery that was covering the army's retreat into Virginia. The 1st VA remained on the south side of the river, guarding the roads, until the 13th of July when the remainder of Pickett's division crossed the river. With the return of the 7th and 11th VA, the brigade was now reunited and they moved off in the direction of Martinsburg, stopping two miles from that place about midnight on the 13th. The brigade was reunited, but they were without their esteemed commander, Gen. Kemper, who because of his injuries was left in Gettysburg. After Kemper's encounter with Gen. Lee immediately following the battle, he was placed in an ambulance and started for the field hospital. The ambulance was upset by an errant Federal shell and the general was thrown to the ground. The severely wounded Kemper was carried to a makeshift

[314] Official Records, Series 1, Volume 27, Part 3, Pgs. 986-87.

hospital where the doctors believed his wound to be mortal. Kemper was among the thousands of Confederate wounded left at Gettysburg when the army retreated. In a communication to Union Gen. Halleck from Gen. Meade on July 6, he reported, "General J. L. Kemper was found mortally wounded on the road to Fairfield." Kemper was eventually moved to the temporary hospital at the Lutheran Seminary in Gettysburg where, against the odds, his condition improved. The general was moved to a hospital in Baltimore and ultimately, on August 24th, sent to Fort McHenry, in that city, as a prisoner of war. It was not until Kemper's arrival in Baltimore that news of his survival reached his family and friends back in Virginia. Up until this time he was presumed dead. He was exchanged on September 22nd at Fortress Monroe and spent the next several months recuperating at his home. Gen. Kemper would never again be physically able take the field in command of his illustrious brigade. In Kemper's absence, Col. Mayo of the 3rd VA assumed temporary command of the brigade.[315]

On the 14th of July, the brigade moved to the south of Martinsburg in a deluge of rain and camped in an open field with no protection from the storm. The men were soaking wet and there was no wood for them to light a fire to dry their clothes. Later in the day, the regiment moved nearer to some woods and soon had large bonfires blazing. The following day they were back on the road and marched seven miles to Bunker Hill, VA. The men rested here for three days before moving to the village of Smithfield in Jefferson County on the 19th of July. The brigade moved out at daybreak on the 20th and passed through Berryville on their way to Millwood where they bivouacked. That night the brigade was placed on picket duty guarding Berry's Ferry from marauding Yankee cavalry. They were relieved from picket duty at four in the morning on the 21st and immediately started off in the direction of Front Royal. The men struggled to cross the strong current of the Shenandoah River that afternoon and camped that night at Chester Gap on the summit of the Blue Ridge Mountains. Enemy cavalry had been in possession of the mountain passes, blocking the Confederates passage into eastern Virginia. Corse's brigade, which was waiting in Winchester to rejoin Pickett's division after missing

[315] Charles Loehr, "War History of the Old First Virginia", Pg. 38: Woodward, "The Confederacy's Forgotten Son", Pgs. 101-104: Official Records, Series 1, Vol. 27, Part 1, Pg. 80.

the battle of Gettysburg, was ordered to move ahead of the army and clear the passes at Chester and Manassas Gaps. After heavy skirmishing they managed to secure the passes on the day before the 1st VA arrived. Late in the afternoon on the 22nd of July, Kemper's brigade moved out to surprise an enemy battery that was reported to have remained on the mountain. After reaching the location and finding the battery gone, the brigade took to the road, reaching Gaines Cross-Roads at dawn on the 23rd. The regiment finally marched into Culpepper Court House on the 24th and rested there for a little over a week. On August 3rd, the brigade moved to Mountain Run on the Rapidan River and camped. While at that place, the regiment returned to a sense of normalcy, resuming regular drill and the regular duties associated with camp life. [316]

While the regiment was making its way back to Virginia the comrades they had to leave behind in Gettysburg were facing a far more harrowing experience. John Dooley left a vivid account of his experience as a Confederate officer in Union captivity after the battle. Dooley had been moved to a field hospital on the afternoon of the 4th of July, one day after being wounded in front of the Federal lines. The unprepared medical staff was completely overwhelmed by the sheer number of patients, both Union and Confederate, who were brought to the makeshift hospitals. The men were unloaded from the ambulances and laid on the wet ground, completely unprotected from the pouring rain. Dooley spotted John Scammell, also from Company "C," standing nearby, wringing out his soaking blanket. Scammell had a shell fragment buried in his chest and was convinced the wound was mortal. While the men waited to receive medical attention, attendants brought crackers and coffee, which the famished rebels devoured. The men spent a dreadful night suffering from their wounds as well as the inclement weather. The moans and shrieks from the suffering soldiers and the constant rumble of the never ending stream of creaking ambulances made sleep impossible. On the morning of July 5th, a Union officer gave Dooley the contents of John Scammell's pockets who, as the wounded Scammell had predicted, died just a short while earlier.

---

[316] Charles Loehr, "War History of the Old First Virginia", Pgs. 39-40: Official Records, Series 1, Vol. 27, Part 3, "Itinerary of Kemper's Brigade" Pg. 1091: Walter Harrison, "Pickett's Men, A Fragment of War History", Pg. 108.

Dooley surveyed the mangled men all around him, many from Kemper's brigade, including Col. Tazewell Patton of the 7th VA. The soldiers suffered from all sorts of hideous wounds and lay unattended as the overworked surgeons applied their craft to the multitude of injured men. One man, obviously in shock and delirious, repeated over and over, "I'm proud I belong to the 1st VA regiment!" On July 9th, Dooley and five or six other officers were placed in a tent and his wounds, which had become infected with maggots, were cleaned and bandaged for the first time. Over the next couple of days, as news of the horrible grief and suffering in Gettysburg circulated, nearby towns and cities began to send help. Medical supplies, food, tents, etc. began to pour into the beleaguered town, helping to relieve the sufferings of the soldiers. Civilians also came to the hospitals, personally bearing gifts of food and other essentials to help ease the pain of the patients. Some were locals from Gettysburg, such as a woman named Farnsworth, who commanded the respect of all who knew her. Others were from out of town, including a woman from New England who claimed to be the sister of Union General John Dix. Dooley was visited by Father Joseph O'Hagan who, prior to the war, was a teacher at Georgetown University when Dooley was there as a student. Father O'Hagan became a chaplain with the seventy-third NY and was serving in that capacity at Gettysburg. He brought Dooley clean shirts, preserved fruit and a bottle of wine also promising to return and have Dooley moved to Gen. Sickles' headquarters where he would be more comfortable. But, on the following day, July 12th, Dooley and his companions were taken by ambulance to the train station and placed in cattle cars destined for Baltimore.

Still unable to walk, Dooley lay on the floor of the train, his clothes caked in dried blood. To make matters worse, it was July 12th, his twenty-first birthday. The slow moving train jostled the injured men, causing excruciating pain to their wounds with each bump. They arrived in Baltimore that evening and were treated to hot coffee and crackers by some of the citizens of that city. The Yankee guards tried to keep the civilians, many of whom had southern sympathies, away from the Confederate prisoners but some managed to negotiate their way to the bedraggled rebels. They spent the night in the cattle cars awaiting transport, which came the following morning. The men were loaded into ambulances and moved through the city streets, under guard, to Fort McHenry. The hospital building on the grounds of the fort had become terribly overcrowded with the wounded from Gettysburg. Dooley and his companions were placed on the second floor of the guardhouse where they spread their blankets on the filthy floor and waited to see if this new location brought any relief to their sufferings.

The staff at Fort McHenry were completely overwhelmed by the enormous influx of prisoners, many of whom had serious wounds. On the 14th of July, Dooley and others were told they would be transferred to Fort Delaware, a prisoner of war camp located on the Delaware River. Still unable to walk, Dooley's comrades procured a stretcher and carried him to the docks where a steamer waited to transport them. The trip was postponed when Union women who were passengers on the boat strenuously objected to traveling with rebel officers. The men returned to their barracks to await their fate. This delay may have been a blessing in disguise for John Dooley. Although the medical attention he received at Fort McHenry was substandard, it undoubtedly exceeded any help he would have received at Fort Delaware. Another benefit to staying at Fort McHenry occurred a few days later when Dooley's uncle, a resident of Baltimore, learned of his incarceration and sent him a basket of food and some books. On the 28th of July, Dooley was moved to a hospital ward which proved to be much cleaner than the barracks. Unfortunately he was assigned to the top bunk on the second floor, lying directly below the buildings tin roof. The mid-summer sun beating down on the roof made his bunk akin to an oven. Fortunately this was a temporary annoyance and Dooley was eventually moved to a bunk on the lower level of the building which was much more comfortable.

The inmates spent their days playing chess and reading Yankee newspapers which they chose not to believe. At night the boredom was alleviated with the singing of songs. On August 22nd, after one month and ten days at Fort McHenry, Dooley and his comrades were taken to the train station in Baltimore and loaded into cars. Their new destination was the Union prisoner of war camp on Johnson Island, which was located in Lake Erie, near Sandusky, Ohio. Like many of those captured on the fields of Gettysburg, Lt. John Dooley would spend most of the remaining months of the war as a prisoner. Fortunately for Dooley, he was an officer.

As unpleasant as his circumstances were, they would have been far worse if he were among the ranks of the enlisted men.[317]

While Dooley was settling into his new home in Ohio, the 1st VA was on the move again back in Virginia. On Sept. 9th they were ordered to move from their camp at Mountain Run and head to Richmond. Unlike previous marches through the city that had more of a party atmosphere, the regiment marched through their hometown at attention. Therefor they were unable to fraternize with the family and friends who had gathered on the streets to witness their passing. After marching through the capital, the regiment moved to Chaffin's farm where they settled into winter quarters that were recently vacated by the men of Gen. Wise's command. On the 25th of September the regiment marched back to Richmond to board the cars of the Richmond, Fredericksburg and Potomac Railroad and moved to Taylorsville.[318]

The regiment, along with the rest of the brigade, commenced regular camp duties when they arrived at Taylorsville. In addition to drilling, the men participated in guarding railroad bridges and performing picket duty along the fords across the North Anna River. The threat of Yankee incursions occasionally triggered false alarms which caused the regiment to form in anticipation of battle. One such alarm was given when nervous pickets mistook a herd of cattle for marauding Yankee cavalry. This produced a good laugh at the embarrassed pickets' expense and the camp returned to a sense of normalcy. The regiment was slowly rejuvenated with the return of wounded soldiers and those prisoners who were fortunate enough to be exchanged and paroled. With the addition of some much needed recruits, the regiment's numbers climbed back to approximately 150. It was believed that the increase in recruits was once again due to the intercession of the commanding General, Robert E. Lee. If true, this was at least the third time that Gen. Lee personally took an interest in maintaining the viability of the 1st VA as a fighting force.

In their spare time, the men were busy building cabins to be used for

---

[317] Robert Emmett Curran, "John Dooley's Civil War, An Irish American's Journey in the First Virginia Infantry Regiment", pgs. 170-189: Joseph T. Durkin, "John Dooley, Confederate Soldier, His War Journal", Pgs. 114-132.

[318] Charles Loehr, "War History of the Old First Virginia Infantry Regiment." Pg. 40: E.P. Reeve letter to his wife, dated Sept. 16, 1863.

winter quarters. Captain Reeve wrote about his cabin, "it is a better one than I have ever had in camp before." While at Taylorsville, the regiment received their pay and a supply of clothing, including overcoats, a gift from the City Council of Richmond. As always, the lack of shoes remained the biggest problem, some of the men being completely barefoot. The food was not very good but was supplemented by the purchase of produce from local farmers. The more resourceful of the men used the bounty of a nearby persimmon field to make beer and coffee. The camp's close proximity to Richmond allowed for short furloughs to visit with family and friends. Another deviation to the boredom of camp life were weekly balls that were held in the nearby town of Ashland and were well attended, especially by the younger men of the 1st VA. A lot of the men remembered their time at Taylorsville as being very pleasant.[319]

The 1st VA, indeed, the entire brigade was a very different unit than it was prior to Gettysburg. Private John Wynn of Company "H" was wounded at 2nd Manassas and was away from the regiment for over a year. Upon his return, in early August 1863, he was amazed at how many of his old comrades were no longer present with the 1st VA. He wrote to his brother, "It is sad to think of how many young and noble boys that have fallen since we left Richmond in May of 61." The high number of casualties among the officers in the regiment led to many changes in its leadership. Major Francis Langley was promoted to Lt. Colonel to replace Col. Williams as commander of the regiment. As of August 31, 1863, Col. Skinner was still listed as the regimental commander but he had not taken the field since being wounded at 2nd Manassas. Lt. Col. Langley was listed as regimental commander of the 1st VA on the organization chart dated October 31, 1863. Captain Norton of Company "D" was promoted to Major and was replaced by Lt. E. P. Reeve as Captain of the Company. With the wounding of Gen. Kemper at Gettysburg, Col. Joseph Mayo of the 3rd VA took over temporary command of the brigade but was eventually replaced by Col. William Terry of the 24th VA, who was promoted to Brig. General. Gen. Kemper was exchanged and returned to Virginia, but the severity of his wound kept him from returning to active duty with the

319 Charles Loehr, "War History of the Old First Virginia Infantry Regiment." Pg. 40: E. P. Reeve letter to his wife, dated October 13, 1863, October 24, 1863 and November 23, 1863, December 29, 1863: B.F. Howard, pg. 44.

brigade that bore his name. Kemper did visit the brigade at least once, in early November, while they were camped at Taylorsville. The other regiments within the brigade also went through command changes in order to replace their many losses at Gettysburg.[320]

It became apparent that the Army of the Potomac and the Army of Northern Virginia were content to go into winter quarters without any further bloodshed. Perhaps the absolute slaughter on the fields of Gettysburg was enough carnage for 1863. The Confederate hierarchy began to look for ways on how best to use their limited manpower during the upcoming winter months. In mid-September, Gen. Longstreet, with Hood's and McLaws's divisions, left Virginia and took the cars for Tennessee to reinforce Gen. Bragg's army. Kemper's brigade, including the 1st VA, remained in camp at Taylorsville. Since their baptism of fire at Bull Run in 1861, when Longstreet was their brigade commander, this was the first time that the 1st VA was not under his command in some form.[321]

Corse's brigade of Pickett's division went with Longstreet to Tennessee. The other brigades of the division were scattered around Virginia. Garnett's old brigade now commanded by Brig. Gen. Eppa Hunton, was stationed at Chaffin's Farm below Richmond. Armistead's old brigade, now commanded by Brig. Gen. Seth Maxwell. Barton, was at Petersburg. Although the brigades were dispersed and each answered to a different commanding General, they were still considered a part of Pickett's division. Pickett himself, on September 23, 1863, was named commander of the Department of North Carolina with his headquarters in Petersburg, VA.[322]

The Coastal Region of North Carolina was an area of concern for the Confederate leadership. Union forces remained in control of most points along the Atlantic coast of the Confederacy, except for the port city of Wilmington, NC. Wilmington, which is located 30 miles up the Cape Fear River from the Atlantic Ocean, was the only major port in the south that was open to blockade runners. The Army of Northern Virginia was

---

320 Official Records, Series 1, Vol. 29. Part 2, Pgs. 682, 783: Charles Loehr, "War History of the Old First Virginia Infantry Regiment." Pg. 40: E.P. Reeve letter to his wife, dated Nov. 16, 1863 "Camp at Taylorsville".

321 James Longstreet, "From Manassas to Appomattox", Pgs. 434-436

322 Walter Harrison, "Pickett's Men", Pgs. 108-109: Official Records, Series 1, Volume 29 Part 2, Pg. 746.

dependent upon Wilmington for all of its imported supplies. The Cape Fear was defended by a series of forts, most notably Fort Fisher and Fort Caswell, which protected the inlet from the blockading Union fleet. In the fall of 1863 it was under the command of Major General W.H.C. Whiting. As early as August 31, 1863, Gen. Whiting began writing to his superiors in Richmond requesting more troops for the defense of Wilmington. In a lengthy letter to the Secretary of War, James A. Seddon, Whiting wrote, "I know of no place now in the Confederacy where the presence of a large body of veteran troops is more necessary or more important than this." Whiting went on to compare the significance of Wilmington to that of Vicksburg, which surrendered two months previous.[323]

Gen. Pickett in his new role as commander of the Department of North Carolina was ordered to cooperate with the sometimes cantankerous Gen. Whiting at Wilmington. When the armies ceased active operations in Northern Virginia, Whiting increased his requests for more troops to be sent to Wilmington. It was Whiting's contention that if the army was going into winter quarters, at least one brigade could spend the winter within his jurisdiction. Pickett agreed with the precaution of moving some troops to North Carolina for the winter. Both men expected the Federals to commence some sort of offensive operations from their bases along the coast in that state. Along with Wilmington, Pickett believed Kinston, NC was key to the defense of the coastal region. It was his belief that no enemy force could move from New Bern toward Wilmington without first seizing Kinston. Pickett wanted to base a large force at Goldsboro where they could be easily transported by rail to Kinston or Wilmington if either place were threatened.[324]

Unbeknownst to Gen. Whiting or Gen. Pickett, however, President Davis and General Lee had their own plans for Kemper's brigade. On January 2, 1864, Gen. Lee wrote to President Davis, "The time is at hand when, if an attempt can be made to capture the enemy's forces at New Bern, it should be done." Lee went on to say he could spare one brigade from the army to augment the force already in the vicinity of Kinston,

---

323 Official Records, Series 1, Volume 33, Pgs. 1071-72.

324 Official Records, Series 1, Volume 33, "Whiting to Cooper" Pg. 1064; "Pickett to Cooper" Pgs. 1067-68; "Whiting to Cooper" Pg. 1069; "Pickett to Cooper" Pgs. 1071-74.

which included Armstead's old brigade now under the command of Brig. Gen. S. M. Barton. The goal of the attack would be to capture New Bern and the large amount of Union supplies that were thought to be there. With the Federal garrison eliminated, the Confederate commissary could also gather food and supplies from the adjacent area. Two days later, President Davis approved Lee's plan and thought the venture important enough to suggest that Lee go to North Carolina to personally oversee the operation. Davis offered to go himself if the General could not get away from the Army of Northern Virginia. A sitting president offering to take the field during an offensive operation leads one to speculate if Davis was losing faith in his military commanders, except of course for Robert E. Lee. It was finally decided that Lee was not comfortable leaving the Army of Northern Virginia when "there was such a struggle to keep the army fed and clothed" and Gen. Pickett was put in overall command of the operation.[325]

The plans of the Confederate high command ended the regiment's time at Taylorsville on January 8, 1864, when together with the rest of the brigade they were ordered to take the cars to Richmond. They arrived in the capital in the early morning hours and marched over snow covered streets to the southern station, where they took the cars and moved off to Petersburg. In Petersburg, the men disembarked, camped near the reservoir for the day and cooked rations for the upcoming journey. That night they switched trains and travelled to Weldon, NC, where they arrived the following day. The brigade was delayed in Weldon while they waited for trains to carry them on to Goldsboro. The Virginians of Kemper's brigade did not get along very well with the local populace at Weldon. Capt. Reeve wrote of "a considerable row which fortunately ended without serious consequences." Prior to leaving the city, however, a member of the 24th VA was shot and killed by a member of the North Carolina provost guard, causing "great excitement among the men." Fearing retaliation by the hardened veterans of Kemper's brigade, the authorities rushed the men onto the trains before many of them knew what had happened. The brigade eventually moved on to camp two miles outside of Goldsboro. As it turned out, this was the same campground they had occupied a year

[325] Official Records, Series 1, Volume 33, "Lee to Davis" pg. 1061, "Davis to Lee" pg. 1064, "Lee to Davis" pg. 1101.

previous. On the 29th of January they moved again, this time to Kinston, where Gen. Pickett was consolidating a force for the attempted attack on New Bern, NC.[326]

New Bern was located at the confluence of the Trent and Neuse Rivers, with the Trent River running to the south of the town and the Neuse River to the north. Gen. Lee, with the advice of Gen. Robert F. Hoke, who was familiar with the area, presented his plan of attack to Gen. Pickett on January 20th. Hoke's brigade was dispatched from the Army of Northern VA and sent to North Carolina, which gave Pickett a total of about thirteen thousand men with which to assault the Federal works. The plan called for a three pronged attack on the town. Gen. Barton was in command of one of the prongs. It was composed of his own brigade, part of Gen. Ransom's brigade and Kemper's brigade, including the 1st VA. He also had fourteen cannon and six hundred cavalry. Barton's force was to move south of the Trent River and cut all enemy communication with reinforcements along the coast. Barton was then to re-cross the Trent River, via the railroad bridge of the Atlantic and North Carolina Railroad, and attack the town from the rear. Col. James Dearing, commanding a second prong, was to move along the north side of the Neuse River with two regiments and capture Fort Anderson, turning the guns in the fort to support the attack. Gen. Hoke, leading the third prong and with Pickett in attendance, was to move between the two rivers with his own brigade, Clingman's brigade and part of Corse's brigade and attack the town from the front. Two hundred naval personnel, under the command of Col. R. Taylor Wood, were to descend the Neuse River in small boats and capture any Union gun boats in the river, using them to support the land attack.[327]

The 1st VA, along with the rest of Kemper's brigade, under the command of Col. William Terry, began the march to New Bern on January 30th. They crossed over to the south side of the Trent River and for two days marched through swamps and over muddy roads. Along the way the Confederates

---

326 Charles Loehr, "War History of the Old First Virginia Infantry Regiment" pgs. 40-41: B. F. Howard, pg. 44: E.P. Reeve letter to his wife, "Camp Near Goldsboro, January 13, 1864".

327 Official Records, Series 1, Volume 33, "Lee to Pickett" pg. 1102; "Report of Maj. Gen. George E. Pickett" pg. 92: John G. Barrett, "The Civil War in North Carolina", The University of North Carolina Press, Chapel Hill NC, 1963, Pg.203.

surprised and overtook several Union outposts. On February 1st the force arrived in front of the Union lines. Skirmishers were sent forward and the brigade formed a line of battle. Artillery within the Union works opened fire on the advancing Confederates. Barton brought up his own guns and an artillery duel ensued. The infantry was halted while Barton conducted a survey of the Union works. Meanwhile the men could hear the muffled sounds of the distant fight that Hoke's column was conducting on the other side of the Trent River in front of New Bern. Barton came to the conclusion that the defenses on this side of the river were much stronger than he was led to believe. He found no point that could be successfully attacked with the force he had at hand. Barton communicated this news to Gen. Pickett, who in turn ordered Barton to cross the river and join Hoke's attack in front of New Bern. Before the forces could be united for a grand assault, however, the enemy garrison in New Bern was reinforced by trains from Morehead City. The trains crossed the very railroad bridge into New Bern that Barton was supposed to capture and use for his own entry into the town. Dearing's attack on the north side of the Neuse River also failed to capture Fort Anderson. The assault by Col. Wood on the river did succeed in capturing the gunboat UNDERWRITER but Wood was forced to burn the boat before they could use her guns on the enemy works. Since the northern and southern columns failed in their objectives, Gen. Pickett decided it was prudent to call off the attack.[328]

The attack was considered a failure but the men under Pickett's command did capture some men and equipment, including two rifled cannon. Pickett and Hoke placed blame for the failure on Gen. Barton for not attacking New Bern from the south and his lack of cooperation. Seven months after their deadly charge across the open fields of Gettysburg, it is not known how the men of the 1st VA felt about Gen. Barton's refusal to assault the fortified fixed position at New Bern. The assault was held in such tight secrecy that the men seemed to be in the dark as to the actual objective of the expedition, but they did recognize that the mission had failed. The regiment, along with the rest of the ill-fated expedition returned to Kinston over the same muddy roads that had deteriorated even further

[328] Official Records, Series 1, Volume 33, "Report of Maj. Gen. George E. Pickett" pg. 92, "Report of Gen. Seth M. Barton" pgs. 97-99: Charles Loehr, "War History of the Old First Virginia Infantry", Pg. 41.

since their arrival. The trek back to Kinston was so bad that even veterans described the march as the most disagreeable they had ever been on. By the time they reached Kinston, they were so caked in mud that they were unrecognizable.[329]

Some of the Federal prisoners captured at New Bern belonged to the 2nd North Carolina Loyal Regiment. Among the members of that regiment were Confederate deserters who had joined the Union army and volunteered to fight against their former comrades. A few of these men were recognized as deserters and in an effort to gain favor with their captors, they identified other members of the regiment who were also Confederate deserters. More and more captives were branded as deserters and eventually thirty-five men were put on trial. About twenty-six of the deserters were sentenced to hang, including the original informants. The executions took place very near Kemper's brigade's camp but it is unclear if any of the men of the 1st VA witnessed the horrid scene. After moving to Goldsboro, a similar event took place that was of a more personal nature and was witnessed by the regiment. A member of the 7th VA was sentenced to be shot by firing squad for desertion. On the 18th of February, the entire brigade including the 1st VA was formed up in a hollow square. The brigade formed three sides of the square and the condemned man rode out in a wagon and was securely tied to a stake at the open end of the square. The firing squad was made up of men from the doomed man's own regiment, the 7th VA, which formed in the middle of the square. The band played a dirge and the chaplain said prayers for the poor man's soul. The command was given and the firing squad discharged their weapons into the deserter's body, killing him instantly. Solemn, gruesome spectacles such as these were intended to reduce the number of desertions from the Confederate ranks.[330]

While at Goldsboro, the regiment drilled twice a day and the normal duties of camp life resumed. Civilians from the city rode out to the camp to watch the soldiers go through their evolutions and dress parades. When camped near Goldsboro the young men of the regiment took delight in

---

329 Official Records, Series 1, Volume 33, pg. 92; E.P. Reeve, Letter to his wife, Feb. 5, 1864 "Camp near Kinston".

330 Walter Harrison, "Pickett's Men", pg. 116-120: David E. Johnston, "Four Years a Soldier"; Pg. 293, Charles Loehr, "War History of the Old First VA" Pg. 41.

visiting town and the young ladies that lived there. They made these outings both with and without official permission. As previously noted, there was no love lost between the North Carolina Provost Guard and the Virginians of Kemper's brigade. The Provost took every opportunity to catch and arrest soldiers who were in town without a pass. Twenty year old Private Delaware McMinn was a regular illicit visitor to Goldsboro and led the Provost on many a chase through the streets of the town, evading the North Carolinians on each occasion. On one such visit, the Provost spotted McMinn and immediately went for him. McMinn led the men on an unusually long race through the streets and alleys of the town. When he was finally hemmed in by the Provost, McMinn halted and with a large grin on his face pulled out a legitimate pass allowing him to visit Goldsboro. The North Carolinians were not amused by the Virginian's shenanigans but were powerless to do anything about it. The 1st VA continued to grow, perhaps through the indulgence of Gen. Lee. Company "D" the largest company in the regiment, boasted nearly sixty members. Numbers this large had not been seen since early in the war. The regiment was also praised for having the best kept camp and weapons in the brigade.[331]

Now that the New Bern expedition was over, Gen. Whiting in Wilmington, NC, resumed his letter writing campaign to bolster the number of troops within his district. On February 28th he wrote, "Kemper's brigade was assigned to me, but the New Bern expedition was ordered, of which that formed part. Since then I am not aware that it is at my disposal. My great need is to have such an addition to the permanent garrison as to enable me to prevent the works at the mouth of the river from being turned or surprised. I cannot do this as things now are." On March 2nd, Kemper's brigade was ordered to Wilmington, NC. The following day Gen. Benjamin Butler's Union army on the James River Peninsula began to move, raising the alarm in Richmond. The fear of an attack on the capital prompted the authorities to call for all available troops, including Kemper's brigade, to be sent to Richmond. The report of the enemy threat turned

---

[331] Charles Loehr, "Only a Private", Paper read before Pickett Camp, CV in 1894, Printed in Richmond Newspaper, March 2, 1894: E. P. Reeve, Letters to his wife, February 23, 1865 "Camp near Kinston"; February 14, 1864, "Camp Near Goldsboro".

out to be incorrect and on March 4th the brigade finally took the cars to Wilmington, where they arrived the next day.[332]

The regiment, along with the entire brigade, marched through the streets of Wilmington on their way to the wharf. Apparently the sight of Kemper's battle tested veterans caused quite a stir among the residents and sailors in the city. Sergeant John Wynne of Company "H" described the scene: "We stopped in Wilmington all night and the next morning early, three fine steamers were in readiness for us. We were soon on board and the steamers moved off very gracefully to a beautiful air played by the 7th regiment's band. It was a grand scene, there were several large blockade steamers in the harbor with all their colors floating in the southern breeze and the neatly dressed sailors were crowded on the decks and rigging to witness our departure and from the windows and porticos throughout the city could be seen the snow white handkerchiefs waved by the hands of Carolina's fair daughters, may the foot of the invader never pollute the streets of their beautiful town. The sun shone in all its brilliancy the river was calm and placid and everything around seemed filled with grandeur and magnificence, we all became enthusiastic and cheer after cheer rolled over the water of the beautiful Cape Fear as onward we flew down its swift and silent current."[333]

The steamers carried the men 30 miles down the Cape Fear River to the town of Smithville. Smithville (now named Southport) sits at the mouth of the river on the western shore. The entrance to the river was protected on the north side by Fort Fisher, located on the tip of the peninsula created by the Cape Fear River and the Atlantic Ocean. On the south side of the inlet sat Fort Caswell, located on Oak Island. The purpose of these two forts, as well as other lesser forts, was to block the Union navy from entering the Cape Fear River and attacking Wilmington. Blockade runners also depended on the forts for support as they attempted to sneak past the Union navy with their vital supplies for the Confederacy. The commander in Wilmington, Gen. Whiting, feared a land attack on the

---

332 Official Records, Series 1, Vol. 33, "Whiting to Bragg" pg. 1200, "Cooper to Whiting", "Cooper to Pickett", "Cooper to Lee" pg. 1206, "Pickett to Cooper" pg. 1210.

333 John Wynne, Letter to his brother, March 15, 1864, Eleanor S. Brockenbrough Library, Museum of the Confederacy/American Civil War Museum, Richmond VA.

forts and it was to counter such a threat that Kemper's brigade was sent to Smithville.

The regiment camped about one mile south of the town and resumed drills and the daily duties of camp life. The surrounding area was very poor and guards were placed at farms and residences to keep the soldiers from foraging. The men mostly dined on the abundant seafood that the area was known for. Crabs, shrimp and especially oysters were a welcome change from their normal army fare. The men spent their free time spectating as blockade runners slipped past the Union fleet and sailed up the river to Wilmington. The Union ships pursued the blockade runners, frequently coming within range of the heavy guns within the surrounding forts. The ensuing barrage produced a show of light and sound for the bored men of the 1st VA who lined the shore to watch these spectacles. The 24th VA was sent across the river to Oak Island where they reinforced the garrison at Fort Caswell. On one occasion the blockade runner LUCY ran aground trying to evade her Federal pursuers. As the Union ships closed in for the kill, men from the 24th VA helped to relocate cannon that eventually drove off the Yankee ship. On the next high tide the LUCY freed herself and continued on to Wilmington with her valuable cargo. The men witnessed the sinking of another Union ship that strayed too close to Fort Caswell and took a direct hit from one of the fort's Whitworth guns. For some, watching the ships, eating seafood and collecting sea shells was very agreeable duty and they were quite content to finish out the war relaxing at the beach. While still others in the regiment were anxious to get back to Virginia and the war.[334]

On March 22nd Gen. Pickett relayed a telegram to Richmond that he received from Gen. Corse in Kinston, NC. In the telegram Corse claimed that Union Gen. Burnside had moved a substantial force to Washington, NC, threatening the Confederate strongholds at Kinston and Goldsboro. Pickett followed up with a similar report that he received from Confederate forces in Tarboro, NC. Pickett ended the dispatch with "Whiting must send troops to me." On March 23rd, Kemper's brigade was ordered to move immediately to Kinston in an attempt to counter this latest threat

[334] David E. Johnston, "Four Years a Soldier", Pg. 294-95: Charles Loehr, "War History of the Old First Virginia" pg. 42: Howard Malcomb Walthall, pgs. 27-28: B.F. Howard, pg. 45.

by the Union Army. The 1st VA's time at the seaside resort came to an end when, along with the rest of the brigade, they boarded the steamer CAPE FEAR on March 24th and sailed back up the river to Wilmington. As this was considered a "case of emergency," the railroad was cleared of all other traffic and the brigade was immediately loaded onto the trains. The men were transported to Goldsboro arriving later that same day.[335]

The 1st VA, along with the rest of the brigade, remained in camp at Goldsboro until April 1st, at which time they received orders to move to Tarboro. That move took three days over muddy and sometimes snow covered roads. Upon reaching Tarboro, they crossed the Tar River and made camp on the eastern bank about one and half miles outside of town. The initial threat from Gen. Burnside subsided and the Confederate generals began to strategize on how to best use their force in North Carolina before Gen. Lee recalled them to the Army of Northern Virginia for the spring campaign. The plan that was decided upon was an attack on the union fortress and supply depot at Plymouth, NC. Kemper's brigade, under the command of Col. William Terry, along with Gen. Robert Ransom's and Hoke's brigades, was ordered to take part in the attack. The force also included the 38th VA Battalion of artillery and Gen. Dearing's Cavalry. Kemper's was the only infantry brigade from Pickett's division to participate in the assault. Overall command of this force was given to Gen. R.F. Hoke, perhaps in reward for his performance at New Bern. The brigade left Tarboro on the 15th of April and marched for 2 ½ days, arriving before Plymouth on the 17th.

Plymouth's location on the southern bank of the Roanoke River near The Albermarle Sound made it an ideal location for a Union supply depot. The river was protected by the U.S. Navy gun boats MIAMI and SOUTHFIELD as well as the smaller boats WHITEHEAD and CERES. The town was protected on the landward side by a semi-circle of forts and earthworks which were manned by Union soldiers from the 16th Connecticut Volunteers, 85th New York Volunteers, 101st Pennsylvania Volunteers, 103rd Pennsylvania Volunteers and two companies of 12th New York Cavalry. Also a part of the garrison were two companies of the 2nd North Carolina Volunteers. These were local troops that like at New

335 Official Records, Series 1, Volume 33, pgs. 1236, 1238, 1240: Charles Loehr, "War History of the Old First Virginia" pg. 42.

Bern, contained some deserters from the Confederate Army. The forts also boasted six guns from the 24th New York Independent Battery and guns manned by the 2nd Massachusetts Heavy Artillery, including a 32 pounder mounted on a naval carriage. The post was under the overall command of Brig. General Henry W. Wessells.[336]

When the 1st VA arrived at Plymouth on the evening of April 17th, they were positioned to the west of town. The western defenses were anchored by three forts. Fort Gray was located two miles from the town on the Roanoke River and was manned by members of the 85th NY and the 2nd Massachusetts Heavy Artillery. Next in the semi-circle to the south was Fort Wessell, also known as the 85th Redoubt, named after the 85th NY who constructed the works. East of Fort Wessell was Fort Williams, the largest of the forts, which commanded the southern approaches and the main roads into the town.

The 1st VA formed a skirmish line and approached Fort Gray with their left flank resting on the river. The skirmishers advanced to within 900 yards of the fort before the defenders opened a robust fire with their cannon. The fire was answered by the Richmond Fayette Artillery, who before the war was Company "F" of the 1st VA. An artillery duel ensued with the shells from both sides flying over the heads of the confederate infantry. According to Capt. Howard of Company "I," the exploding shells forced the line of skirmishers "to hug mother earth very close." At one point the Union gun boat CERES made a run down the river, attracting fire from both the Confederate batteries and infantry alike. The cannonade continued till approximately 8 PM when things quieted down across the battlefield. At 9 PM the CERES made another run up the river but this time the rebels heard the boat approaching and were prepared to unleash a terrific fire into her, causing damage to the boat and killing or wounding nine Union sailors.[337]

After the firing died down, a detachment of men from the 1st VA took refuge in a recently abandoned house near the river. The men were happily surprised to find a variety of food within the house that had been left by

---

336 Official Records, Series 1, Volume 33, pgs. 296-297 "Report of Gen. Wessells": John G. Barrett, "The Civil War in North Carolina", 213-14.

337 B.F. Howard, Pgs. 45-46: David E. Johnston, "Four Years a Soldier", Pg. 46: Official Records, Series 1, Volume 33, pgs. 296-297 "Report of Gen. Wessells".

the former occupants. A fire was lit and the hungry soldiers began to cook their new found bounty. The light from the cook fire shone through the window facing the Confederate lines who mistook it for another Union gun boat. Confederate artillery began lobbing shells in the direction of the frame house and its Rebel occupants. Word was quickly sent back, informing the gunners of their deadly mistake. Fortunately no one was hurt in the mishap but the following morning Union guns in Fort Gray began their own bombardment of the little house. One of the first shells struck the stairs on which two members of the 1st VA, Lt. Jesse Payne and Private Tom Minor, were standing, toppling the two men to the ground. Seeing that the two men were unhurt, Delaware McMinn of Company "D" found their ungainly fall to be hysterical. As he stood laughing at his comrades' misfortune, a second shell came through the wall, killing McMinn instantly.[338]

The cannonade resumed on the 18th of April between the forts and the Confederate batteries. Sharpshooters on both sides of the struggle also continued their deadly craft. The armed transport BOMBSHELL moved down river toward Fort Gray and was fired upon by the rebel guns. She received damage below the water line and returned to the docks of Plymouth where she sunk. The 1st VA remained in front of Fort Gray until 4 PM when they were relieved by the 11th VA. With the remainder of the brigade they moved six miles around the semi-circle to the south and east. The route of march took them through swamps and bogs but they managed to arrive in front of Fort Wessells about 8 PM. Fort Wessells was located approximately 1000 yards to the southwest of the town and contained several heavy guns. Sharpshooters were mounted on the parapet of the fort which was surrounded by a deep ditch and heavy abatis.

Fort Wessells had been under siege during the day and had successfully repelled every attempt to seize it. In an earlier assault, Col. Mercer of the 21st GA was killed while leading his men in a failed attempt to breach the breastworks. Kemper's brigade arrived in front of the fort and was forced to counter march to get into their proper position. The maneuver was done under a severe fire from the enemy but was done in good order. After

---

338 Charles Loehr, "War History of the Old First Virginia" pg. 43: Charles Loehr, Paper read before Pickett Camp C.V. and printed in a Richmond Newspaper, March 2, 1894.

the infantry lines were established, the Confederate artillery was pushed up closer to the fort and began a furious bombardment. Hoke's brigade attacked the works and once again were repulsed by the defenders who used hand grenades, a relatively new and seldom used weapon, to help hold off the invaders. The Confederates, who were also under fire from the gun boats in the river and the artillery in Fort Williams, continued to maneuver until Fort Wessells was completely cut off from the town and any Union support. The Confederate bombardment and musket fire eventually proved to be too much for the defenders and the fort surrendered during the night.[339]

The final piece of Gen. Hokes' plan to capture Plymouth came into play during the early morning hours of the 19th with the arrival of the Confederate iron plated ram ALBERMARLE under the command of Commander James W. Cooke. Hoke knew he must take control of the river if he was to successfully attack the town. Fortunately the Confederate Navy had been in the process of building an iron clad further up the Roanoke River at Edwards Ferry. The construction of the ALBERMARLE was completed just in time for her to take part in the attack. In fact workmen were still aboard the ram completing the final touches when she started up the river to take part in the operation against Plymouth. At 3 AM on the 19th of April the guns of Fort Gray announced the arrival of the ALBERMARLE. The ship ignored the fire coming from the fort. Instead, Cooke steered a course directly toward the Union gun boats that were waiting to take on the larger Confederate vessel. The ALBERMARLE rammed the SOUTHFIELD, penetrating nine feet of her prow into the hapless boat. At the same time she fired a broadside into the MIAMI, killing many of her crew, including Lt. Commander Flusser, who was in command of the Union flotilla. The SOUTHFIELD sunk so quickly she threatened to take the entangled ALBEMARLE down with her. Cooke managed to extricate the prow of the ALBERMARLE from the sinking boat and immediately turned his attention to the remaining Union gun boats. Realizing their wooden boats were no match for the iron plated ram,

339 John Wynne, Letter to his Father, "Near Plymouth NC April 24/64": David E. Johnston, "Four Years a Soldier", Pg. 297-298: Official Records, Series 1, Volume 33, pgs. 296-297 "Report of Gen. Wessells".

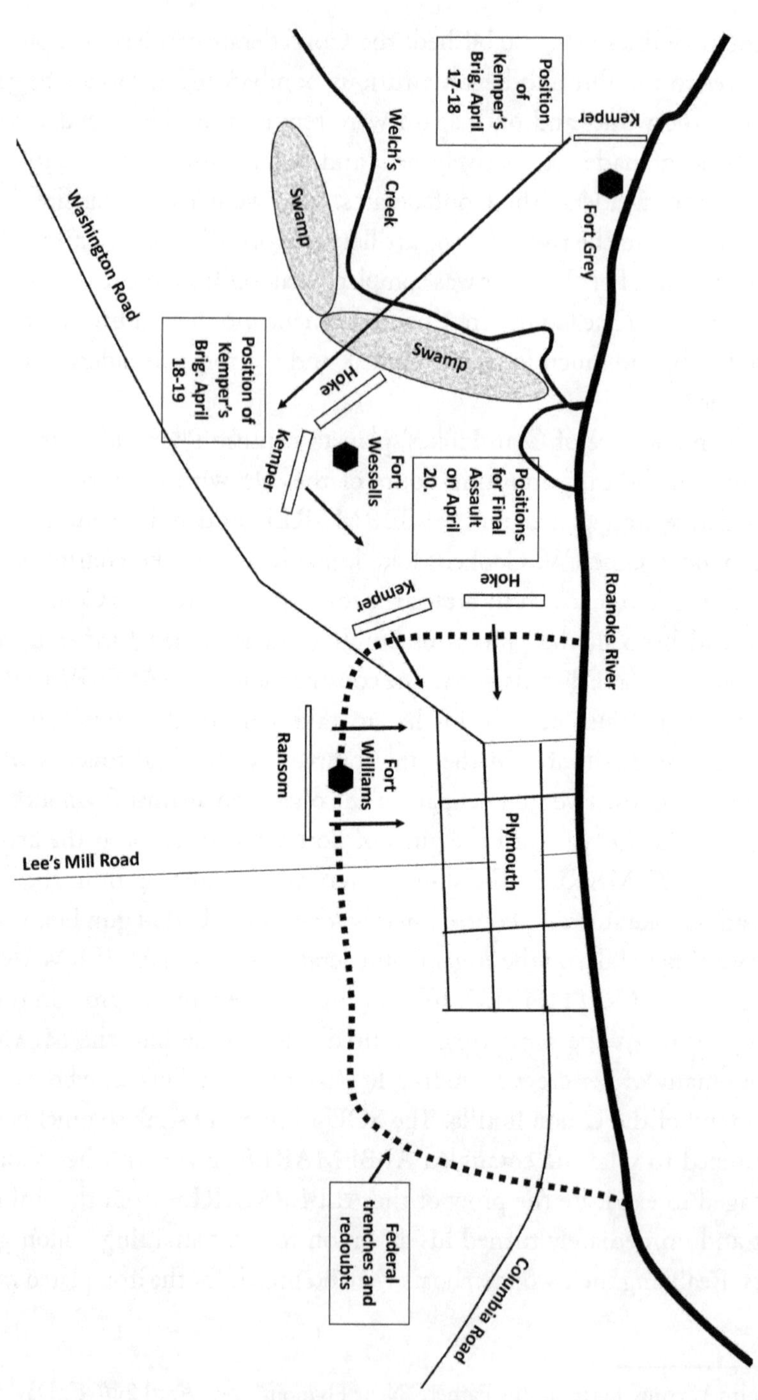

The Battle of Plymouth
April 17 – 20, 1864

the Federals retreated up the river toward Albermarle Sound, leaving the river in control of the Confederates and sealing the fate of Plymouth.[340]

Now that the threat from the Union gun boats had been removed and the additional fire power of the ALBERMARLE was added to his force, Gen. Hoke began to formulate his plans for the final assault on Fort Williams. Fort Williams was the largest of the forts. It sat due south of town and controlled the main roads coming from that direction. The 1st VA spent the remainder of April 19th skirmishing with the enemy riflemen in the breastworks of that fort. Another member of the regiment, 29 year old Michael Consadine, was killed during the skirmishing. Like McMinn who was killed the day before, Consadine was a member of the original group who enlisted in the 1st VA three years earlier, almost to the day, on April 21, 1861.

The following morning, April 20th, under a flag of truce, Gen. Hoke asked for the surrender of the Union garrison. Even though his situation seemed hopeless, Gen. Wessells refused to surrender. For the final assault, Kemper's brigade was in the center with Hoke's brigade to the left, and Ransom's brigade to the right. The Confederate artillery working in concert with the guns on the ALBERMARLE, opened a terrific barrage on Fort Williams. The cannonade was so intense that the gunners inside the fort could not man their own guns without being killed. The infantry advanced, shooting at anything that moved inside the fort. Eventually Ransom's men worked their way around the fort and into the town. At 10 AM a white flag was hoisted over the beleaguered Fort Williams and the battle of Plymouth came to an end.[341]

After three years of hardship, a lack of food, clothing and equipment, the men were allowed to take whatever they desired from the vast stores of Union supplies found within the town. The 1st VA stacked arms, dumped the meagre contents of their haversacks and began to fill them with all

---

340 J. Thomas Scharf, "History of the Confederate States Navy", Gramercy Books a division of Random House Value Publishing Inc. 40 Engelhard Ave., Avenel, New Jersey 17001, 1996: John G. Barrett, "The Civil War in North Carolina", Pg. 218.

341 Official Records, Series 1, Volume 33, pgs. 298-299 "Report of Gen. Wessells": John Wynne, Letter to his Father, "Near Plymouth NC April 24/64": Charles Loehr, "War History of the Old First Virginia" Pgs. 43-44: David E. Johnston, "Four Years a Soldier", Pg. 299-301.

sorts of foodstuffs and delicacies. Men were seen carrying several pairs of shoes and boots, blankets and all types of clothing. For many it was their first opportunity to acquire a rifled musket, discarding their less accurate smoothbores. The Confederacy also benefited from the surrender of Plymouth. Besides approximately 2,500 prisoners of war, the captured items included wagons, 500 horses, 5,000 stands of small arms, 28 pieces of artillery, a large amount of ordinance and vast amounts of commissary and quartermaster stores. All of which would benefit the Army of Northern Virginia greatly in the upcoming campaign.[342]

The thanks of the Confederacy was demonstrated in the following joint resolution from the Confederate Congress issued on May 17, 1864*:*

Resolved by the Congress of the Confederate States of America. That the thanks of Congress and the country are due and are tendered to Maj. Gen. Robert F. Hoke and Commander James W. Cooke, and the officers and men under their command, for the brilliant victory over the enemy at Plymouth N.C.[343]

A partial list of casualties in the 1st VA during the battle for Plymouth are as follows:

Killed – Privates Delaware McMinn of Company "D" and Michael Consadine of Company "C."

Wounded – Lieutenant J. A. Payne of Company "B"; Privates Theoderick J. Robertson of Company "D", Wilson B. Joseph, Henry H. Toler and Isham Belcher of Company "H".

The regiment remained in the vicinity of Plymouth until the 25th of April when the brigade and the rest of Hoke's command marched to Jamesville. The following day they arrived in front of Washington, NC. Gen. Hoke had hoped to capitalize on his success by driving the Federals out of Washington and then moving on for another attempt to capture the Union force at New Bern.[344]

Gen. Hoke delayed the assault on Washington when he learned the

---

342 Charles Loehr, "War History of the Old First Virginia" Pg. 44: John G. Barrett, "The Civil War in North Carolina", Pg. 220.

343 Official Records, Series 1, Volume 33, Pg. 305.

344 Lee Wallace, "1st Virginia Infantry", Pgs. 81-123: "Record of the Richmond City and Henrico Co. Virginia Troops", Compiled by E. H. Chamberlayne, Jr., Richmond 1879.Charles Loehr, "War History of the Old First Virginia" Pg. 44

Union garrison was vacating the town. When the Confederate troops entered Washington they were sickened by the scenes of wanton destruction that the Yankees had left in their wake. Upon learning of their impending abandonment of Washington, some of the Federal troops had begun to loot the town. The criminal behavior became wide spread, the looters not only pillaging government property but also private homes and businesses. Fires had been started and quickly spread, destroying half of the town. Not only were the Confederate soldiers outraged by the devastation found in Washington, the Union commander was equally disgusted with the conduct of the soldiers under his own command. In General Orders No. 5, Brig. Gen. I. N. Palmer wrote:

"The commanding general had until this time believed it impossible that any troops in his command could have committed so disgraceful an act as this which now blackens the fare fame of the Army of North Carolina. He finds, however, that he was sadly mistaken, and that the ranks are disgraced by men who are not soldiers, but thieves and scoundrels, dead to all sense of honor and humanity, for whom no punishment can be too severe."[345]

Although Washington was captured without firing a shot in anger, the 1st VA nevertheless suffered a casualty. Lt. Adolphus Blair of Company "D," accidentally shot himself in the leg with his pistol. The wound was quite serious and removed Blair from service with the regiment.

The 3rd VA was left in Washington to garrison the town while the rest of the brigade moved off in the direction of New Bern on April 28th. The route of march took them through Greenville and then on to the Neuse River which they crossed on pontoons twelve miles below Kinston. They crossed the Trent River on pontoons and passed through Pollocksville before arriving at New Bern on the 4th of May. The following morning the regiment took up a position on Colonel Hill's farm, the same position they had occupied on the previous expedition to New Bern, three months earlier. They were pushed forward as skirmishers that evening and came within sight of the town. The 1st VA remained in this position, conducting picket duty along the river, until the night of the 6th, when they were abruptly ordered to abandon the attack and move back to Kinston.[346]

While the 1st VA was moving from Washington to New Bern, Gen.

---

345 Official Records, Series 1 Volume 33, Pg. 310, "General Orders #5".

346 Charles Loehr, "War History of the Old First Virginia" Pg. 44-45.

Kemper was assigned to the command of the reserve forces of the State of Virginia. This order removed Kemper from command of the brigade that had won so much glory in his name. The wounds he suffered at Gettysburg made it impossible for him to return to field duty in command of the brigade. Col. William R. Terry, also wounded at Gettysburg, had been in temporary command of the brigade during the absence of Gen. Kemper since recovering from his own wounds, including during this most recent campaign in NC. Terry, a graduate of both the Virginia Military Institute and the University of Virginia, had been made Colonel of the 24th VA back in September of 1861 and was now promoted to Brigadier General. His official promotion came on May 31, 1864, and, in time, Kemper's Brigade would come to be known as Terry's Brigade.[347]

In early May, Gen. Kemper issued the following farewell address to the devoted men of his brigade:

Richmond, May 2nd 1864

To the Officers and Men of Kemper's Brigade,

For months it has been my fixed expectation and purpose to resume my old command at the opening of this campaign. But at the last moment my plans have been thwarted by an over ruling necessity. I am now warned by eminent medical advisers that my condition is such as positively incapacitates me for the duties of a field commander and for doing justice to yourselves in the relation that further service in the saddle must result in the ruin of my constitution if not the destruction of my life – without enuring to the benefit of the country.

Under these circumstances I have been assigned to the command of the Reserved Forces of the State of Virginia. I have not sought the position: but struck down by the casualties of war and unable longer to lead your veteran battalions, I believe it an imperative duty to accept it.

It is the most painful duty of my life to sever the relations which for three years have harmoniously unite us; which carried us together through memorable and fiery trials, and bound you to my heart with ties stronger than "hooks of steel". No portion of our armies will present to the world more splendid annals of valor than the First, Third, Seventh, Eleventh, and

[347] Official Records, Series 1, Volume 51, Part 2, Pg. 881: "Historical Times, Encyclopedia of the Civil War" Patricia Faust, Editor, Pg. 750.

Twenty-Fourth Regiments of Virginia Infantry. Let us ever remember also, as honored comrades, though now separated from us, the noble Seventeenth Virginia – identified with us by two years of common toils and achievements. It were enough of honor to have shared the fortunes of any of these regiments. Any soldiers might will be proud to possess the command of them all. Stouter heroes have not trod the field of battle. In your torn flags, your scarred persons, your rolls of gallant dead, you bear the memorials of a long succession of glorious conflicts: but from the smoke and fire of not one of them have you emerged without honor.

I will not tell you to preserve unsullied in the future the reputation, above all price, which the past has secured. The veteran brigade which Longstreet, Ewell, and A. P. Hill were proud successively to command at the beginning of the war, as dauntless as the Imperial Guard, know how to die but not to surrender.

Fellow soldiers, I bid each of you an affectionate adieu. I cease to be your commander but firmly and forever remain your friend. I shall, as heretofore, watch your career with the profoundest solicitude for your welfare. May the God of Battles steel your nerves and shelter your forms amid the perils of the field. May peaceful homes, a stable government, an admiring country, be at once the monuments and rewards of your valor.

James L. Kemper[348]

[348] Albert and Shirley Small Special Collections Library, University of Virginia, Charlottesville, VA.

THE TRENCHES OF VIRGINIA

The situation in Virginia had grown ominous for the Confederacy. President Lincoln had placed Gen. Ulysses S. Grant, the hero of Vicksburg, in command of all the Union armies on March 3, 1864. With the arrival of milder weather, Grant put his armies in motion. On May 4th the Army of the Potomac crossed the Rapidan River with more than 120,000 men. Gen. Lee began to consolidate his forces to meet this Union onslaught. At the same time, Union Gen. Benjamin Butler's Army of the James was making preparations to sail up the James River toward Richmond and Petersburg. Other than reserve forces and militias, there was nothing to stop him from reaching the capital. Gen. Pickett, who had been replaced by Gen. Beauregard as commander of North Carolina, was still in Petersburg and began to organize what few troops were on hand as a defense against Butler's advance.[349]

It was the threat of Butler's move down the James River that halted the attack on New Bern and put the 1st VA back on the road, headed toward Petersburg. The regiment left New Bern and marched throughout the pitch black night. After a short rest at Pollocksville, they continued for about sixteen miles and halted along the Neuse River on the night of the 7th. The rapid pace of the forced march and the ever increasing warm weather fatigued the weary soldiers. Many took advantage of a refreshing bath in the Neuse River during their brief stop. The following day they reached Kinston and waited for transportation. On the 9th of May they took the cars, passing through Goldsboro, and after travelling through the night reached Jarratt's station on the morning of the 10th. Union cavalry

349 E. B. Long, "The Civil War Day by Day, An Almanac 1861-1865", Doubleday and Company Inc., Garden City, New York, 1971, Pg.492.

had raided the station two days earlier and tore up the tracks and burned a bridge forcing the regiment to disembark and march the next eleven miles to Stony Creek. All available trains were sent from Petersburg to pick up the stranded brigades. The 1st VA arrived in Petersburg at 4 PM on the 10th of May.[350]

As the brigade entered the city, the grateful citizens of Petersburg were much relieved to see battle hardened troops arrive for their defense. Union Gen. Butler's reputation as a harsh occupier was well known throughout the south and the residents of Petersburg feared for their lives and property if he were to capture their city. The government in Richmond was also genuinely worried about this latest threat to the capital. They took the extraordinary step of releasing prisoners from the military prison and forming them into a battalion in an effort to supplement the defenses. On May 5th, Butler sailed down the James River and landed 30,000 troops of his Army of the James at City Point and Bermuda Hundred and planned on moving toward Petersburg and Richmond. The timely arrival of Kemper's (Terry's) Brigade along with the other troops from North Carolina, helped to ease the fears of the populace. The civilians cooked government rations for the arriving troops and presented them with gifts of their own food that could be spared.[351]

On May 5, 1864, the day that Butler landed his troops on the south bank of the James River, the armies of Grant and Lee came together in the conflagration that would become known as the "Battle of the Wilderness." The bloodbath would claim more than 25,000 casualties between the two armies. Unlike his predecessors, who normally withdrew after such a costly battle, Grant continued his movement deeper into Virginia. This movement and Lee's countermove brought on the Battle of Spotsylvania, which started on May 10th, the same day the 1st VA arrived in Petersburg. These events made the speedy elimination of Butler's advance a most pressing matter, seeing as Gen. Lee would soon need the troops then congregating in Petersburg for his campaign against Grant and the Army of the Potomac.

---

[350] Charles Loehr, "War History of the Old First Virginia": Pg. 45; B.F. Howard, Pgs. 50-51.

[351] David E. Johnston, "Four Years a Soldier", Pgs. 303-304; Official Records, Series 1, Volume 36, pg. 1023.

Up until this point, Gen. Pickett, with a meagre force, had managed to hold off Gen. Butler's half-hearted attempts to seriously cut the railroad and communications between Richmond, Petersburg and the Deep South. Butler's cavalry did manage to disrupt communications and cut the railroad in a few places but he missed his chance to break the railroad completely and capture Petersburg, which was lightly defended at the time. With each passing train, Confederate troops were pouring into the city, negating Butler's early advantage. Eventually Butler fell back to the James River at Drewry's Bluff. Gen. Beauregard arrived in Petersburg and took over command of the forces assembling there. As the various brigades arrived on the scene, they were grouped together into temporary ad hoc divisions. This situation had the potential for serious problems since commanders were forced to work with unfamiliar colleagues and staff personnel. Kemper's (Terry's) brigade was placed in a division commanded by Gen. Robert Ransom. Also in Ransom's division was Barton's (formerly Armstead's) brigade, Hoke's old brigade of North Carolinians now under the command of Col. William G. Lewis and Gen. Archibald Gracie's brigade made up of men from Alabama. It was Beauregard's plan for this division, under Ransom, to attack the right flank of Butler's Union position driving it back onto its center. The center and left would be attacked by two divisions commanded by Maj. Gen. Hoke and Brig. Gen. Alfred Colquitt. Gen. Whiting, who was recently transferred from Wilmington, was to advance from Petersburg with a separate force of 4,500 men and get into the Union rear, blocking Butler from returning to his base of operations at Bermuda Hundred [352]

The 1st VA, along with the rest of the brigade, moved out of Petersburg on the 11th of May and spent the night near Port Walthall Junction. The following day they moved to Half Way House, on the turnpike mid-way to Richmond. While here the enemy attacked the rear guard of the column, causing the brigade to halt and form a line of battle in a soaking rain storm. The Yankees backed off and the column moved on to the outer works near Drewry's Bluff. Heavy skirmishing took place along the lines that evening and the men slept on their arms. On the 13th, the brigade moved to Broad Rock Race Track where, because of a rumor that the enemy was

[352] Walter Harrison, "Pickett's Men", Pg. 124-126: Official Records, Series 1, Volume 36, Pg. 207 and "Report of Gen. Beauregard" Pgs. 199-200.

advancing, they halted in a line of trenches. In fact, Militia Cavalry from Richmond mistook a scouting party from the 1st VA for Yankees and sounded the alarm. The following day they moved closer to Drewry's Bluff and occupied a line of trenches where they remained until 9 PM on the 15th of May. That night the men were issued 60 cartridges apiece, which was a sure sign of an imminent engagement. Later that night they moved to a wood line closer to the Federal position and laid down for an uneasy sleep.[353]

It was 2 o'clock in the morning, on the 16th of May when 17,300 Confederate soldiers began forming up to assault approximately 38,000 Union soldiers at Drewry's Bluff on the James River. The men were quietly awoken, no drums or bugles to sound reveille. They lined up and began to move out, everything done in a hush so as not to alert the Yankees of their coming. They crossed Kingsland Creek and formed their battle lines. Once again, Kemper's (Terry's) brigade was placed in a position on the extreme flank, this time the far left, of the attacking force. The brigade was behind the battle line of approximately 1,100 Alabamians under the command of Gen. Gracie. The regiments within Kemper's (Terry's) brigade were positioned as follows: The 1st VA was astride the Stage Road, the 7th VA was to their left and the 11th VA and the 24th VA were to their right. Gen. Terry was shorthanded, by one regiment, because the 3rd VA was left in Washington, NC and had not yet returned to their comrades in the brigade. Terry had approximately 900 men in his brigade at Drewry's Bluff. To the left of the 7th was a small contingent of Confederate cavalry between the brigade and the James River. To the right of the brigade was a battery of four brass Napoleons.[354]

The field of battle was blanketed by a fog so thick the men could not see 10 paces in front of them. Voices of unknown officers, trying to position their troops, pierced the heavy mist. Finally at about 4:30 in the morning, Gen. Gracie's voice rang out from in front of the 1st VA, "Skirmishers, Forward March." The men in the 1st VA could not see but they heard the line of men in their front begin to move as Gracie's brigade stepped off toward the waiting Yankees. After allowing for Gracie's brigade

---

353 B. F. Howard, Pg. 52: Charles Loehr, "War History of the Old 1st VA" Pg. 46.

354 SHSP, Volume 19, "Charles Loehr", Battle of Drewry's Bluff, Pgs.101-104: David E. Johnston, "Four Years a Soldier", Pgs. 309

to obtain the proper distance in front of his own, Gen. Terry gave the command that put his own brigade in motion. It was not very long before single musket shots rang out, signifying the skirmishers had met the enemy. The volume of fire increased dramatically as Gracie's main battle line came within range of the Federal works. The four brass Napoleons of Martin's battery were placed on a slight knoll and began a rapid fire over the advancing Confederates into the Union lines.[355]

As the sun rose higher in the sky and the density of the fog lessened, the Union lines became more visible to the attacking Confederates. The Yankees had taken a position in a wood line overlooking an open field. They enhanced the defensibility of their position by piling up logs in front of their lines. Directly in front of Gracie's and Kemper's (Terry's) brigades, the lines were held by the 23rd, 25th and 27th Massachusetts and the 9th NJ, known as the "Star Brigade" and under the command of Brig. Gen. Charles Heckman. Heckman's brigade totaled approximately 2,700 men. Heckman's men fired volley after volley into Gracie's Alabamians, causing gaps to form in their lines. Errant shots were passing through and over Gracie's men and causing casualties in Terry's line, which had halted about 50 yards behind the Alabamians. One of those struck during the advance was Archibald Govan, who was known as Darby. Darby, one of the regiment's favorite singers, was wrapped in several U.S. Army blankets that were spoils of war he obtained at Plymouth. During the advance, Darby remarked to one of his comrades, "Don't you think this is a good breastwork?" referring to the heavy wool blankets wrapped around his body. Moments later he was shot through the heart and died instantly.[356]

Eventually the enemy fire began to take its toll on the Alabamians and the advance came to a halt. Gen. Gracie requested help from Gen. Terry who ordered the 24th VA and the 11th VA to advance. The Virginians went forward with a yell, passed through the Alabamians and crashed into the Union lines, taking casualties with every step. Among them was Col. Maury of the 24th VA who went down with a serious wound. Next in line

---

355 SHSP, Volume 19, "Charles Loehr", Battle of Drewry's Bluff, Pgs.102-103.

356 Major George Norton, from his papers, published in an unknown Richmond newspaper after the war: SHSP, Volume 19, "Charles Loehr", Battle of Drewry's Bluff, Pgs.102-103: Charles Loehr, "Only a Private", Paper read before Pickett Camp, CV in 1894, Printed in Richmond Newspaper, March 2, 1894:

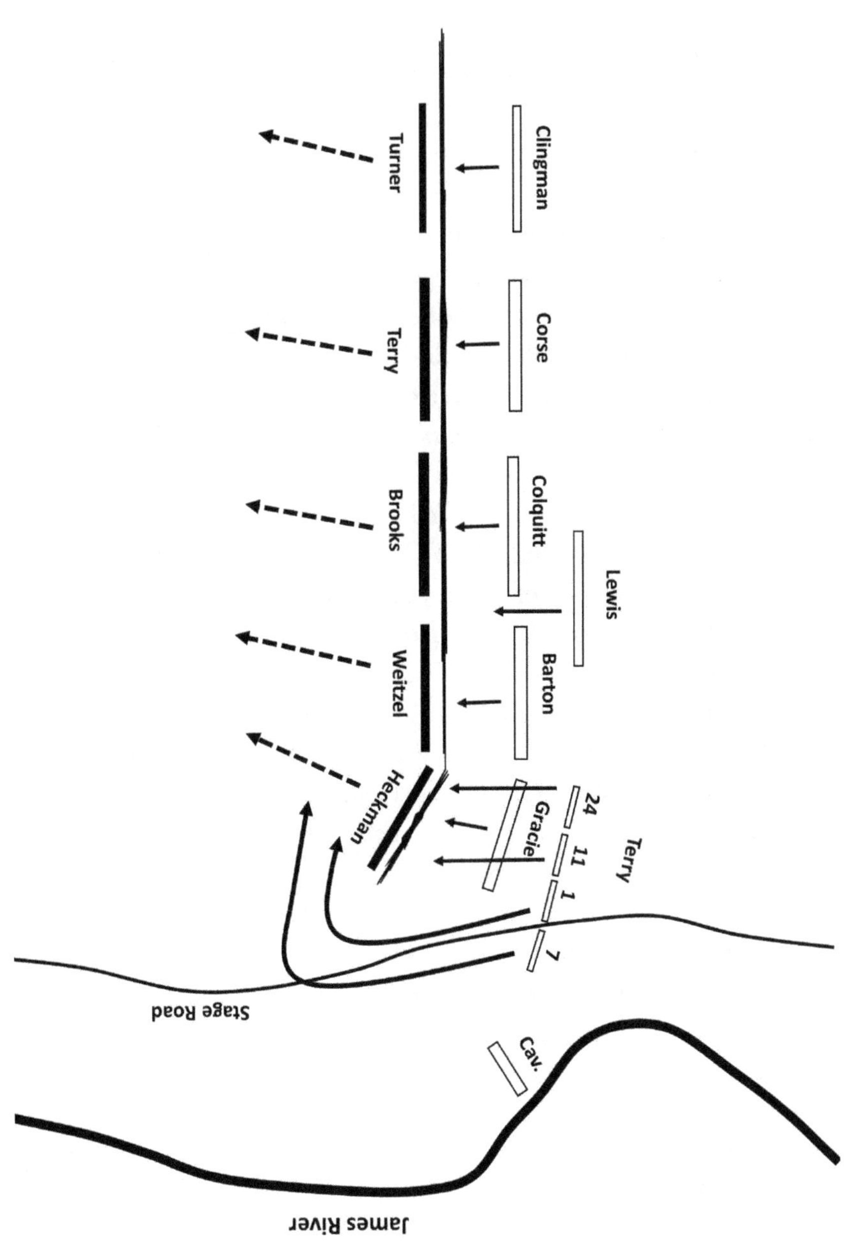

Battle of Drewry's Bluff
May 16, 1864

was the 1st VA who advanced quickly down the Stage Road. Their path was blocked by a pond on one side of the road and tangled underbrush on the other. The men crowded onto the road to get past the natural obstacles. The color bearer, John Quigg, bravely led the regiment further down the road and surprisingly met no resistance whatsoever. After traveling several hundred yards, the sound of the battle seemed to come from their right and rear. The new direction of the reverberations of the fight meant the regiment had somehow managed to get on the Union flank and rear. They turned and marched to the sound of the guns. Feeling their way through the thick woods, they arrived in a clearing that must have been an enemy camp from the night before. A dozen coffee pots were boiling on the fires. Genuine coffee had become such a rarity in the south that the men could not resist the temptation to stop and fill their cups with the delicious brew as they passed through the empty Federal camp.[357]

With hot coffee in hand, the 1st VA continued on, making contact with Federal troops, many of whom were so surprised to see rebels behind their lines they surrendered immediately. As they moved deeper into the Union lines, resistance became stiffer. A group of Yankees were ordered to surrender but instead they yelled out, "What regiment is that?" To which came the answer, "The First Virginia." This was immediately met by a volley at point blank range. Nine members of the 1st VA were killed instantly. The volley was returned and the Virginians charged into the Yankees, capturing most of those still standing. Not long after, the much reduced ranks of the 11th and 24th VA came through the works and linked up with the 1st VA. The 11th and 24th had to fight their way through and over the Federal works and paid dearly for the heroic assault, with approximately one-third of their numbers left on the field as casualties.[358]

Meanwhile, the 7th VA had swung even further to the left of the 1st VA and farther behind the Union lines. The Federal soldiers of Heckman's Star Brigade who were fleeing the fight with the 11th and 24th and managed to elude the 1st VA ran into the 7th VA and were captured. The 7th pushed on, capturing more men, including some officers. An officer in an overcoat

[357] E.P. Reeve, "Civil War Reminiscences": Major George Norton, from his papers, published in an unknown Richmond newspaper after the war: SHSP, Volume 19, "Charles Loehr", Battle of Drewry's Bluff, pgs.104-105.

[358] SHSP, Volume 19, "Charles Loehr", Battle of Drewry's Bluff, Pgs.106-107.

was watching as the chaotic scene unfolded before him. Thinking him an officer from Gracie's Alabama brigade, a member of the 7th VA asked if his regiment was in front of them "Yes," the officer answered, "go ahead you are driving them." A more skeptical Sgt. Blakely of the 7th inquired of the unknown officer, what was his regiment. When the officer did not answer, Sgt. Blakely said, "You are my prisoner." The sergeant asked the man for his weapons, to which the officer replied, "I am a General officer and prefer to surrender them to a field officer." Blakely took the man to Col. Floweree to whom the General surrendered. At that time his true identity became known, they had captured General Heckman, the Union brigade commander. The 7th also managed to capture 4 stands of colors.[359]

The fighting subsided on this section of the battlefield, although it continued on the far right for a couple of hours. Details were organized to escort the prisoners from the field. Four members of the 1st VA took control of one group of prisoners and headed to the Confederate rear. Because of the smoke, fog or simply an unfamiliarity of the area, they walked off in the wrong direction, unknowingly toward the Union lines. When challenged by sentries "Who are you?" Jeff Vaughan haughtily answered, "None of your business, I belong to the Old First, who are you?" He was invited to come forward and the captors instantly became the captives. Now that the battle was over, the dead and wounded needed to be cared for. Howard Malcomb Walthall had watched as his brother Ryland fell, dead, with a bullet in his brain. After the battle, Howard, with the help of others, carried his brother's limp body in a blanket to the rear. He sent a message to his father in Richmond and waited all day on the side of the road for him to arrive. Howard's father borrowed a wagon and rode to Drewry's Bluff to retrieve his dead son. The father and son eventually removed Ryland's body to Richmond where he was buried in Hollywood Cemetery. Those that could not be sent home to Richmond were buried on the battlefield.[360]

A partial list of those killed and wounded in the 1st VA at Drewry's Bluff were:

---

359 David E. Johnston, "Four Years a Soldier", Pgs. 309

360 Howard Malcomb Walthall, A Memoir, pg. 30: SHSP, Volume 19, "Charles Loehr", Battle of Drewry's Bluff, Pgs.107-108.

Company "B" – Killed: Corporals William A. Stoeber and Jerry Toomey; Private William H. Crigger. Wounded: Private Joseph R. Daniels.
Company "C" – Killed: Private Samuel H. Gillespie. Wounded: Private Jackson Trueman.
Company "D" – Killed: Private Archibald D. Govan. Wounded: Sergeant George E. Craig; Private William W. Turner. Captured: Private Nathaniel F. Wheat.
Company "G" – Killed: Private Robert Ryland Walthall and Thomas P. Harvey. Wounded: Captain Eldridge Morris; Private Thomas W. Miles. Captured: Private Alfred Jeff Vaughan and Daniel M. Walker.
Company "H" – Killed: Sergeant John W. Wynne; Corporals James A. Via. Wounded; Lieutenant Ellerson William Martin; Corporal Robert N. Dunn; Privates A.B. Morgan and Allen O. Clayton.
Company "I" - Killed: Corporal Alphonso A. Figner; Privates Charles A. Wills and J. R. Wesley. Wounded: Sergeant William F. Terry; Corporal Edwin B. Loving; Privates Richard A. Ashby, Martin Hodges, and William P. Smith.

This being a partial list, estimates put the killed and wounded for the 1st VA at approximately 40. Of the killed, five men were original members of the regiment who enlisted in April of 1861. They were Stoeber, Toomey, Walthall, Govan and Figner.[361]

The brigade lost approximately 47 killed, 200 wounded, and 10 missing for a total of 257 casualties. The majority of the losses within the brigade came from the 11th and 24th VA who had the unenviable task of attacking the enemy works from the front. Gracie's brigade who attacked in front of Kemper's (Terry's) had approximately 314 total casualties. One Confederate casualty of interest was the death of Col. Joseph Cabell of the 38th VA in Barton's Brigade. Cabell was the only field officer in Pickett's division to escape from Gettysburg unhurt but his luck ran out while leading his men at Drewry's Bluff. On the Union side, Heckman's brigade

---

361 Lee Wallace, "1st Virginia Infantry", Pgs. 81-123: "Record of the Richmond City and Henrico Co. Virginia Troops", Compiled by E. H. Chamberlayne, Jr., Richmond 1879. Charles Loehr, "War History of the Old First Virginia", Pg.48.

suffered approximately 42 killed, 188 wounded and 458 captured, for a total of 688.[362]

Union Gen. Butler withdrew his battered force back to his base of operations at Bermuda Hundred, thereby relieving the pressure on Richmond, Petersburg and the railroads which connected those cities with the south. In that sense the battle at Drewry's Bluff was a success. Gen. Beauregard, however, had hoped to encircle and completely destroy Butler's army at Drewry's Bluff. Gen. Whiting's force of more than 4,000 men coming from Petersburg was supposed to block Butler's escape, but his column never arrived and took no part in the battle. Whiting cited poor intelligence and bad communications among his reasons for not reaching the battlefield on May 16th. Nonetheless, Beauregard and members of the 1st VA blamed Whiting for the escape of Butler's Union Army.[363]

That night, after caring for the dead and wounded, the regiment bivouacked on the battlefield fully expecting a resumption of hostilities in the morning. With the light of day on May 17th it was discovered that the Yankees had retreated back to their fortified base at Bermuda Hundred, ending any opportunity of further engaging them. The regiment moved up the James River in the direction of Bermuda Hundred, halting at Howlett House. Gen. Beauregard planned to build earthworks at this location on the James River and man them with rifled cannon, thereby preventing any Union transports from landing troops behind the Confederate lines.[364]

Construction of the earthworks had already begun but Union gun boats anchored in the river continued to drive off the work parties. The 1st VA and the 7th VA were ordered to continue the work. Getting to the work site was in itself a dangerous proposition. The men had to cross an open field in broad daylight, within sight and range of the Yankee gun boats. The men crossed the field at a dead run in open order, "every man on his own hook." Upon reaching the works they put aside their weapons and grabbed the picks and shovels. The phrase of the day was "spades being trumps." The gun boats opened fire on the position, causing tremendous explosions among the men. They went to work in earnest and soon had

---

362 SHSP, Volume 19, "Charles Loehr", Battle of Drewry's Bluff, Pg. 110: Walter Harrison, "Pickett's Men", pg. 126.

363 Official Records, Series 1, Volume 36, Pgs. 196-204, Pgs. 256-260.

364 Official Records, Series 1, Volume 36. Pg. 198.

enough dirt piled up to give them some protection while they completed the gun emplacements. The large shells fired from the naval guns caused such huge eruptions of dirt and rock to fly in the air that it buried the men in the trenches and made it difficult for some of them to extricate themselves. One shot that was left intact after impact was measured at forty-five inches in circumference. The shells continued to plough into the work area, wounding and even killing some of the men. What made it worse for soldiers who were well acquainted with the trials of combat was the realization that they had no way of fighting back. The dirt covered, exhausted men worked until after dark, finally laying down in the trenches and going to sleep. They were awakened by a new group of workers who had crossed the field in darkness to relieve them. The gun boats, unable to dislodge the Virginians from their burden, had moved off during the night, leaving the unfinished fort in an eerie silence. Looking like coal miners, the men of the 1st VA climbed out of the trenches, picked up their muskets and started out across the dark open field.

A partial list of casualties suffered by 1st VA in the trenches of Howlett House were:

Killed: Corporal Alonzo A. Chappell of Company "I." Wounded: Private Ezekial Priddy of Company "D," Lieutenant Paul C. Cabell and Sergeant Richard E. Armstrong of Company "H," Captain Benjamin F. Howard, Privates George W. Boler, and Andrew T. Minor of Company "I." Most of those wounded were stunned from the concussion of the large caliber shells.[365]

With Gen. Butler's Army of the James bottled up at Bermuda Hundred, the Confederacy's attention was now completely directed to the juggernaut that was the Army of the Potomac, being led by Gen. U.S. Grant. After the battle of Spotsylvania, Grant continued his move south into Virginia toward the Richmond/Petersburg corridor. Petersburg is located 25 miles to the south of Richmond and the two cities were connected by the

[365] Major George Norton, from his papers, published in an unknown Richmond newspaper after the war: E. P. Reeve, Letter to his wife dated, May 19, 1864, "Near the James River": B.F. Howard, pg. 53: Charles Loehr, "War History of the Old First Virginia", pg. 49.

Richmond Petersburg turnpike and the Richmond Petersburg Railroad. Since Petersburg was an essential railway junction with several rail lines running into the Deep South, it was imperative that the corridor between Petersburg and the capital be kept open. The defenses along this corridor consisted of a series of extensive trench works, in most places at least two lines deep, known as the inner and outer works, running parallel and to the east of the turnpike and rail line. It was here that the 1st VA, along with the rest of the brigade, was sent on the 19th of May. The regiment took up a position in the trenches near the Clay house, just south of the James River.[366]

For at least the previous two weeks Gen. Lee had been trying to reassemble Pickett's scattered division and return them to the Army of Northern Virginia. Butler's invasion along the James River and the need to repel it with every available regiment put those plans on hold. On May 20th, Special Orders No. 117 was issued which ordered: "Kemper's, Hunton's, Barton's, and Corse's, and also Hoke's old brigade, will proceed immediately by railroad to the headquarters Army of Northern Virginia and report to the general commanding." In anticipation of this reuniting of Pickett's division, the 1st VA and the rest of Kemper's brigade were ordered out of the trenches just a few hours after they had arrived. They marched all night and reached Richmond on the morning of May 20th.[367]

That day the four regiments of the brigade that were present, the 1st VA, 7th VA, 11th VA and 24th VA, paraded through the streets of Richmond. Each regiment, carried one of the captured Union flags from the battle at Drewry's Bluff. After being away from Richmond for many months, a large portion of the 1st VA took it upon themselves to visit friends and family while they were in the city. That evening, about 60 men from the 1st VA, and men from the 7th VA and 11th VA were loaded onto flat cars and sent toward Fredericksburg. At about 9PM they reached Milford Station, the

---

366 "Atlas to accompany the Official Records of the Union and Confederate Armies", Compiled by Capt. Calvin D. Cowles, 23rd U.S. Infantry, Originally published by The Government Printing Office, Washington DC, 1891-1895, Republished by Barnes and Noble Publishing Inc., 2003, Plate 100, pg. 241 and plate 77-1, pg. 194: B.F. Howard, Pg. 53

367 Official Records, Series 1, Volume 36 Part 2, Pg. 95, Part 3, Pg. 799: B. F. Howard, Pg. 53.

northern most point that the trains could go due to Yankee occupation of the railroad. The small force, approximately 450 men, under the command of Major Norton of the 1st VA, left the depot and camped outside of the town near the plank bridge over the Mattapony River.[368]

The men awoke on the morning of the 21st and began to stir about their camp. A small detachment of Confederate cavalry rode into town and announced that Yankee cavalry had been seen in Bowling Green and was headed their way. Major Norton deployed the men of the 1st VA in and around the few buildings of the small village. The 7th and 11th VA formed a skirmish line behind the town. Shortly after taking their position, Union Cavalry belonging to the division commanded by Gen. Alfred Thomas Torbert were seen trotting down the dusty road leading into Milford. The men of the 1st VA waited for the cavalrymen to get close and then opened fire. The Yankees retreated, regrouped and charged into the town again, only to be met with another volley from the Virginians who were protected within the buildings. More and more cavalryman were appearing before the town. After a third failed attempt at charging the town, the Yankees dismounted and formed a skirmish line. As their numbers continued to grow, so did their fire power. The dismounted soldiers were pushing ever closer to the town when Major Norton ordered the 11th VA to charge into the advancing enemy. The 11th pushed the Federals back and formed a line of battle in front of the town.

After being pushed back again the Union commander brought up artillery and began to launch shells into the Confederate position. It was not much longer before Major Norton could see large columns of enemy infantry also moving on his position. Norton realized his small command was about to be overwhelmed by a sea of blue and he ordered a retreat across the bridge. The Confederates conducted a fighting withdraw retreating toward the bridge and the river. Part of the 11th VA in their advanced position in front of the town did not get the order to withdraw and approximately 60 of their men were surrounded and captured. The remainder of the 11th VA and their comrades in the 1st and 7th VA took up positions on the far side of the river and kept up a stiff fire to hold back the enemy. Members of the 7th VA began tearing up planks on the bridge to slow the Yankee advance. Norton then fell back to a ridgeline and formed

---

368 SHSP, Vol. 26, "The battle of Milford Station" by Charles Loehr, Pg. 111

a line of battle in the hopes of repelling any further advance by the enemy. Seeing Norton's battle line and not knowing what was in his front, Gen. Torbert halted the Union force on his side of the river. Tolbert telegraphed his superior, Gen Winfield Scott Hancock, "I have driven the enemy (all infantry) across the Milford Bridge, and am holding the bridge. The enemy's infantry are on the opposite side of the river, and I doubt whether I can drive them away." With no attack forthcoming, Norton eventually drew off his force and moved toward the Confederate lines.[369]

This relatively small skirmish had far reaching consequences in the overall strategy between the armies of Lee and Grant. The Union force at Milford was the lead column of Gen. Hancock's 2nd Corps, which was the lead element of The Army of the Potomac. Hancock was attempting to get his corps to Hanover Junction before Lee, thereby cutting the Confederates off from Richmond and forcing Lee to attack under unfavorable circumstances. The action at Milford Station and subsequent stand on the nearby ridgeline halted Hancock's column long enough for Lee to win the deadly race to Hanover Junction and the defenses around Richmond. Unbeknownst to Norton and the rest of the men from Kemper's brigade, Gen. Corse's brigade was about a mile away on another hilltop possibly in view of Milford Station. If Torbert had a view of both Kemper's and Corse's brigades, he may have thought he was up against a much larger force, thereby prompting his telegram to Hancock stating, "I doubt whether I can drive them away." The men in the brigade were later told that Gen. Lee congratulated Major Norton in person for the heroic defense of Milford Station by the men of the 1st, 7th and 11th VA.[370]

After leaving Milford Station, the regiment moved toward Hanover Junction where they reunited with the remainder of the brigade. Pickett's division, now reformed, took its place among the ranks in Longstreet's Corps, now under the temporary command of Lt. Gen. Richard Anderson while Longstreet recovered from the wound he received at the Battle of the Wilderness. On May 22nd, the 3rd VA was recalled from North Carolina, completing the reunification of Kemper's (Terry's) brigade. On the 28th of

---

369 SHSP, Vol. 26, "The battle of Milford Station" by Charles Loehr, Pg. 111-114: Official Records, Series 1, Volume 36, part 3, Pg. 48: B.F. Howard, pg. 53: David E. Johnston, "Four Years a Soldier", Pgs. 325-327.

370 SHSP, Vol. 26, "The battle of Milford Station" by Charles Loehr, Pg. 115

May they were camped at Hanover Town awaiting their supply wagons. The wagons finally arrived at 10 o'clock that night and rations were issued. It was the first food the men had eaten in twenty-four hours. On May 30th, the brigade moved to the Confederate lines outside of Cold Harbor. As they filed into the trenches, the 1st VA was sent forward as skirmishers to feel out the enemy position. The regiment moved into a wood line in pitch black darkness. Contact was made with enemy pickets and a minor skirmish ensued. The regiment captured a couple of prisoners who, in the confused darkness, wandered into their midst. The brigade was moved farther to the right and spent the rest of the night fortifying their position. By the following morning they had a "formidable breastwork thrown up."[371]

The 1st of June found the regiment in the trenches in front of Cold Harbor. Once again they were sent out as skirmishers. The skirmish line was moved back and forth, left and right and with each move came the task of digging new rifle pits. The opposing skirmish lines were in such close proximity that it was extremely dangerous for skirmishers to show themselves. The enemy attacked the lines to the right of the 1st VA and was repulsed with heavy loss by Hoke's brigade. The men were on alert for the next couple of days as a general attack by the enemy was expected at any time. Heavy skirmishing and artillery duels continued on the 2nd of June. The following day Gen. Grant launched a massive assault involving three Union corps but again the majority of the heavy fighting took place to the right of the position held by Kemper's (Terry's) brigade. And again the attack was repulsed with heavy losses to Grant's men. David Johnston of the 7th VA travelled down the lines to visit friends in another regiment and witnessed the result of Grant's frontal assault at Cold Harbor. After the war he wrote of the devastation that littered the terrain in front of the Confederate lines. The landscape was strewn with the corpses of Union soldiers, in some places the bodies lay in heaps upon the ground. Late in the day on the 5th of June the enemy launched another attack to the right of the brigade. There was heavy skirmishing in their immediate front and every man was ordered into the trenches in anticipation of a general assault.

---

371 Official Records, Series 1, Volume 36, Part, 3, Pg. 800: E.P. Reeve, "Civil War Reminiscences": B. F. Howard, Pg. 54.

The attack was repulsed and a relative calm settled over the battlefield, allowing the men to lie down in the trenches and sleep.[372]

Skirmishes, fortifying the breastworks and the occasional alarms continued through the early part of June. On June 12th, the Yankees began an enfilade fire into Pickett's line. This barrage caused the men to once again gather their spades and picks and begin digging new breastworks and bombproofs to protect them from the direction of this new threat. On the following morning it was discovered that the Union army had moved off to their left in the direction of the James River. The 1st VA, along with the rest of Pickett's division, began to move off in a parallel line toward the James River in an effort to block the enemy from flanking the Confederate army and capturing Petersburg. On that first day of the march, they passed over the old battlefields of Gaines' Mills and Seven Pines before they reached the scene of their fight at Frazier's Farm, where they bivouacked for the night.[373]

The division's trek to the James River continued on the 14th and 15th of June. Gen. Lee was riding with Pickett's division when they reached Chaffin's bluff on the north side of the James River on June 16th. They passed over to the south shore, across a pontoon bridge, a full day behind the lead elements of the Union army. They continued moving south, passing through their old battlefield at Drewry's Bluff. In conjunction with the southern movement of the Army of the Potomac, Butler's Army of the James left their fortifications at Bermuda Hundred and attacked toward Petersburg. This attack prompted Gen. Beauregard, who was still in command at Petersburg, to strip the defenses near the James River and move those troops to the city. Butler's attack was repelled but Grant's men took possession of the unoccupied Confederate trenches as they crossed the James River. Union occupation of this section of the line caused a serious threat to the communications between Richmond and Petersburg as the Yankees immediately went to work destroying the railroad. It also caused a severe threat to Pickett's column since Lee had no viable information that the Union army had crossed the river and was on Pickett's flank. [374]

---

372 B.F, Howard, Pg. 55: David Johnston, "Four Years a Soldier", Pg. 331: E.P. Reeve, Letter to his wife, "Trenches nears Gaines Mills, June 10, 1864.

373 B. F. Howard, Pg. 56.

374 Official Records, Series 1, Volume 40, Part 2, Pg. 99, 106-107, 658-659: E. B. Long, "The Civil War Day by Day, An Almanac 1861-1865", Pg. 523.

The column was moving at the route step and was strung out along the Petersburg Turnpike. A small detachment of Confederate cavalry was met and from them it was learned that Yankees were operating in the area. Believing the Yankees were merely a scouting party or perhaps a detachment tearing up the railroad, this news did not alarm the officers or the men. Eventually sporadic musket fire was heard coming from the front of the column, prompting the officers to close ranks. As this was taking place, a terrific volley of fire came from the wood line to the immediate left of the road and Pickett's column. An unexpected flanking fire such as this into an unsuspecting column of troops could have caused terror and panic among novice or green soldiers. But the core of these men were battle hardened veterans who did not scare easily. Each regiment, including the 1st VA, turned to the left, instantly forming a line of battle. Skirmishers advanced to the front and the line began to move in the direction of their hidden assailants. The Confederates pushed forward into the woods, driving the Yankees before them. The Union soldiers were forced back to the inner works that Gen. Beauregard had abandoned in order to defend Petersburg. The 1st VA, along with the rest of Pickett's division, continued to drive the Yankees and eventually forced them out of the trench works after dark. The Federals fell back again, this time to the outer line of trenches, while the Confederates sent out skirmishers and strengthened their position in the newly recaptured inner line.

Heavy skirmishing and artillery fire exploded all along the lines on the following morning and continued until early in the afternoon. At approximately 3 PM an assault was ordered and the men of Pickett's division clambered out of the security of their trenches and charged across the open field. The 1st VA attacked near the Clay house and although the Union defenders commenced a heavy fire, the Confederates got into the trenches and drove them out, thereby regaining all of the works that had been abandoned in the previous days by Gen. Beauregard. Pickett's division now occupied the trenches between Howlett house and the Clay house. Had Grant been allowed to occupy and reinforce this section of the trenches, the communication lines between Richmond and Petersburg in all probability would have been in great peril. Pickett's capture of the works safeguarded those communications. Gen. Lee feared the attack would prove to be too costly in human life and sent orders to cancel the charge but by the time the message arrived, the breastworks were already under Confederate control.[375]

Gen. Lee wrote to Gen. Anderson, who was still in command of the 1st Corps while Longstreet recuperated:

"General I take great pleasure in presenting to you my congratulations upon the conduct of the men of your corps. I believe that they will carry anything they are put against. We tried very hard to stop Pickett's men from capturing the breastworks of the enemy, but couldn't do it. I hope his loss is small.

R.E. Lee, General

Official: G. M. Sorrel, Lieut-Col., A. A. Gen.
For Major-Gen. G. E. Pickett, Commanding Division"[376]

Prior to the attack the men of the 1st VA received some comical relief from Benjamin Nobles of Company "C." A bullet went through his canteen and feeling the liquid flowing down over his "unmentionables," he began to scream for the ambulance to take him from the field. His comrades had a good laugh when it was discovered the liquid was water from his canteen and not blood from a wound to his groin. Unfortunately the regiment did suffer the following casualties in the retaking of the Confederate lines:
Wounded:
Company "D" – Corporal George L. Meenley; Privates Thomas W. Taylor, Ezekial Priddy.
Company "H" – Private George E. Redford.
Company "I" – Privates James K. Yancy and John H. James.[377]

Pickett's division occupied the Confederate trenches between Port Walthall at Swift Creek northward to Howlett House on the James River, a distance of about three miles. Pickett had between four and five thousand men to cover that distance. The 1st VA spent the remainder of June moving

---

375 Edward Payson Reeve, "Civil War Reminiscences of Captain Edward Payson Reeve": Walter Harrison, "Pickett's Men", Pg. 130: David Johnston, "Four Years a Soldier", pgs. 333-334: Charles Loehr, "War History of the Old First Virginia", Pg. 52: B. F. Howard, Pgs. 56-57.

376 Official Records, Series 1, Volume 40, Part 1, Pg. 749.

377 Charles Loehr, "War History of the Old First Virginia", Pg. 52.

to various positions along Pickett's section of the line. Skirmishers manned the rifle pits in front of the main lines and engaged in clashes with the enemy pickets, some of which were quite heavy. These skirmishes continued to cause casualties among the men of the 1st VA. The regiment received quite a few new recruits during this period of time. Most of the recruits were conscripts and although many of them turned into good soldiers, others were unfit for duty in a front line combat unit. In July the regiment settled down in a position near the Clay house, at about the middle of Pickett's line. When not on picket duty, their time was spent fortifying their position. Aside from the constant digging of trenches, abatis and Chevaux de fries were built and placed in front of the breastworks.[378]

The month of July brought more of the same for the 1st VA. Picket duty remained the most dangerous job endured by the men, but, bombardment by Federal artillery was also a constant deadly threat to the soldiers manning the lines. So much so that when the Confederate artillery was looking to recycle expended Union shells, an artillery officer wrote to General Pendleton, the Chief of Artillery for the Army of Northern Virginia, "I write particularly to call your attention to the fact that there are a large number in the vicinity of General Pickett's line."[379]

With the Union army being in such close proximity to the suburbs of Richmond and Petersburg, it added an additional level of stress to the men of the 1st VA. For many, their families and homes were in imminent danger of being overrun by the Yankee army. Captain E. P. Reeve obtained a two day pass to collect his family in Dinwiddie. While waiting for a train in Petersburg to carry them back to Richmond, Reeve and his wife watched as Union shells lit up the night sky as they streaked into the city. After a somewhat scary night in Petersburg, he was successful in getting his wife and child safely to the capital. For enlisted men it was not so easy to get passes to check on the safety of their families. For some, who were willing to bear the trials of combat and soldier life for themselves, the fear for their family's safety was too much to bear and they simply walked off the line.[380]

---

[378] Charles Loehr, "War History of the Old First Virginia", Pg. 53: David Johnston, "Four Years a soldier", Pg. 338: B. F. Howard, Pgs. 57-58.

[379] Official Records, Series 1, Volume 40, Part 3, Pg. 748.

[380] Edward Payson Reeve "Civil War Reminiscences of Captain Edward Payson Reeve": B. F. Howard, Pg. 59.

Desertions were becoming more numerous within Pickett's division as the days in the trenches dragged on. Some of the conscripts who were drafted to fill the ranks of the army were not quite as devoted to the cause of the Confederacy as those that volunteered and therefore were more inclined to walk away from their posts. Even veterans, after three years of bloody war, may have found it unbearable to remain in the trenches. The increased number of desertions caused a high level of concern among the commanding officers of the army. Confederate soldiers who deserted to the enemy were also giving valuable intelligence in regards to the location and condition of their former units. In an attempt to stem the flow of desertions, public executions were conducted for those who attempted to flee to the enemy. On July 25th, a detail from each brigade in the division, including men from the 1st VA, were sent to witness the execution by firing squad of two men from Barton's Brigade. Within Kemper's (Terry's) brigade, a young man of about 17 from the 7th VA was arrested at his house and tried for desertion. After being found guilty he was sentenced to death by firing squad. His regiment formed a three sided hollow square and the condemned man was tied to a stake at the open end. Twelve members of his own company were picked to be the executioners. Six of the twelve guns were loaded with blank cartridges so that no man would know who fired the fatal shot. When the command was given, the detail fired, killing the young man instantly. The 1st VA was not immune to this type of behavior. Private James B. Wallis, a 38 year old conscript in Company "I" was charged with being absent without leave. He was sentenced to carry a fence rail on the parapet wall four hours each day for fifteen days. Wallis also was fined one month's in addition to the pay for the time he was absent. Fortunately for Wallis he was not charged with desertion. Lesser crimes also brought severe punishment to the perpetrator. Private James Robinson of Company "I" was taken one-half mile behind the lines, and given 39 lashes on his bare back for "numerous bad acts," including thievery. Robinson was then expelled from the company and told not to return. This sentence was imposed by a unanimous vote of his own company. [381]

On the 16th of August, the 1st VA and the 11th VA were pulled out of the south side defenses and moved across the James River to the north

381 Official Records, Series 1, Volume 40, Part 2, pgs. 71,201: David Johnston, "Four Years a Soldier", Pgs. 345-46: B. F. Howard, Pg. 59.

side. They bivouacked that night near Chaffin's bluff on the north shore. The following day they continued moving north along the lines. The column stopped to rest when Gen. Lee rode up and inquired as to who they were. When told they were the 1st and 11th VA from Pickett's division, he remarked, "All right, I know these men, and they will do their duty."

On the 18th they took up a position in the trenches near Fussell's Mills where they remained for the night in the pouring rain. During the previous months while manning the rifle pits and advanced positions along the lines, it was common practice to strike up conversations and even unofficial truces with the enemy in the opposing forward positions. Yanks and Rebs would meet and trade articles such as tobacco and coffee. This practice was resumed in the new position. When the rain cleared and the sun rose on the 19th, it was evident the opposing lines were very near. Members of the 1st VA yelled over to the Yanks "not to shoot they had men from Pickett's division in their front." The Federal soldiers agreed and a round of bartering ensued and not a shot was fired while the 1st VA manned that section of the line. During one conversation a Yank inquired if the Rebs wanted to trade a copy of the New York Herald for the Richmond Dispatch. Sgt. Pat Woods of Company "C" good naturedly replied that if they could get the NY Herald to print the truth, the Virginians would happily swap papers with them. This brief period of unofficial peace between veteran troops amazed the Richmond Militiamen who were positioned behind the 1st VA and witnessed the entire affair. Later that day the regiment was relieved and began the long march back to the south side of the river. They arrived back at their old camp late on the 20th completely exhausted after their long march and lack of sleep during the previous five days.[382]

In mid-September the regiment moved into a new line of stronger breastworks that were constructed in the rear of their current position. After further strengthening the new position, the men went to work on building winter quarters for themselves. The rows of wooden cabins, built by each regiment behind the lines, took on the appearance of small

[382] Charles Loehr, "War History of the Old First Virginia", Pgs. 53-54: B. F. Howard, Pg. 58-59: E. P. Reeve, Letter to his wife, "South Side Defenses, August 22, 1864": "Reunion of the Blue and the Gray", John W. Frazier, Ware Brothers, Company Printers, Philadelphia PA, 1906, Reprint from the collection of the University of Michigan Library, Pg. 57.

villages. By all accounts their quarters were considered quite pleasant and comfortable. The men of the 1st VA built a chapel and had planned to build a Masonic Lodge but could not get authorization for the project. Life along the lines settled into a dull routine of manning and strengthening the trenches. Drilling, guard duty, dress parades and inspections also helped to fill their days. Details were sent out to the rifle pits, forward of the main line, to keep watch for any aggressive movement by the enemy. Interaction between the opposing pickets continued despite the objections of the commanding officers. In their off time, writing and receiving letters and packages helped to cheer the men. Regular church services and the formation of a bible class aided in the spiritual well-being of the regiment.[383]

The regiment remained on this part of the line for the remainder of 1864. During this time the concern for their families in and around Richmond was increasing with each letter from home. Aside from the looming threat of Grant's massive Union army that was poised to attack the capital, the costs for the necessities of life were skyrocketing in the city. The fear of mortal combat was compounded by the continued anxiety for their family's well-being at home. The last three months of 1864 saw many serious setbacks to the fortunes of the Confederacy. On the military front, Gen. Early's loss at Cedar Creek in the Shenandoah Valley, the fall of Atlanta and Sherman's march to the sea which culminated in the loss of Savanah all pointed to tough times ahead for the Confederacy. Additionally, on January 15th, Fort Fisher finally surrendered. As the men of the 1st VA well knew, this meant the closure of the port of Wilmington, the only port open to foreign goods for the Army of Northern Virginia. Politically, the re-election of Lincoln in November assured the men in the trenches at Petersburg that the war would continue. These events were extremely disheartening to many of the men of the regiment, the brigade and the entire army who had struggled for nearly four years.[384]

On January 8th the regiment moved to the left of the line to a position near Howlett House on the James River. The quarters they found awaiting

---

383 B. F. Howard, Pg. 59: E. P. Reeve, Letters to his wife, "Sept. 30, 1864", "Nov. 24, 1864", "Nov. 27, 1864".

384 E. P. Reeve, Letter to his wife, "January 19, 1865": David Johnston, "Four Years a Soldier", Pg. 354.

them were not near as large or well-constructed as the houses they built for themselves at their previous location. They immediately went to work in an attempt to improve their new living conditions. The monotony was broken on the 22nd of January when the men of the regiment witnessed a naval battle on the river between Union and Confederate iron clads. In February, news reached the lines of the failed Peace Conference between President Lincoln and emissaries of the Confederacy. Any residual hope of a peaceful settlement to the war was crushed with the failure of that conference. On February 15th the entire regiment met under the chairmanship of Colonel Langley to discuss the unfavorable situation. Even with the bleak state of affairs, the regiment adopted the following resolutions:

"Resolved, That to the humiliating propositions for peace made by President Lincoln to our companions, we enter our indignant protest that while we would be rejoiced to stop the effusion of blood and the desolation of our country, we will assent to no terms short of independence and separate nationality.

Resolved, That in as much as we have tendered the olive branch to our foes, which they have trampled in the dust, no alternative is left us but to defend our homes, our property and lives, as long as the foot of a vandal pollutes the soil of the South.

Resolved, That while recognizing our dependence on Almighty God, who defends the cause of just, we again dedicate ourselves to the cause. Again we unfurl a banner which we have borne from Bull Run to Bermuda Hundreds, and again we swear to "die freemen rather than slaves."

Resolved, That we hail with pleasure the appointment of R. E. Lee General-in-Chief; that we have an abiding confidence in his judgment, patriotism, and valor, and wherever he orders we will go with joyful acclamation.

Resolved, That the people at home be exhorted to sustain the army, to drive back the skulker, to aid in feeding and clothing the soldiers, to send the best men into councils of the nation, that energy and ability by be infused into the different departments, State and Confederate.

Resolved, That though disaster and gloom now hovers over us, we believe all things will be so ordered in the coming campaign, that our wrongs will be avenged, our rights secured, and those who now claim us as slaves will own us as victors.

Resolved, That we would hail with acclamation the enrolment into our armies of Negro troops; we therefore recommend to our representatives in Congress assembled, to use their endeavors for the immediate accomplishment of that end."

With these resolutions, the men of the 1st VA pledged to fight on to the bitter end.[385]

With the territorial losses of the Confederacy came the reduction of the bureaucracy within the Confederate government. Since every man was needed on the front lines, many of those that were detailed to work in Richmond early on in the war were sent back to their respective commands, much to their chagrin. Along with the return of these detailed men, the regiment also received approximately 80 recruits. Company "K" was reformed with some of the new recruits and put under the command of Lt. William Lawson who had been promoted after losing his arm carrying the regimental colors at Gettysburg. Upon returning to duty, Lawson was originally assigned to the Presidential guard in Richmond. He gave up that relatively safe assignment to rejoin his comrades in the 1st VA. On February 24th the brigade returned to their original position on the lines near Swift Creek. But, they would not remain there long.[386]

---

385 Charles Loehr, "War History of the Old First Virginia", Pgs. 54-55.

386 Charles Loehr, "War History of the Old First Virginia", Pgs. 55-56

THE FINAL BATTLES

On March 5th, Pickett's division was relieved in the trenches by the men of Mahone's division. On March 8th, a grand review was held by Gen. Pickett in preparation for the division's return to active operations. On the 9th they moved to Manchester where they camped for the night. The following day they marched through Richmond and filed into a section of trenches in the outer works near Brook Road. Union General Philip Sheridan's cavalry, after completing their successful campaign in the Shenandoah Valley, was active to the north of Richmond and on the 14th, Pickett's division left the lines at Brook Road and marched toward Ashland, VA, to meet this new threat. Gen. Longstreet, now recuperated from his wound, was once again in command of this force. For four days in bad weather, Longstreet maneuvered his troops in an attempt to bring Sheridan's cavalry to battle. Sheridan stayed out of reach and eventually left the area to join up with Grant's army. Pickett's division returned to the lines near Nine Mile Road around the 18th of March.[387]

During this period, March 9 – 18, Terry's brigade suffered the disgrace of having 40 soldiers desert their ranks. It is not known how many, if any of the 40 were from the 1st VA. If there was any consolation to the officers of the brigade, this was the lowest amount of desertions for any brigade in Pickett's division. During the same period, Hunton's brigade had 183 desertions, Steuart's brigade had 145 desertions, and Corse's brigade had 144. The desertions for the four brigades in Pickett's division totaled 512, the largest amount of any division in the army. Gen. Lee was extremely concerned about the recent spike in desertions from his army. In a letter to the Secretary of War on the subject of desertions, he noted that Pickett's

[387] B. F. Howard, Pg. 64: E.P. Reeve, "Civil War Reminiscences".

division had been on the move around Richmond and it was his hope that "some of his men only availed themselves of the opportunity to visit their homes and will return." To help encourage Confederate soldiers to desert, Gen. Grant was paying bounties to any Rebel who deserted to the Union army and brought his musket with him.[388]

On the 23rd of March, Gen. Longstreet held another, and as it turned out the last, grand review of Pickett's division and the 1st VA. The following day a flurry of telegrams between Lee's and Longstreet's headquarters ordered Pickett's division to move to Petersburg. On the 25th the brigade left the trenches at Nine Mile Road and marched to Richmond where they took the cars on the Richmond/Petersburg Railroad to Dunlop Station, north of Petersburg. They remained in this vicinity until the 29th when Pickett was ordered to move his division to Sutherland Station, south and west of the city, to support Gen. Lee's right flank.

At this time Pickett's division was a bit scattered. Corse's brigade was with Terry's at Dunlop Station. Armstead's old brigade, which had been commanded by Gen. Barton but was now under the command of Brig. Gen. George H. Steuart of Maryland, was to the south of Petersburg. Steuart was ordered to join Pickett on his way to Sutherland Station. Hunton's brigade remained north of the James River with Longstreet awaiting transport to Petersburg. The railroad could not accommodate Pickett's entire force so the 1st and 7th VA had to walk most of the 10 miles to Sutherland Station. The three available brigades of Pickett's division, (Terry's, Corse's and Steuart) were consolidated at Sutherland Tavern that night.[389]

While the regiment was riding the cars from Richmond to Dunlop Station on the 25th of March, Gen. Lee launched a major attack on the Union held Fort Steadman. The fort was overrun and initially the attack appeared to be a huge success. But, a Union counterattack retook the fort and inflicted heavy casualties on the Confederate force. It was reported that Private Joseph B. Chambers of Company "F," 100th PA, captured the colors of the 1st VA Infantry. Private Chambers was awarded the Congressional

388 Official Records, Series 1, Volume 46, Pgs. 1332, 1353, 38 and 42. (The author can find no record of a member of the 1st VA deserting during this periosd).

389 Walter Harrison, "Pickett's Men", Pg. 135: Charles Loehr, "War History of the Old First Virginia" Pg. 58.

Medal of Honor for this heroic deed. It is possible, even probable, that Private Chambers did indeed capture the colors of a Confederate regiment, but it is doubtful that it was the flag of the 1st VA. There is absolutely no evidence that any part of the 1st VA took part in the attack on Fort Steadman. As previously stated, the regiment was travelling on the railroad from Richmond on that day.[390]

The strategic situation that prompted Pickett's deployment to Lee's right flank had become critical. The Confederate lines from Richmond to Petersburg were stretched so thin that they had become increasingly difficult to defend. Grant sent Sheridan's cavalry to the south and west of Petersburg, causing a catastrophic threat to Lee's right flank. If Sheridan were allowed to operate freely, the two remaining rail lines to the Deep South would be threatened. The loss of those rail lines would force the retreat of the Army of Northern Virginia from their defenses and the evacuation of Richmond. It was Grant's wish to force Lee out of his defensive works and into the open field where Grant's overwhelming numbers could strike a fatal blow to the Army of Northern Virginia and in effect end the war. Unlike Grant, Lee had no more troops to extend his stationary lines without dangerously weakening other sections. It was Gen. Longstreet who proposed sending Pickett's division with all of the Confederate cavalry to the right flank of the army. Pickett's infantry and Fitz Lee's cavalry were to cooperate as a mobile force to contend with Sheridan's large cavalry corps. Lee approved of the plan and Pickett's division, including the 1st VA, was sent to the right of the lines.[391]

Pickett's force consisted of his three infantry brigades (Terry's, Corse's and Steuart's) totaling approximately 5,000 men. Added to that were two small brigades, Ransom's and Wallace's, from Bushrod Johnson's division, adding another 1,400 infantry. Rooney Lee's and Thomas Rosser's cavalry divisions were ordered to report to Fitz Lee who was already operating in the area. This gave Fitz Lee a total of 4,200 cavalry, a far cry from Sheridan's 9,000 Union horsemen who had the added advantage of being armed with Spencer repeating carbines. The Confederate force was augmented with the addition of Pegram's artillery battalion of twenty guns. It was hoped

---

390 Official Records, Series 1, Volume 46, Part 1, Pgs. 335, 342, 380, 1033.

391 Douglas Southall Freeman, "R. E. Lee", Volume 4, Pg. 27, Charles Scribner's and Sons, New York, 1936: Official Records, Series 1, Volume 46, Part 3, Pgs. 1357, 1360.

that this combined force would be able to stem the Union onslaught that was enveloping Gen. Lee's right flank.[392]

After the division arrived at Dunlop Tavern on the night of the 29th of March, Pickett received orders from Gen. R. H. Anderson to push on to White Oak Road. There he was to take up a position to the right of Gen. Johnson's division, which was the extreme right of the Confederate Petersburg line. The division conducted a forced march through the night in the pouring rain and arrived at White Oak Road at sunrise. While the soaking wet men rested, Gen. Lee arrived on the line. Lee was consulting with the General officers present when word came from Fitz Lee that a heavy enemy cavalry force was present at the road junction known as Five Forks. Pickett was ordered to take the infantry and six guns of Pegram's artillery and drive the Union cavalry out of Five Forks. Once completed he was to combine forces with Fitz Lee and move on Dinwiddie C. H. where it was believed that Sheridan's main force was located.[393]

On their way to Five Forks, the division was continuously harassed by Yankee cavalry on both their front and their flanks. Skirmishing as they moved along the road slowed the pace of the column. At one point the blue clad horseman attacked the accompanying ammunition wagons but were driven off before they could cause any mischief. When the column arrived at Five Forks, the 1st VA and the 7th VA were pushed out in front to drive off the enemy cavalry that occupied the Forks. This they did "in handsome style" and the two regiments remained on picket duty in front of the division. Rooney Lee and Rosser had yet to arrive with their cavalry and the infantry was exhausted after marching and skirmishing for the better part of the past 18 hours. Since it was also getting dark, the two commanders, Pickett and Fitz Lee, agreed to stay at Five Forks for the night and move on to Dinwiddie C. H. in the morning.[394]

After spending a rainy night at Five Forks, Pickett's force moved toward Dinwiddie C. H. at 10 AM on the morning of March 31st. Fitz Lee's cavalry protected their flanks as the infantry trudged through muddy

---

392 Freeman, "R. E. Lee", Volume 4, Pgs. 28-31.

393 Walter Harrison, "Pickett's Men", Pgs. 135-136

394 "Report of Major-Gen. Georg Pickett" as quoted in "Pickett's Men", Walter Harrison, Pgs. 142-151: Charles Loehr, "War History of the Old First Virginia", Pg. 58.

fields and roads. They arrived at Chamberlain's Creek, or Chamberlain's Bed as it was known locally, and found it running very high from the recent heavy rains. A fordable spot was found near an old mill that was defended by dismounted Union cavalry of the 1st Brigade, 2nd Division, under the command of Brig. Gen. Henry Davies. The 3rd VA waded through the waist deep water under a heavy fire and forced their way onto the far bank but suffered severe casualties in the process. The 1st VA followed across the creek and after a brisk fight drove off the Union defenders. The remainder of Pickett's force crossed the creek, reformed their lines and continued the move on Dinwiddie C. H.[395]

Davies brought up his entire brigade and attempted to halt the rebel attack. Davies troopers let loose a ferocious fire with their repeating rifles but it was not enough to stop the determined Confederate offensive and Davies was once again forced to retire. Brig. Gen. Thomas Devin, who was in command of the 1st Division of the Cavalry Corps, began throwing brigades of dismounted Union cavalry in the path of the advancing rebels. These piecemeal attempts slowed the advance but were not enough to stop it. The 1st VA, along with the rest of the division, continued the running battle, overcoming each obstacle that the Union commanders placed in their path. As the Confederates passed over dead and wounded Yankees, they picked up their carbines and fired them until empty.[396]

Union commanders continued to bring up reinforcements as fast as possible and placing them in advantageous positions between the Confederates and Dinwiddie C. H. Each Union line encountered was eventually pushed back onto the ensuing line in their rear. When stubborn resistance was encountered by the infantry, Fitz Lee's cavalry rode around the flank of the determined defenders, forcing another withdraw. The battle persisted in this manner until late in the afternoon when Pickett's force was within one mile of Dinwiddie C. H. Gen. Sheridan, who was personally at Dinwiddie, placed troopers of the third division under the

---

[395] David Johnston, "Four Years a Soldier". Pg. 384: Charles Loehr, "War History of the Old First Virginia", Pg. 58: Official Records, Series 1, Volume 46, Part 1, "Report of Brig. Gen. Henry Davies", Pg. 1143-1144.

[396] Official Records, Series 1, Volume 46, Part 1, "Report of Brig. Gen. Henry Davies", Pg. 1143-1144: "Report of Brig. Gen. Thomas C. Devin, U. S. Army Commanding First Division", pgs. 1122-23.

command of Brevet Major Gen. George Custer in a strong position on which the retreating troopers could rally. Custer's line was augmented with a battery of four, 3-inch rifles of Battery "A," 2nd U.S. Light Artillery. With darkness fast approaching, Pickett reformed his men in one last attempt to reach Dinwiddie C. H. before nightfall. The rebels attacked, but this time Custer's line held until darkness brought an end to the contest. Each force maintained their position, the combatants so close that opposing pickets were within pistol shot of each other. That night the men of the 1st VA helped to gather and care for the many wounded of both armies that littered the battlefield. The regiment itself suffered few casualties in the all-day fight but the brigade suffered the loss of their commander, Gen. Terry. Terry's horse was killed and fell on the General, injuring him severely. Col. Mayo of the 3rd VA, as he did after Gettysburg, once again took over command of the brigade.[397]

Sheridan spent the night communicating with Generals Grant and Meade in regards to his situation at Dinwiddie C. H. The Union commanders on the scene overestimated the force that Pickett had in their front. Major Gen. Merritt believed Pickett's men numbered over 14,000, when in fact Pickett and Fitz Lee combined numbered approximately 10,600. Sheridan wrote to Grant, "This force it too strong for us. I will hold out at Dinwiddie Court House until I am compelled to leave." Grant had already put things in motion to support Sheridan's position. As Sheridan knew, approximately 12,000 men of the Union V Corps, under the command of Gen. Gouverneur Warren, had been trying to reach his position during the day. Although Warren could hear the sounds of the fight taking place in the distance, the running battle continued to move away from his position. Bad roads, destroyed bridges, confusing orders and Warren's cautious nature kept him from arriving at Dinwiddie C. H. in time to take part in the fight. Gen. Meade, in an effort to speed Warren's approach, wrote, "Time is of the utmost importance. Sheridan cannot maintain himself at Dinwiddie without re-enforcements, and yours are

[397] Ed Bears & Chris Calkins, "The Battle of Five Forks", H. E. Howard, Lynchburg VA, 1985, Pgs. 44-46: Official Records, Series 1, Volume 46, "Report of Bvt. Maj. Gen. George A. Custer", Pgs. 1129-1131: E.P. Reeve, "Civil War Reminiscences.

the only ones that can be sent. Use every exertion to get the troops to him as soon as possible."[398]

Through the capture of two prisoners by his scouts, Pickett learned late in the night of the arrival of lead elements of Warren's V Corps. It was also apparent that Sheridan's entire cavalry corps was at Dinwiddie C. H. If he remained in his current position, both his rear and flank would be open to attack from the massive corps of infantry that was approaching ever closer by the hour. In the early morning hours, Pickett began to draw off his force and fall back on the more defensible position at Five Forks. The move was done in good order, the Confederates removed all of their wounded and buried their dead before leaving their position at Dinwiddie. Pickett telegrammed Gen. Lee and explained the situation to him. Gen. Lee replied to hold Five Forks at all costs and to keep the enemy away from the Southside Railroad. Upon reaching Five Forks, the men of the 1st VA, along with the rest of Pickett's division, began to stack logs and fence rails in an attempt to build crude breastworks.[399]

Pickett's troops occupied approximately a mile and three-quarters section of White Oak Road, which ran east and west. Ford's Church Road ran perpendicular, north and south, through the center of his line. On the extreme right of his line, facing south, Pickett placed Corse's brigade. To the left of Corse was Terry's brigade (Mayo) which included the 1st VA. Mayo's left rested on Ford's Church Road. To Mayo's left was Steuart's brigade and to his left were the two brigades from Johnson's division, Wallace's and Ransom's, which constituted the extreme left of the line. Rooney Lee's cavalry protected the right flank and Munford's cavalry the left. The only thing between Pickett's left and the far right flank of the Petersburg defenses was Robert's undermanned cavalry brigade patrolling the area. A battery of Pegram's guns were placed between Mayo and Steuart on Ford's Church Road. Other guns were placed on each flank.

Having placed his troops in line, Pickett and Fitz Lee accepted an invitation from Gen. Rosser to take part in a lunch of baked shad. The generals, like all of their men, were hungry and even with an impending

---

398 Official Records, Series 1, Volume 46, Part 1, Pg. 1110, 1111, 1116, 816-825, 367.

399 "Report of Major-Gen. Georg Pickett" as quoted in "Pickett's Men", Walter Harrison, Pgs. 142-151; Charles Loehr, "War History of the Old First Virginia", Pg. 59.

battle found it hard to turn down such an enticing invitation. Prior to leaving, Fitz Lee received a report that Robert's troopers on the left of the line had been driven off. If true this meant that Pickett's force was completely cut off from the rest of the Confederate army. Fitz Lee sent Munford to confirm the report and he rode off with Pickett to Rosser's headquarters and fresh baked shad.[400]

Sheridan's cavalry began arriving on the scene in the early afternoon. A skirmish line from the 1st VA made up of men from Company "C" were surprised in their forward position by the fast moving cavalry and captured. The few who escaped ran back to the main line and gave warning of the impending peril. Union cavalry made several attempts to charge the Confederate line but in each case were repulsed. Sheridan's troopers continued to skirmish with the Confederate infantry throughout the afternoon. While this action was taking place, Gen. Warren deployed the three divisions of his corps, out of sight of the rebel lines. Warren's divisions were eventually spotted by Confederate pickets and word spread to the lines of the forthcoming infantry attack. Pickett and Fitz Lee had not yet returned from their lunch with Rosser and each brigade commander was on his own to prepare for the impending assault by the Union V Corps. His preparations being made, Warren's corps burst from the woods a little after 4 PM and approached the extreme left of the Confederate lines. Through some misinterpretation of the terrain, the V Corps was actually past the breastworks and needed a series of left oblique marches to align themselves with the rebel trenches. [401]

The V Corps battle line from left to right was composed of the divisions of Generals Romeyn B. Ayres, Charles Griffin and Samuel Crawford, approximately 12,000 men in all. Ayres' division turned to the left and moved up White Oak Road, advancing toward Ransom's small brigade of North Carolinians. Ransom refused his line in an attempt to protect his left flank. He also had four guns of McGregor's battery positioned on the flank. The North Carolinians launched a deadly fire into Ayres' division as they approached the lines. The Union troops hesitated and then pushed on into the maelstrom. The weight of musket fire and McGregor's

---

400 Ed Bears & Chris Calkins, "The Battle of Five Forks", Pgs. 77, 81.

401 Charles Loehr, "War History of the Old First Virginia", Pg. 59: Official Records, Series 1, Volume 46, "Warren's Report on the Action of April 1, 1865", Pgs. 828-837.

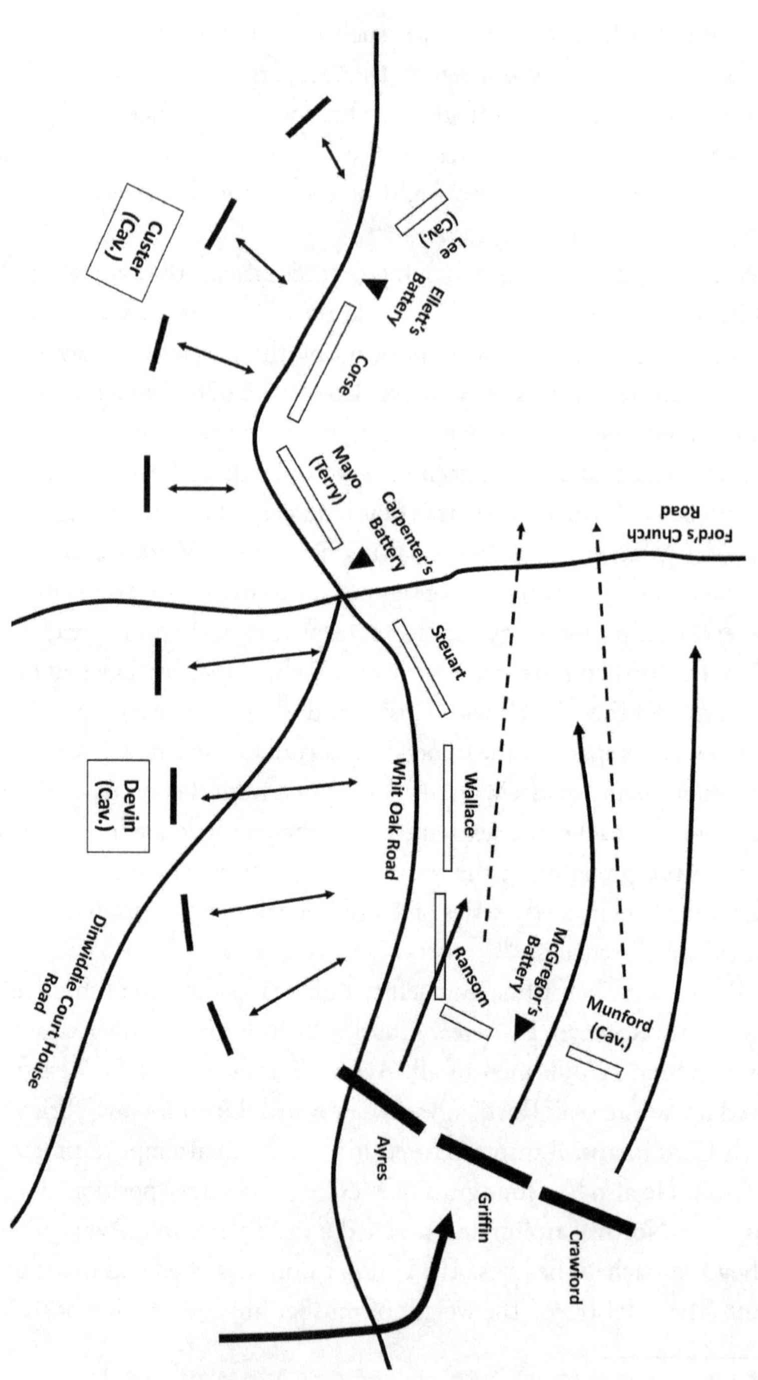

The Battle of Five Forks,
The Union Advance, April 1, 1865

guns recoiled the division again and it appeared to stall in front of the Confederate works. In order to keep the Rebels from re-enforcing the threatened left flank, Sheridan's cavalry, approximately 9,000 strong, both mounted and dismounted, attacked all along the Confederate line. Sheridan, himself, saw the Union infantry halt, and in some cases began to retrace their steps. He grabbed his headquarters flag and charged into the infantrymen, riding up and down the lines screaming encouragement to the reluctant soldiers, in a scene reminiscent of his actions at Cedar Creek the previous October. Like at Cedar Creek, his example succeeded and the blue line continued to push forward.[402]

Munson's Confederate cavalry took up a position to the left of Ransom's refused line but it was not enough to save the exposed flank. As the wave of blue clad soldiers neared their lines, some of the North Carolinians dropped their weapons and headed for the rear, but the vast majority stood ready to meet the assault. Ayres' division crashed into the rebel flank and carried the works, pushing all that was before it. Prisoners were sent to the rear so quickly that they could not be counted, but it was estimated to be near 1,000. Those of Ransom's men not killed or captured fell back onto Wallace's brigade, which was next in line. As Ayres fought his way up the White Oak Road, Griffin moved his division to Ayres' right, which was behind the rebel works. To his right and far behind the Confederate lines was Crawford's Union division.[403]

Crawford was so far behind the Confederate lines that he found very little resistance as he moved though the pine forests that were indicative of this part of Virginia. Crawford came to Ford's Church Road where he captured some wagons and ambulances. Gen. Warren arrived at this point and ordered Crawford to turn his division to the left and march down the Ford's Church Road into the center of the Confederate rear. The Rebel line along White Oak Road was steadily collapsing. Ransom's remnants and Wallace's brigade were now being pushed back onto Steuart's brigade. Pickett, who had raced to the scene, pulled Mayo's brigade, including the 1st VA, out of line and shifted them to the rear to face Crawford's division coming down Ford's Church Road. The brigade rushed to their new

---

402 Ed Bears & Chris Calkins, "The Battle of Five Forks", Pgs. 93-94.

403 "Report of Major-Gen. Georg Pickett" as quoted in "Pickett's Men", Walter Harrison, Pgs. 146.

position with a scream, scooping up stragglers from the decimated left and pushing them back into line as they went.[404]

The 1st VA, along with the rest of the brigade, took up a position straddling the Ford's Church Road, facing north. They were supported by some of McGregor's guns which were saved when Ransom's line collapsed. Crawford's lead brigade, commanded by Gen. Coulter, collided with Mayo's Virginians and a terrific fire fight ensued causing severe casualties to Coulter's brigade. The 1st VA and their comrades in the 3rd, 7th, 11th and 24th VA regiments put up a gallant defense but the small brigade had no chance of stopping such overwhelming numbers as they were confronted with in Crawford's entire Union division. The Yankees moved on both flanks of Mayo's brigade and the Confederates were close to being completely surrounded. The brigade began to waver and fall back, many of those who were trapped dropped their weapons and became prisoners of war. Those that could escape fell back and rallied on Corse's brigade which had turned to face the enemy and was the only infantry brigade left with any semblance of order. Standing with Corse's brigade was the ensign and color guard protecting the flag of the 1st VA which proudly waved above the chaotic scene below. In a bizarre sight, standing next to the Color Guard was an ad hoc glee club singing "Rally Round the Flag." As the sun was finally setting, survivors from every brigade were flocking to the line of Corse's steadfast men and taking a position in line hoping to hold off the Yankees long enough to escape. Rooney Lee's Cavalry charged into Custer's division, driving them back and allowing the remains of Pickett's command to break out and leave the field as darkness fell.[405]

The Battle at Five Forks was absolutely devastating to the Confederacy. Grant now had an opening to push his army in behind the lines at Petersburg

---

[404] Official Records, Series 1, Volume 46, Part 1, "Report of Gen. Samual Crawford", Pgs. 879-881: E.P. Reeve, Reminiscences: David Johnston, "Four Years a Soldier", Pg. 390.

[405] Official Records, Series 1, Volume 46, Part 1, Pgs. 879-881, 835: "Report of Major-Gen. George Pickett" as quoted in "Pickett's Men", Walter Harrison, Pgs. 147: Davis Johnston, "Four Years a Soldier", Pg. 392.

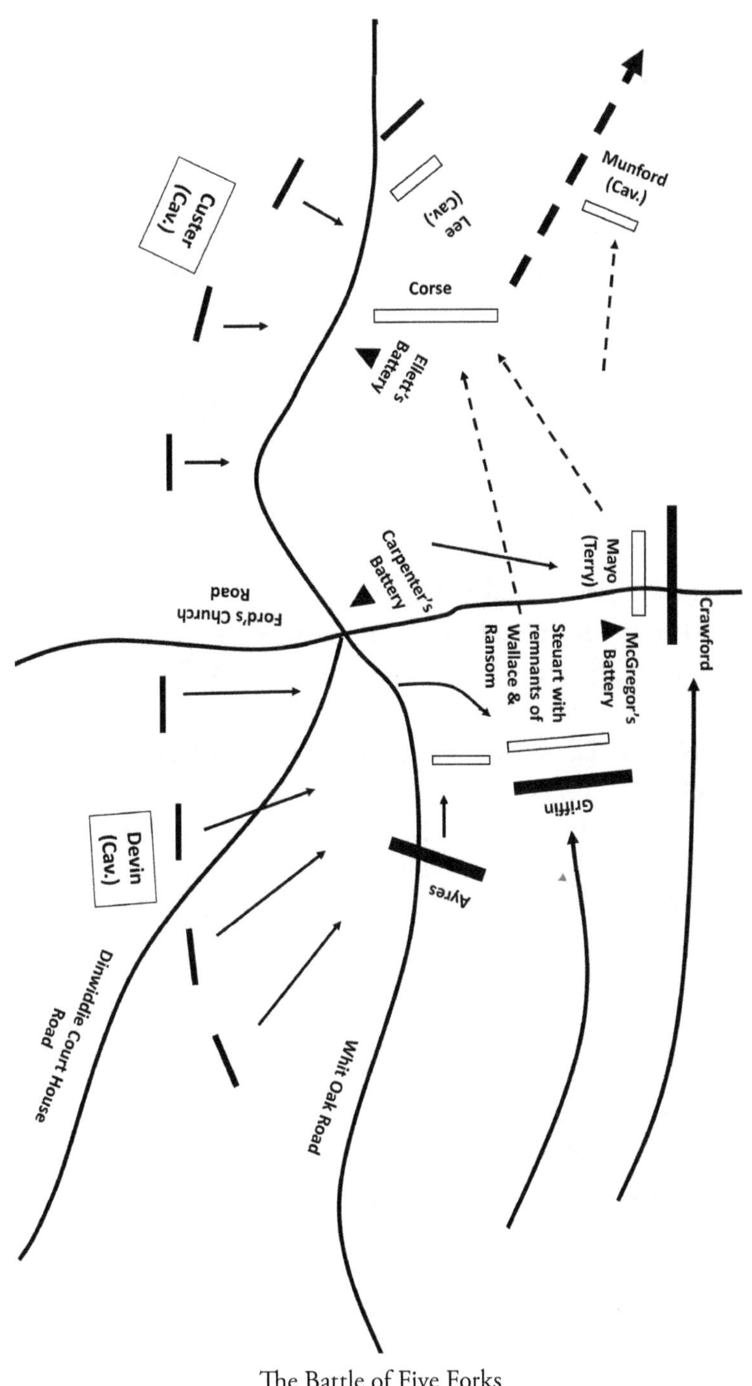

The Battle of Five Forks
The Confederate Collapse

and cut all railroad lines into the city. This made Lee's position along the Richmond/Petersburg corridor untenable. On the morning following the battle, Lee wrote to Secretary of War Breckinridge, "I see no prospect of doing more than holding our position here till night. I am not certain I can do that." Lee also recommended "that all preparation be made for leaving Richmond tonight." Later that day Lee again wrote to Breckinridge, "It is absolutely necessary that we should abandon our position tonight or run the risk of being cut off in the morning." As everyone knew, this telegram meant the loss of Petersburg and Richmond and more importantly it took the Army of Northern Virginia out from behind its breastworks and into the open field where Grant's overwhelming numbers could destroy it.[406]

The losses within Pickett's division are pure speculation. Walter Harrison, Pickett's Inspector General, wrote that on the 3rd of April, the division mustered 1,300 men from those who were at Five Forks. On the assumption the division had 3,900 before the battle, the losses at Five Forks amounted to 2,600 men. Union Gen. Warren reported the capture of 3,244 men but that number included the men of Wallace's and Ransom's brigades and the cavalry divisions which were not part of Pickett's division. Among the many officers lost in the battle was the brilliant, young artillery officer Col. Willie Pegram who was shot from his horse while defending his cannon. The 1st VA lost about 100 men, most of whom were captured in their attempt to stop Crawford's division. Incredibly the regiment suffered only two fatalities. Following is a partial list of casualties within the regiment (All captured unless otherwise noted):

Captured:
Field and Staff – Assistant Surgeon Dr. Henry H. Seargent.
Company "B" – Sergeants John L. Littlepage, Benjamin M. Crow; Privates J. H. Daniels, Thomas G. Harlow, John Hazelwood, William J. Mallory, and Philip S. Roberts.

Company "C" – Corporal Richard C. Price (Wounded); Privates William H. Brock, Nathanial A. Bernstein, William G. Burton (Wounded), James W. Corcoran, Thomas Collins, Hillery W. Collins, William A. Collins, James Edwards, Thomas E. Farrar, Benjamin L. Hargraves, Jabez M.

[406] Official Records, Series 1, Volume 46, Part 1, Pgs. 1264-65.

Gravely, John H. Goulder, William P. Ingram, John N. Johnson, E. R. Marden, James McCrossen, Benjamin J. McCary, Thomas Murphy, Michael Nolan, Benjamin R. Nobles, George A. Pinnell, George. W. Pollard, Alex E. Powell, Calvin Rainey, James A. Thorpe, Jackson Trueman, E. L. White and Abram J. Williams.

Company "D" – Sergeants John H. Keplar, Charles T. Loehr, Junius Perrin (Killed); Corporals William J. Armstrong, George L. Meanley; Privates J. N. Andrews, Henry C. Bowe, James G. Braton, George W. Crow, Andrew J. Draper, John T. Farmer, D. R. Foushee, Peter P. Fuqua, Benjamin K. Garrett, John W. Harris, John P. Hendrick, William P. Mahane, Charles L. Melson, George W. Mitchell, Alexander G. Moss, Robert H. Redman, Chasteen M. Sublett, Henry W. Watson.

Company "G" – Sergeants Geo. W. Ball, William. H. Deane; Corporal Richard D. Jordan, James R. Atkinson (Wounded and captured); Privates William Anderson, Benjamin Ashby, Charles W. Bell, Gustavus A. Chapman, Thomas W. Hay, Vernon E. Hodges, Pleasant H. Payne, Edwin Robinson, William H. Wilson, William. A. Wood, Patrick Woods, Edwin J. Gray (Wounded).

Company "H" – Lieutenant Paul C. Cabell; Sergeant Thomas S. Riddick, Theodore R. Martin; Privates, W. D. Burchell, John H. Daniel, William H. Duerson, James A. Ford, James Kingsy, George A. Nolting, Edward G. Nuckols, Marcus A. Rose, Charles F. Sims, and John J. Sinnott, Nicholas L. Vaughn (Killed).

Company "I" – Sergeants Thomas E. Traylor, William T. White (Wounded and captured); Corporal John T. Crew; Privates; Richard A. Ashby, John L. Ashworth, George W. Boler, C. H. Chappell, John C. Head, Harvey Hodges, Martin Hodges, Thomas P. Lester, Patrick Quinn, James E. Robinson, James B. Wallace.

Company "K" – (Serving with another company) Private Ballard E. Ward.[407]

The fields and forests to the west and north of Five Forks were littered with small groups of men who managed to escape from the battle. Throughout the night men banded together and some semblance of military order was restored to the fragments of Pickett's shattered division. The remnants of the regiment picked up the march on April 2nd, moving about twelve miles and camping near the Appomattox River. On this day many of the scattered units found their way back to Pickett's division and their brigades. Eppa Hunton's brigade also rejoined the division with nine hundred men, giving Pickett a total of only about twenty-four hundred muskets. On the 3rd they continued the retreat to Amelia Court House. After a brief rest at Amelia C. H., they moved off in the direction of Farmville on the 4th of April. Gen. Lee's entire army was moving across this section of Virginia after evacuating Petersburg and Richmond. Pickett's column joined up with Gen. Ewell's Corps who had withdrawn from their position on the Petersburg line during the night of April 2nd. On the night of April 5th the division camped near Sailor's Creek.[408]

The march to Sailor's Creek were some of the most arduous days of the entire war for the men of the 1st VA. Throughout the march there was the constant threat of Union cavalry attacking their column and skirmishing with the blue clad horseman was commonplace. The urgency of the situation allowed very little time for sleep halts in the retreat were few and short lived and food was almost non-existent, save for a bit of parched corn and a small ration of bread. The wagons were being pulled by starving animals and greatly slowed the pace, increasing the risk of capture by the Union army that was making every attempt to cut off Gen Lee's retreat. During the retreat, on the evening of April 3rd, word reached the Virginians of the surrender and subsequent burning of Richmond. For those who called the capital home, anxiety over their family's well-being

---

407 Walter Harrison, "Pickett's Men", Pg. 153: Lee Wallace, "1st Virginia Infantry", Pgs. 81-123: "Record of the Richmond City and Henrico Co. Virginia Troops", Compiled by E. H. Chamberlayne, Jr., Richmond 1879. Charles Loehr, "War History of the Old First Virginia", Pgs. 59-60.

408 B. F. Howard, Pg. 65: Walter Harrison, "Pickett's Men", Pgs. 152-153.

compounded the misery of an already unbearable situation. Perhaps it was the mental and physical burden of the march or the slow realization that all was now lost but some of the men remembered this march as worse than all of their trials and tribulations over the past four years combined.[409]

On the 6th of April, the 1st VA as a part of Terry's brigade in Pickett's division crossed over Little Sailor's Creek on the Deatonville Road heading in the direction of Farmville. The division was marching with what was left of Anderson's Corps, followed by Ewell's Corps. An attack by Union cavalry halted Anderson and Ewell. The attack was repulsed but a gap opened up between Anderson and the rest of the army which continued forward when Anderson halted. The gap was quickly exploited by the Federals. A battalion of Confederate artillery tried to cross the gap and was quickly attacked and captured by Union horsemen. Pickett sent his brigades to rescue the artillery and while the Virginians did drive off the enemy, they were not in time to save the guns or gunners. The confederates quickly began to build breastworks from fence posts and logs anticipating an attack on their exposed position. Anderson and Ewell found themselves blocked in front by a large force of Sheridan's cavalry and infantry from General Horatio Wright's Union VI corps coming up from the rear. Wright placed 20 cannon across the creek at the Hillsman house and at 5:00 PM began a fierce shelling of the Confederate position.[410]

As the Union VI Corps crashed into Ewell's men in the rear, Sheridan's cavalry attacked Anderson in the front. The fighting became confused and brutal. Gen. Custer's division attacked in Pickett's front and was repulsed several times. The enemy horsemen filled the air with hot lead from their repeating rifles and the Confederates laid behind their improvised breastworks firing as fast as possible in response. In some places the combatants were in such close proximity to one another that the fighting was hand to hand. Eventually Custer's troopers broke through the lines and the Confederate position collapsed. There were wholesale surrenders on parts of the line while the struggle continued on at other sections. Eventually, the 1st VA, in their last battle of the war, found themselves

---

409 "Civil War Reminiscences of Captain Edward Payson Reeve", Edward Payson Reeve: David Johnston, "Four Years a Soldier", Pgs. 399-402.

410 Chris Calkins, "The Appomattox Campaign", Pgs. 106-111, Schroeder Publications, 131 Tanglewood Drive, Lynchburg, VA 24502, 2008.

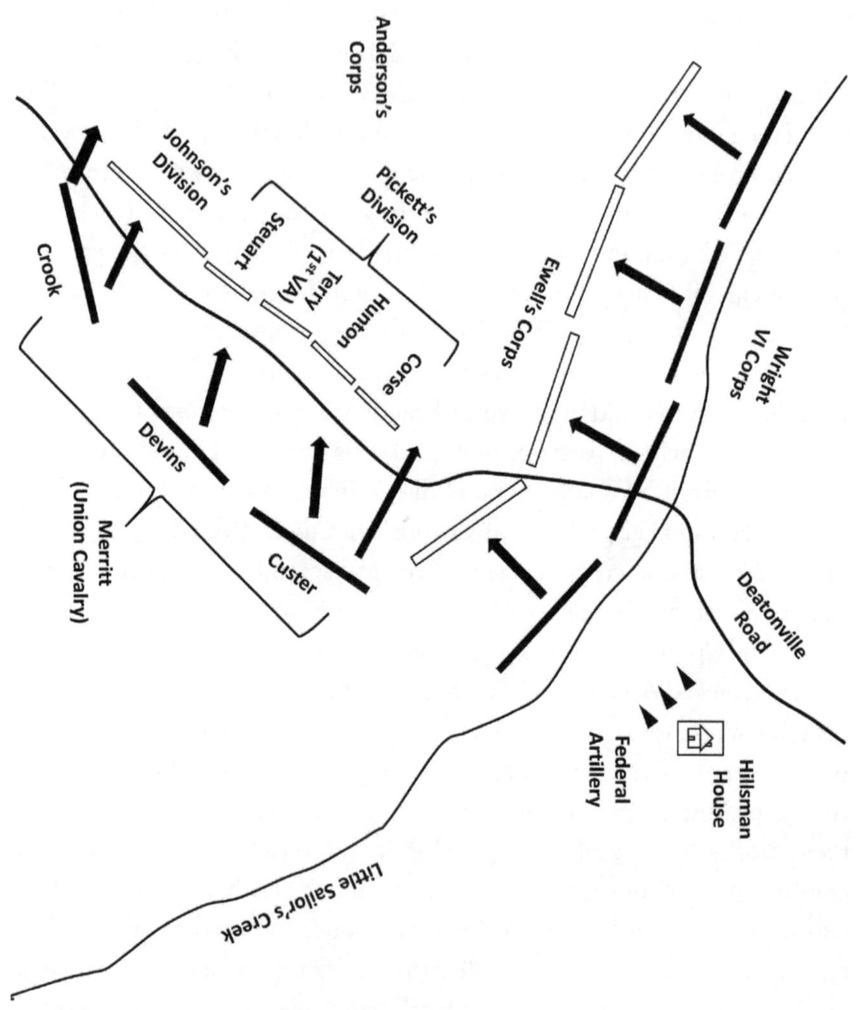

Battle of Sailor's Creek
April 6, 1865

completely surrounded and Lt. Col. Langley was compelled to surrender the regiment.[411]

Most of Pickett's division was forced to do the same. Gen. Pickett and several of his staff were being chased by Union cavalry but were saved from capture by a well-placed volley from a nearby unit of Confederate infantry. Pickett managed to escape but his division ceased to exist as an effective military unit. Generals Corse and Hunton were taken prisoner but Generals Steuart and Terry managed to slip through the Federal lines and escape. The only members of the 1st VA not captured were those who were with the wagon train. Following is a partial list of casualties, the majority captured, at Sailor's Creek:

Field and Staff – Lt. Colonel F. H. Langley; Major G. F. Norton.

Company "B" – Captain Thomas H. Davis; Lieutenant Logan S. Robins; Sergeant John Q, Figg; Corporal Mungo P. Buchanan, Nathaniel Earnest (Killed); Privates J. W. Cauthorn, William J. Gravett, James A. Green, George R. Heath, Charles Mitchell.

Company "C" – Sergeants John Moriarty, Patrick Woods; Corporals Lawrence Carroll, Richard Price; Privates Benjamin R. Nobles, L. Notlin.

Company "D" – Captain Edward P. Reeve; Lieutenant Robert McCandish Jones; Corporal George E. Craig; Privates Meyer Angle, Henry W. Furcron, Corbin Pettit, Thomas W. Traylor, W. R. Wilkins, W. A. Westmoreland, Samuel L. Wingfield, C. H. Wheeler.

Company "G" – Captain Eldridge Morris; Lieutenant William T. Woody; Sergeant Elijah Wright, Corporal John Allen; Privates Edward C. Atkins, Joseph R. Epps, Charles W. Gentry, Thomas W. Miles, Alfred Jeff Vaughan.

Company "H" – Lieutenant William M. Lawson; Sergeant Ryland H. Norvell; Corporals Robert N. Dunn, F. M. Smith; Privates Isham Belcher,

---

411 Chris Calkins, "The Appomattox Campaign", Pgs. 106-111: David Johnston, "Four Years a Soldier", Pgs. 406-407.

William M. Belcher, M. H. Burton, E. F. Davidson, Robert E. Dignum, Henry H. Tolar, Jesse W. Viar.

Company "I" – Lieutenant Henry C. Ballow; Sergeant William F. Terry; Corporal Edwin B. Loving; Privates Samuel Clark, Thomas B. Huffman, William P. Smith, William C. Taliaferro. Wounded and Captured Fred R. Pugh.

Company "K" – Privates J. W. Bumgarner, Washington Musser, Gordon Respass, Alfred J. Rosenbaum, Jacob Smith, Steven Umbarger."[412]

There were only seventeen men from the 1st VA who managed to escape the disasters at Five Forks and Sailor's Creek. As no officers were present, the small group was under the command of Sergeant Major Andrew J. Simpson. These men followed the army to Appomattox C. H. where they took part in the surrender of the Army of Northern Virginia on April 9, 1865. Of these seventeen men, ten were members of the original 1st VA who had enlisted almost exactly 4 years earlier on April 21, 1861. Unfortunately, none of them left any known written account of their experience. The Seventeen sole surviving members of the 1st VA were:

"Sergeant Major Andrew J. Simpson in command; Quartermaster Sergeant William Harper Deane; Ordnance Sergeant Elias P. Hudgins.
Company "B" – Privates James Stagg, John F. Snyder, George C. Hancock, George Earnest, John R. Garrett.
Company "C" – John N. Johnson.
Company "D" – Privates Thomas A. Howard, John F. Wheeley, Lemuel R. Wingfield.
Company "G" – Private John K. Wilkinson, James P. Mahone.
Company "H" – Private Robert E. Womack.

---

412 Walter Harrison "Pickett's Men", Pgs. 156-157: Lee Wallace, "1st Virginia Infantry", Pgs. 81-123: "Record of the Richmond City and Henrico Co. Virginia Troops", Compiled by E. H. Chamberlayne, Jr., Richmond 1879: Charles Loehr, "War History of the Old First Virginia" Pg. 62.

Company "I" – Privates Martin Oeters, R. L. Carter."[413]

It was fitting that the 1st VA, the regiment that was first to meet the Union advance at Bull Run almost four long years before, was represented at the final surrender of the Army of Northern Virginia. There is no record of the flag of the 1st VA being surrendered at Appomattox. Color bearer Patrick Woods is said to have ripped the flag from its staff and concealed it at Sailor's Creek before he was captured. For those captured at Five Forks and Sailor's Creek, the suffering and death that they had endured throughout the war was not yet over. After being captured they were marched off to various prisoner of war camps in the Northern states.[414]

For many of the enlisted men in the 1st VA, that meant a journey to the nightmare that was Point Lookout, MD. This prisoner of war camp was located on a low lying peninsula at the confluence of the Potomac River and the Chesapeake Bay. The camp was created after the Battle of Gettysburg to house the many prisoners captured there. With the U.S. government's policy of severely limiting paroles and exchanges coupled with the misfortunes of the southern armies in 1864-65, the number of prisoners at the camp soon far outnumbered its intended capacity. When those captured at Five Forks and Sailor's Creek arrived, the populace of the prison was in excess of 20,000.[415]

Those prisoners of the 1st VA, along with thousands of additional Confederate soldiers captured during Gen. Lee's retreat from the lines at Petersburg, were marched back to that city where they boarded steamers at City Point. Although the Confederates were mostly treated with kindness by the front line troops who captured them, their treatment worsened as they were transferred to rear echelon troops who never witnessed the horrors of battle. Upon reaching the wharf at Point Lookout, the men were ordered to place all of their belongings on the dock. Union soldiers kicked into the water any article that had U.S. stamped on it, including blankets, coats, etc., claiming it was stolen property from the Union Army. Since the

---

[413] Lee Wallace, "1st Virginia Infantry", Pgs. 81-123: "Record of the Richmond City and Henrico Co. Virginia Troops", Compiled by E. H. Chamberlayne, Jr., Richmond 1879. Charles Loehr, "War History of the Old First Virginia", Pg. 62.

[414] Richmond newspaper, Dated 7/21/1875.

[415] www.nps.gov, Point Lookout Confederate Cemetery.

men of the 1st VA were almost completely outfitted with items procured from Plymouth and other battlefields, they were left standing on the docks with nothing to protect them from the elements.

The captives were then marched off to the "bull pen," a large fenced in field which housed the thousands and thousands of prisoners. Those that were fortunate managed to find shelter in one of the small tents that lined the muddy streets. If no tents were available, the men were forced to lie on the wet ground with nothing more than a thin blanket to protect them. The perimeter of the camp was lined with a fifteen foot wooden wall, the top of which was adorned with a platform that was patrolled by trigger happy guards. Fifteen feet inside the wall was a ditch known as the "dead line," any prisoner who crossed the ditch was immediately shot by the guards on the wall. The rations issued to the Confederates were barely enough to keep the men from starvation and the drinking water was brackish and unhealthy. These conditions when combined with the mosquito infested low lying ground, led to the outbreak of many deadly diseases among the prisoners. To make matters worse, the camp hospital which had been built to accommodate only twelve hundred patients was overwhelmed by the many thousands of sick and dying men. [416]

Although estimates of Confederate prisoners who died at Point Lookout vary greatly, approximately 4,000 are thought to be buried in the cemetery there. Of those, no less than seven are from the 1st VA: William J. Gravett of Company "B;" Alexander G. Moss and John W. Harris from Company "D;" William Hammett. Deane and William A. Wood, from company "G;" Steven Umburger and Gordon Respass from Company "K;"[417]

When captured, the officers were separated from the enlisted men and sent to different camps. Many of the captured officers of the 1st VA were sent to Johnson's Island in Lake Erie, near Sandusky Ohio. The officers fared better than the enlisted men in as much as they at least had barracks on the island and were not forced to sleep on the muddy ground.

---

416 Southern Historical Society Papers, Volume 18, "Point Lookout", by Charles Loehr, Pgs. 113-120: www.plpow.com, Descendants of Point Lookout, POW organization.

417 Lee Wallace, "1st Virginia Infantry", Pgs. 81-123: www.plpow.com, Descendants of Point Lookout, POW organization: https://old.findagrave.com, Find-A-Grave: http://www.interment.net, Internment.net.

They too were stripped of any articles that formerly belonged to the U. S. Government as they went into captivity. Like Point Lookout, Johnson's Island soon became overcrowded in the months following Gettysburg. The rations issued to the prisoners there were just as inadequate as well, forcing the officers, like their enlisted counterparts at Point Lookout, to eat rats which were in abundance at both camps.

As the war was winding down the prisoners were processed for release. After swearing allegiance to the United States and promising not to take up arms against the government, the men at Point Lookout were transferred to a holding pen, which in fact was nothing more than a large open field, to await transportation. When enough men were processed, the emaciated, ragged former soldiers were crowded onto steamers and sent to Richmond. The officers at Johnson's Island and other prisons were also allowed to take the oath of allegiance and were likewise sent back to Richmond by trains and boats. [418]

[418] Charles Loehr, "War History of the Old First Virginia", Pg. 61.

POSTWAR

In 1861 the 1st VA marched out of Richmond in grand style to the sounds of cheering crowds and marching bands. The naïve young soldiers dressed in their finest uniforms, all marching in step to the beat of the drums. Their return to Richmond was in sharp contrast to those heady days that must have seemed a lifetime ago. Instead of the regiment returning in a triumphant parade, the veterans of the 1st VA arrived a few at a time. Some arrived on overcrowded steamers and trains, others rode in wagons pulled by mules, and still others walked to the former capital of the Confederacy from wherever they happened to be when the long bloody war finally came to an end. Most of them wore ragged threadbare uniforms and they arrived hungry and penniless to their former homes. Their city had been partially destroyed by fire when the Confederates evacuated in April and was now occupied by Union troops. It was now left to these intrepid men who were so heroic in war to pick up the pieces of their shattered lives and build anew.

After a decade of rebuilding their lives as peaceful citizens of the United States, the men of the 1st VA decided it was time to renew their relationships with the comrades whom they had shared so many trials and tribulations. In April of 1875 notices were published in the newspapers requesting that all surviving members of the 1st VA assemble at the Virginia Opera House on April 23rd. The purpose of the meeting was the formation of a regimental veterans association. About one hundred of the former soldiers attended the meeting, as well as many spectators from Richmond who sat attentively in the galleries of the Opera House. Captain Joseph Griswold called the meeting to order promptly at 8:30 PM. James Dooley of Company "C," the son of Major John Dooley, was unanimously elected temporary chairman of the proceedings. A committee made up of one representative from each of the former companies was appointed to draft a constitution and by-laws for the association. It was discussed and decided to extend membership to any person who served honorably prior to or during the war. This ruling opened membership to the three infantry companies who were transferred at the beginning of the war as well as the Richmond Howitzers and Fayette Artillery. The appointed committee then left the room to attend to their duties.

While the committee debated the proposed constitution and by-laws in private, the meeting continued in the main hall. Several dignitaries in attendance were introduced and given "seats of honor" on the stage. Among them were Mayor Anthony Keiley, Gen. Patrick Moore, Gen. George E. Pickett, Col. William Palmer, and Dr. John. S. D. Cullen. Members of the 1st VA band were also in attendance and throughout the night they entertained those in the hall with patriotic songs. Several speeches were given before the committee returned to the floor and offered their proposals for by-laws, which were accepted. Elections for officers of the association were held and Gen. Patrick Moore was elected President. Col. Palmer was elected 1st Vice-President, Major Norton was elected 2nd Vice-President and Col. Langley was elected 3rd Vice-President. According to their new by-laws, the object of the association was to "revive friendships and memories of our army life; to visit and relieve our comrades in distress, and to provide for a history of our regiment." Any person who served honorably in the regiment during the war, from April 19, 1861 or thereafter, was eligible for "active" membership. Those who served in the regiment prior to the war were eligible for membership but were not allowed to vote or hold office. After the close of business, many of those in attendance paid their one dollar initiation fee and the first meeting of the "Old First Virginia Infantry Association" was adjourned.[419]

The Old First Virginia Infantry Association was formed as a civilian organization without uniforms, weapons or drill. The Association would parade on special occasions, most notably Memorial Day, and the funerals of deceased members. The Association had no official connection with the First Regiment of Virginia Volunteers that was reconstituted four years earlier on October 25, 1871. This regiment was reformed from numerous

---

419 Unknown Richmond newspaper, April 24, 1875: "Constitution and By-Laws of Old First Va. Infantry", Richmond, Baughman Brothers Printers, 1876.

companies of Virginia militia much the same as it was formed prior to the war. Although there was no official link between the Association and the new regiment, the two organizations did participate in many of the same events in the Richmond area.[420]

It was determined that the Association would hold monthly business meetings throughout the year. It was also decided that the anniversary of their first engagement, the Battle of Bull Run, July 18, 1861, would be celebrated each year with a reunion and banquet.

The first such celebration was held in 1875. The surviving men of the regiment assembled in front of City Hall and as they had done countless times before, they formed a column. Similarly, Smith's band was in the lead playing martial tunes. Sergeant Pat Woods unfurled the regimental battle flag that he had hidden and preserved when the regiment surrendered in April of 1865. The battle flag, alongside the Virginia State flag, once again proudly waved over the heads of the regiment in peace as it had done on so many fields of war. Under the command of Gen. Patrick Moore, the regiment stepped off and marched through the city to the docks at the Packet House where the men boarded canal boats. The boats carried the men of the 1st VA to the city's Pump House whose park like setting doubled as a gathering spot for parties and celebrations.

The day was spent renewing old friendships and no doubt the rehashing of the many campaigns of days gone by. One of the highlights was the target shooting competition which was won by Capt. E. P. Reeve of Company "D" and who received a silver medal for his efforts. Private John Lloyd of Company "E" received the leather medal for worst shot. Rain forced the festivities indoors where the large assembly crowded into the banquet hall for dinner. A round of toasts were read before the gathering: "The First Virginia Regiment: First of all in rank and second to none in renown; the old First today renews the memory of her earliest engagement – the happy opening of a glorious career."

Numerous toasts followed including one by Anthony Keiley, the Mayor of Richmond and a veteran of the 12th VA.

Many dignitaries and absent members sent letters of regret at not being able to attend the reunion. Among them were Col. Frederick Skinner who

---

420 "Constitution and By-Laws of Old First Va. Infantry": "Daily Dispatch" newspaper, October 27, 1871.

wrote, "*I beg you will assure them that though absent in person my heart will be with them and that wherever I may be and so long as I may live, my greatest pride will be the consciousness that like themselves, I too, can claim to be a veteran of the Old First Virginia.*" Other letters were received from such notables as Gen. George Pickett, who was confined to his bed, Gen. Kemper, who was serving as Governor of Virginia, and Gen. Beauregard, who was in New Orleans. At the conclusion of the evening the men and their families boarded the boats and returned to the city.[421]

The autumn of 1875 found the Old First Virginia Association front and center during two massive events in Richmond. On September 23rd, the veterans of the Old First Virginia along with the current First Regiment of Virginia Volunteers and other veteran groups assembled at the docks of the Powhatan Steamboat Company to take possession of a crate containing the statue of Gen. Thomas "Stonewall" Jackson. The statue, created by renowned Irish sculptor John Henry Foley, was a gift from "English gentlemen" to the people of Virginia. The crate was loaded onto a wagon and covered with the flags of Great Britain and Virginia. Among others, members of the Old First Virginia picked up the long ropes that were attached to the wagon and proceeded to pull the carriage and its valuable cargo through the streets of Richmond to the Capital building. Governor Kemper met the procession in front of the Capital and on behalf of the people of Virginia took possession of the statue. The bronze seventeen foot high sculpture was placed in the basement of the Capital building to await the completion of the pedestal on which it was to be mounted.[422]

On July 30th of 1875, Gen. George E. Pickett died from an illness at his home in Norfolk, VA. The General was temporarily interred at Cedar Grove Cemetery in that city. On October 23rd, his remains were disinterred in preparation for their removal to Hollywood Cemetery in Richmond, to be buried alongside many of his men who died at Gettysburg in the charge that bears his name. It was the Old First Virginia who bore the singular honor of travelling to Norfolk and escorting Pickett's remains back to Richmond. The eight men chosen for that solemn duty were:

---

[421] Unknown Richmond newspaper, July 21, 1875, July 26, 1875: Richmond Enquirer, Friday Morning July 20, 1877.

[422] The Alexandria Gazette Newspaper, September 24, 1875: Emergingcivilwar.com, Statues of Stonewall: Virginia State Capital Grounds, Richmond.

Captain William English, Captain Eldridge Morris, Charles Loehr, John A. Lloyd, Wilson B. Joseph, John Tyree, Herman Paul, and John Howard Childrey. Gen. Pickett's remains were placed in the Capital building where they laid in state for one day. On the following day, the funeral procession, estimated at five thousand participants, which included the Old First Virginia wound through the streets of Richmond in front of the forty thousand spectators who lined the roof tops and sidewalks. Homes and businesses were tastefully decorated with black bunting to honor one of Virginia's more famous generals. The procession entered Hollywood Cemetery and the men of the Old First Virginia watched as their old division commander, who they followed in that immortal charge, was laid to rest in the section of the cemetery known as "Gettysburg Hill."[423]

Two days after Gen. Pickett's funeral, the city of Richmond turned out once again to honor one of Virginia's favorite sons. The day had finally arrived for the unveiling of the Stonewall Jackson monument in front of the Capital building. The high regard in which the memory of Gen. Jackson was held in Virginia, second only to Robert E. Lee, was evident by the massive crowds that inundated Richmond. The entire populace of the capital, coupled with the estimated thirty thousand out of towners, crowded onto the streets to witness the celebration. The entire city was decorated in a manner as had never been seen before. Prevalent among the decorations were the stars and stripes of the American flag to which these ex-confederates now bore their allegiance. The procession, which was three miles in length, was led by Gen. Joseph E. Johnston and his staff. Following Johnston were the men of the reconstituted 1st VA Infantry Regiment. The parade consisted of all manner of military organizations, including militia companies and cadets from the military academies such as VMI, where Jackson served as a professor before the war. The parade also featured Dignitaries and politicians who rode in handsome carriages.[424]

Seventy-eight veterans of The Old First Virginia Association marched in the parade under the command of Col. Frederick Skinner who traveled from his home in New York for the festivities. Col. Skinner had been named as one of the Marshals for the parade, but after meeting with his

[423] The Alexandria Gazette Newspaper, October 25, 1875.

[424] The Alexandria Gazette, October 26, 1875: Turf, Field and Farm Magazine, November 12, 1875, written by F. G. Skinner.

comrades in the Old First he decided to march with his former regiment. Skinner wrote of his experience in the third person for a magazine that he was working for at the time: "*Our Field Editor had been appointed a Marshal by General Heth, and reported for duty on the day before the inauguration, but the scarred remnant of his own regiment, the "Old First Virginia," claimed him with an affectionate importunity not to be refused by a heart which in those four long years of alternate triumph and disastrous defeat had learned to admire and respect them as brave soldiers, and love them as comrades and brothers. He felt honored at being selected as one of the Marshals from among that army of Southern veterans, but he held it to be a still greater honor to march on that supreme occasion at the head of the few gallant survivors of such a regiment as the immortal Old First.*" The men of the Old First Virginia were quite accustomed to marching through the streets of Richmond to wild applause from the citizens of the city, but on this day the most boisterous ovations were reserved for the veterans of Gen. Jackson's own "Stonewall Brigade." Upon reaching the Capital building the crowd was greeted by several speeches including one by the Old First's former brigade commander, Gen. Kemper, who was now Governor of Virginia. Finally the beautiful statue of Gen. Jackson was unveiled before many teary eyed veterans of the former Army of Northern Virginia.[425]

It was not only deceased generals that drew the attention of the Old First Virginia. Members also took part in Memorial Day ceremonies at Oakwood and Hollywood cemeteries, where they placed flowers on the graves of fellow Confederate veterans. In a magnanimous gesture, the Association formed a committee to care for the graves of what were thought to be Union soldiers who were held as prisoners on Belle Island in the James River. The Association contacted the Federal authorities and it was later ascertained by the U. S. Army that the graves in question on Belle Island were not Union soldiers after all. Never the less, the Old First's cordial offer was gratefully acknowledged by Captain Rockwell of the U. S. Army, who was in charge of the National Cemetery.

Another example which demonstrates how these men who gave so much for the Confederacy were now ready to move forward as loyal citizens of the United States occurred at one of their annual reunions at Yuengling's Brewery Park on the James River. Captain B. F. Howard had

---

[425] Turf, Field and Farm Magazine, November 12, 1875, written by F. G. Skinner.

come into possession of the United States flag that the regiment carried prior to the secession of Virginia. Colonel Palmer accepted the flag on behalf of the Old First Virginia and had it hoisted above the pavilion. The Stars and Stripes unfurled to the breeze coming off the river amid loud cheers from the Confederate veterans below.[426]

Throughout the following years more and more veteran associations began to form across the country and members of the Old First Virginia Association began to meet informally with other veterans from Pickett's division. In early 1887, this led to the formation of the Pickett's Division Association of which the men of the Old First Virginia played a large role. No less than two veterans of the regiment, Charles Loehr and Edward Reeve, served as Commander of the newly formed association. Shortly after their incorporation, Pickett's Division Association received an invitation from a most unlikely source, the Philadelphia Brigade of Union Veterans located in Philadelphia, PA. The Philadelphia Brigade was made up of veterans from the 69th PA, 71st PA, 72nd PA and the 106th PA, the very men who withstood the onslaught of Pickett's Division on Cemetery Hill in Gettysburg. The Philadelphia Brigade was planning a reunion in Gettysburg to dedicate monuments to the 69th and 71st PA Regiments. It was their sincere hope that by inviting the men of Pickett's Division they could further the healing of the nation. They would meet the Virginians in a spirit of "Fraternity, Charity and Loyalty."[427]

During the intervening years since the end of the war, the Battle of Gettysburg in general and the assault known as Pickett's Charge specifically had taken on an almost mythological status. The soldiers of the Philadelphia Brigade and Pickett's Division were glorified in books, articles and speeches, much to the chagrin of the thousands of other soldiers on both sides who took part in the assault on July 3, 1863. The two units who clashed so violently on Cemetery Hill were ranked among the great fighting men in history, such as Napoleon's Old Guard at Waterloo and the Spartans who fought at Thermopylae. Therefore a reunion between these

---

[426] Alexandria Gazette, August 7, 1875: Letter from Captain J. T. Rockwell to the Old First VA Association, dated September 18, 1875: Unknown Richmond Newspaper.

[427] Carol Reardon, "Pickett's Charge in History and Memory", University of North Carolina Press, Chapel Hill NC, 1997, Pg. 93

two vaunted units on the blood stained fields of Gettysburg would be a symbol of national unity that the entire nation would notice.

Coincidentally, the Virginians of Pickett's Division had plans for a monument and reunion of their own at the site of their greatest struggle. It was their hope to place a monument dedicated to Gen. Pickett within the Bloody Angle, near the site where Gen. Armistead was mortally wounded. The monument was intended to mark the spot of the furthest penetration of the Union lines by Pickett's Division. A committee was formed which included Charles Loehr, who at the time was the Secretary of The Pickett's Division Association. After corresponding with the Gettysburg Memorial Association, which oversaw the placement of all monuments on the battlefield, the Virginians were told they would not be allowed to place a Confederate marker within the Union lines at Gettysburg. It was the policy of the Gettysburg Memorial Association to only allow monuments on original lines of battle and not on temporary positions. A three man delegation that included Edward P. Reeve travelled to Gettysburg to plead their case before Col. Batchelder of the Gettysburg Memorial Association. Batchelder informed the men that he had received bushels of letters from concerned citizens in opposition to the Confederate monument and even to an organized Confederate reunion in Gettysburg which had taken on the aura of hallowed ground. Their mission unfulfilled, the delegation returned to Richmond and reported their findings to the Pickett's Division Association.[428]

The executive committee held a meeting on May 7, 1887, to review the unfavorable response that was received from the Gettysburg Memorial Association. The following resolution was adopted by the committee:

"Whereas, the committee having heard the report of the sub-committee sent to Gettysburg to confer with the committee of the Gettysburg Memorial Association, and having learned that they will not be allowed to locate the proposed monument upon the spot to which the Division penetrated within the Federal lines in their charge, therefore,

Resolved, that it is inexpedient to erect our monument upon the Gettysburg Battlefield.

---

[428] John Tregaskis, "Souvenir of the Re-Union of The Blue and The Gray, on the Battlefield of Gettysburg, July 1, 2, 3, and 4,1888", Tregaskis and Co.,767 Broadway, Room 8, New York, 1888. Pg. 205.

Resolved, that the proposed reunion of Pickett's Division, at Gettysburg, on July 3rd, be not held.

Resolved, that a copy of these resolutions be sent to the secretary of the Gettysburg Memorial Association."[429]

With this resolution it looked as though the historic reunion between the former foes at Gettysburg would not take place. But the men of the Philadelphia Brigade were not prepared to throw in the towel on the proposed reunion. They were determined to heal the wounds of war even if some of their northern brethren disagreed. The Secretary of the Philadelphia Brigade, John W. Frazier, sent the following letter to Charles Loehr the Secretary of the Pickett's Division Association:

"Sergeant Chas. T. Loehr,

Secretary Pickett's Division, Richmond Va.

My Dear Comrade: The very agreeable duty of communicating with your Association, relative to the reunion at Gettysburg, has been assigned to me.

At a meeting of the Philadelphia Brigade held May 4th, a committee of nine was appointed to make all arrangements necessary to extend a fitting welcome to Pickett's Division at Gettysburg. At a meeting of the committee held May 10th, I was directed to officially inform your Association of our deep regret at the possibility of the contemplated reunion between your Division and our Brigade Association, not taking place in July next at Gettysburg.

We regret this all the more because we had intended to extend such a welcome as your unsurpassed bravery merited, and I was instructed to earnestly request you not to forego your desire to hold your first reunion at Gettysburg, July 3rd, but to meet there as the guests of the Philadelphia Brigade, to enjoy the hospitality we will extend to you, and with the fraternal feelings created by that reunion - the first of the kind held since the War - and with our sincere sympathy and co-operation, unitedly complete the arrangements you have begun, towards dedicating an imperishable monument to commemorate American Heroism, of which none are more proud than they who withstood the shock of your charge - a charge not surpassed in its unfaltering courage in the annals of war, since time began.

---

[429] John W. Frazier, "Reunion of the Blue and Gray, Philadelphia brigade and Pickett's division, July 2, 3, 4, 1887 and September 15, 16, 17, 1906", Ware Bros. Company, Philadelphia PA, 1906, Pg. 74.

Please lay my letter before you're Association at its meeting on Saturday next, and urge your comrades to meet us at Gettysburg, July 3, 1887, and assure them for the Brigade, I have the honor to represent, that we will be pleased to greet as many as will meet with us, whether it be 100 or 1,000 and the great good to all will result from that reunion.

Please let me hear from you at the earliest moment, as your acceptance will necessitate some immediate and pleasant work on our part. With renewed assurance of the soldierly regard, believe me,

Yours Fraternally,
John W. Frazier,

Secretary, Pro Tem, Philadelphia Brigade.
Philadelphia, May 11, 1887."[430]

In response, Charles Loehr wrote on May 14th:

"Your cordial invitation, of 11th inst., extended to our Division by the Philadelphia Brigade was laid before our committee, and in reply I am requested to tender you our sincere and grateful thanks for the fraternal welcome, and the very flattering terms therein contained, and to express to your Association the assurance that while this committee does not feel itself now authorized to accept the invitation so generously tendered, for the reason that their functions have ceased, when at their last meeting they decided not to hold their reunion at Gettysburg, they deeply feel and appreciate all your kind intentions and efforts for friendship sake.

We hope and trust that the day may come when all lines between the North and the South – the Blue and the Gray – shall have forever disappeared, and the survivors of our old Division and those of your gallant Brigade will meet – as you indicate in your letter – at Gettysburg to dedicate a Union monument (not alone for what was once called the Union side) but a memorial to the gallant men of both sides, expressive of the true American motto: 'A large country and a warm Heart,' remembering only the devotion and courage of

430 John W. Frazier, "Reunion of the Blue and the Gray", Pgs. 78-81.

the men who dared to sacrifice their lives and limbs for their principles and their country."[431]

Undeterred in his quest to bring about this historic reunion, John Frazier wrote to Charles Loehr on the 23rd of May asking the Secretary to present his letter to the membership of Pickett's Division at their next meeting and persuade them to override the committee's decision. In his letter he wrote:

"*We have been so long anticipating, with so much pleasure, the renewal of an acquaintance begun and ended so unceremoniously, twenty-four years ago, that we know not how to take any disappointment of our hopes and plans, and if not all your Association, we still hope a strong committee – not less than one hundred – will be appointed at your meeting on June 1st, to represent your Association, at Gettysburg, as the honored guests of the Philadelphia Brigade. If your Association could understand how very anxious we are to meet and welcome you, I am sure you would not fail in coming.*"[432]

Loehr had Frazier's gracious invitation published in the Richmond Dispatch and he received such a positive response from the members of the Pickett's Division Association that he wrote John Frazier on May 26, "*From the calls I have had to-day I am sure that when your fraternal invitation is submitted at our general meeting on June 1st, we shall succeed in getting a respectable delegation to join you in revisiting the spot where more history was made in three days than we can now make in 30 years.*" The two Secretaries were not disappointed when the membership of Pickett's Division Association met on June 1st, 1887. The Association voted that all members accept the invitation from the Philadelphia Brigade and attend the reunion in Gettysburg.[433]

For the first time in the now united country, two organized bodies of men who had fought so fiercely against each other would meet under the auspice of fraternity and friendship. The novelty of this event drew the attention of the press and thousands of people descended upon Gettysburg

[431] John W. Frazier, "Reunion of the Blue and the Gray", Pg. 81
[432] John W. Frazier, "Reunion of the Blue and the Gray", Pgs. 82
[433] John W. Frazier, "Reunion of the Blue and the Gray", Pg. 84-85

to witness this historic reunion. Adding to the frenzy was the spectacle of Mrs. George Pickett and her son George who traveled to Gettysburg with the troops her husband once commanded. The Virginians arrived in Gettysburg on July 2, 1887, much to the delight of their Northern hosts. The two associations formed up and marched through the town which had seen so much death and destruction just twenty-four years before. Instead of the roar of cannon and the buzz of bullets, the men listened to cheers and applause from the crowds of people who lined the streets of the small town. A band playing military airs accompanied the veterans on their march through Gettysburg. When the column reached the town square, Pickett's men marched up alongside the Philadelphia Brigade. The order was given "Right or Left face" and the sky was lit up with fireworks. Next came the command "Advance" and the two lines converged on each other in a flurry of handshakes and well wishes from the former combatants while the band played "Dixie." The teary eyed greetings continued under a night sky lit with fireworks and the air full of deafening cheers.[434]

The crowd moved into the local courthouse where the evening was filled with speeches commemorating the heroic deeds of both organizations on this field and throughout the war. The orators spoke of patriotism, devotion to one flag and the new found friendships that filled the room and should be an example for the entire country. It was fitting that John Frazier, whose determination and persistence made this reunion a reality, opened the proceedings. Captain E. P. Reeve from the Old First Virginia was also one of the speakers.[435]

The following day, Sunday, July 3rd, the veterans of both armies attended the dedication of the monuments to the 69th and 71st PA Volunteers, a marker on the spot where Lt. Cushing fell defending his guns and a monument to Cowan's NY battery. During the dedication, the Philadelphia Brigade presented a floral arrangement in the design of the trefoil badge of the Second Corps to Mrs. Pickett, who had captured the hearts of the northern men as well as the southern. Mrs. Pickett was also presented with a ribbon badge of blue and gray, with tears in her eyes she pinned the badge to her chest amid wild cheers from all in attendance. During the dedication of the monument to Cowan's Battery, Captain

---

434 John Tregaskis, "Souvenir of the Re-Union of The Blue and The Gray", Pg. 209

435 John W. Frazier, "Reunion of the Blue and the Gray", Pg. 90.

Cowan returned a sword to Pickett's men. Cowan claimed the sword belonged to a young Virginian officer who fell dead in front of his guns and it was his wish that the sword could be returned to the dead officer's family. In yet another show of solidarity, the Union veterans also pledged their support to erect a stone to mark the spot where Gen. Armistead fell on that fateful day. [436]

On Monday, July 4th, Mrs. Pickett hosted a reception on Seminary Ridge along the lines where Pickett's Division formed up for their historic charge. Following the reception, the veterans toured the entire battlefield in one hundred carriages procured by the Philadelphia Brigade. When the group circled back to the foot of Cemetery Ridge, they disembarked from the carriages, formed a line and, marching arm in arm, the men of the blue and gray moved in the direction of the infamous Stone Wall. Upon reaching the wall where so many of their comrades paid the ultimate price of war, the Union men took up positions on their side of the wall while the former Confederates waited on the other. As the Philadelphia Brigade took their positions, the men of Pickett's Division advanced, but instead of death and destruction, the men, with tears in their eyes, clasped hands in "Fraternity, Charity and Loyalty." That evening was full of speeches, fireworks and general good will among the veterans as they spent their last night together in the small town that their deeds had made famous twenty-four years before.[437]

By any standards, this, the first reunion between soldiers of the Blue and the Gray was a huge success. The press in both the north and the south took notice of the event and praised the veterans of the two associations for promoting peace and good will among the sections of the nation who had fought a great civil war. Journalists hoped that the actions of the veterans would help to silence those who continued to "stir up the embers of sectional hatred." It was hoped that the success achieved at this reunion would carry over to the twenty-fifth anniversary grand reunion planned for the following year. And by all accounts the success of this historic event was due to the diligence of two men, John Frazier of the Philadelphia

---

[436] John Tregaskis, "Souvenir of the Re-Union of The Blue and The Gray", Pgs. 211-212

[437] John W. Frazier, "Reunion of the Blue and the Gray", Pg. 113.

Brigade and Charles Loehr of Pickett's Division Association, who of course was a proud member of the 1st VA.[438]

Much to the delight of the Confederate veterans, eight days after the close of the reunion the Gettysburg Battlefield Memorial Association approved the request to place a marker on the spot where Gen. Armistead was wounded. The granite marker was made by the Thomas Nawn Company of Concord, New Hampshire and placed on the battlefield in early 1888. It could be argued that without the persuasion of men like Charles Loehr and E. P. Reeve of the 1st VA, along with their comrades in Pickett's Division Association and the Philadelphia Brigade, the monument to Armistead would never have been placed on Cemetery Ridge in Gettysburg.[439]

Although they were denied permission to erect a monument to Gen. Pickett within the Union lines at Gettysburg, the men of his former division continued in their quest to honor their former commander. The new plan was to erect a monument at Hollywood Cemetery where it would mark the grave of the Confederate General. This project was also managed by a member of the 1st VA., Capt. E. P. Reeve, who became commander of the Pickett's Division Association. In addition to corresponding with the artisans in relation to the construction of the monument, Reeve helped with the planning of the festivities associated with the dedication. The Association invited the Philadelphia Brigade to attend, inadvertently stirring up the hard liners from both north and south. Determined not to allow their detractors to foster hate between the regions, the Philadelphia Brigade accepted and attended the dedication on October 5, 1888. The Philadelphians were welcomed in Richmond and treated with the same genuine hospitality by the Virginians as they had been shown in Gettysburg.[440]

Prior to the dedication, a committee of members from the Pickett Division Association met at the monument on Sept. 24th to place a "time capsule" within the corner stone of the monument. The copper box contained a roster of all living members of Pickett's Division, a copy of the

---

[438] Carol Reardon, "Pickett's Charge in History and Memory", Pg. 99.

[439] David G. Martin, "Confederate Monuments at Gettysburg", Combined Books, Inc., 151 E. 10th Avenue, Conshohocken, PA 19428, 1995.

[440] E. P. Reeve Papers, University of North Carolina, Chapel Hill; Carol Reardon, "Pickett's Charge in History and Memory", Pgs.104-105.

book by Walter Harrison "Pickett's Men a Fragment of History," a copy of the book by Charles Loehr "War History of the First Virginia," a history of the challenges involved in building the monument and a list of those who promoted its construction. Cabinet portraits of E. P. Reeve, Charles Loehr and many other members of the Association, buttons from a coat owned by Gen. Robert E. Lee, and copies of all the major Richmond newspapers were also placed in the box. Lastly, several items from Gettysburg itself were put in the time capsule including a Blue and Gray Badge from the Philadelphia Brigade which had been designed for the 1887 reunion, a piece of the stone wall where so many of Pickett's men perished, and pressed cedar and daisies from the spot where Armistead fell. The box was placed without ceremony but with a reverenced silence.[441]

The two organizations continued their relationship and they met again in Washington, D.C., in March of 1889. And once again members of the Old First Virginia, along with Mrs. Pickett and her son, were in attendance. The group visited landmarks in the capital including the White House where they met with President Harrison. The veterans retired to Willard's Hotel where they conducted a meeting, at which time the Philadelphia Brigade presented the Pickett's Division Association with a magnificent forty-two star U.S. flag.[442]

Aside from their participation within the Pickett's Division Association, the members of the 1st VA continued their work with the Old First Virginia. They continued to hold their regular business meetings at the Exchange Hotel in Richmond and their yearly reunions at various venues and parks outside the capital. And of course they continued in their mission to honor their dead comrades. In February of 1896, a delegation of members from the Old First Virginia including Col. William H. Palmer, Capt. E. P. Reeve, Charles T. Loehr, Major James E. Phillips, Lt. James T. Vaughan, Lt. W. Thomas Wood, Lt. E. W. Martin, A. Jeff Vaughan, John T. Hughes, Charles H. Epps, and S. R. Gates, boarded the steamer DANVILLE and sailed to Baltimore. Their mission was to escort the remains of their heroic Colonel, Lewis B. Williams, back to Richmond. Col. Williams had been shot off his horse while leading the regiment during Pickett's Charge and died two days after. His remains had been sent to Baltimore where they

441 Richmond Newspaper, September 25, 1888.

442 Richmond Newspaper, March 23, 1889.

rested in a vault owned by Baltimore business man, William Gittings, at Greenmount Cemetery. Now, almost 33 years later, his comrades had come to take him home. The delegation was met by a committee of former Confederates from Baltimore. The Virginians were taken to the Equitable Building where they were the guests of honor at a dinner. Afterwards the group moved to the cemetery where the Old First Virginia Association took charge of their Colonel's remains. They returned to the docks, bid their hosts a fond farewell and boarded the DANVILLE for the return journey to Richmond.

Upon reaching Richmond, the Colonel's remains were taken to the Capital where they laid in state overnight at the Rotunda. The following day a large funeral procession, attended by veterans associations, military units and dignitaries, including Governor Charles O'Ferrell, wound its way through the streets of Richmond to Hollywood Cemetery. There, Col. Williams was buried with full military honors next to the grave of his former commander, Gen. George E. Pickett.[443]

When Col. Williams was killed in Gettysburg, his personal belongings eventually made their way back to his family in Virginia. Among them was the original silk battle flag carried by the regiment from October of 1861 until it was replaced on the way to Gettysburg in June of 1863. This sacred relic of the regiment was held by the Colonel's family until, at the request of Governor Fitzhugh Lee, it was carried in the parade for the unveiling of the Robert E. Lee monument in 1890. It was then deposited in the state library where the flag remained until the Old First Virginia Association conducted a search for it. With the help of Col. Williams' family, the Association again took possession of this honored symbol that they had followed through so many struggles in the first two years of war. The flag was unfurled at some of the Association's reunions before being placed into the hands of the Museum of the Confederacy* where it still resides to this day.[444]

At the annual reunion of the 1st VA in July of 1892, Col. Frederick

---

443 Baltimore American, February 16, 1896; Richmond Dispatch, February 18, 1896.

444 Richmond Times, September 6, 1894; Richmond Times, July of 1909. *What was once the Museum of the Confederacy is now the American Civil War Museum in Richmond, VA.

Skinner presented his comrades with another symbol of their heroic deeds during the war. The Colonel donated his oversized sword to the Old First Virginia Association. The same sword he wielded so lethally at 2nd Manassas when he rode among the Union cannoneers on Chinn Ridge. The sword was accepted by the Association and placed in the Museum of the Confederacy. It was the Colonel's wish that the sword be returned to his grandson if he were to ever request it. The Colonel died two years later in 1894. His grandson, F. S. Green of New York, attended the 1903 reunion and requested the sword be returned to his family. The Old First Virginia Association contacted the Museum of the Confederacy and the sword was returned. The sword surfaced again many years later in 1993, almost one hundred years after his death, when Colonel Skinner was honored with a memorial plaque on his tomb at Westminster Cemetery in Baltimore, MD. The ceremony was hosted by the local Sons of Confederate Veterans Chapter, The Harry Gilmore Camp. Descendants of Col. Skinner were the guests of honor and they brought the famous sword to display during the ceremony.[445]

The relationship between the veterans of the Pickett's Division Association and the Philadelphia Brigade continued through correspondence and visits to each other's home cities. On June 12, 1906, at a meeting of the Philadelphia Brigade, it was agreed that the Brigade would make a trip to Gettysburg with a side trip to Sharpsburg on September 15 – 18 of that year. The following day, John Frazier, who was now Adjutant of the Philadelphia Brigade, wrote to Charles Loehr and invited the Pickett's Division Association to join them at Gettysburg. The Association accepted the invitation and a second reunion between the former enemies was planned. The veterans of both organizations arrived in Gettysburg on the afternoon of September 15, 1906. After dinner they gathered at the High Water Mark, the site of their bloody contest 43 years before. In a magnanimous gesture, the sword of Gen. Armistead was returned to the men of Pickett's Division. Sergeant Michael Specht of the 72nd PA, present when Gen. Armistead was carried from the field after suffering a mortal wound on that fateful day, picked up the General's sword and preserved

---

445 Richmond Newspaper, July 15, 1903; Marsha Raeder, Civil War News, November 1993, Pg. 33: Conversations with Mr. Robert Lyons, one of the organizers of the 1993 dedication of Col. Skinner's tomb.

it for all those years. As the bonds of comradeship grew between the Virginians and the Pennsylvanians, Specht felt the time was right to return the sword to the men who stood with Armistead at the Bloody Angle. Captain Thomas Jeffress, the current President of the Pickett's Division Association, accepted the sword and assured those in attendance the relic would be placed in the Museum of the Confederacy in Richmond.[446]

That night, the group assembled in the Court House for what was known as a "camp fire." As the meeting started, letters of regret were read by John Frazier. The first being by none other than the President of the United States, Theodore Roosevelt. In his note, Roosevelt reinforced the sentiment that these two organizations had done so much to foster throughout the land. He wrote; *"Surely there never was such a war as ours, where the men who fought against one another are now knit together by the closest ties of brotherly love, and have left to their children and their children's children, as a heritage in common, the memory of the valor and the self-devotion alike of those who wore the blue and those who wore the gray."*[447]

There was another benefit of this friendship, a friendship that was due in no small part to the men of the 1st VA, which was of national importance and of great value to the south. It was because of this relationship that the movement was begun to return the captured battle flags held by the War Department to the southern states. In a lengthy speech that night in the court house in Gettysburg, John Frazier addressed this issue: *"When the Philadelphia Brigade and Pickett's Division were about to hold their first Re-union at Gettysburg on July 3, 1887, some of the comrades of the Old Brigade thought it would enhance the spirit of fraternity to return the two or three battle flags left by Pickett's Division at the Bloody Angle, after all their color-bearers had been shot to death and, we accordingly wrote to the War Department requesting that those flags be returned to the Philadelphia Brigade for that purpose."*

"The suggestion raised a mighty protest from Hon. Lucius Fairchild, at that time Commander-in-Chief of the Grand Army of the Republic, and Hon. Jos. B. Foraker, then Governor of Ohio, who threatened to invade Washington with the National Guard of Ohio, if necessary, to prevent such "sacrilege." Since then Mr. Foraker, as a Senator, presented a resolution in the United

446 John W. Frazier, "Reunion of the Blue and the Gray", Pg. 5 – 17.

447 John W. Frazier, "Reunion of the Blue and the Gray", Pg. 21

States Senate, providing for a return of all the Confederate battle-flags held by the War Department; the Foraker resolution was unanimously adopted, and not a Grand Army protest was entered against it."

"I mention this as one of a hundred instances, evidencing the growing feeling of fraternity between the North and the South that has taken place since that Re-union of the Blue and Gray – The Philadelphia Brigade and Pickett's Division – in 1887 at the "Bloody Angle' of Gettysburg." It was obvious that the cooperation between these two veteran organizations was having far reaching results.[448]

Commander Worman of the Philadelphia Brigade then recognized the efforts of John Frazier and Charles Loehr in bringing about the reunions. Worman said; *"It was almost to their single and untiring efforts that the reunion of the Blue and the Gray of 1887 took place, of which this reunion is a natural sequence."* Worman then introduced Charles Loehr who spoke on behalf of the Virginians. Also in attendance and on the list of speakers was Mrs. George Pickett, who never missed an opportunity to travel with the men of Pickett's Division. She was so loved by the men of both organizations that during the reunion of 1906, the Philadelphia Brigade voted her an honorary member of the Brigade, which drew wild cheers from all in attendance.[449]

At least seven members of the 1st VA took part in the 1906 reunion, they were Charles Loehr, James B. Angle, Howard Malcomb Walthall, Meyer Angle, Ed B. Loving, Lt. William M. Lawson, and Samuel L. Wingfield. At the end of the reunion the aging veterans bid each other a fond farewell, realizing that for many this would be the last time they would see each other face to face. The 50th anniversary of the battle took place in 1913 and was open to not just the members of Pickett's Division and the Philadelphia Brigade but to all surviving participants of the famous battle. Enough surviving members of the 1st VA attended that they cancelled their annual July reunion in Richmond, and while it is quite possible that some men were able to renew their acquaintances at that time with the Philadelphia Brigade, no record of such meetings exist.[450]

---

448 John W. Frazier, "Reunion of the Blue and the Gray", Pg. 41.

449 John W. Frazier, "Reunion of the Blue and the Gray", Pg. 42; The Times-Dispatch, September 16, 1906.

450 John W. Frazier, "Reunion of the Blue and the Gray", Pg. 62.

The mutual admiration and respect of the two organizations was demonstrated in a letter written by John Frazier of the Philadelphia Brigade to Charles Loehr's son upon the death of his father in 1915:

Philadelphia, March 18, 1915

William Loehr, Esq.
My dear friend:

Your letter of the 16th received, and I write to say that I was never more shocked in all my life than in being informed of your father's death.

There never was a soldier of the Union or Confederate Army – a citizen of the North or of the South – whom I held in higher esteem than I did my friend and comrade, Sergeant Charles T. Loehr of Pickett's Division. He was a manly man in all the attributes that contribute to true American manhood.

Charles T. Loehr, Secretary of the Pickett's Division Association, and I, as Secretary of a Committee of the Philadelphia Brigade Association, almost single-handed and alone, brought about the great Reunion of the Blue and Gray – survivors of the Philadelphia Brigade and Pickett's Division at the Bloody Angle of Gettysburg on July 1, 2, 3, and 4, 1887, a Reunion, such as had never before been witnessed upon any battle-field in the history of the world.

If ever the angels of Heaven came near to Earth – since the Birth of the Babe of Bethlehem – singing again in celestial strains, "Peace on Earth, Good-Will to Men, Hosanna in the Highest Glory", they were round and about us with their invisible presence as the Blue and the Gray – the grizzled veterans of Pickett's Division and the Philadelphia Brigade – clasped hands across the stone wall of Cemetery Ridge on that afternoon of July 3, 1887 – the self-same stone wall that the heroic men of Pickett's Division fought so valiantly to gain, and the equally heroic veterans of the Philadelphia Brigade fought just as desperately to maintain on that afternoon of July 3, 1863.

In order to gain that stone-wall, by your father's command, and to maintain it by ours, the veterans of those two commands, fought with clubbed muskets, and their mingled blood reddened the stones of that low stone-wall on July 3, 1863, while on the afternoon of July 3, 1887, the mingled tears of manly men, fell upon those stones as they looked into each other's eyes, with hands clasped in Fraternity."[451]

The Old First Virginia Association continued with their meetings and they continued with their annual reunions commemorating their baptism of fire at Bull Run. Each year there were fewer and fewer of the old veterans as they joined their comrades who fell in battle so many years before. Little did they know when they marched out of Richmond back in 1861 the journey they were about to undertake. They proved themselves valiant soldiers in war and exceptional citizens in peace. They kept alive the memory and the honor of the 1st VA Volunteer Infantry till their last days. Perhaps the most fitting description of this band of brothers comes from their former brigade commander Gen. James Lawson Kemper, who as Governor of Virginia wrote in 1875, *"You know I was identified with the First through many bloody vicissitudes. Jollier men in camp, braver soldiers in battle were not found in the Army of Northern Virginia. Stouter heroes never tread the field of Mars. Present my acknowledgements and my homage to the scarred survivors of that immortal band."*[452]

The End

[451] Excerpt of letter from John W. Frazier to William Loehr, March 18, 1915.

[452] Richmond Newspaper, July 21, 1875.

EPILOGUE

As previously stated in the text, the 1st VA was reconstituted in 1871 and served the state of Virginia until May of 1898 when four companies (A, B, C and F) were mustered into Federal Service during the Spanish American War. Companies A, B and C served as Companies M, B, and I of the 2nd Virginia Volunteer Infantry, respectively. Company F served as Company M of the 3rd Virginia Volunteer Infantry. All four companies served within the boundaries of the United States during the Spanish American War.

Several companies served under different designations until September 1, 1908, when they were reconstituted as the 1st Infantry of the Virginia Volunteers. On June 3, 1916, they were redesignated as the Virginia National Guard. From June 1916 to January 1917 the 1st VA was mustered into Federal service and was stationed on the Mexican border.

They were again called into Federal Service on August 5, 1917. On October 4, 1917, the regiment was combined with the 2nd and 4th VA to form the 116th Infantry as a component of the 29th Division. In that capacity they served in France as part of the American Expeditionary Force during World War I. The regiment took part in the Meuse-Argonne Operation and defended the lines in Alsace. The 1st VA was demobilized from Federal Service on May 30, 1919.

Between the World Wars the 1st VA went through several reorganizations and designations until they were mustered into Federal service on February 3, 1941, as 2nd Battalion, 176th Infantry, 29th Division. On March 11, 1942, they were removed from the 29th Division and sent to Fort Benning, GA, as the Infantry Demonstration Regiment. They remained in that capacity until July 10, 1944, when they were inactivated.

On November 20, 1946, the 1st VA was reorganized as 3rd Battalion,

176th Infantry. They served within the 176th Infantry until March 22, 1963, when they were converted into the 276th Engineer Battalion, with their headquarters in Richmond. They continue in that capacity to this very day, serving as part of the Virginia National Guard, and have also done their part in the war against terror, serving in both Iraq and Afghanistan. While serving in Iraq in 2004, a suicide bomber detonated his device in the mess tent killing two members of the battalion.[453]

The continued service of these brave men from Virginia make it one of, if not "THE", oldest military unit in the nation.

[453] M. C. Jackson, Captain 1st Infantry, Virginia National Guard, "The Romantic Record of the First Virginia Infantry", Pgs. 6-8, 1931; United States Army Center of Military History, Lineage and Honors Information. https://history.army.mil/html/forcestruc/lineages/branches/eng/0276enbn.htm

MAJOR ENGAGEMENTS - 1st VA, 1861 - 1865

July 18, 1861 – Bull Run

July 21, 1861 – 1st Manassas

May 5, 1862 – Williamsburg

May 31, 1862 – Seven Pines

June 30, 1862 – Frazier's Farm

August 30, 1862 – 2nd Manassas

September 14, 1862 – South Mountain

September 17, 1862 - Sharpsburg/Antietam

December 13, 1862 – Fredericksburg

April 13, 1863 – Suffolk

July 3, 1863 – Gettysburg

February 1, 1864 – New Bern

April 20, 1864 – Plymouth

May 16, 1864 - Drewry's Bluff

May 18, 1864 – Howlett House

May 21, 1864 – Milford Station

June 3, 1864 – Cold Harbor

June 17, 1864 – Clay Farm/Howlett Line

March 31, 1865 – Dinwiddie C. H.

April 1, 1865 – Five Forks

April 6, 1865 – Sailor's Creek

April 9, 1865 – Appomattox C. H.

BIBLIOGRAPHY

"The American Civil War, An English View", Field Marshal Viscount Wolseley, Published by Stackpole Books, 5067 Ritter Road, Mechanicsburg, PA, 17055, 2002.

"An introduction to Civil War Small Arms" by Earl J. Coates and Dean S. Thomas, Published by Thomas Publications, P.O. Box 3031, Gettysburg, PA 17325, 1990

"The Appomattox Campaign", Chris M. Calkins, Schroeder Publications, 131 Tanglewood Drive, Lynchburg, VA 24502, 2008.

"Arms and Equipment of the Confederacy", "Echoes of Glory", Editor Henry Woodhead, Time Life in conjunction with Borders Press, a division of Borders Inc., 311 Maynard, Ann Arbor, Michigan 48104.

"Battles and Leaders of the Civil War", Four Volumes, Published by arrangement with A.S. Barnes and Co. Inc. Copyright 1956 by Thomas Yoseloff, Inc.

"Battle of Five Forks", Ed Bears and Chris Calkins, Published by H. E. Howard, Lynchburg, VA 1985.

"Before Antietam, The Battle for South Mountain", John Michael Priest, White Mane Publishing Company, P.O. Box 152, Shippensburg, PA 17257, 1992.

"The Civil War in Maryland", Daniel Carroll Toomey, Publisher Toomey Press, Baltimore, MD. 1993.

"The Civil War in North Carolina", John G. Barrett, University of North Carolina Press, Chapel Hill, NC, 1963

"Confederate Monuments at Gettysburg", David G. Martin, Combined Books Inc. 151 E. 10th Avenue, Conshohocken, PA19428, 1995.

"First Virginia Infantry" by Lee A. Wallace, Published by H.E. Howard Inc. Lynchburg, VA' 1985.

"From Cedar Mountain to Antietam", Edward J. Stackpole, Publisher Stackpole Books, Cameron and Kelker Streets, PO Box 1831, Harrisburg, PA 17105, 1993.

"From Manassas to Appomattox", Gen. James Longstreet C.S.A.", Mallard Press, An imprint of BDD Promotional Book Company, Inc., 666 Fifth Ave, New York, NY 10103, 1991.

"History of the Confederate States Navy", J. Thomas Scharf, Gramercy Books a division of Random House Value Publishing Inc. 40 Engelhard Ave., Avenel, New Jersey 17001, 1996

"History of the Seventeenth Virginia Infantry" by George Wise, Originally published by Baltimore, Kelly, Piet and Company, 1870, Digitized by Cornell University Library.

"John Dooley, Confederate Soldier, His War Journal", John Dooley, Edited by Joseph T. Durkin, S.J., Publisher Georgetown University Press, 1945.

"John Dooley's Civil War, An Irish American's Journey in the First Virginia Infantry Regiment", Edited by Robert Emmett Curran, Copyright 2012 by The University of Tennessee Press/Knoxville.

"Landscape Turned Red", Stephen W. Sears, Poplar Library Edition, Warner Books Inc., 666 Fifth Avenue, New York, NY 10103, 1983.

"Longstreet's Assault – Pickett's Charge, The Lost Record of Pickett's Wounded", Donald J. Frey, White Mane Publishing Company Inc. P.O. Box 152, Shippensburg, PA 17257-0152 USA.

"Maymont History Interpretation Handbook," by Herbert S. Wheary. Maymont Foundation, 2012. 1700 Hampton Street, Richmond VA, 23220

"Nothing But Glory", by Kathy Georg Harrison, Thomas Publications, P.O. Box 3031, Gettysburg, PA17325, 2001.

"Nothing But Glory", by Kathleen R. Georg and John W. Busey, Published for Longstreet House by Gateway Press, Inc., 1001 N. Charles St., Baltimore, MD 21202, 1987.

"Pickett's Charge, Eyewitness Accounts", Edited by Richard Rollins, Rank and File Publications, 1926 South Pacific Coast Highway Suite 228, Redondo Beach, California 90277, 1994.

"Pickett's Charge in History and Memory", Carol Reardon, University of North Carolina Press, Chapel Hill NC. 1997.

"Recollections of a Confederate Staff Officer", Gen. G. Moxley Sorrel, Bantam Books, 666 Fifth Ave, New York, NY 10103. 1992.

"Return to Bull Run, The Campaign and Battle of Second Manassas", John J. Hennessy, Publisher Simon and Schuster, 1230 Avenue of the Americas, New York, NY 10020, 1993.

"Reunion of the Blue and Gray, Philadelphia Brigade and Pickett's Division, July 2, 3, 4, 1887 and September 15, 16, 17, 1906", John W. Frazier, Ware Bros. Company, Philadelphia, PA 1906.

"Richmond Ambulance Co., Herbig's Infirmary Co. and The Virginia Public Guard and Armory Band" by Jeffrey C. Weaver and Lee A. Wallace, Jr., Published by H.E. Howard Inc. Lynchburg, VA 1985.

"Souvenir of the Re-Union of the Blue and the Gray on the Battlefield of Gettysburg, July 1, 2, 3, and 4, 1888". John Tregaskis, Tregaskis and Company, 767 Broadway, Room 8, New York, 1888.

"The Confederacy's Forgotten Son, Major General James Lawson Kemper, C.S.A.", Harold R. Woodward, Rockbridge Publishing Company, Post Office Box 70, Natural Bridge Station, VA 24579, 1993.

"The Damned Red Flags of the Rebellion", by Richard Rollins, Rank and File Publications, 1926 South Pacific Coast Highway, Suite 228, Redondo Beach, California 90277.

"The Fredericksburg Campaign", by Edward J. Stackpole, Published by Stackpole Books, Cameron and Kelker Streets, P.O. Box 1831, Harrisburg, PA 17105. 1991.

"The Gettysburg Companion", by Mark Adkin, Published by Stackpole Books, 5067 Ritter Road, Mechanicsburg, PA 17055, 2008,

"The Maps of Antietam: An Atlas of the Antietam (Sharpsburg) Campaign, Including the Battle of South Mountain, September 2-20, 1862", by Bradley M. Gottfried, Published by Savas Beatie LLC, 989 Governor Drive, Suite 102, El Dorado Hills, CA 95762.

"The Maps of First Bull Run", by Bradley M. Gottfried, Publisher Savas Beatie LLC, PO Box 4527, Eldorado Hills, CA 95762, 2009

"The Maps of Gettysburg: An Atlas of the Gettysburg Campaign, June 3 – July 13, 1863" by Bradley M. Gottfried, Published by Savas Beatie LLC, P.O. Box4527, El Dorado Hills, CA 95762. 2007.

"The Maryland Campaign of September, 1862", Volume 1, "South Mountain", by Ezra A. Carmen, Edited and annotated by Thomas G. Clemens, Published by Savas Beatie LLC, 521 Fifth Ave, Suite 1700, New York, NY 10175. 2010.

"The Third Day at Gettysburg and Beyond", edited by Gary Gallagher, University of North Carolina Press, Chapel Hill, NC. 1994.

"The U.S. Army War College Guide to the Battle of Antietam" Edited by Luvaas and Nelson, Published by Harper Collins Publishers, Inc. 10 East 53rd Street, New York, NY 10022. 1987.

"The U.S. Army War College Guide to the Battles of Chancellorsville and Fredericksburg", edited by Jay Luvaas and Harold Nelson, Published by Harper Collins Publishers, Inc. 10 East 53rd Street, New York, NY 10022. 1989.

"The U.S. Army War College Guide to the Battle of Gettysburg", Edited by Jay Luvaas and Harold W. Nelson, Published by South Mountain Press, Inc., 17 West Pomfret Street, Carlisle, PA 17013.

"The War of the Rebellion: A compilation of the Official Records of the Union and Confederate Armies", Washington Printing Office, 1884, Reprinted by The National Historical Society, Harrisburg PA, 1971, Reprinted 1985 by Historical Time, Inc.

"They Called Him Stonewall, A Life of Lt. General T. J. Jackson C.S.A.", by Burke Davis, Published by Wings Books, A Random House Company, 40 Engelhard Avenue, Avenal, New Jersey 07001, 1954,

"Through the Perilous Fight, Six Weeks that Saved the Nation", by Steve Vogel, Random House Publishing, New York, NY 2013.

"To Appomattox, Nine April Days, 1865", Burke Davis, Eastern Acorn Press, 1992.

"To the Gates of Richmond, The Peninsula Campaign", Stephen W. Sears, Publisher Houghton Mifflin Company, 215 Park Ave. South, New York, NY 10003, First Mariner Books Edition 2001.

"War History of the Old First Virginia Infantry Regiment", Charles T. Loehr, Publisher Wm. Ellis Jones, Book and Job Printer, Richmond VA, 1884.

"The West Point Atlas of War, The Civil War", Chief Editor: Brigadier General Vincent J. Esposito, Published by Tess Press an imprint of Black Dog and Leventhal Publishers, Inc., 151 West 19th Street, New York, NY 10011

Websites:

American Civil War Museum: http://acwm.org/

Citrus County Schools, Slang of the American Civil War: http://www.citrus.k12.fl.us/staffdev/social%20studies/PDF/Slang%20of%20the%20American%20Civil%20War.pdf

Civil War Richmond: http://www.mdgorman.com/search.htm

Civil War Trust: http://www.civilwar.org/

Find A Grave, Millions of Cemetery Records: https://www.findagrave.com/

Gettysburg Stone Sentinels: http://gettysburg.stonesentinels.com/confederate-headquarters/kempers-brigade/

Historical Marker Database: http://www.hmdb.org/

Historical Military Records: https://www.fold3.com/

Internet Archive Search; http://archive.org

Library of Congress: http://chroniclingamerica.loc.gov/

Military Records On-line: http://civilwarintheeast.com/confederate-regiments/virginia/1st-virginia-infantry-regiment/

National Park Service, Soldiers and Sailors Database:

https://www.nps.gov/civilwar/soldiers-and-sailors-database.htm

National Archives: https://www.archives.gov

The Codori Family: http://codorifamily.com/farm_house_worksheet_1975.html

The online Books Page, Confederate Veteran Magazine: http://onlinebooks.library.upenn.edu/webbin/serial?id=confedvet

University of Memphis, Historical Newspapers On-line: http://libguides.memphis.edu/c.php?g=94219&p=611022#s-lg-box-1816897

University of North Carolina Libraries: http://webcat.lib.unc.edu/

University of Virginia, A Guide to the Papers of James Lawson Kemper: http://ead.lib.virginia.edu/vivaxtf/view?docId=uva-sc/viu03342.xml;query=Kemper;brand=default

Virginia Historical Society: http://www.jstor.org/publisher/vhs

INDEX

Symbols

A

B

C

D

E

F

G

H

M

N

O

P

Q

R

S

T

V

W

Y

CPSIA information can be obtained
at www.ICGtesting.com
Printed in the USA
LVHW02s1843280518
578746LV00002BA/498/P

9 781489 716569